Lake Superior

The Ultimate Guide to the Region

by Hugh E. Bishop

Lake Superior Port Cities Inc.

First Edition: May 2005

LAKE SUPERIOR PORT CITIES INC.
P.O. Box 16417
Duluth, Minnesota 55816-0417 USA
888-BIG LAKE (888-244-5253) • www.lakesuperior.com
Publishers of *Lake Superior Magazine* and *Lake Superior Travel Guide*

5 4 3 2 1

Library of Congress Cataloging-in-Publication Data

Bishop, Hugh E., 1940-
     Lake Superior: the ultimate guide to the region / by Hugh E. Bishop. – 1st ed.
     p. cm.
     Includes index.
     ISBN 0-942235-66-5
     1. Superior, Lake, Region – Guidebooks. I. Title.
     F552 .B57 2005
     977.4/9 22   2005040809

Printed in Canada

              Editors: Paul Hayden, Konnie LeMay, Wendy Webb
     Book Design: Mathew Pawlak
     Cover Design: Roberta Baker
     Inside Photos: *Lake Superior Magazine*
          Printer: Friesens Book Division, Winnipeg, Manitoba

Cover: Split Rock Lighthouse on the Minnesota shore of Lake Superior is among the lake's most recognized, photographed and beloved landmarks. Photo by Paul Sundberg.

Back cover: Marquette, Michigan's red lighthouse attracts attention and the nearby beach attracts summer bathers. The Aerial Lift Bridge in Duluth, Minnesota, is a focal point for waterfront activity like the Vista Fleet tour boats. Photos by Paul Hayden.

LAKE SUPERIOR
Contents

Alphabetical Listings

Introduction

Welcome to Lake Superior. It's a grand region that takes you through some of the most scenic, at times glorious, territory on earth. It's an outdoors enthusiast's dream world, but is also a civilized area with several cosmopolitan centers that offer all the dining, lodging and amenities a traveler could desire.

In compiling this travel guide, we present experiences and information gathered during more than 25 years of traveling the Big Lake to produce our *Lake Superior Magazine.* You'll find frequent references to the Circle Tour route throughout this volume. I did this to tempt you to explore more widely. In 12 years of poking around Lake Superior, I'm still discovering new places and new information, so don't be timid about exploring on your own.

The information presented here is as current as frequent checking can make it. The alphabetical listings should prove a handy and easy guide to whatever area you explore in the Lake Superior region. To help with future editions, we encourage you to send your impressions or suggestions by logging onto our Website at www.lakesuperior.com.

In all areas around Lake Superior, you'll find very friendly folks in the tourist information centers. Nearly always, they'll go out of their way to make your visit as pleasant and interesting as possible. They're real professionals at it.

Be assured that our recommendations are as unbiased as possible. We have scrupulously refused any incentive – that is to say free food, lodging, etc. – from any entity that we may recommend in this guide. Basically, our travels are the same as yours – we pay our own way.

Enjoy your lake journeys ... and come back often.

Hugh E. Bishop

Great Lakes Region

Lake Superior Region

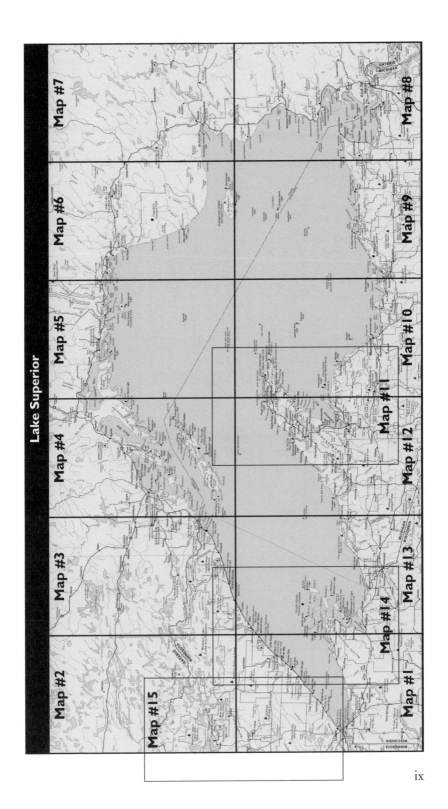

How to Use this Guide

Lake Superior can be – and has been – circled by just about any mode of transportation imaginable: by car, by kayak, bus, snowmobile, bicycle, motorcycle, horseback, powerboat, sailboat, canoe, on foot.

We know of kayakers who have taken two months to paddle around the edges of the lake and of one Iron Butt Association motorcyclist who completed the circle (legally) in 21 hours.

But undertaking the full Lake Superior Circle Tour is certainly not the only way to enjoy and visit the Big Lake.

This guide is designed to enhance your trip whether you plan a one-night getaway, a couple days at one location or a week or more enjoying a leisurely tour of the whole basin.

The region's cities and towns – along with a special parks and public destinations – are listed alphabetically. Many of the entries include a directory that gives basic contact numbers for tourism and information bureaus and often for places to stay or eateries serving up a local flavor. Most larger towns have bus service and many connect by air service to larger metropolitan areas. Car rentals are readily available. Although most lake area highways are two lanes, driving is extremely comfortable.

Throughout this section of the guide, you will find a series of maps, arranged clockwise from the Head of the Lakes, Duluth, Minnesota. The map showing the entire Lake Superior region on page ix outlines the number for each map presented. References within individual listings direct you to those more detailed maps. You will also find a few suggested mini-tours of specific regions and a fun section with a checklist of 50 lifetime lake experiences.

The opening section of this book also gives you a lake basin full of information, tidbits and tips for traveling or getting to know this region.

As you travel, remember, this is a safe and friendly part of the continent. Feel free to ask for help or directions if you need them.

You will see small tidbits like these on the bottoms and sides of some pages in this guide. They will introduce you to especially worthy places to visit or will offer a bit more information to enhance your stay.

Map I Lake Superior - Southeastern Section

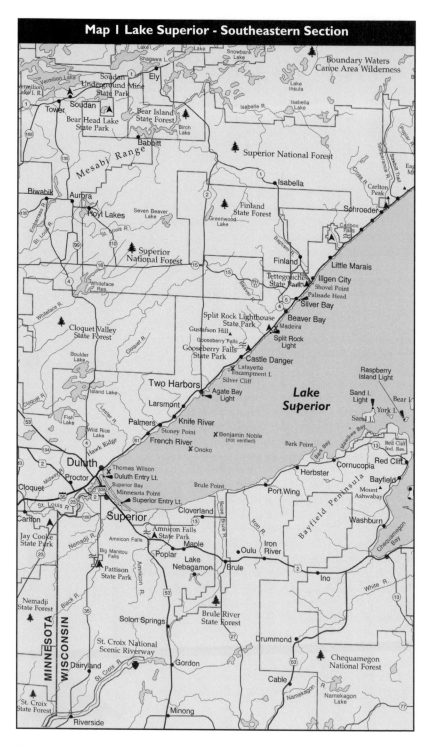

Basics & Beyond

AREA CODES

Thunder Bay/North of Superior, Ontario – Area Code 807.
Algoma Region/Sault Ste. Marie, Ontario – Area Code 705.
Michigan's Upper Peninsula – Area Code 906.
Northern Wisconsin – Area Code 715.
Northern Minnesota – Area Code 218.

METRIC CONVERSION

The Metric System is used in Canada and is applied to measurements and temperatures. The English System is used in the United States and is applied to measurements and temperatures. Use these simple conversions:

English	Metric
1 inch = 2.54 centimeters	1 centimeter = .039 inches
1 foot = 30 centimeters	1 meter = 3.28 feet
1 yard = 0.91 meters	1 meter = 1.09 yards (3.3 feet)
1 mile = 1.61 kilometers	1 kilometer = 0.62 miles
1 pound = 0.45 kilograms	1 kilogram = 2.2 pounds
1 pint = 0.47 liters	1 liter = 2.1 pints
1 gallon (U.S.) = 3.79 liters	1 liter = 0.26 gallons (U.S.)

To convert temperature:
0 degrees Celsius is equivalent to 32 degrees Fahrenheit.
Celsius to Fahrenheit: Degrees C x 9 ÷ 5 + 32 = degrees F.
Fahrenheit to Celsius: Degrees F -32 x 5 ÷ 9 = degrees C.

TIME ZONES

ONTARIO – All of Ontario near Lake Superior is in the Eastern Time Zone, however the extreme northwestern part of the province, west of 90 degrees west longitude (Shebandowan on Highway 11), is in the Central Time Zone.
MICHIGAN – Most of the Upper Peninsula of Michigan is in the Eastern Time Zone, however the southwestern U.P. counties of Gogebic, Iron, Dickinson and Menominee are in the Central Time Zone.
MINNESOTA – The entire state is in the Central Zone.
WISCONSIN – The entire state is in the Central Zone.

ONTARIO TRAFFIC LAWS

SPEED LIMITS – all roads and highways, unless otherwise posted:
Passenger car – 80 km/h (50 mph) except on designated, signed Trans Canada routes or freeways – 90 or 100 km/h (56 or 62 mph)
Urban area – 40 to 60 km/h (25 to 37 mph)
Safety belts required – if the car is designed with them, for

Map 2 Lake Superior - Northwestern Section

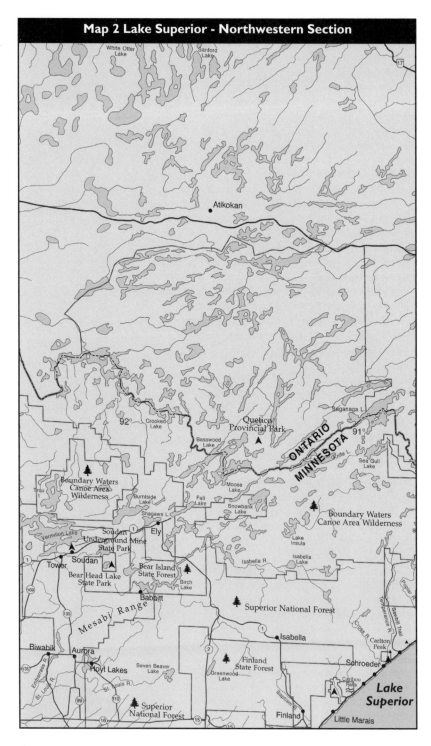

adults and all children over 18 kg. (40 lbs.) in weight.
Radar warning devices are prohibited by law and might be
confiscated, even if not in use.
Ontario Provincial Emergency Assistance: Dial 911.

UNITED STATES TRAFFIC LAWS
SPEED LIMITS – all roads and highways, unless otherwise
posted:
Passenger car – 55 mph (88 km/h)
except on designated, signed rural freeways – 65 mph
(104 km/h)
Truck – 55 mph (88 km/h)
School buses – 50 mph (80 km/h)
Child restraint required for children younger than 4 years and for
all children younger than 12. Children younger than 1 year old
must be fastened in an approved infant carrier in the back seat.
Between 1 and 4, children must be fastened in an approved child
passenger restraint system, preferably in the back seat.
Safety belts required for driver and all front-seat passengers.
Michigan Statewide Emergency Assistance –
800-525-5555. Call 911 where available.
Minnesota Statewide Emergency Assistance: Call 911.
Wisconsin Statewide Emergency Assistance: Call 911.

LICENSES, PERMITS AND SUCH
To fish, hunt, camp or otherwise use a state or provincial
park various licenses and/or permits are required. If you're
entering state or provincial parks, you can usually just get one
day or multi-day use permit onsite. You can get a fishing
license just about anywhere in season (ask at any convenience
store) but hunting licenses require a bit more effort. The
ability to hunt some animals, like bear, sometimes requires
applying for a lottery. Regulations vary from state to state to
province. So, if you want to hunt in the Lake Superior region,
inquire at the local department or ministry of natural resources.

CROSSING BORDERS
Crossing the international border is fairly straightforward,
but in 2005 as an effort of Homeland Security, border
officials are beginning to fingerprint those of foreign
citizenship who enter into the United States at certain border
crossings. Be aware that such changes might add time and
require patience.
You do need proper identification. A valid driver's license
with a picture is usually enough, but another proof of identity
might be requested in rare cases. A passport or birth certificate
will do. Identification may also be required for children, so
it's best to have a copy of their birth certificates, just in case.

When you reach the border, you can expect a couple of general questions about where you live, where you're going, and what, if anything, you've purchased on your travels. A word of warning: In this new age of homeland security, it's wise to be simple, straightforward and friendly with your answers.

You may take your pet across the border, but proof of immunization is required. Also, some public areas, like Isle Royale, don't allow pets in order to protect wildlife.

IT'S GOOD TO KNOW THAT:

Gasoline in Canada is sold by the liter rather than by the U.S. gallon. A liter equals about one quarter of a gallon. Be advised of this at the pump.

Depending on how long you stay, you may take up to a $400 personal exemption on purchases in Canada that you bring back to the United States, and $300 Canadian (CAD) for U.S. purchases brought back into Canada. If you shop in Canada and are not a citizen, you can claim a rebate on the 7 percent federal goods and services tax if you spend $100 CAD or more – and that includes accommodations. Ask for a form at the border, in a duty free shop or at most motels and inns in the province.

LAKE SUPERIOR

Covers about 31,700 square miles (82,170 square kilometers) – an area equal to Massachusetts, Connecticut, Rhode Island, Vermont and New Hampshire combined.

Stretches 382 miles (615 kilometers) east-west and 160 miles (258 kilometers) north-south.

Reaches to 1,279 feet (389.6 meters) deep, averaging 489 feet (148 meters).

Totals 2,725 miles (4,387 kilometers) of shoreline on its edges and islands.

Is the largest and deepest of the Great Lakes and could hold all the water of the other four, plus three more Lake Eries.

Is head of an ancient river system we call "the Great Lakes." Duluth-Superior is "Head of the Lakes" and Thunder Bay is the "Lakehead" city. From there to the Atlantic Ocean on the St. Lawrence Seaway is more than 2,300 miles (3,700 kilometers) – seven days of travel for a typical shipping vessel.

Takes 30 minutes for sunrise (and set) to arc east to west over the lake.

Has a drainage area of 49,300 square miles (127,791 square kilometers).

Has a periodic seiche (SAYSH) that sloshes water from side to side, rapidly raising water levels on one side while lowering them on the other. This shift is caused by rain, wind, barometric pressure and other natural phenomena.

Turns over its water at a rate of 199 years. (The smallest Great Lake, Lake Erie, takes only about 3 years.)

WHAT YOU'LL FIND HERE

The Lake Superior region is home to spectacular natural scenery the likes of which you won't find anywhere else in the world. Above all else, get out and enjoy it. Wherever your destination, plan to spend some time outdoors. You can find an adventure for any fitness level hiking, biking, kayaking, canoeing, sailing, boating, skiing, snowshoeing, dogsledding, snowmobiling … there is an endless amount of outdoor fun to be had here in any season.

MAKE RESERVATIONS BEFORE YOU GO

The peak tourist season around much of Lake Superior is summer through fall colors. However, winter sports enthusiasts flock to many parts of the lake to take advantage of the snow. Bottom line: Make reservations for hotels or camping well in advance, no matter the season.

LAKE SUPERIOR SEASONS

Spring (generally starts late April): It's short and sweet. As the ice and snow melt and the world comes alive again, it's a perfect time for dedicated "birders" to hunt for their favorite feathered friends. The coming of spring means just one thing

LAKE SUPERIOR

Contains 10 percent of the earth's surface fresh water and more than half of all the water in the Great Lakes combined. (Only 3 percent of the earth's surface water is fresh water.)

Holds 3 quadrillion gallons of water. (Enough to flood North and South America under 1 foot of water.) It was filled with glacial melt 10,000 years ago.

Is called "an ocean in a test tube" by some researchers because it often acts more like an ocean than a lake.

Is about 601 feet above sea level.

Averages a water temperature of 40 degrees Fahrenheit (4.4 degrees Celsius). Its bays and inlets can warm to 70 F (16 to 21 C). It can freeze "completely" for short periods (hours) as in 1979.

Is considered "ultra-oligotrophic" by limnologists (lake scientists) because it has few nutrients, sediment and other material in its water.

Has two major natural tributaries – Nipigon River in Ontario and St. Louis River at Duluth-Superior – plus a diverted source of water from Ontario's Ogoki and Longlac rivers that together almost equals the flow of each natural tributary.

Anchors a basin 89 percent forest-covered and rich in resources. A wealth of minerals plus iron, gold, silver, copper, zinc and even diamonds have been found. Lake Superior has its "gems" – agates, amethyst, greenstone and Thomsonite.

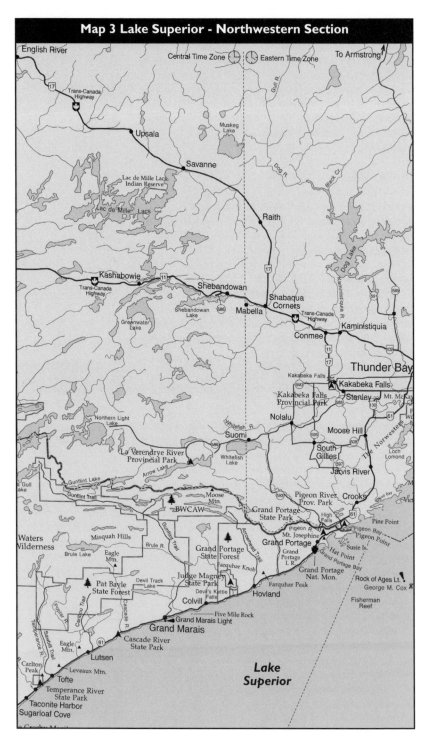

Map 3 Lake Superior - Northwestern Section

Central Time Zone | Eastern Time Zone | To Armstrong

English River

17 Trans-Canada Highway

Upsala

Savanne

Muskeg Lake

Lac de Mille Lacs Indian Reserve

Lac de Mille Lacs

Raith

Greenwater Lake

Kashabowie

11 Trans-Canada Highway

Shebandowan

Shebandowan Lake

Mabella

Shabaqua Corners

Trans-Canada Highway

Conmee

Kaministiquia

Northern Light Lake

Kakabeka Falls

Kakabeka Falls

Kakabeka Falls Provincial Park

Stanley Mt. McKay

Thunder Bay

Nolalu

Whitefish R.

Suomi

Moose Hill

La Verendrye River Provincial Park

Whitefish Lake

South Gillies

Jarvis River

Gunflint Lake

Arrow Lake

Moose Mtn.

Pigeon River Prov. Park

Crooks

Gunflint Trail

BWCAW

Grand Portage State Park

High Falls

Pine Point

Pigeon Bay

Waters Wilderness

Misquah Hills

Brule R.

Brule Lake

Eagle Mtn.

Gunflint Trail

Grand Portage State Forest

Arrowhead Trail

Pigeon R.

Mt. Josephine

Grand Portage

Grand Portage I. R.

Susie Is.

Pigeon Point

Farquhar Knob

Hat Point

Grand Portage Bay

Pat Bayle State Forest

Devil Track Lake

Judge Magney State Park

Devil's Kettle Falls

Farquhar Peak

Grand Portage Nat. Mon.

Rock of Ages Lt.

George M. Cox

Colvill

Hovland

Fisherman Reef

Five Mile Rock

Grand Marais Light

Grand Marais

Cascade River State Park

Lake Superior

Eagle Mtn.

Lutsen

Leveaux Mtn.

Carlton Peak

Tofte

Temperance River State Park

Taconite Harbor

Sugarloaf Cove

8

to many lake lovers – fishing opener! (That's the start of the fishing season). Many resorts around the lake have springtime specials, and some fabulous deals can be found during this time. This season can be a bit wet and muddy, so, if you're planning outdoor activities, it's wise to bring proper footwear, rain gear and several changes of clothes.

Summer (generally mid-June through August): During this season, the weather varies, depending where on the lake you are. On the southern part of the lake, summers can get downright hot. But the farther north you go in Minnesota and Ontario, summer weather can range from hot to mild to chilly, especially at night. It's best to bring a light sweater, sweatshirt, long pants and a jacket, just in case the weather turns cold. Locals know that even on the hottest days, the weather will be cooler on the lakeshore than it is inland.

Summer is the time to get out and explore the vast wilderness that surrounds this great lake, whether its on foot on one of the myriad of hiking trails, on a bike, or by canoe, sailboat or something a little larger. Take a guided cruise out onto the big lake from many tourist spots or slip your own kayak into the water. It's a busy tourist season and virtually all of the lake's inns, hotels, resorts and tourist attractions are filled with visitors. If you're planning a summer trip to the lake, make reservations early.

Fall (generally September through mid-November): Autumn is a spectacular time around Lake Superior, with fall colors starting to appear in early September; in some areas, in late August. Many resorts and inns lakewide cater to "leaf spotters," and most weekends, especially in Michigan's Keweenaw Peninsula where some of the most awesome fall colors are found, are booked solid, sometimes months in advance. Another fabulous time to vacation on the lake is in the late fall, a time locals call "the Gales of November." It's that less stunning time when the leaves have fallen off the trees and the winds pick up … locals know that the lake in all its fury is the most awe-inspiring during this time when waves pummel the shoreline. Find a hotel or resort right on the water, curl up with a glass of wine and a fire in the fireplace and watch nature's awesome show. Many lakeside resorts offer specials during this time.

Winter (generally mid-November into April): Anyone who lives around this lake needs to love (or at least be at peace with) winter. It's not only long, it's often cold. January is notorious for extremely cold temperatures (double-digits below zero Fahrenheit) and the winds create "wind chill," that feels even colder than the actual temperature.

That's the bad news. The good news is, winter is beautiful here, with some gloriously sunny days. Lake Superior creates its own weather patterns, and in the winter it blankets the

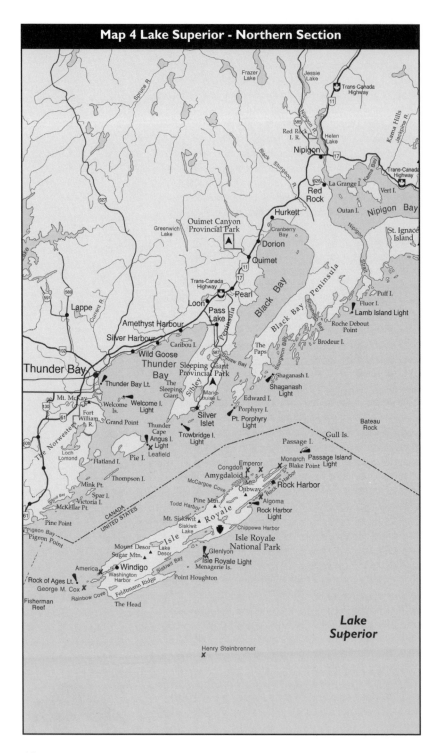

Map 4 Lake Superior - Northern Section

Lake
Superior

10

area with what locals call "lake effect" snow. Many areas around the lake get hundreds of inches of snow each year, making it a mecca for winter sports enthusiasts. You'll find plenty of resources for downhill and cross-country skiing, dog sledding, snowshoeing, snowmobiling, skating, ice fishing … anything that floats your, er, sled.

Locals know that, in the winter, temperatures are warmer on the lakeshore than they are inland.

WINTER SURVIVAL GUIDE

Cold temperatures and snow like that found here on Lake Superior are nothing with which to trifle. Pay attention to the storm warnings when driving and be aware of weather conditions. People who have long lived in this area know how to survive the extreme weather, even if they're caught outdoors. Visitors may not. Here is a list of survival tips to keep you safe, snug and warm during our harshest of seasons.

• Dress appropriately. If you're planning on outdoor activities, make sure you've got a jacket, hat, mittens or gloves and boots that are made to protect you in this environment. A sturdy jean jacket isn't going to do the job. Think goosedown or Thinsulate. When you're warm, you can enjoy the region to its fullest.

• Respect the temperature. Even if you've planned your skiing vacation for months, if you get here and the temperature dips below zero (Fahrenheit), take extra caution. A chair lift ride on a cold, windy day can be brutal. Plan on heading into the chalet often. Ditto for other winter sports. Also, remember that wind chill is real. It may freeze your skin. Take it seriously and cover up fingers, ears, nose and cheeks on windy days.

WINTER DRIVING 101

Most times of the year, the roadways around the Lake Superior region are not only highly driveable, they are beautiful ways to get from here to there. In winter, however, conditions can change quickly. Here are some tips for those who don't habitually spend six months of the year in snow:

• Is your car ready to travel in the snow? Make sure it's tuned up and in good shape, including the tires. Also, stock it with a scraper and brush, jumper cables in case your battery dies, a tow chain, shovel and a bag of sand for traction in case you get stuck in the snow or on ice. Also, throw a blanket and a working flashlight in the trunk, just in case.

• Keep a survival kit in your trunk. It should include a coffee can (melt snow inside of it for water), a candle with matches or a lighter, a brightly colored cloth to use as a flag, a first aid kit and high energy, non-perishable foods.

Map 5 Lake Superior - Northern Section

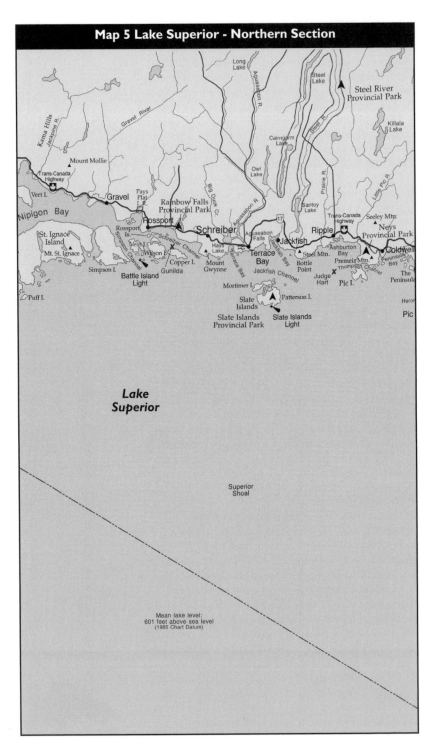

• Front-wheel drive or four-wheel drive are most adaptable in trickier weather conditions, but even four-wheel vehicles can't handle blizzard and extremely icy conditions. Be aware of the weather as you travel in winter and don't travel when you should not. If you travel little-used backroads, realize that a four-wheel drive vehicle might be the best or even necessary. Obviously, the main roadways are well kept and safe, but again be aware of road conditions and drive accordingly.

• Drive slowly, as conditions warrant. Overpasses and bridges, along with on and off ramps, are often slippery.

• Understand your vehicle's brake system – be it anti-lock or another – and what the best methods are for avoiding or driving out of a skid on ice.

• If you do get stranded, stay in your car. Run the engine for five minutes each hour, taking care to keep your exhaust pipe free of snow. Open the windows a bit to get fresh air.

• Some areas around Lake Superior have cell phone coverage, but not all do. Take that into consideration as you make your travel plans for any season.

THE LAKE SUPERIOR DRESS CODE

There isn't one. This is a casual place, where blue jeans and a T-shirt are welcomed just about anywhere. That's not to say you won't find elegant restaurants, museums and high culture, especially in the larger cities like Duluth-Superior, Thunder Bay, Sault Ste. Marie and Marquette, so pack depending on your trip itinerary. But if you're planning to simply "get away from it all" at a resort and experience the lake's fabulous natural environment, leave your suit coat or cocktail dress at home.

WHAT TO BRING?

When packing for a trip to Lake Superior, expect the unexpected. It might turn cold in summer, or warm up nicely in the fall. Pack at least one "off season" outfit, and you'll be prepared for anything. Make sure you have the proper shoes and other outdoor gear for exploring the lake's beautiful parks and wilderness, and bring at least one change of footwear in case yours gets wet or muddy while hiking on a trail. For those whose hands feel the chill, light gloves might be good to pack even during summer in case the night turns nippy.

LOCAL FLAVOR

When traveling around Lake Superior, there are some regional culinary specialties that you just shouldn't miss. Much of the traditional food around Lake Superior comes from our immigrant forebears. Depending on where you are, you'll find strong Swedish, Norwegian, Finnish, German,

Map 6 Lake Superior - Northeastern Section

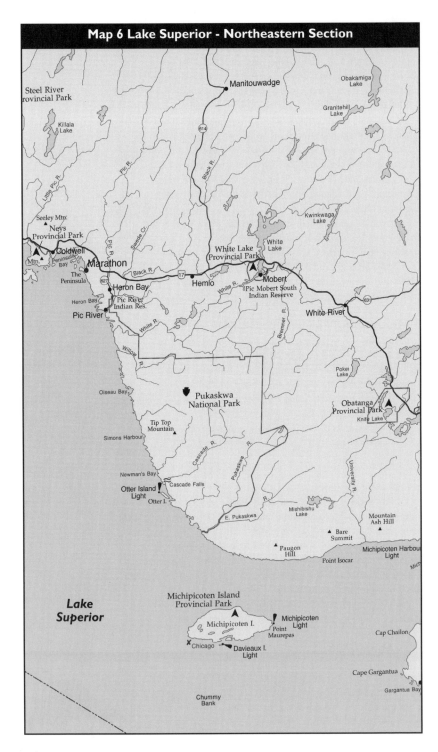

Steel River
Provincial Park

Manitouwadge

Obakamiga
Lake

Killala
Lake

Granitehill
Lake

614

Little Pic R.

Pic R.

Black R.

Kwinkwaga
Lake

Seeley Mtn.

Neys
Provincial Park

Coldwell

Swede Cr.

Pic R.

White
Lake

White Lake
Provincial Park

Mtn.

Peninsula
Bay

Marathon

Black R.

17

Hemlo

Mobert

Pic Mobert South
Indian Reserve

The
Peninsula

627

Heron Bay

White R.

631

Heron Bay

Pic River
Indian Res.

White R.

Bremner R.

White River

Pic River

Willow R.

Pokei
Lake

Obatanga
Provincial Park

Oiseau Bay

Pukaskwa
National Park

Knife Lake

Tip Top
Mountain

Cascade R.

Pukaskwa R.

University R.

Simons Harbour

Newman's Bay

Otter Island
Light

Cascade Falls

Otter I.

E. Pukaskwa

Mishibishu
Lake

Mountain
Ash Hill

Bare
Summit

Paugon
Hill

Michipicoten Harbour
Light

Point Isocar

Mich

Lake
Superior

Michipicoten Island
Provincial Park

Michipicoten I.

Michipicoten
Light

Point
Maurepas

Cap Chaillon

Chicago

Davieaux I.
Light

Cape Gargantua

Gargantua Bay

Chummy
Bank

Polish and Italian communities, and excellent examples of that cuisine in many local restaurants. These are closely held traditions of families sitting down together for dinner. If you see any of these regional specialties advertised or on menus, by all means, give them a try:

Wild rice: Wild rice is native to the cold rivers and lakes in Minnesota, Wisconsin and Ontario. It isn't a rice at all, but a long-grain water grass growing in shallow, marshy waters. Cooked and used like white or brown rice, wild rice has a nutty flavor that pairs well with many dishes. Wild rice was a staple in the Native American diet in the Lake Superior region and is still harvested today using traditional methods. The temperamental grain has also been hybridized and farmed commercially. Wild rice afficionados prefer the naturally grown product.

Pasty: It's pronounced "PASS-tee," and this is a Cornish-inspired dish made popular in this region by Scandinavian (especially Finnish) immigrants. It's a meat pie, consisting of beef, potatoes, carrots, onions and sometimes rutabaga inside a flaky crust. You'll find the best pasties around the lake in Michigan's Upper Peninsula, where they're a staple in most every household.

Fish fry: The Friday night fish fry is nearly a religion in Wisconsin, upper Michigan and Minnesota, stemming from the Catholic tradition of not eating meat on Fridays. For generations, families have been gathering in taverns and restaurants around the region for fish fry, which usually consists of white fish dipped in batter and deep fried.

Fish boil: This is the fish fry's cholesterol-free cousin. Fish boils originated when Lake Superior was home to an armada of fishing boats and scores of people made their living fishing this inland sea. The men would bring home their catches, women would throw them in an outdoor cauldron of boiling water along with potatoes and other veggies they'd happen to have on hand, and while the whole thing was boiling, people talked, played music and generally had a great time with their community. You'll find this tradition still alive around the lake, mainly on weekends during the summer. Make sure to partake of this lake tradition.

Walleye: While Lake Superior doesn't have one regional specialty, this could be nominated for that title. People here love their walleye, especially if they've caught it themselves.

Lefse: In Minnesota, lefse is as common as is a tortilla in Mexico. Lefse is flat bread, about the thickness of its Mexican cousin, made from potatoes. It's a Scandinavian specialty, and it still can be found in most Scandinavian homes of which there are many in this region. Try it warm with a little butter and sugar sprinkled on it, and you'll be hooked.

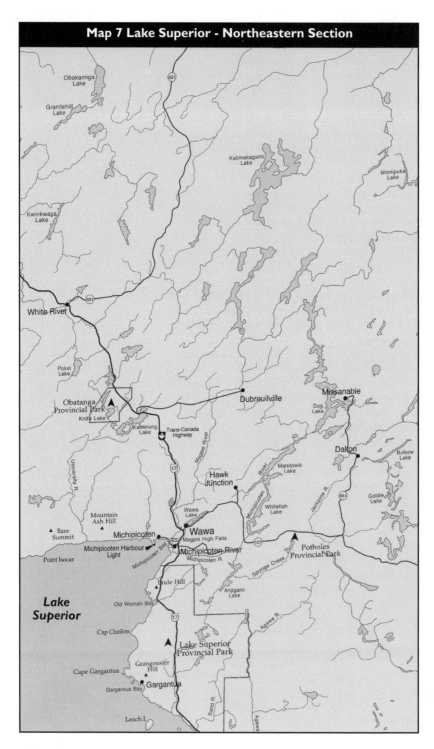

Map 7 Lake Superior - Northeastern Section

16

Lutefisk: Another traditional Scandinavian food, lutefisk is loved and hated with great passion in this region. It's fish soaked in lye. Yes, you heard right. You won't find it on many menus, but if you should, try it once, just to say you've had it.

LOOKING AT LAKERS, SEEING THE SALTIES

Big ships on the big lake are a common sight. The ships travel the lake from about mid-March when the ice breaks to December or January when the lake's surface begins to freeze.

Locals call these ships "lakers," and "salties." Lakers sail only on the Great Lakes. These vessels ride low in the water and are larger and more common than salties, which are ocean-going ships visiting Lake Superior to drop cargo or take on iron ore, grain or coal. Salties generally ride higher in the water and have cranes on their decks. Salties often carry cargo, while Lakers mostly transport bulk commodities.

The best places to watch the ships is in the large ports of Duluth, Superior, Thunder Bay or Sault Ste. Marie. Witnessing one of these monster boats maneuver its way through the Soo Locks is quite a memorable sight, as is standing near the canal in Duluth and watching an enormous ship slip by, almost close enough to touch.

GIFTS FROM THE LAKE:
ROCK PICKING ON THE SUPERIOR SHORE

Okay, we admit it. Collecting rocks is an obsession for many people who live near (or love) Lake Superior. Hey, they're our sea shells.

You'll find them decorating many Lake Superior homes and businesses. People use them as literal touchstones to remind them of a favorite trip, an especially memorable excursion to the lake, or simply as a focal point for the spiritual pull Lake Superior has on many people who love it. These are the gray, flat, speckled or multicolored rocks you'll find on nearly any beach. But here's a quick rundown of more exotic rocks you might encounter:

Lake Superior agate – The official gemstone of Minnesota, an agate is a quartz with red, brown, gray and translucent bands. These stones are a favorite of collectors who slice and polish them into solid rainbows. Hot spots to check for agates: stream beds, gravel pits, gravel beaches and river mouths from Two Harbors through Grand Marais Minnesota, and beaches in Michigan's Upper Peninsula. There are agate mines in Ontario as well.

Amethyst – This purple quartz adorns expensive jewelry and can be found along Minnesota's Gunflint Trail and Michigan's Isle Royale, but they're in Ontario in abundance. The province has five amethyst mines, and you can "pick your own"

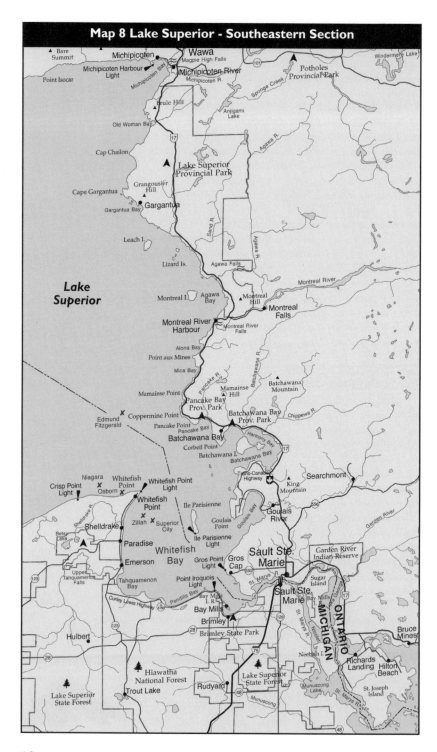

Map 8 Lake Superior - Southeastern Section

18

amethyst there like other people pick their own apples in an orchard. Not surprisingly, it's Ontario's provincial gemstone.

Isle Royale Greenstone – Greenstones are billions of years old and are aptly named. This dark green rock is the state gemstone of Michigan. The easiest place to look for them is Isle Royale, of course, but be warned, it is not legal to take them from this national park.

Thomsonite – Formed by steam bubbles in lava, Thomsonite has striped eyes of brilliant colors. Found only in a few spots around the world, the most lucrative happens to be in Good Harbor Bay, just west of Grand Marais, Minnesota. There are several Thomsonite mines in that area.

LAKE SUPERIOR WILDLIFE

Much of the land around Lake Superior is wilderness, and there you'll encounter wildlife, one of the treats of visiting or living around here. The best time to see animals is from dusk to dawn. Catching the unexpected glimpse of magnificent creatures like bears and moose is thrilling, to be sure, but use caution. Remember: When you're in the wild, you're a guest in their home.

While you might see a variety of small critters or deer on any walk in a park or along a trail in the woods, here's a list of some of larger animals you'll just might encounter along with safety tips for keeping it friendly.

• **Black bears** are omnivores, meaning they'll eat nearly everything. Many bears in the Lake Superior region have learned to troll campsites and portages for food left out by careless human visitors. Don't be one of them. Keep food at your campsite high in a tree, 10 feet from the ground and 10 feet from the tree trunk, well out of a bear's reach. Most campgrounds in bear territory have special trash containers and you should make sure to use those. Never keep any food – even a candy bar – in your tent, or you might awaken to find a hungry bear standing over you wondering what, exactly, smells so good.

Most black bears are wary of humans and will shy away if encountered. There are exceptions. Coming upon a mother bear and her cubs can be dangerous; never get between them. If a bear wanders into your campsite, do not feed it. Make noise, lots of it. That will usually drive off a bear. When hiking in the woods, make noise (talk to your companion or wear a bell, for example) so you won't surprise a bear. If you find yourself face to face with a black bear, do not run or panic. Black bear attacks on humans are rare. Talk in a loud voice, and back away slowly, making sure to leave the bear an avenue of escape. If it woofs, slaps the ground or bluff charges toward you, just continue backing away in a calm manner.

Map 9 Lake Superior - Southeastern Section

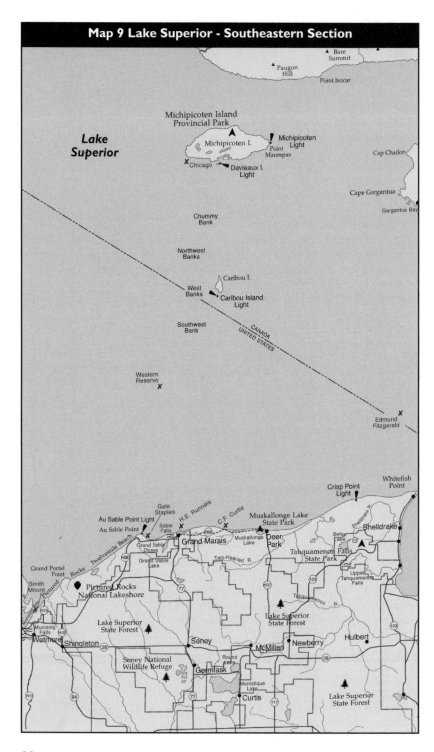

"Bear spray," similar to mace, is growing in popularity, but you need to be within a few feet of the animal to use it.

• **Timber wolves** are plentiful in northern Minnesota and Ontario, and their numbers are on the rise in Michigan and Wisconsin. Though many live in the woods around the lake, it's very rare to see one. Wolves don't want to see you. However, especially in the Boundary Waters Canoe Area Wilderness, it's not uncommon to hear packs howling at night and you might spot some tracks. If you happen to encounter one of these magnificent animals, consider yourself fortunate, and remember, wolf attacks on humans are extremely rare. However, wolves have been known to attack unattended dogs in the region. Keep your pet on a leash while hiking.

• **Moose** are plentiful in many parts of the Lake Superior region, and encounters are not unusual, especially in wild, untamed areas. These normally shy gentle giants gait through boggy terrain with poor eyesight. If you come upon a moose, remain still and it probably won't flee, but may continue with whatever it was doing. Have a camera close at hand, and you're sure to get some good shots. In the fall during "rut," or mating season, exercise extreme caution around the bull moose especially. Locals say the moose go a bit insane in the fall, and they're more likely to charge and attack humans – even cars!

If you're journeying by car through our wild areas in winter, take it slow. Moose, while generally not aggressive during this time of year, enjoy licking the salt used on many roadways. You just might take a sharp turn to find a moose in the middle of your path.

• **Cougars** are indeed returning Lake Superior residents, though not in great numbers. If you encounter one, it is a rare enough event to warrant a call to the local department or ministry of natural resources. They'll want to know about it. Be aware that these great cats are in the wild, especially if you're on foot in a remote area. If you find yourself face to face with a cougar, do not run. This will cause the cougar to give chase. Stand your ground, make yourself look as large as possible by opening your jacket and putting your arms above your head, wide. Pick up children or keep them close. Do your best to convince the cougar you are not prey. If a cougar attacks, fight back hard and do not play dead. You may use "bear spray" on cougars, but best not to get that close.

• Other animals you might encounter in our forests include skunks, raccoons, bobcats, lynx, badgers, fishers, porcupines, foxes and the ever-present deer. Be respectful in all cases and remember that they are not tame animals and should not be fed or harassed.

Map 10 Lake Superior - Southern Section

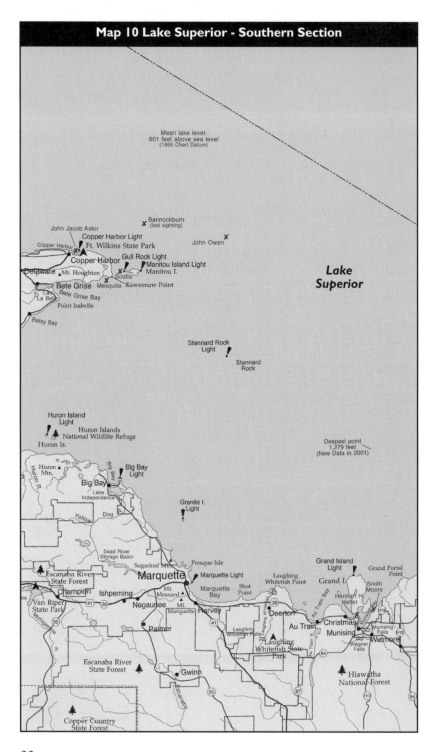

Mean lake level:
601 feet above sea level
(1985 Chart Datum)

Bannockburn
(last sighting)

John Jacob Astor
Copper Harbor Light
Ft. Wilkins State Park

John Owen

Copper Harbor
Copper Harbor
Gull Rock Light
Manitou Island Light

Lake Superior

Delaware
Mt. Houghton
Manitou I.
Scotia

Bete Grise
Mesquite
Keweenaw Point

Lac
La Belle
Bete Grise Bay
Point Isabelle

Betsy Bay

Stannard Rock
Light

Stannard
Rock

Huron Island
Light
Huron Islands
National Wildlife Refuge
Huron Is.

Deepest point
1,279 feet
(New Data in 2001)

Huron ▲
Mtn.
Big Bay
Light

Big Bay

Big Bay
Lake
Independence

Yellow
Dog

Granite I.
Light

Dead River
Storage Basin

Sugarloaf Mtn.
Presque Isle

Grand Island
Light
Grand Portal
Point

Escanaba River
State Forest
Champion
Ishpeming

Marquette
Marquette Light

Marquette
Bay

Shot
Point

Laughing
Whitefish Point

Grand I.
Smith
Moore

Van Riper
State Park

Mt.
Mesnard ▲

Negaunee
Mt.
Marquette

Harvey

Herman H.
Hetler

Deerton
Au Train
Christmas
Munising

Munising
Falls

Wetmore

Palmer

Laughing
Whitefish Falls

Laughing
Whitefish State
Park

Wagner
Falls

Escanaba River
State Forest

Gwinn

Hiawatha
National Forest

Copper Country
State Forest

Deer in the Headlights

One creature you're virtually certain to encounter around Lake Superior is deer, oftentimes in great numbers. Deer are most active in the morning and at dusk, but you can find them nibbling the grass along the roadside at nearly any time of the day or night. They're gentle animals and fun to watch, especially as they leap and bound along ... unless that leaping and bounding is directly into the path of your car.

Deer-car accidents are common, especially in wooded or rural areas. Here's what locals do to avoid hitting a deer: Scan the ditches on either side of the road as you drive, especially at dusk and dawn. Seeing deer before they're square in your headlights makes all the difference. If possible, ask a passenger to act as a "deer spotter." If, despite your best efforts, a deer leaps out into your path, do not swerve wildly to avoid it. Law enforcement officials lakewide report that most of the human fatalities that result from deer-car accidents happen when people swerve, lose control of their cars and veer into oncoming traffic or roll down an embankment.

Lake Superior Birds

Birding is a popular pastime lakewide. While it's fun to see the smaller feathered creatures, much of the excitement around birding comes when you spot one of the majestic raptors that soar here. There are some great flyway hot spots for birding around the Lake Superior region. Some special spots include Whitefish Point, Michigan, Hawk Ridge in Duluth, Minnesota, and Thunder Cape in Ontario. While great varieties of feather residents abound, here are some of the larger birds that might be encountered:

• **Bald eagles,** once threatened, have come back in great numbers around Lake Superior. It isn't uncommon to look into the sky and see this enormous bird soaring. Better yet is to witness one diving into the lake for food.

• **Ospreys,** with their black and white feathers, are also highly skilled fishermen. Look for their huge nests in the treetops in remote areas.

• **Owls** live in the area, and also migrate through in the fall. When the leaves have fallen off the trees, it's a good time to look for these mysterious birds.

• **Hawks** of several types live and hunt in the Lake Superior region. Look for them sitting sentinel on top of telephone poles and in solitary branches on treetops.

• **Loons** don't fall into the raptor category, but there is no sound more identifiable with the Lake Superior wilderness than the loon's haunting call ... unless it's the wolf's howl. These black and white waterfowl live on large lakes throughout the region.

Map II Lake Superior - Keweenaw Peninsula Section

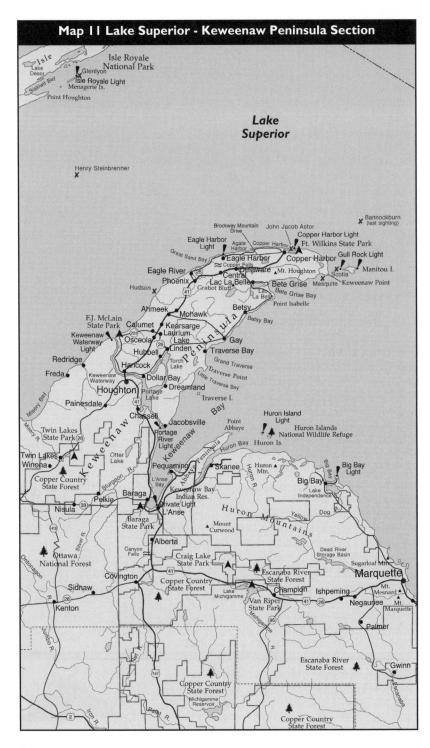

Isle Royale
National Park

Isle
Lake
Desor

Glenlyon

Isle Royale Light

Menagerie Is.

Siskiwit Bay

Point Houghton

Lake
Superior

Henry Steinbrenner
✗

Bannockburn
(last sighting) ✗

Brockway Mountain
Drive

John Jacob Astor

Copper Harbor Light

Eagle Harbor
Light

Agate
Harbor

Copper Harbor

Ft. Wilkins State Park

Eagle Harbor

Gull Rock Light

Great Sand Bay

Copper Harbor

Copper Falls

Eagle River (26)

Delaware

Mt. Houghton

Scotia ✗

Manitou I.

Phoenix

Central

Mesquite ✗

Keweenaw Point

Hudson ✗

Lac La Belle

Bete Grise

(41)

Gratiot Bluff

Lac
La Belle

Bete Grise Bay

Ahmeek

Point Isabelle

Mohawk

Betsy

F.J. McLain
State Park

Calumet

Kearsarge

Betsy Bay

Keweenaw
Waterway
Light

(203)

Laurium

Osceola

Lake

Gay

Redridge

Hubbell

Linden

(26)

Traverse Bay

Torch
Lake

Grand Traverse

Hancock

Traverse Point

Freda

Keweenaw
Waterway

Dollar Bay

Little Traverse Bay

Houghton

Portage
Lake

Dreamland

Traverse I.

Painesdale

(41)

Bay

Misery Bay

Chassell

Jacobsville

Point
Abbaye

Huron Island
Light

Misery R.

Twin Lakes
State Park (26)

Portage
River
Light

Huron Islands
National Wildlife Refuge

Twin Lakes

Otter
Lake

Huron Is.

Winona

Pequaming

Skanee

Huron
Mtn.

Big Bay
Light

Copper Country
State Forest

Sturgeon R.

L'Anse
Bay

Baraga

Keweenaw Bay
Indian Res.

Big Bay

Nisula

(38)

Pelkie

Private Light

Lake
Independence

Silver R.

L'Anse

Huron

Mountains

(H16)

Baraga
State Park

Mount
Curwood

Yellow

Dog R.

Ottawa
National Forest

Canyon
Falls

Alberta

Dead River
Storage Basin

Sugarloaf Mtn.

Ontonagon

Covington

Craig Lake
State Park

Escanaba River
State Forest

Marquette

Sidnaw

(41)

Copper Country
State Forest

Champlin

Ishpeming

Mt.
Mesnard

Kenton

(28)

Lake
Michigamme

Van Riper
State Park

(41) (28)

Negaunee

Mt.
Marquette

(95)

Palmer

Jumbo R.

Escanaba River
State Forest

Gwinn

(141)

Copper Country
State Forest

Michigamme
Reservoir

(2)

Iron R.

Paint R.

Copper Country
State Forest

50 Experiences of a Lifetime on Lake Superior

(Reprinted from *Lake Superior Magazine*)

Maybe we're a little biased, but here at *Lake Superior Magazine*, we find every moment spent on the big lake suitable as a "Best of the Lake." For these pages, we narrow the selection to a manageable 50 Lake Superior experiences of a lifetime. May they inspire you to try something new or to create your own list.

1. Do the Circle Tour – Clockwise or counterclockwise? Car, bicycle, motorcycle or shoes? Who cares! Just make sure to circle the entire lake at least once in your life. (Check out other people's circular experiences at www.lakesuperiorcircletour.com.)

2. Sail, cruise or paddle – In a powerboat, in a kayak or under a sail, the lake is different from out there. If you don't have your own boat to float, try options like Vista Fleet and the *Grampa Woo* in Minnesota; Pictured Rocks Cruises and Shipwreck Tours in Michigan; Soo Locks Tours and Lock Tours Canada in the two Sault Ste. Maries, or the Madeline Island Ferry and Apostle Islands Cruise Service in Wisconsin.

3. Take a trip to an island – Pick an island, any island. Try an Apostle in Wisconsin for a short ferry ride or Isle Royale in Michigan for a long excursion. Or head north to Ontario for a ride to a wilder island.

4. Attend a festival – How can you say you've truly "done" Lake Superior without a fest on your itinerary? You can celebrate the independence of the United States and the creation of Canada, or hail blueberries, winter, apples, St. Urho, fish boils, blues music, theater and so much more.

5. Swim on a hot August (or any) day or dip your toes into the water – There's nothing quite like a swim in the biggest freshwater lake in the world. Or simply toe-dipping. It's not all that cold. Really.

Map 12 Lake Superior - Southern Section

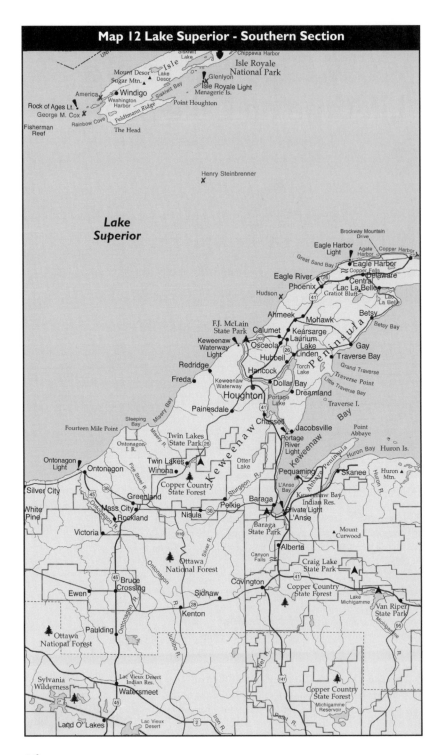

Isle Royale
National Park

Isle Royale Light

Siskiwit
Lake

Chippewa Harbor

Mount Desor
Sugar Mtn.

Lake
Desor

Glenlyon

Menagerie Is.

America

Windigo

Washington
Harbor

Siskiwit Bay

Point Houghton

Rock of Ages Lt.
George M. Cox

Rainbow Cove

Feldtmann Ridge

Washington
Harbor

Fisherman
Reef

The Head

Henry Steinbrenner

Lake
Superior

Brockway Mountain
Drive

Eagle Harbor
Light

Agate
Harbor

Copper Harbor

Great Sand Bay

Eagle Harbor

Copper Falls

Eagle River

Delaware

Phoenix

Central

Lac La Belle

Lac
La Belle

Hudson

Gratiot Bluff

Ahmeek

Mohawk

Betsy

F.J. McLain
State Park

Calumet

Kearsarge

Laurium

Betsy Bay

Keweenaw
Waterway
Light

Osceola

Lake

Linden

Gay

Redridge

Hubbell

Torch
Lake

Traverse Bay

Grand Traverse

Keweenaw
Waterway

Hancock

Traverse Point

Freda

Dollar Bay

Little Traverse Bay

Houghton

Dreamland

Traverse I.

Portage
Lake

Painesdale

Bay

Chassell

Jacobsville

Point
Abbaye

Sleeping
Bay

Fourteen Mile Point

Portage
River
Light

Ontonagon
I.R.

Twin Lakes
State Park

Otter
Lake

Pequaming

Huron Bay

Huron Is.

Ontonagon
Light

Twin Lakes

Winoha

Skanee

Huron
Mtn.

Silver City

Ontonagon

Copper Country
State Forest

L'Anse
Bay

Huron R.

Greenland

Sturgeon R.

Baraga

Keweenaw Bay
Indian Res.

White
Pine

Mass City

Rockland

Nisula

Pelkie

Private Light

L'Anse

Victoria

Baraga
State Park

Mount
Curwood

Alberta

Canyon
Falls

Craig Lake
State Park

Ottawa
National Forest

Copper Country
State Forest

Bruce
Crossing

Covington

Lake
Michigamme

Van Riper
State Park

Ewen

Sidnaw

Kenton

Ottawa
National Forest

Paulding

Sylvania
Wilderness

Lac Vieux Desert
Indian Res.

Watersmeet

Copper Country
State Forest

Michigamme
Reservoir

Land O' Lakes

Lac Vieux
Desert

6. Watch a storm – Marvel at the awesome power of the wind and the waves. A waterfront resort, cabin or hotel gives comfortable views of those gales in November (or in April).

7. See the northern lights – If you don't believe in magic, the spectral sight of the aurora borealis on a crisp evening just might change your mind.

8. Visit in all four seasons – Cross-country ski in winter, hike in spring, paddle in summer, take a leaf tour in fall or simply hang out and watch as each season unveils its qualities. If you only visit in one season, you haven't had a full lake experience. The seasons are why we live here.

9. Tour a lighthouse – The many lighthouses dotting the shores once served mainly as aids to navigation (many still do), but now they are time machines taking us back in the lake's history. Some are historic sites, some are bed-and-breakfast inns, all are marvelous reminders of the past.

10. Listen to a fog horn – Is it the sound of the horn, the fog itself or the combination of the two that creates the unsettling effect both comforting and chilling at the same time. Most places with a lighthouse have a fog signal. Duluth, Minnesota, has perhaps the last official old diaphone with a distinctive "BEE-Oh."

11. Watch a ship coming into a port – Magnificent ore- and coal-bearing lakers or ocean-going salties never fail to inspire and delight. Check them out at Thunder Bay, Ontario; the Sault Ste. Maries, (Ontario & Michigan); Marquette, Michigan; and Duluth, Two Harbors and Silver Bay, Minnesota, and at various other points around the lake.

12. Watch a sunrise or a sunset over the lake – That big red ball, whether it's coming or going, is an awesome sight to see.

13. Ditto watching a full moon rise – An enormous orange moon hanging in the autumn sky over the calm lake, you on the rocks with a campfire and s'mores. What s'more needs to be said?

14. Savor regional specialties – Lake trout, wild rice, cranberries ... pasties. To get a real taste of the region, you've got to taste the regional fare. Heck, you may want to try a lutefisk church dinner ... maybe.

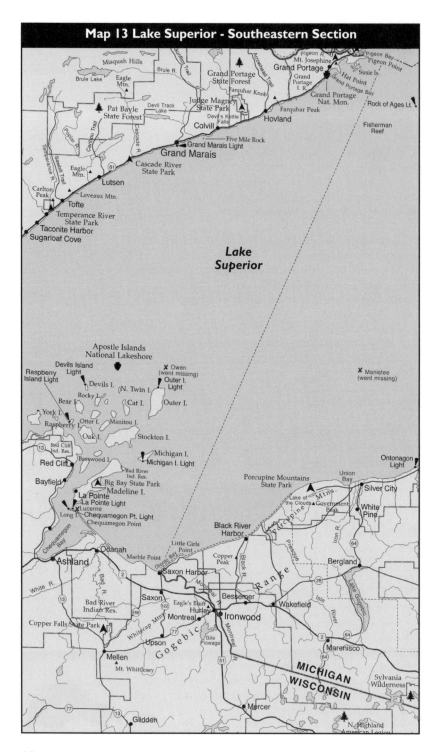

Map 13 Lake Superior - Southeastern Section

Misquah Hills

Brule Lake

Eagle Mtn.

Brule R.

Gunflint Trail

Arrowhead Trail

Pigeon R.

Mt. Josephine

Grand Portage

Pigeon Bay

Pigeon Point

Grand Portage State Forest

Grand Portage I. R.

Susie Is.

Hat Point

Grand Portage Bay

Farquhar Knob

Grand Portage Nat. Mon.

Rock of Ages Lt.

Judge Magney State Park

Devil's Kettle Falls

Farquhar Peak

Fisherman Reef

Pat Bayle State Forest

Devil Track Lake

Colvill

Hovland

Caribou Trail

Poplar R.

Cascade R.

Five Mile Rock

Grand Marais Light

Superior Hiking Trail

Grand Marais

Temperance R.

Eagle Mtn.

61

Cascade River State Park

Lutsen

Leveaux Mtn.

Carlton Peak

Tofte

Temperance River State Park

Taconite Harbor

Sugarloaf Cove

Lake Superior

Apostle Islands National Lakeshore

Devils Island Light

Raspberry Island Light

Devils I.

Rocky I.

N. Twin I.

Cat I.

✗ Owen (went missing)

Outer I. Light

Outer I.

✗ Manistee (went missing)

Bear I.

York I.

Raspberry I.

Otter I.

Manitou I.

Oak I.

Stockton I.

Red Cliff Ind. Res.

13

Red Cliff

Basswood I.

Michigan I.

Michigan I. Light

Ontonagon Light

Bayfield

Big Bay State Park

Madeline I.

Bad River Ind. Res.

Porcupine Mountains State Park

Union Bay

Silver City

La Pointe

La Pointe Light

Lucerne

Chequamegon Pt. Light

Long I.

Chequamegon Point

Lake of the Clouds

Government Peak

White Pine

Chequamegon Bay

Black River Harbor

Porcupine Mtns.

Iron R.

Odanah

Marble Point

Little Girls Point

Oronto Bay

Bergland

Ashland

Bad R.

2

Saxon Harbor

Copper Peak

Black R.

Presque

64

Range

28

Lake Gogebic

White R.

13

Bad River Indian Res.

Saxon

169

122

Eagle's Bluff

Hurley

Montreal R.

Bessemer

Wakefield

Isle

River

Copper Falls State Park

Whitecap Mtn.

77

Montreal

Ironwood

Gile Flowage

Montreal R.

2

64

Upson

Gogebic

51

Marenisco

64

Mellen

Mt. Whittlesey

MICHIGAN

WISCONSIN

Sylvania Wilderness

2

77

13

Glidden

Mercer

N. Highland American Legion

15. Stroll along a waterfront – Many small and large towns created paths along the water. It's great to people and lake watch. For example, Sault Ste. Marie, Ontario's boardwalk features funky statuary while Duluth's lakewalk has hiking, biking and skating.

16. Seek out wildlife – Seeing bear, fox, moose, deer, woodland caribou or raptors and other birds tells us we're not the only ones who love the lake. Many trails afford wildlife watching. Migration flights, like Hawk Ridge in Duluth, Whitefish Point in Michigan or Thunder Bay, offer prime birding. If sea gulls are your thing, you can feed or scatter a flock in many lake locales.

17. Seek out a really BIG critter – These animals are easy to spot because they don't move much. Take the goose at Wawa or the Winnie-the-Pooh at White River, both Ontario. Another favorite is the huge muskie at Hayward, Wisconsin, which is the National Fresh Water Fishing Hall of Fame. The one-half city block long and $4^{1}/_{2}$ stories tall concrete, steel and fiberglass structure is a wonder.

18. Sit on a beach at night and listen to the waves – Whooosh, whooosh, whooosh.

19. Beachcomb – Pick rocks (there are agates in there somewhere), find treasures left by the lake or by earlier beach visitors, feel the sand between your toes, roam without specific purpose. Ahhh. That feels good.

20. Skip rocks on the lake – This is an experience unto itself. If you've never found a flat skipping rock, hefted it for the right balance and then launched it across the water for one, two, three maybe four or more skips, well, then you just haven't.

21. Hike, bike, inline skate, cross-country ski or snowmobile on any trail – Hundreds of miles of woodland trails exist around the lake. Make friends with some of them. Take friends on them!

22. Rent a lakeside cabin – Maybe just for a week or a weekend, pretend it's your home and get to know the lake like a local … without having to go to work every day. In winter, of course, living like a local means shoveling the front stoop.

23. Camp lakeside or north woods – It's an intimate way to get up close and personal with the lake.

29

Map 14 Lake Superior - Apostle Islands/Bayfield Area Section

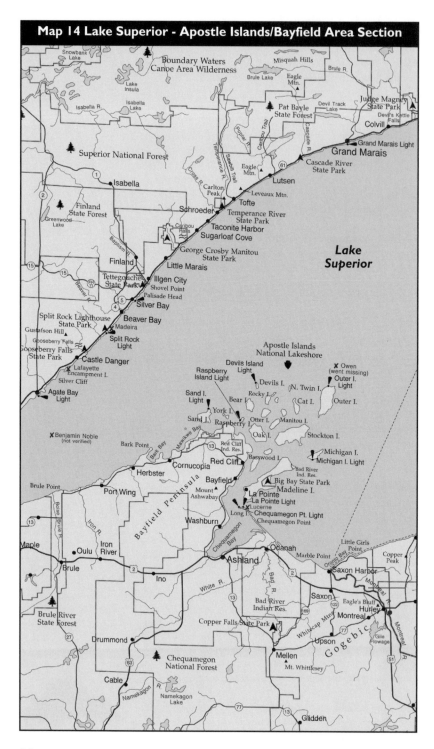

Snowbank Lake
Boundary Waters Canoe Area Wilderness
Misquah Hills
Lake Insula
Brule R.
Brule Lake
Eagle Mtn.
Isabella R.
Isabella Lake
Pat Bayle State Forest
Devil Track Lake
Judge Magney State Park
Devil's Kettle Falls
Colvill
Superior National Forest
Grand Marais Light
Grand Marais
61
Cascade R.
Cascade River State Park
1
Isabella
Eagle Mtn.
Carlton Peak
Lutsen
Leveaux Mtn.
2
Finland State Forest
Greenwood Lake
Tofte
Schroeder
Temperance River State Park
Caribou Falls
Taconite Harbor
Sugarloaf Cove
Baptism R.
Finland
George Crosby Manitou State Park
Little Marais
Lake Superior
15
15
Tettegouche State Park
Illgen City
Shovel Point
Palisade Head
Beaver R.
FH 11
5
Silver Bay
4
Split Rock Lighthouse State Park
Beaver Bay
Madeira
Gustafson Hill
Split Rock Light
Gooseberry Falls
Gooseberry Falls State Park
Castle Danger
Apostle Islands National Lakeshore
Devils Island Light
Owen (went missing)
Lafayette Encampment I.
Silver Cliff
Raspberry Island Light
Devils I.
Outer I. Light
Sand I. Light
Bear I.
Rocky I.
N. Twin I.
Agate Bay Light
Cat I.
Outer I.
York I.
Sand I.
Raspberry I.
Otter I.
Manitou I.
Benjamin Noble (not verified)
Bark Point
Bad Bay
Mawikwe Bay
Oak I.
Stockton I.
Red Cliff Ind. Res.
13
Basswood I.
Michigan I.
Michigan I. Light
Cornucopia
Red Cliff
Herbster
Bayfield
Big Bay State Park
Brule Point
Port Wing
Mount Ashwabay
Madeline I.
La Pointe
La Pointe Light
Lucerne
Bad River Ind. Res.
Bois Brule R.
Iron R.
Washburn
Long I.
Chequamegon Pt. Light
Chequamegon Point
13
Maple
Oulu
Iron River
Chequamegon Bay
Odanah
Little Girls Point
Copper Peak
Brule
2
Ino
Ashland
Marble Point
Orienta Bay
Saxon Harbor
Saxon
White R.
Bad R.
2
Montreal R.
Brule River State Forest
13
Bad River Indian Res.
189
Saxon
122
Eagle's Bluff
Hurley
Montreal
27
Drummond
Copper Falls State Park
77
Upson
Gile Flowage
63
Chequamegon National Forest
Mellen
Mt. Whittlesey
Gogebic
51
Cable
Namekagon R.
Namekagon Lake
77
13
Glidden

24. Stay for a week in one spot – Sample the wide variety of accommodations – big lodge, family-run resort, small motel or fancy hotel. The key is to plan enough time to explore, to get to know the staff and feel the real flavor of the area.

25. Visit a waterfall – So many waterfalls, so little time. Almost every direction has a waterfall in there somewhere.

26. Watch a dog sled, dragon boat, snowmobile, snowshoe or running race. Or even better, volunteer to help – Check out local calendars (or our events in each issue or online at www.lakesuperior.com). There's something about watching folks go, go, go that harkens to life on our lake.

27. Bring your dog on a road trip – Don't be selfish with your lake time; bring the pup to the world's largest water dish.

28. Visit the Great Lakes Aquarium – Have an environmental Circle Tour of Lake Superior in a couple of hours. It's the biggest fresh-water aquarium in the world located on the biggest fresh-water lake in the world. Don't miss it.

29. Tour the locks at Sault Ste. Marie, Ontario & Michigan – You simply have to see what opened Lake Superior to the world in 1855. These aren't the original locks, but shipping remains impressive and you can practically touch a boat as it goes by.

30. Take a walk in the fog – Definitely a lake experience. Pick the right, safe path (not a road). If it's too thick to walk, simply sitting by the lapping lake will suffice.

31. Travel a side road – Get off the well-beaten paths. Especially at the northern shores in Ontario, the only way to reach the lake is to take a side road.

32. Slow down to lake time – If you plan to visit for one day, plan for two. Don't rush in the car; don't rush in general. If you're counting, you'll notice fewer stoplights and traffic jams than you might be used to.

33. Stop at a visitor center – Get directions, pick up some brochures, talk to the folks there about what to do and see. Knowing more is good and you can relive the experience with the stuff you pick up.

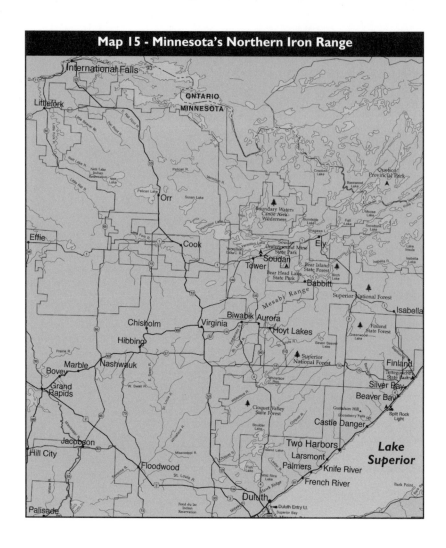

Map 15 - Minnesota's Northern Iron Range

34. Picnic on the lakeshore – Pack your own or pick up something (like smoked salmon) en route. Food does taste better with a lake breeze and splashing waves for company.

35. Experience winter in Big Snow Country – Just once, learn what it really means to be snowed in.

36. Charter a fishing boat – Play Old Man and the Sea for a day with an experienced fishing guide. (Your ending will be happier than the book's.) Visitor information centers can direct you to the local charters.

37. Ride a scenic train – Several spots along the lake connect to the rails. Sault Ste. Marie and White River, Ontario, and Spooner, Wisconsin, have connections. Duluth, Minnesota, hosts two scenic trains.

38. Simply find a view to enjoy and enjoy it – 'Nuff said.

39. Visit a national, state or provincial park – With more than 50 parks, public forests or wildlife refuges of one sort or another, there is practically one around ever corner of Lake Superior. Don't miss 'em.

40. Do the tour with someone special – It's one thing to have great experiences; it's a better thing to share them with someone.

41. Create memories for your children – Lake and north woods holidays (or living) should mean no stuffy can't-touch-can't-talk-just-can't-only-for-grown-ups activities.

42. Breathe it all in – The sense of smell is the best memory trigger, we are told. Remember the smells of campfire smoke and fresh, clean lake air or moist deep woods vegetation. Locals thrill to that first "spring" day when air is warm enough to let the sniffer work after a long winter's nap.

43. Shop a local specialty store – Need a mini moose for the mantel, a jar of lingonberries to take home, a regional book or local artwork? Check out the shops that feature local foods, artists and trinkets.

44. Get to know some locals – We're very friendly. Feel free to say "hi" and chat at a walkway or in a local eating establishment. Conversing with clerks is cool. Knowing us helps you know the lake region.

45. Visit a historic re-enactment or a local museum – Living history enlightens visitors and residents. Fort William Historic Park in Thunder Bay, Ontario, and Fort Wilkins in Copper Harbor, Michigan, are two good examples. Small historic museums abound, like the one on Madeline Island, Wisconsin.

46. Tour a lakeside mansion – Past lifestyles of the rich and famous always intrigue and we've got some good ones. Check out places like Glensheen Historic Estate in Duluth, Minnesota, Fairlawn Mansion in Superior, Wisconsin, or bed-and-breakfast inns like Laurium Manor in Laurium, Michigan, or the Old Rittenhouse in Bayfield, Wisconsin.

47. Cross the border – Going north or going south, it's a lake experience to see both countries and realize the differences and similarities.

48. Sample a marine museum – Several reveal our maritime heritage. Try Great Lakes Shipwreck Museum at Whitefish Point or Marquette Maritime Museum in Michigan or the Lake Superior Maritime Visitor Center in Duluth, Minnesota. There are some smaller local examples to be sampled.

49. Do something nostalgic – Sure, you can do these things anywhere, but by the lake is better, trust us. What's nostalgic? Stop at a local diner or family restaurant on a shore. Go to a north woods resort where the kids can learn to paddle a canoe. Get a fishing license and drop a line into the water. You have your own childhood memories to go by.

50. This one, we leave to you – Consider this one for the road … fill it in as you find your own lifetime experience on Lake Superior's shores.

Recommended Drives

ircling Lake Superior, while a wonderful, must-do experience, is but one way to make your lake visit. Following below are sections of the Circle Tour and region, any one of which would make a magical getaway for a few days or longer. These drives simply outline stretches of the larger Circle Tour that offer manageable shorter trips and sometimes give you a little bit of history to boot. Specifics for the towns and cities traversed by these drives can be found by checking the individual, alphabetical listings in the main body of this guide. So pack up the family and take to the road....

MINNESOTA'S NORTH SHORE SCENIC DRIVE

A scenic stretch of the Lake Superior Circle Tour follows along Highway 61 into Minnesota's Arrowhead, beginning at the Lester River bridge within the city limits of Duluth extending along Lake Superior to Canada's border, or southwesterly from the border to Duluth. For this description, begin at the eastern end of Duluth, where the Lake Superior North Shore Association operates an information stand at Lester River daily from May to September. Visitors will find a wealth of material to enhance their journey and can also check on road projects along the north shore.

Of particular interest to hikers and bikers, the first section of Gitchi-Gami Trail was completed from Split Rock to Beaver Bay in 2002 and additional segments are finished at Gooseberry Falls and Tofte. This non-motorized, 10-foot paved route is the first leg of a planned route from Two Harbors to Grand Marais. The trail is a joint effort of the Minnesota Department of Transportation and the Department of Natural Resources with the Lake Superior Touring Trail Association. Reconstruction of the former road bed for Highway 61 around Silver Creek Cliff was undertaken in 2004 to create an exciting ride taking in the panoramic lake view to the south, along with a rest stop at the top of the cliff. In the Lutsen-Tofte area, several former

hiking trails have changed to accommodate multiple use by bikers and snowmobilers.

Visitors in the winter months will be interested in the more than 900 miles of snowmobile trails and the equally impressive cross-country ski trail system along Minnesota's north shore.

Kitchi-Gammi Park at Brighton Beach is a popular swimming and picnicking area with access just past the information stand at Lester River. A lot of good skipping stones can be found along the beach, with smooth rocks to the water's edge.

The Minnesota shoreline of Lake Superior is targeted for a series of non-impact camping and rest sites for canoeists and kayakers known as the Lake Superior Water Trail. A nonprofit volunteer organization hopes to eventually have sites in place all along the shore from Duluth to the Canadian border. More information is available from the Lake Superior Water Trail Association of Minnesota at Grand Marais.

Skyline Parkway in Duluth, the Superior National Forest Scenic Byway (Forest Highway 11) from Silver Bay to the Iron Range and the Gunflint Trail out of Grand Marais are all designated as State Scenic Byways. The entire north shore route from Canal Park's Aerial Lift Bridge to the International Bridge at the Pigeon River is designated as an All-American Road by the U.S. Department of Transportation, only one of 20 such designated routes in the country.

For the first 20 miles (32 kilometers), the highway route splits into two roads. Minnesota 61 becomes a four-lane divided expressway one-quarter mile or more away from the view of the lake, although at intervals it has spurs down to the lakeshore. The expressway has no accommodations and the scenery is much less enticing than the alternate route closer to the lake.

Parallel to and above the scenic route and the expressway is the North Shore Corridor Trail, a designated recreation trail that runs from Duluth to Grand Marais. The trail offers opportunities for hiking in summer and cross-country skiing, dog sledding and snowmobiling in winter. No motorized vehicles are permitted on the trail in summer.

County 61 runs right next to the lake, within yards of the shoreline, and is the preferred scenic route, having been designated the North Shore Scenic Drive. A marked bicycle route accompanies the entire Scenic Drive. Traveler pullouts are located conveniently close to Lake Superior, although there are no formal toilet facilities except at Knife River, near the expressway. The Duluth Water Plant offers free cold and filtered water at the roadside pulloff adjacent to the plant. Access to the shore makes for a restful stop.

The North Shore Scenic Drive route has restaurants, lodging, great shops and many locations to stop and dip your feet in the cool water. It also passes over numerous streams that empty into the lake, most of which offer excellent fishing at all times of the year. The most popular are the Lester, French and Sucker rivers. Air conditioning, courtesy of the lake, is cheap, automatic and mechanically trouble-free. Ideal photographs can be made from almost any location.

The scenic north shore accommodations have a tendency to fill up early in the day during summer and fall, so advance reservations are always the best idea.

Businesses and residents on the route have planted thousands of flowering plants along the roadway as an additional showy welcome to warm-weather visitors. Berry pickers are a common sight seeking wild strawberries, chokecherries and gooseberries in June, followed by raspberries in July and then the esteemed blueberries, which ripen in late July inland and early August along the shore.

The North Shore Scenic Railroad travels parallel to the North Shore Scenic Drive between Duluth and Two Harbors with shorter rides between The Depot in downtown Duluth and the Lester River area of Duluth.

Extensive stands of aspen from Lester River to Knife River are an indication that this area was once devastated by fire. This occurred in a series of forest fires in 1918. Aspen (poplar) and birch are referred to as "disturbance community" by foresters. Both trees begin new growth quickly after an area has been logged or burned.

Just before Lakeview Castle Restaurant and Lounge, construction is moving on an inland harbor of refuge for boaters.

At the mouth of the beautiful French River just past Lakeview Castle, the Minnesota Department of Natural Resources operates a modern cold water hatchery, the French River Fish Hatchery. Numerous species of fish such as sucker, walleye, steelhead and other strains of rainbow trout are incubated at the hatchery, using the cool, clear water available in this location to help ensure that the fishery continues to be healthy. Visitors are welcome for self-guided tours weekdays.

Rita B and nephew Scott Graden offer a tantalizing cuisine at the New Scenic Café. The Shorecrest Supper Club and Motel offers a bit of the old north shore with an emphasis on fish and other local favorites. Both locations offer excellent views of Lake Superior as you dine.

Make time for gift shop browsing, since each store along the Scenic Drive has a unique personality. Tom's Logging Camp and Trading Post is a gift shop surrounded by a re-creation of an 1800s North West Fur Company camp. Traditional gifts, clothing and footwear. There is a fee to

enter the camp where there are tame deer and a trout pond.

A half mile from Tom's is Stoney Point, site of several shipwrecks in the late 1800s and early 1900s. This jut of land, although unimproved, is a dandy spot to watch large ships on their way to port.

The drive between Duluth and Two Harbors offers lodging opportunities, most with views of Lake Superior. Several new bed-and-breakfast inns and cabins have been added in recent years. And a couple of nice campgrounds offer additional overnight options.

Five miles (8 kilometers) northeast of the French River, a historic plaque commemorates the settlement of Buchanan, named after President James Buchanan (1857-61). Platted in 1856, the townsite was the home of the north shore's first post office. The following year the first of the region's newspapers, the *North Shore Advocate*, was published here. Copper mining was the promise, but it never materialized, and the town was eventually abandoned and later destroyed by fire.

At numerous locations along the north shore route from Knife River to the Canadian border there is entry to the Superior Hiking Trail, planned eventually to also connect to Duluth. Earning high praise from hikers and hiking organizations, additional sections of the trail are being completed by volunteers, allowing free and easy access from many places of lodging along the way. More than 240 miles (350 kilometers) of trail are well-signed and maintained by volunteers to provide hikers with challenges at whatever level they desire. In fact, the Superior Hiking Trail has become a part of a lodge-to-lodge hiking system on the shore. Superior Shuttle service is available on Fridays, Saturdays and Sundays at many of the participating lodges, as well as numerous pickup and drop-off points along the trail from May to late October. Watch for the signs. Superior Hiking Trail Association has information at its office and store on Seventh Avenue in Two Harbors.

For information on specific areas of Minnesota's north shore, turn to the listing for the various towns, but don't allow the border between the United States and Canada to stop you from continuing on the Circle Tour.

Canada has a differing terrain presenting majestic views of Lake Superior, sandy beach access and excellent fishing experiences. Just across the border and customs gate you can obtain more current information about your trip into Canada at the Visitor Information Centre. Official maps and detailed brochures of locations in this region of Ontario are available at the center, which is open from mid-May through Labour Day.

Crossing the border is a simple process, but there are regulations regarding what you can take with you, which are explained in some detail at the front of this publication. In general dogs and cats older than 3 months will need certification signed by a licensed veterinarian that they have been vaccinated against rabies. You may also be asked to prove your citizenship with documents like a driver's license,

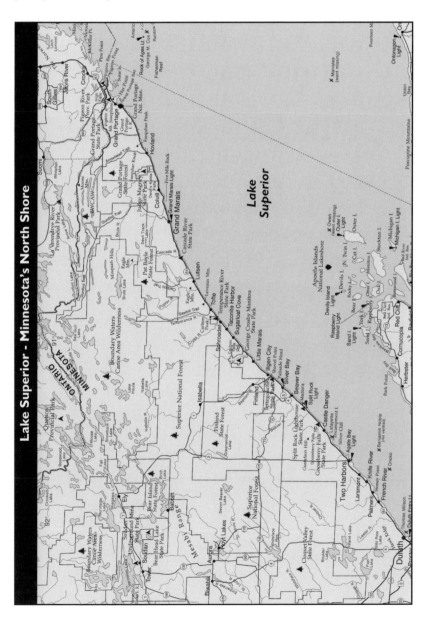

Lake Superior - Minnesota's North Shore

passport or a birth or baptismal certificate. Just a driver's license alone may not be enough.

Be aware that Ontario runs on the metric system, so road signs, speed and other measurements might be a little strange to you if you're from the United States: kilometers per hour, liters instead of gallons. Also, radar warning devices are forbidden in Ontario, even if turned off and only being transported in your vehicle. Police may confiscate such devices. The Lake Superior area of Ontario is in the Eastern Time Zone. Also, as in the United States, many Ontario municipalities have adopted no-smoking ordinances of varying degrees, so it's best to check before lighting up in most establishments.

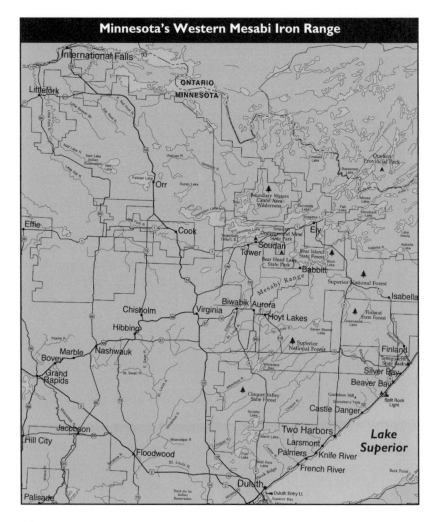

Minnesota's Western Mesabi Iron Range

WESTERN MESABI IRON RANGE, MINNESOTA

The Western Mesabi lies along Highway 169 between Hibbing and Grand Rapids, passing by or through the smaller mining towns of Keewatin, Nashwauk, Marble, Calumet, Bovey and Coleraine. Calumet is the unofficial gateway to the western Mesabi Range and home to the last intact iron ore pit mine in Minnesota that can be toured. Listed on the National Historic Register, the Hill Annex Mine is a good history stop. (See the Calumet, Minnesota, listing)

West of Calumet, winter skiers will want to visit Mont Itasca at Coleraine, which is now designated as a U.S. biathlon training center and also offers ski jumping, snowboarding, downhill and cross-country trails. Coleraine was built as a model town for Oliver Iron Mining Company employees working in the mines and mining plants near the cities of Bovey and Coleraine.

The westernmost city on the Mesabi Iron Range is Grand Rapids, where timber and tourism have traditionally played a much more significant role than mining in the economy of the area. See details in the separate listing for Grand Rapids, Minnesota.

SUNSET COUNTRY, ONTARIO

The Lake Superior Circle Tour follows Highway 61 northerly from the International Border at Pigeon River through Thunder Bay to Nipigon, but travelers with an extra day or two and a spirit of exploration may want to consider a round-trip side jaunt from Thunder Bay west to the twin border cities of Fort Frances, Ontario, and International Falls, Minnesota. Along the way, the landscape is dotted with fish-filled lakes and covered with thick boreal forest. This area is designated as Sunset Country for promotional purposes.

A short jaunt from Kakabeka Falls on Highway 11/17 heading west from Thunder Bay brings you to Shebandowan, where the highway divides to become two routes into the far western haunts of Ontario. Highway 11 takes a southerly route and Highway 17 wends its way to the north.

The largest cities on the two routes are Fort Frances (population 8,560) on Rainy Lake and Kenora (population 9,600) on Lake of the Woods. This trip, we'll focus on the Highway 11 route.

LaVerendrye River Provincial Park occupies a large area to the south of the highway and is a complete wilderness area accessed from the Thunder Bay area by taking Highway 588 through Nolalu. Located between Lake Superior and the eastern boundary of Quetico Wilderness Provincial Park, the park is bounded to the south in the United States by the Boundary Waters Canoe Area Wilderness (BWCAW). LaVer-

endrye Park is undeveloped and, with no staff or campgrounds, open primarily for those hardy campers who desire a true wilderness experience. Crown land camping permits are required.

Quetico Wilderness Provincial Park is a wilderness area of lakes, streams and woods that has changed little since the voyageurs paddled the waters three centuries ago.

The park covers 4,662 square kilometers that include more than 1,500 kilometers (930 miles) of canoe routes. The park is adjacent to the U.S. Boundary Waters Canoe Area Wilderness and many visitors enjoy both parks in one trip. Due to the popularity of back country travel, reservations to paddle the interior are advisable well in advance.

Aside from canoeing, Quetico offers hiking trails, campgrounds, picnic areas and beaches and summer interpretative programs at its Dawson Trail Campground (accessed from Highway 11). In winter, a few hardy skiers and snowshoers share Quetico with the wolves and moose. The park contains the largest concentration of pictographs between Lake Superior and Manitoba, with 30 known sites. Use of Quetico's interior is by limited permit, with numerous regulations regarding what can be taken into the park. Visitors moving into the park via water from the U.S. side must register with park rangers. Open mid-May to early October.

Atikokan (population 4,400), just north of the park on Highway 11, has complete services for park visitors. Numerous outfitters and stores stock everything that canoeists, backpackers, anglers and campers need.

For those who prefer a few wilderness conveniences, there are hotels and restaurants. The town is a jumping off point to deeper wilderness – the Canadian equivalent of Ely, Minnesota.

At the western terminus of our side trek is Fort Frances (population, 8,315). Just across the Rainy River, International Falls, Minnesota, (population 5,620) joins its Canadian twin in producing a huge volume of paper products. This is also prime fishing and water recreation country, with the Rainy River and Rainy Lake serving as a boundary between the U.S. and Canada and Lake Kabetogama in the back yard.

To return to our Lake Superior Circle Tour, either retrace your track coming in or, about 30 kilometers (20 miles) northeast of Fort Frances, take Highway 502 northward to visit Dryden and Ignace, then back to Thunder Bay by way of Highway 17. There are several other worthwhile stops and points of interest

DIRECTORY

Tourist Information – Fort Frances, Ontario, Chamber of Commerce, 807-274-5773, 800-820-3678

Lake Superior - Sunset Country, Ontario

along the way. Highway 11/17 brings you into the western part of Thunder Bay.

ONTARIO'S NORTHWEST SHORE

Near Pearl on Trans Canada Highway 11/17 between Thunder Bay and Nipigon, keep a sharp eye out for signs pointing the way to amethyst mines. Amethyst is Ontario's official gemstone, as well as the February birthstone. The semiprecious gem can be found at the Blue Points Amethyst Mine, Ontario Gem Amethyst Mine, which has a gift shop, and the Panorama Amethyst Mine, the largest amethyst mine on the continent.

In the same vicinity, don't miss stopping at Ouimet Canyon Provincial Park, whose walls stand 165 meters (500 feet) apart and 115 meters (350 feet) high and face each other for 3 kilometers (2 miles). See side story.

Don't blink or you'll pass the Dorion Loop taking you to the village of Dorion, home of Ontario's largest fish hatchery and Canada's largest wildlife mural on the walls of the Canyon Country Store. There's an annual Fall Fair and Festival.

Hurkett Cove Conservation Area lies just 3 kilometers (2 miles) east of the Wolf River and south of the highway and is home to a variety of songbirds, waterfowl and other wildlife.

The community of Hurkett is situated on Black Bay. Take the Hurkett Loop from Highway 11/17. If you're not in a hurry, this little side trip should yield some interesting photo opportunities. Hurkett is the site of the gigantic A&R Greenhouse tree nursery, which offers guided tours upon request. Hurkett hosts a winter carnival the second week of February.

You're now in what is called North of Superior and the most northerly point on Lake Superior.

To the east is Algoma Country and the twin cities of Sault Ste. Marie, Ontario and Michigan. This entire stretch of the Circle Tour is the northern part of the Great Lakes Heritage Coast under an Ontario Ministry of Natural Resources initiative.

En route, you'll have the opportunity to see lots of wildlife, papermaking, gold mining and visit numerous provincial parks, many with campgrounds operated by Ontario Parks, and a national park.

This portion of Lake Superior is home to some of the most dramatic coastlines and waterscapes, yet you'll seldom be more than a few kilometers from good food, lodging, stores and gift shops, fuel or anything else you need. Along the route, many of the municipalities have passed no-smoking or restricted smoking bylaws, so it's best to check before lighting up.

LAKE NIPIGON, FRONTIER TRAIL, ONTARIO

From Nipigon, Trans Canada Highway 11 heads northeastward and is called the Frontier Trail-Circuit du Nord Tourist Route.

This side trip takes a lazy arc up the Clay Belt and across the northern spruce bush, opening the north to thousands of anglers, hunters and other outdoor enthusiasts. This is a vast watershed area for Lake Superior, with Lake Nipigon, the Nipigon River and the Longlac Water Diversion project providing the greatest source of flow into the big lake.

Take the 50-kilometer (31-mile) drive from Nipigon up to Orient Bay on Lake Nipigon, where the rocks of the Canadian Shield are called the Pititawabik Palisades.

Many of the Lake Nipigon beaches consist of black sand that has been eroded from Lake Nipigon's basaltic cliffs and gathered by wave action on the shorelines.

44

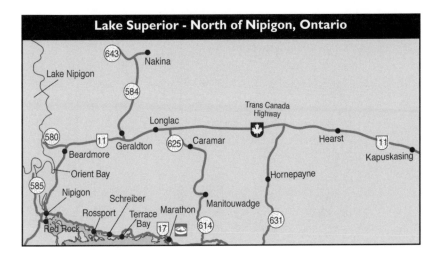

The southeast corner of Lake Nipigon/Orient Bay has many waterfalls that freeze in the winter and attract hearty visitors interested in climbing the icy precipices. An annual Ice Fest in March celebrates the phenomena.

For more locations along the Frontier Trail, see the special side trip map.

SOUTHERN UPPER PENINSULA, MICHIGAN

From Sault Ste. Marie, you can continue directly on the Lake Superior Circle Tour route, but you might want to consider a slight detour, if you have time. An interesting side trip from the Sault area is toward St. Ignace and the Mackinac Bridge (MACK-i-naw).

You can drive directly south for about 45 minutes on Interstate 75 from Sault Ste. Marie to St. Ignace and the bridge, which connects the Upper and Lower peninsulas of Michigan. A nice alternate route east from the Soo on M-129 opens the eastern U.P. for exploration.

While the southern U.P. trip can obviously go either west to east or vice versa, we will describe the trip from east to west here, with a number of the towns also being referenced in their own alphabetical listing.

From the Sault area, Michigan 129 gives access to Sugar, Neebish and Drummond islands on the U.S. side of the St. Marys River waterway. A fourth island in the chain, St. Joseph, is discussed under the alphabetical heading and lies on the Canadian side of the international border.

Sugar Island is accessible from Sault Ste. Marie. To reach Neebish Island, stop at Barbeau, where a car ferry takes the visitor across the channel. The island sits between Lake Nicolet and Munuscong Lake, both of which offer

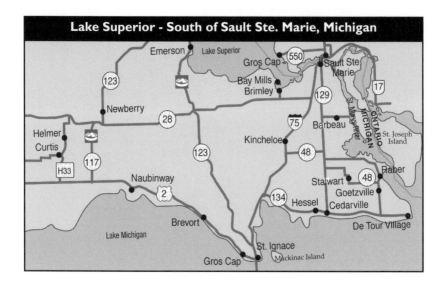

recreational opportunities. At Barbeau, Cozy Corners restaurant offers good food for hungry travelers.

Before reaching the last island, you'll pass the Raber Bay area, which includes the small towns of Stalwart, Goetzville and Raber. This is an area of fine lodging and restaurants and our route is now along a portion of the Lake Huron Circle Tour.

The third island is Drummond Island, the largest of the group, which is accessed by ferry from De Tour Village on Highway 134 at the very eastern tip of the U.P. See alphabetized listing for more detail.

From De Tour, M-134 takes you to Cedarville and Hessel in the Les Cheneaux Islands area. There are 36 islands in the group, with marinas, beaches and waterfront walks to delight the visitor. Visit the Les Cheneaux Historical Museum for insight into the lake-oriented culture of the region. On the second Saturday in August, attend the Antique Boat Show, Art Festival and Regatta in Hessel. Cedarville's annual Les Cheneaux Snowfest in February is also famed for its festive nature. Golfers will want to try out Hessel Ridge Golf Course. From here, we head for a junction with I-75 to visit St. Ignace, Mackinac Island (see separate listing) and the Mackinac Bridge, described in the St. Ignace section. Take U.S. Highway 2 west from St. Ignace toward Gros Cap. The Gros Cap Church was built in 1918. Brevort has several campgrounds and offers access to Lake Michigan's dunes. Lake Michigan's shorelines are nearly all sandy, with dunes as a common feature.

You'll pass communities steeped in the traditions of fishing. Naubinway is known as the "Land of Echoes" and

has a marina, complete with charter
fishing. The Fishermen's Memorial
honors local fishermen who lost their lives
on Lake Michigan. Naubinway is also
home to Garlyn Zoological Park right on
Highway 2, featuring the U.P.'s largest
variety of live animals, all in a natural
setting. Open daily 11 a.m.-7 p.m.
summer and fall, weekends in winter.

If you want to return to the Lake
Superior Circle Tour, a number of routes turn north off
Highway 2 and allow you to rejoin the Lake Superior route
wherever you choose. In this particular area, Highway 117 is a
straight shot to Highway 28 just west of Newberry.

For a more scenic route, County Road H33 at the
junction in Gould City heads north toward Curtis and the
Manistique Lakes area for excellent recreation.

A bit farther north on H33, Helmer is home to the
Helmer House, a historic bed-and-breakfast and restaurant
that you'll want to put on your agenda. After renovation in
1982, it is a favorite destination for those who want to escape
the cares of the world. The restaurant specializes in fresh-
caught whitefish. One of Lake Superior's best places to eat
and stay. Open May through October.

U.S.Highway 2 travels nearly straight west from
Naubinway past Gould City and Blaney Park, before bearing
southwest toward Gulliver. The sights at Gulliver are
described in the town's listing.

Traveling Highway 2 west from Gulliver, the shoreline
city of Manistique offers a good selection of lodging facilities,
including several state or private campgrounds, and dining for
whatever your taste may be. (See separate listing.)

At Garden Corners on Highway 2 in Michigan's southern
U.P., catch vistas of Big Bay de Noc as you pass the small
towns of Isabella, Nahma Junction and Ensign to Rapid River
at the north end of Little Bay de Noc. Follow Highway 2/41
along the shoreline southwesterly to Gladstone (population
4,565) and Escanaba (population 13,660). See the Escanaba
listing for more detail on this area.

On Highway 2/41 through the southern U.P. west of
Escanaba/Gladstone, you pass through a number of small
towns, but will want to watch for signs directing you to Chip-
In's Island Resort and Casino about 13 miles (17 kilometers)
west of Escanaba at Harris, with 113-rooms, RV park,
restaurants and a wide variety of gaming. It's operated by the
Hannahville Tribe on the Michigan Potawatomi Reservation.

On Highway 2/41 about midway between Escanaba and
Iron Mountain, keep an eye out for Hermansville to visit the

IXL Historic Museum, housed in the 1882 headquarters building of the Wisconsin Land and Lumber Company. Open Memorial Day through Labor Day, with group tour arrangements during the off-season. See the separate listing under Hermansville.

You are well away from the shores of both Lake Superior and Lake Michigan at this point, heading for the western U.P. where iron ore mines once fostered an abundant economy. Although the mines are long since depleted, many of the smallish communities you pass were mining locations where the families of employees lived, worked and did most of their day-to-day business.

Plan to stop at Vulcan for an underground tour by train of the Iron Mountain Iron Mine, where you'll travel 2,600 feet (800 meters) through the drifts and stopes (tunnels and roomlike areas) of the mine. Nearby in Norway (population 2,910), the Jake Menghini Historical Museum is housed in a historic log cabin that once served as a carriage stopping place. The museum is open free of charge Memorial Day through the Saturday prior to Columbus Day in October, although donations are accepted.

Waterfall aficionados can check out Piers Gorge in Norway, where white water tumbles over a 10-foot falls and roars wildly through canyon walls. A bit farther on Highway 2, a roadside park with tables, water and toilets at Quinnesec gives a nice view of Fumee Falls.

Iron Mountain snuggles into a large bend of the Menominee River that forms the boundary between Michigan and Wisconsin. Like a mother hen with chicks, a number of smaller towns in both Wisconsin and Michigan surround Iron Mountain. See Iron Mountain listing for more details.

Highway 2/141 jogs into Wisconsin for a brief sojourn just west of Iron Mountain and passes through two small towns, the interestingly named Spread Eagle and Florence, before re-entering Michigan in Iron County.

A 15-minute drive brings you to Crystal Falls, the Iron County seat and a crossroads community where you can catch Highway 141 north to rejoin the Lake Superior Circle Tour. See the listing under Crystal Falls for details.

Another hen-and-chick community, with the former mining locations of Gaastra, Caspian, Stambaugh and Mineral Hills nearby, Iron River offers travelers a number of lodging, shopping and dining options. See Iron River in the listings.

In nearby Caspian, the Iron County Historical Museum features 20 pioneer buildings reflecting logging, mining, transportation and other aspects of settling the area. See Iron River, Michigan, listing for details.

Lake Superior - Upper Peninsula of Michigan & Northeastern Wisconsin

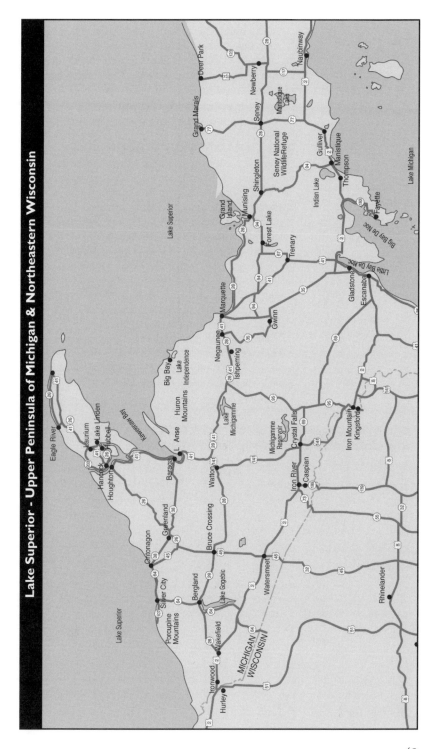

As you again head westward, traveling through the Ottawa National Forest, a huge area of the western U.P. set aside for multiple-use. The Ottawa Visitor Center in Watersmeet can provide full information on recreational facilities within this wonderfully scenic area. See the Watersmeet listing for detail.

The route westward along Highway 2 is now well into Big Snow Country, heading for Wakefield, Bessemer and Ironwood.

INDIANHEAD REGION, WISCONSIN

From U.S. Highway-2 at Brule we recommend an interesting side trip that travels south via Highway 27. If you have time, turn east on County N to visit Barnes and Drummond, which has an interesting museum of local history.

Continuing south on Highway 27 leads to Hayward, the home of the National Fresh Water Fishing Hall of Fame, documenting the exploits of noteworthy anglers and their prizewinning catches. This is also home to the World Lumberjack Championships. Just east east of town, the Lac Courte Oreilles Band of Lake Superior Ojibway operates Lac Courte Oreilles Casino, Lodge and Convention Center, offering many amenities and gaming fun.

From Hayward, catch Highway 77 westward through areas dotted by inland lakes and interesting towns to reconnect to the Circle Tour via Highway 35. Just to the south of the junction with Highway 35, Forts Folle Avoine Historical Park between Webster and Danbury is a worthwhile stop, recreating an early fur trading post situated on the site. Area lodging information is available from Burnett County Resort and Campground Association. Also in the area is Hole in the Wall Casino for gaming fun, a hotel and pool. There are several good good restaurants in Danbury.

Lake Superior - Wisconsin Indianhead

Alberta Village - Aurora

ALBERTA VILLAGE, MICHIGAN

The museum village of Alberta and the Ford Forestry Center are part of Michigan Technological University in Houghton. The site, about 9 miles south of L'Anse on U.S. 41, is comprised of nearly 2,000 acres of forest around the original townsite, which now serves as a research facility and conference center of MTU. An integral part of the site is the Ford Historic Sawmill, open as an exhibit by the Alberta Village and Museum Board, with a guided tour following the path of lumber from logs to finished boards. A house nearby is also open for tours. A gift shop welcomes visitors seeking a memento of their visit. Open Mondays, Tuesdays and Fridays.

Alberta Village, Michigan, regional map – page 24.

Travelers wanting to pick up M-28 to the east or west will find the intersection with U.S. 41 about four miles south. To visit L'Anse, take the highway north about nine miles.

A Bit of History

To ensure a steady supply of hardwood lumber needed in manufacturing cars by his company, Henry Ford established five sawmill sites in the northern Upper Peninsula, with Alberta being established last in 1935 as a satellite mill to his larger operation in L'Anse. The site was cleared in dense forestland and a village, steam-powered sawmill and a dam for a mill pond were constructed. While not grand by today's standards, the homes were comfortable and workers and their families were apparently quite happy to have both good jobs and decent housing and schools. The mill was a model of its time – clean, safe, efficient and pleasant to work in with good lighting, a varnished interior and painted floors with clearly marked pathways. Converted to electrical power after the site was donated to Michigan Technological University, the mill operated part time as a teaching site for forestry students until about 1980. It is now an interesting look at how logs were turned into 15,000 board feet of lumber per day in the 1930s.

A

Today

The public is welcome to stop by and partake of the trails, wander through the model townsite that housed workers at the sawmill, tour the mill and view the historic memorabilia. A trail takes you from the townsite to Canyon Falls and another circles Plumbago Lake, a pleasant way to spend an hour or so.

DIRECTORY

Tourist Information – Baraga County Tourism Association, 906-524-7444, 800-743-4908; Alberta Village Museum and Gift Shop, 906-524-7900 (summer)

What to See and Do

Near Alberta is Canyon Falls, the Grand Canyon of the Upper Peninsula. Look for the signs for the Sturgeon River Roadside Park off Highway 41, which has a 10-minute self-guided hiking trail to the gorge and waterfalls. There is also a hiking trail to the falls from Alberta Village.

The museum holds a "Tin Lizzie" show in early summer and an art sale and music festival in August.

What's Next

From Alberta Village, U.S. Highway 61 heads 8 miles north toward L'Anse or south about five miles to a junction with Michigan Highway 28/141.

APOSTLE ISLANDS
NATIONAL LAKESHORE, WISCONSIN

Twenty-one of the 22 islands (Madeline Island excluded, see separate entry) and 2,500 acres of the Bayfield Peninsula mainland make up the Apostle Islands National Lakeshore area, one of only four national lakeshores in the country (two of which are on Lake Superior). It is operated out of Bayfield by the National Park Service and is available for visitors to enjoy. The park includes historic fish camps, lighthouses, beaches, sandstone cliffs, "sea caves" and remnant virgin timber. The lakeshore covers 69,372 acres, of which 42,140 are above the waterline.

Apostle Islands, Wisconsin, regional map – page 30.

Stop at the Lakeshore's Visitor Center in the Old County Courthouse in Bayfield, where you'll see the Fresnel lens from the Michigan Island Lighthouse exhibited. Turn north off Wisconsin 13, one block to Washington Avenue.

Other visitor or contact centers are located at Little Sand Bay and Stockton Island. The Park Service maintains the Manitou Island Fish Camp, Hokenson Historic Site at Little Sand Bay and Raspberry Island Lighthouse and gardens, where extensive work has stabilized the eroding cliff that threatened the historic lighthouse. Similar work was undertaken in 2004 to stabilize the Outer Island Lighthouse cliff. National Park Service volunteers occupy the light

stations at Sand, Devils, Michigan and Outer islands. Tours are available daily when personnel are present.

From the west, we suggest approaching the Apostles via the western Bayfield Peninsula by taking Wisconsin Highway 13 from U.S. Highway 2 through the small villages of Port Wing, Cornucopia and Red Cliff to Bayfield. From the east, catch Highway 13 north to Washburn and Bayfield just west of Ashland.

Boats, boats and more boats make up Bayfield, Wisconsin's waterfront as it is a major water access for the Apostle Islands.

– Lake Superior Magazine

A Bit of History

Long known to Native Americans and voyageurs, the Apostle Islands and more particularly Madeline Island were important in the fur trade from about 1700 until about 1850. Commercial fishing commenced for a few years in the 1830s by the American Fur Company, but it would be the late 1800s before it became a major source of income to local fishermen. Logging was also important in the economy for a period in the late 1800s and early 1900s before the timber was depleted. Fishing remained a primary economic factor until the late 1900s, when the industry was devastated by the invasion of the lamprey eel. Meanwhile, the islands, again particularly Madeline, began attracting visitors. Some built summer homes, while others came back year after year to relish the fabulous scenery and the mild, healthful air. By 1970, enough support had been generated that the U.S. Park Service designated 21 islands and a sizable acreage of mainland as Apostle Islands National Lakeshore to protect

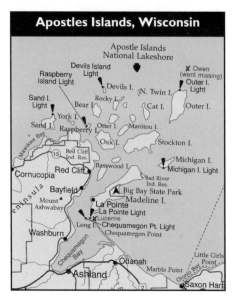

Apostles Islands, Wisconsin

and preserve the natural and historic qualities found there.

Today

Today, a few fishermen still eke out income by setting nets, but recreation and tourism have become the mainstay of the local economy. The National Lakeshore attracts thousands of visitors each year and the communities of the Bayfield Peninsula have done much to accent their amenities for visitors.

What to See and Do

More than 50 miles (80 kilometers) of trails are maintained in the national lakeshore. Camping is permitted on 18 of the 21 islands. A fee is charged for camping permits. The Apostle Islands Cruise Service is one way to get to the Apostle Islands aboard the *Island Princess* or *Ashland Bay Express*. The tours offer three-hour narrated boat excursions around 19 of the 22 Apostle Islands mid-May through mid-October. Beginning in mid-June through Labor Day, choose from a variety of cruises, including sunset cruises and island shuttles for camping, day hiking or touring a lighthouse.

The Apostles are the site of numerous shipwrecks. Divers will appreciate the installation of mooring buoys at two of the more popular wrecks. A number of wrecks are visible from the surface in good weather. Contact Apostle Islands National Lakeshore for free diving permits and a brochure describing dive sites.

Notable Events

• Round the Islands Race Week celebrates the marine heritage of the area with exciting sailing action each year in June.

• Apostle Island Lighthouse Celebration through most of September is an annual celebration of the historic lights that shone the way through the island for early mariners

• Chequamegon Chef's Exhibition in June gives visitors and residents to Madeline Island a chance to sample the best of the area's cookery.

• Annual Star Bar Softball Tournament is a fun competition on Madeline Island challenging top teams from the area.

ASHLAND, WISCONSIN

Population 8,695

Ashland is situated on the southern shore of Chequamegon (Shu-kwa-ma-gon) Bay of Lake Superior right on U.S. Highway 2 from either the east or west. The city is the home of Northland College and the Sigurd Olson Environmental Institute. The college specializes in environmental and Native American studies in a liberal arts setting. The Ashland campus of Wisconsin Indianhead Technical College offers training in many vocational and specialty areas of study and houses a state-of-the-art Technology Center.

Ashland, Wisconsin, regional map – page 24.

Visitors will receive a warm welcome and the Ashland Area Chamber of Commerce, located on the lake side of West U.S. Highway 2 in the center of town, is a good place to start. It's fully equipped with brochures, pamphlets, books, maps and guides on all of the towns and attractions in this area. The Chequamegon Bay area offers a wealth of delightful birding opportunities for those seeking to add species to their list of sightings. A "Birding by the Bay" brochure guides birders to the best sites and is available at area information centers and other outlets.

Shopping, lodging and dining are terrific in this historic city, which celebrated its 150th anniversary in 2004. Ashland has public bus service between 6 a.m. and 4:30 p.m. through the Bay Area Rural Transit system. The BART system services the entire Chequamegon Bay area from Odanah and Ashland to Red Cliff on the Bayfield Peninsula. Ashland's JFK Airport is home to the only full-service "log" terminal in the state, constructed of red pine logs from Bayfield County.

Check Ashland's *Daily Press* for the latest news and events. Visitors are reminded that smoking in restaurants is prohibited by Ashland city ordinance. Bars and special sections of some restaurants may allow it, but it's best to check before lighting up.

A Bit of History

The historical record of Ashland traces back to 1658 when the French explorers and fur traders Radisson and Groseilliers built a cabin on the waterfront of Chequamegon Bay and spent the winter there before going on to collect furs at other stops on Lake Superior. The cabin is the first residence known to have been built on Lake Superior by non-native people. In the intervening period to the present, Ashland has been successively important in the fur trade (circa 1700-1840), logging and lumbering (1880-1900), the quarrying of brownstone (1880-1900), transportation (1860s-present), manufacturing and tourism. Founded by Asaph Whittlesey in 1854, the town was almost immediately abandoned by all but one family in 1857 until the Civil War ended. The announcement that a

55

A

railroad was planned through the city revived the hopes of pioneers and the 1877 arrival of that railroad assured the future of the settlement.

By the 1880s, Ashland became an important producer of lumber products, and Frederick Prentice started quarrying brownstone along Chequamegon Bay and the Apostle Islands for use in building construction. A significant number of buildings in the city reflect the importance of that enterprise.

Commercial fishing became significant in the 1890s and remained active until the lamprey eel invasion all but killed off the native fish species. A few fishermen still set nets, but their market is largely the area's eateries.

With mid-1880s development of the Gogebic Iron Range to the east, Ashland's harbor became a focal point of shipping interests, which had previously been devoted to handling lumber cargoes. With depletion of the iron ore in the 1950s, the harbor's importance waned, but the waterfront was rejuvenated by building a large marina and other attractions in the latter 20th century. Today, it's a vital player in the promotion of tourism, which increased significantly through the 1900s as visitors discovered the beauty and magic of the Lake Superior region.

Today

As the county seat of Ashland County, the city retains its role as the vibrant hub of government, business and retail for the sizable surrounding area to the present. Several manufacturing firms are located in and around the city, providing employment for a sizable number of skilled workers. In addition, Ashland's Memorial Medical Center is a regional facility for the area and a significant employer, as is Northland College and Wisconsin Indianhead Technical College. Timber remains a viable product in the area, with a number of successful logging firms and manufacturers of logging equipment located in the area. And, as the area's tourism industry has grown, the number of facilities geared to visitors has grown apace. Northern Great Lakes Visitor Center is just one example of impressive amenities added in the area during the past decade or two.

What to See and Do

Ashland is home to seven historical wall-sized murals located throughout the downtown. These paintings depict the heritage and early life of the area. A brochure describing each of the murals can be picked up at the Chamber office.

Baldwin Locomotive *#950*, the largest in the world when it was built, is exhibited at the Depot site. It is the only Decapod (10-wheel drive) to serve the Soo Line Railroad in various locations from 1900 until 1954, when steam locomotion was

DIRECTORY

A

Tourism Information – Ashland (Wisconsin) Area Chamber of Commerce, 715-682-2500, 800-284-9484; Northern Great Lakes Visitor Center, 715-685-9983

Where to Stay

Hotel Chequamegon, 715-682-9095, 101 Lake Shore Dr., is a modern structure built in the grand old tradition. Superbly decorated with 65 rooms, the hotel overlooks the water. Dining in-house. AmericInn, 715-682-9950, 3009 Lake Shore Dr. E., offers nice rooms with a view of Lake Superior. Anderson's Chequamegon Motel,

715-682-4658, 2200 Lake Shore Dr. W., is a long-time visitor favorite, with wonderful views of Lake Superior.

For a bed-and-breakfast stay, contact The Residenz B&B, 715-682-2425, or the Inn at Timber Cove, 715-682-9600.

Where to Eat with a Local Flavor

L.C. Wilmarth's Deep Water Grille, 715-682-4200, 808 W. Main St., offers a full menu that includes Lake Superior fish and wild rice soup. Located in a historic building on West Main Street that also houses South Shore Brewery, which produces and markets hand-crafted beers, stouts, ales and porters on site.

retired from service by the railroad. An important workhorse in Ashland ore dock operations from 1942 to 1954, it was dedicated as a historical display by the city in 1957. A playground for children in nearby Central Railyard Park offers a welcome chance for travel weary kids to burn energy.

Ashland Historical Society Museum holds the history of the first century and a half of the city in the 500 block of West Main Street. Open daily.

Behind the Chequamegon Hotel, the 140-slip, full-service Ashland Harbor and Marina reflects the beauty of Chequamegon Bay. It has annual dockage, moorings, transient slips and full fuel and pumpout facilities. Seaplane dockage is available.

The Band Shell on the waterfront at Memorial Park has open air concerts on Thursday evenings during the summer. Its benches offer pleasant surroundings for a picnic. The park is the focal point for the annual Ashland Bay Days Festival in July. Ashland's Lakewalk is a delightful way to stretch travel-weary legs.

Ashland Ore Dock was constructed in 1916, with an addition made in 1925. It is 1,800 feet long, 80 feet high and 59 feet wide and is the world's largest concrete structure of its kind. At one time there were five similar docks in Ashland. Shipping of Wisconsin and Michigan iron ore from these docks ended in the mid-1960s.

A stone marker on Maslowski Beach commemorates the site of the first cabin built by Europeans in Wisconsin, erected by French explorers Radisson and Groseilliers in the fall of 1658.

A

The historic Soo Line Depot was destroyed by fire in 2000, but has been renovated and once again serves the public. Turn south off U.S. Highway 2 two blocks on Third Avenue.

Each October, the city celebrates its heritage as a rail and shipping center with the Ashland WhistleStop Festival, a two-day observance marked with many fun activities centering in a huge heated tent in the downtown area.

Northern Great Lakes Visitor Center provides information and services year-round, seven days a week. Located west of Ashland on Highway 2, the four-season, 36,000-square-foot center gives visitors an over-the-trees panoramic view of Lake Superior and the nearby Ashland's Fish Creek Slough from a 70-foot (21-meter) observation tower. A closer look at the Sloughs can be had with a kayak trip or ask to arrange an experience on Lake Superior in a war canoe. Exhibits and a 100-seat theater are used to further the interpretative and educational goals of the facility, besides providing regional visitor information and trip planning areas. A series of trails allows visitors access to the wetland area near the center, which is abundant with wildlife, and welcomes snowshoers and cross-country skiers in winter. A snowmobile trail comes right to the door of the center. The center houses historical archives and a Wisconsin Historical Society research area. The Northern Wisconsin History Center is located here and shows an audio-visual musical history in the auditorium. It's also the site of the annual Chequamegon Bay Rendezvous, sponsored by Northern Wisconsin Heritage Connection.

The city sports the Chequamegon Bay Golf Course, an 18-hole, par 72 course. Although owned by the Ashland Elks Lodge, which makes its home there, the course is open to the public.

During the winter, Ashland receives a good share of the white stuff, which makes snowmobiling and winter sports most attractive. An annual ice fishing event is held on the bay, along with the Ashland Snowcross and Terrain X Race. Auto racing on the ice is also a popular sport. Cross-country skiing is available nearby.

Parks and Public Areas

Prentice Park is a historic area and the largest of Ashland's 12 parks. A secluded area perfect for picnics, it offers the pure cold water of artesian wells and there are hiking trails, viewing platforms, a playground and tent camping – all adjacent to wildlife that live in Fish Creek Slough.

Other parks you may want to check out are Bayview on the east end, Kreher nearer the downtown and Maslowski in the western side of town.

Swimming beaches, some with lifeguards, are available along Highway 2 at Bayview Park on Ashland's east end,

Kreher Park near the ore dock in the center of town and
Maslowski Beach at the west end of Ashland.

Notable Events

• Winter Lake Fest/Book Across the Bay Ski/Snowshoe
Tour and Race in February attracts hundreds of winter
enthusiasts for outdoor fun and a chance to race or tour
across the bay by candlelight.

• Top of North Farm and Garden Show in February
celebrates the upcoming growing season with the latest
products for farmers and gardeners.

• Home & Sport Show in April showcases everything
from appliances to outdoor gear.

• Wisconsin's Largest House-to-House Garage Sale in
May is a citywide "housecleaning" where you may find just
about anything for sale.

• Chequamegon Woods to Water Relay in late May is a
race by teams from Cable in Chequamegon National Forest
to the waterfront in Ashland.

• Chequamegon Bay Rendezvous in mid-June is a family
education and fun recreation of the past on the grounds of
Northern Great Lakes Visitor Center.

• Big Granite Inline Marathon/Half Marathon in mid-
June challenges skaters to post the fastest time from Marengo
to Ashland.

• Ice Cream Social on the Courthouse Lawn is held in
conjunction with the city's July 4 celebration, parade and
fireworks.

• Bay Days in mid-July pulls out all the stops to celebrate
life along Lake Superior and Chequamegon Bay.

• Red Clay Classic Stock Car Races and Racers' Ball in
early October is the final auto racing challenge of the season
at ABC Raceway.

• WhistleStop Festival in early October celebrates the
city's heritage as an important railroading center.

• Garland City of the North Parade in early December
anticipates the approaching holidays with fun family events
and a giant parade in the downtown.

Where to Shop

A plenitude of shops offer a wide variety of regional gifts.
Many of the city's businesses are located in historic buildings
constructed of locally quarried brownstone. The city of
Ashland offers many shopping opportunities both on
Lakeshore Drive (U.S. 2) and one block above on historic
Main Street. The designs of old Ashland have been preserved
in a historic district, including the Courthouse, City Hall and
Post Office, and an artistic effort has created a number of

A

wall-sized murals in Historic Downtown. Guides to the murals are available at the info center.

The Artisan Shop offers works of regional artists, Native artists and local craftspeople. Superior Framing and Gallery has works by local, regional and national artists, framing by certified craftspeople and home decor items.

Gifts, collectables and fine area products are available at Superior House, New England Store, Country Treasures or Spirit of the North Gift Shop in the Northern Great Lakes Visitor Center.

Toward the west end of town, stop at Bodin's on the Lake for smoked fish, sports outfitting equipment and other Lake Superior related materials.

What's Next
From Ashland, take Highway 2 east on the way to Hurley, Wisconsin, and Ironwood, Michigan. To the west lie several small towns on the way to Superior, Wisconsin, and Duluth, Minnesota. Highway 13 just west of Ashland leads to the Washburn, Bayfield and the Bayfield Peninsula

AU TRAIN, MICHIGAN
Population 570

Au Train, Michigan, regional map – page 22.

Au Train River generously scoops patterned pools in the sand at its access to Lake Superior between Marquette and Munising. Here, you are entering the Central Upper Peninsula. A half-mile east of Au Train is a beachside picnic park with Scott Falls, a low waterfall, across the highway. At Au Train Campground, wander down the Song Bird Trail for a live concert along an interpretative path. A campground is on U.S. Forest Service Road 2276, south of M-28 about 6 miles (10 kilometers) on County Road H-03. Open from late spring into October. Those desiring indoor accommodations will want to contact Pinewood Lodge bed-and-breakfast inn. Nearby, the Brownstone Inn offers a tempting array of homemade entrees, handcut steaks and fresh fish.

What's Next
Along M-28 to the east you'll come to Munising. To the west there are several scenic lakeshore turnoffs between Au Train and Marquette.

AURORA, MINNESOTA
Population: 2,000

At the eastern tip of the Mesabi Iron Range are the towns of Aurora, Biwabik and Hoyt Lakes, each important in the history of Minnesota iron mining. Aurora and Biwabik were early mining locations when the rich Mesabi hematite ore was being mined. Hoyt Lakes was built as housing for employees concurrent with the construction of the giant Erie Mining Company taconite plant a few miles north of the townsite. The plant was shut down in 2000.

Aurora, Minnesota, regional map – page 2.

A Bit of History

Aurora was once the site of several important iron ore mines that have long since been shut down. An early taconite test plant was located at Aurora and developed many proven processes by which the abundant, flintlike low-grade taconite iron ore could be upgraded to a usable product. That pilot plant was the precursor of Erie Mining Company, which was built a few miles northeast of town in the mid-1950s. The plant produced up to 14 millions tons of iron ore a year until it was closed in 2000. Although it was already an active city when the taconite plant was built, Aurora was bypassed by the mining company for residential development and Hoyt Lakes was built a few miles east to house workers and their families.

Today

A resilient town that has seen many economic ups and downs through its more than 100-year history, Aurora retains much of the robust character that has sustained it through boom and bust. Its main street is dotted with several saloons. Some like Rudy's Bar and Grill in the middle of downtown have long histories of serving miners, construction workers, loggers and folks from the large rural area south of town.

Aurora can fill any need, from emergency health care to novelty gifts and good restaurants. A stop at Zup's Grocery meets every grocery need and is sure to reward the shopper with specialty meats for any occasion, from campfire cooking to holiday feasts. Ron's Bakery on Main Street has provided baked goodies to generations of residents and visitors. Cherro's Italian Market provides specialty items for the Mediterranean taste and a couple of times each summer the A&W Drive In on South Main sponsors Classic Car Cruise Nights that are a must for classic car buffs throughout northeastern Minnesota.

What's Next

To the east is Hoyt Lakes (population 2,200) and to the west is Biwabik (population about 1,000), each described in separate listings

LAKE SUPERIOR
Bad River - Brule

BAD RIVER RESERVATION, WISCONSIN
Population: 1,500

Bad River Reservation, Wisconsin, regional map – page 28.

Traveling U.S. Highway 2 in northern Wisconsin, you'll go through the Bad River Indian Reservation, home of the Bad River Band of Lake Superior Chippewa. With the Red Cliff Chippewa tribal reservation, this is one of two reservations in Apostle Islands Country and the largest in Wisconsin. In Odanah, you can enjoy gaming at the Bad River Lodge and Casino. It's one of the log buildings beside the highway. The tribe also operates a grocery/convenience store near the casino and construction has expanded convention and restaurant space at the lodge. The restaurant offers a variety of dining, from burgers to fine cuisine.

The band is known for its operation of a fish hatchery and wild rice gathering at the nearby Kakagon Sloughs. In mid- to later August each year, the tribe sponsors its Wild Rice Festival and Powwow.

Boaters will find a refurbished harbor of refuge, short-term dockage, parking, boat launch and rest-room facilities at the western edge of the Bad River Reservation. Second Landing is at the foot of Reykdahl Road about 2 miles (3 kilometers) east of Ashland.

What's Next

Traveling east on Highway 2 from Bad River takes you to Hurley and Ironwood, Michigan. Westerly, you're heading for Ashland.

BARAGA, MICHIGAN
Population: 1,285

On Highway 41 east of Houghton and west from L'Anse, Baraga (BEAR-a-ga) sits snugly in the southeast corner of Keweenaw Bay. Named for Catholic missionary Bishop Frederic Baraga, who ministered to Native Americans from 1831 to 1868, often on snowshoes, his memory is preserved at the Shrine of the Snowshoe Priest, an impressive 35-foot (11-meter) copper statue that overlooks Keweenaw Bay from a 25-foot (7-meter) pedestal at the top of Red Rock Bluff between L'Anse and Baraga. There is a nice gift shop offering mementos of your visit.

Most visitors never seem to tire of looking out over Keweenaw Bay, and the town seems to agree, with much of it located either on the waterfront or on the gently rising hillside to the west that presents panoramic views of the shore.

A Bit of History

The early history of Baraga mentions fur trading outposts in the area, but it was the 1881 arrival of Thomas Nestor and his construction of a huge modern sawmill that spurred development in the area. Capable of producing 46 million board feet of timber products per year, Nestor established his own fleet of lumber barges. By his death in 1890 at Baraga, his operation was the bull of the woods in a huge surrounding area. The company became Estate of Thomas Nestor after his death and logging by that peculiarly named lumber company continued until the surrounding pinery was depleted. Subsequently, the Detroit-based company acquired huge stands of pine in Wisconsin and in the Gooseberry River watershed in northeastern Minnesota, rafting logs to Baraga until about 1910, when those western pineries were also gone.

During the same period, commercial fishing became important in the Baraga area and remained a source of income for many fishermen until the invasion by lamprey eels caused fish populations to dramatically decrease by the 1970s. Farming was also possible in the area and histories record that several large cheese factories were located in the surrounding area. By that time, tourists began to visit and became an economic factor that remains important to the present.

Baraga, Michigan, regional map – page 24.

B

DIRECTORY

Tourist Information – Baraga County Tourist and Recreation Association, 906-524-7444, 800-743-4908

Where to Stay
Ojibwa Casino Resort, 906-353-7611, 800-323-8045, M-38 and Beartown Rd., offers nice rooms, exciting gaming and in-house dining.
Best Western Baraga Lakeside Inn, 906-353-7123, 800-528-1234, 900 U.S. Hwy. 41 S., has lakefront rooms, a marina, a good restaurant and lounge.
Super 8 Motel, 906-353-6680,

800-800-8000, M-38 (across from Ojibwa Casino), is only a short distance from town, gaming, trail access. This lodging also offers parking for large vehicles.

Where to Eat with a Local Flavor
Baraga Lakeside Inn, 906-353-7123, 900 U.S. Hwy. 41., overlooks the bay and features great views and a good menu.
Four Star Restaurant, 906-353-7633, M-38 and Beartown Rd. (Ojibwa Casino), offers a full-service menu in a family atmosphere.

Today

The Keweenaw Bay Indian Community's development of Ojibwa Casino along with other visitor amenities became an important employer in the latter 1900s and remains important to the area's economy.

What to See and Do

A fun activity is the Ojibwa Casino Resort on M-38 with the latest Las Vegas-style casino games, Big Bucks Bingo, lodging, a restaurant and other amenities.

There are various routes to Sturgeon River Gorge, one of the Upper Peninsula's most spectacular rustic scenic lookouts. A comparatively easy route follows M-38 west to Prickett Dam Road, then 9 miles (14 kilometers) south along the Sturgeon River to the gorge, falls and Silver Mountain. Silver Mountain Trail leads up to cool moss- and fern-covered boulders and through deep forests to a scenic view of the western Upper Peninsula with falls at the bottom. Don't stray too close to the edge. This is a wilderness setting. It is not handicapped accessible.

Notable Museums

Baraga County Museum is right on the Lake Superior waterfront in Baraga, displaying interesting prehistoric culture and recorded history from the Ice Age forward. Open May to mid-October, Tuesday through Sunday.

About 5 miles north of Baraga at Arnheim, turn left for 6 miles (9.5 kilometers) to visit the Hanka Homestead, a living outdoor Finnish museum that takes you back to the 1920s. Fee.

Parks and Public Areas

Baraga State Park has modern campgrounds across U.S. 41 from the head of Keweenaw Bay and the boat launch site. Fishing, swimming, hiking, picnicking. Admission by park permit.

Notable Events

• Keweenaw Bay Indian Community hosts a major powwow, open to the public, in the county park each year on the fourth weekend in July.

Campgrounds

Campers will want to check the Ojibway Campgrounds, also operated by the Keweenaw Bay Indian Community.

What's Next

If your direction of travel is west from Baraga, M-38 travels past Nisula and across the Keweenaw, ending in Ontonagon. Our recommended Circle Tour route follows U.S. 41. For several miles north of Baraga, the highway hugs the sandy shoreline of Lake Superior. To the east, it's about a 5-mile drive to L'Anse.

BATCHAWANA BAY, ONTARIO

Population 100

The village of Batchawana Bay is just off Trans Canada Highway 17 on the eastern Lake Superior shore and starts where Highway 563 meets the Carp River. At the end of H-563 is the Ontario Government Dock, which serves as a safe port for commercial and pleasure craft. The bay stretches out to Batchawana Island, with a backdrop of Batchawana Mountain, which at 665 meters (2,195 feet) is the undisputed highest peak on the Ontario shores of Lake Superior.

Batchawana Bay, Ontario, regional map – page 18.

What to See and Do

Batchawana Bay is a large inland bay 56 kilometers (35 miles) of shoreline in circumference, featuring the warmest swimming waters on Lake Superior at Batchawana Bay Provincial Park. It also offers exceptional island exploration, sailing, boating, windsurfing and sightseeing. Lodging, a post office and the picturesque St. Isaac Catholic Church are located in the village.

Visitors can rent canoes, participate in outdoor adventures or winter recreation at Voyageurs' Lodge and Cookhouse. Groups can relive the voyageur experience in a 26-foot Montreal canoe. Three miles of pristine sand beach on Batchawana Bay are within a short walk.

South on Highway 17, watch for Chippewa River Falls. This spectacular Circle Tour landmark is the halfway point of the Trans Canada Highway and features a foot trail to great

DIRECTORY

Tourist Information – Batchawana Bay Tourist Information, 705-882-2235; Ontario Tourism, 800-668-2746

Where to Stay
Lake Shore Resort and Salzburger Hof, 705-882-2503, offers chalet lodgings with a great view of Lake Superior.
Sunset Inn and RV Park, 705-882-2231, on the banks of the Batchawana River has

spaces for camping or RV parking, with modern cabins and great river fishing.

Where to Eat with a Local Flavor
Lake Shore Resort and Salzburger Hof, 705-882-2323, has a fine German-Austrian menu and a magnificent view of the big lake. Voyageurs' Lodge and Cookhouse, 705-882-2504, has good lake trout and whitefish dinners and also offers lodging.

camera shots, a cut-stone monument, clean provincial outhouses and plenty of parking.

Parks and Public Areas
The day-use Batchawana Bay Provincial Park has 5 kilometers (3 miles) of sandy beaches for swimming, picnicking and walking. A modern Tourist Information Centre houses the Batchawana Bay Tourist Association. Open early June to early September.

What's Next
Your Circle Tour route leaving Batchawana Bay either to the north or south follows Highway 17, with the northward route heading for Montreal River Harbor and Wawa. The southern route passes Heyden and Searchmont on the way to Sault Ste. Marie.

BAYFIELD, WISCONSIN
Population 610

Bayfield, Wisconsin, regional map – page 30.

Bayfield is a New England-style town, nestled into a Lake Superior hillside and sporting a sparkling bayfront on the eastern shoreline of Wisconsin's Bayfield Peninsula. One of the favorite destinations on Lake Superior, the population swells during summer.

Steeped in water heritage, Bayfield, closest town to the Apostle Islands, holds an annual apple festival the first weekend in October and presents original arts and crafts in all forms.

Called the Gateway to the Apostles, Bayfield was named the Best Little Town in the Midwest by the *Chicago Tribune*. Bayfield's waterborne commerce includes fishing, tour boating and ferryboats. Its bent for the arts has it boasting 14 galleries displaying a wide choice of items. This is also right in the heart of some of the best birding opportunities around

Lake Superior. A "Birding by the Bay" brochure guides birders to the best sites and is available at area information centers and other outlets.

The Circle Tour route follows Highway 13 from Bayfield, with westbound travelers heading northward to Red Cliff and the western Bayfield Peninsula villages of Cornucopia, Herbster and Port Wing. Eastbound travelers will head south out of Bayfield toward Washburn and Ashland to continue on their trip.

A Bit of History

Although nearby La Pointe on Madeline Island (see separate listings) is one of Lake Superior's oldest settlements, the area around Bayfield is the traditional homeland of the Ojibway people and was important during the voyageur and fur trade eras. By the latter 1800s, Bayfield had also become important in both the lumber industry (briefly) and commercial fishing, which is still taking place today. Many of the large homes in town date from that period. In the second half of the 20th century, tourism became a dominant economic factor, as visitors discovered the romantic charm and terrific scenic beauty of the Bayfield Peninsula.

Today

Visitors will find dozens of shops, bayfront lodgings, eateries and other amenities in the downtown area. A plethora of bed-and-breakfast inns welcome overnighters, but advance reservations are strongly advised. Museums, nearly every service a visitor might desire and friendly, attentive people make this a favorite destination. The turn-of-the-century mansions, churches and commercial buildings house the shops, galleries and bed-and-breakfast inns for which the town is known, quaint lodgings of every pleasure.

What to See and Do

A 50-block area of this charming hillside community has been designated as a historic district on the National Register of Historic Places. The Chamber of Commerce office has information on a self-guided walking tour that will give you an afternoon of history as well as some exercise. The Chamber office also offers information on 90-minute Bayfield Heritage Tours, a guided, narrated walking trek that visits 24 historic Bayfield structures listed on the National Register. The tour is lighted by lanterns.

For music lovers, Christ Episcopal Church is the venue for the Bayfield (Mostly) Schubert Festival Thursday evenings mid-June through mid-August.

Apostle Islands National Lakeshore

With headquarters and main information center in Bayfield, Apostle Islands National Lakeshore gives visitors a unique opportunity to visit isolated lighthouse sites, beautifully forested islands and to learn the history of this scenic area.

Accessible by either private boat or by boats from the Apostle Islands Cruise Service in Bayfield, the National Lakeshore encompasses 21 of the 22 islands in the archipelago, with Madeline Island being the only one not included. A good deal of mainland is also included in the Lakeshore. (See separate listing for Apostle Islands Lakeshore.)

B

On to Madeline Island

Lying a tantalizing 2.5 miles (4 kilometers) across open water from Bayfield, Wisconsin, La Pointe and Madeline Island are magnets for visitors. For those who arrive in their own boats, getting to the island is a matter of less than a half-hour trip. For those without a boat, the crossing can be made on one of the ferries operated by Madeline Island Ferry from docks in Bayfield and La Pointe. You simply walk, bike or drive your car aboard, relax and enjoy the scenery. More than two dozen crossings are made per day in the busy summer season. In winter, an ice road is maintained after freeze-up that yes, cars can drive on, but a wind sled also provides service when ice conditions warrant it. There is a lighted, paved, uncontrolled air strip for visitors arriving by air. It's located 1.5 miles east of La Pointe. (See separate Madeline Island listing.)

During the summer, a Farmers Market is open near Maggie's restaurant on Manypenny Avenue each Saturday.

Do take a tour of apple orchards along the hilltop above town. Stop at Erickson's Orchard for good food, gifts and classic antiques. You can pick your own. Hauser's Superior View Farm takes its name from the view, 600 feet (183 meters) above lake level. A variety of plants, flowers and trees and, of course, apples are available here, as well as homemade jams and jellies and dried flowers. It is home to the Bayfield Winery, which produces hard ciders and wines concocted from local fruits and berries. Check out the miniature tractor collection and farm antiques in the hayloft of the historic Sears-Roebuck mail-order barn. Good Earth Gardens offers dried flowers, fresh herbs and you can pick your own berries in season. Blue Vista Farm overlooks the lake. You'll love the fields of lupine in the early summer. And the Olsens at Bayfield Apple Company have experimented with several interesting combinations of fruits and you can watch them concoct their juices, jellies, jams and apple mustard (absolutely delicious). Other orchards and farms to check for specialty produce include Highland Valley, Apple Hill and Rabideaux.

Eight miles (13 kilometers) southwestward from Bayfield on Wisconsin 13, wax your skis and enjoy 40 miles (65 kilometers) of groomed cross-country trails at Mount Ashwabay, a ski area with an acronym name made from the first syllables of Ashland, Washburn and Bayfield. Turn west on Ski Hill Road off State Highway 13. Trails vary from old logging roads to hilly slopes. Mt. Ashwabay has 14 downhill runs for all skill levels, snowmaking capability, ski rental, instruction, food and a chalet. Open Wednesday through Saturday for downhill and daily for cross-country skiing.

Also at Mt. Ashwabay, signs will direct you to where Lake Superior Big Top Chautauqua offers unique professional summer entertainment – culture under canvas. The Big Top features the popular historical musicals of Bayfield, Washburn and the Chequamegon region and well-known performers under the mirthful artistry of impresario Warren Nelson. The season runs from early June through Labor Day. Bay Area Rural Transit buses provide pickup from various locations in the area.

A series of hiking and biking trails begins near the Chamber offices, which are located one block south of the main street at Manypenny and Broad. Of particular interest are the Brownstone and Iron Bridge walking trails. Visitors with kids will appreciate the new playground near the Coast Guard station.

Apostle Islands Cruise Service offers water-level views among the Apostle Islands on its *Island Princess* or *Ashland Bay Express*. The three-hour narrated excursions around 19 of

DIRECTORY

Tourist Information – Bayfield Area Chamber of Commerce, 715-779-3335, 800-447-4094; Bayfield Country Tourism, 800-472-6338; Apostle Islands Information, 715-682-2500, 800-284-9484 ext. 9

Where to Stay
Old Rittenhouse Inn, 715-779-5111, 301 Rittenhouse Ave., is Bayfield's oldest and best-known bed-and-breakfast inn, with exquisite meals and many special annual events. Bayfield is rife with historic to modern inns, many in former mansions and residences. Call the Chamber for additional listings.
Bay Front Inn and Gifts, 715-779-3330, 15 Front St., is a recently built, 16 room waterfront lodging with good dining adjacent.

Seagull Bay Motel, 715-779-5558, 325 7th St., offers nice motel units with a friendly, knowledgeable staff.

Where to Eat with a Local Flavor
Greunke's First Street Inn and Restaurant, 715-779-5480, 17 Rittenhouse Ave., offers lodging and is a home of traditional fish boils during the summer.
Maggie's Restaurant, 715-779-5641, 257 Manypenny Ave., has especially fine hamburgers, gourmet pasta or pizza in a decor flooded with flamingos.
Wild Rice Restaurant, 715-779-9881, 84860 Old San Rd. (a mile south on Hwy. 13), offers gourmet dining and a great wine selection during the summer months.
Portside Bar & Restaurant, 715-779-5380, 34475 Port Superior Rd. (about a mile south on Hwy. 13), has nice dining right at the marina's waterfront.

B

the 22 islands are offered mid-May through mid-October. From mid-June through Labor Day, a variety of cruises include sunset and island shuttles.

Co-owner Craig Locey at Thimbleberry Inn B&B on the way to Red Cliff serves as licensed captain of the *Sandpiper*, a 35-foot wooden sailing ketch that makes regular tours of the Apostle Islands from the inn's dock.

Madeline Island Ferry Service provides a regular schedule of vehicle and passenger service between Bayfield and La Pointe on Madeline Island during the time when the water is open. In winter, a windsled provides service until the ice freezes hard enough to support traffic, when an ice road is maintained between the towns. The ferry is a great way to see both towns, as well as the countryside around them. It's especially grand during the fall color season.

Golfers will enjoy Apostle Highlands Golf Course. It has golfers teeing off over a miniature Lake Superior on the first hole and offers a great panorama of the Apostle Islands and the entire bay area from 500 feet above the lake.

Outdoor enthusiasts will want to check out the services of Trek & Trail, which offers adventures year-round. Also worth

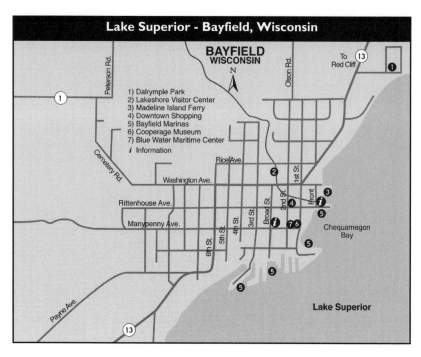

Lake Superior - Bayfield, Wisconsin

BAYFIELD
WISCONSIN

1) Dalrymple Park
2) Lakeshore Visitor Center
3) Madeline Island Ferry
4) Downtown Shopping
5) Bayfield Marinas
6) Cooperage Museum
7) Blue Water Maritime Center
i Information

checking are Living Adventure, with a nice selection of
adventure possibilities, and Apostle Islands Outfitters, which
can help plan and equip an outing. Bayview Riding Stables
can fill the needs of the "horsey set." Scuba enthusiasts will
want to check with Superior Adventures for information on
local diving hotspots.

Visitors wanting to stay fit or to get into shape can check
out the Bayfield Recreation Center, offering a fitness center,
swimming pool, whirlpool and racquetball court.

Anglers looking for Lake Superior fishing action should
contact Nourse's Sport Fishing or Roberta's Charters.

Notable Museums

Bayfield Heritage Association Center on North Broad
Street is a good place to delve into the past and present of this
charming town. Fee.

Bayfield Maritime Museum at the corner of Wilson Avenue
and First Street is an interesting stop, featuring exhibits of a
wide range of nautical paraphernalia, items from Bayfield's
commercial fishing industry and Great Lakes artifacts.
Summers only. Fee.

Parks and Public Areas

Apostle Islands National Lakeshore is the predominant
parkland of the area, encompassing nearly 70,000 acres of

which 42,140 are above the water. With 21 of the 22 Apostle Islands and a sizable chunk of mainland within its boundary, this is one of two areas on Lake Superior to carry the national lakeshore designation (the other being Pictured Rocks in Michigan's Upper Peninsula). Stop at the Lakeshore's Visitor Center in the Old County Courthouse for information and to check out the Fresnel lens from the Michigan Island Lighthouse. For additional information, see the Apostle Islands National Lakeshore listing.

Notable Events

• Bayfield in Bloom from mid-May to mid-June is a monthlong celebration of all things horticultural, featuring gardening tips and other activities for gardeners. The area's many orchards and wildflower farms are spotlighted.

• Apostle Islands Lighthouse Celebration, which was selected as one of the American Bus Association's top 100 events in North America, is scheduled from early to late September each year, with cruises offering views or guided tours of the lighthouses and other related events. Contact the Keeper of the Light (715-779-5619) gift shop for information.

• The first full weekend (Friday-Sunday) of October each year, the Bayfield Apple Festival transforms the town into a bustling festival city, loaded to the gills with people honoring King Apple. There are parades, contests, fish boils, a carnival, food booths, arts and crafts and waterfront regalia. Book lodging early; thousands pack this festival every year. Weekend highlights include a Venetian Boat Parade and the 500-member Wisconsin Mass Band.

• Old-Fashioned Christmas lasts from Thanksgiving until New Year's, complete with Santa arriving by boat and a tour of decorated historic and new homes.

• Apostle Islands Sled Dog Race is a mushing competition set in and around the islands in February.

• Annual Run on Water and Asaph Whittlesey Snowshoe Race gives competitors a chance to race on Lakes Superior's iced surface in February.

• Blessing of the Fleet is a mid-June rite that features a line-up of many boaters seeking the blessing of their various vessels.

• Festival of Arts gives local artists the opportunity to exhibit their works on the waterfront in late July.

Where to Shop

The downtown waterfront area is loaded with shops, galleries and showrooms for the artistic creations of many talented artists and artisans. Fine art with a Native American emphasis is available from some studios.

B

Split Rock Lighthouse

Just down the road from Beaver Bay, Minnesota, the oft-photographed sentinel, Split Rock Lighthouse, stands regally atop its 130-foot cliff where it served as a beacon for thousands of ships from 1909 until its decommissioning in 1968. When the highway opened in 1924, the lighthouse became a popular stop and today has more than 150,000 visitors annually to its 25-acre site. Take in the exhibits, outbuildings and ascend the tower to the lamproom for a look at the original Fresnel lens.

The 2,500-acre Split Rock Lighthouse State Park surrounds the site. Fees apply for park and some parts of lighthouse visit. (See separate listing for Split Rock Lighthouse.)

Keeper of the Light on the waterfront has a fine collection of Apostle Islands and general lighthouse memorabilia and is full of interesting books and nautical stuff.

Kerr Studio & Gallery has jewelry and sculptures right in the downtown on Front Street.

Just at the south edge of Bayfield, Eckels Pottery offers excellent stoneware and porcelain and encourages shoppers to watch the potters at work.

Campgrounds

Campers in the area will want to check on Apostle Islands Area Campground or the city-owned Dalrymple Campground, where there are limited sites for larger RVs, but ample spaces for tenters and smaller RVs and spectacular views.

What's Next

Leaving Bayfield, you will take Highway 13 either north to Red Cliff and then southwesterly through the small towns of Cornucopia, Herbster and Port Wing on the way to Superior. To the south, Highway 13 passes through Washburn on the road to Ashland to rejoin Highway 2.

BEAVER BAY, MINNESOTA

Population 150

Beaver Bay is the oldest settlement with a continuous existence on Minnesota's Lake Superior shore. It was founded in 1856 by German immigrants, who opened the region's first successful sawmill. In addition to townspeople, they employed many Ojibway people in the area. Look for the chainsaw-carved beaver that welcomes visitors. For information, check the Visitors Center operated by Bay Area Historical Society.

Considered sacred ground, an Indian cemetery sits beside County Road 4 on the east side of town. John Beargrease, best known as one of the early mail carriers who made the weekly trip between Two Harbors and Grand Portage, is buried here. The annual John Beargrease Sled Dog Marathon held in February between Duluth and Grand Marais is named in honor of Beargrease, who became a north shore legend for his dependability, no matter what the weather.

Where to Shop

A small town, Beaver Bay is loaded with fun shops. Several are located in the Beaver Bay Mini-Mall. The Beaver Bay Agate Shop is the best rock shop on the shore. The town

DIRECTORY

Tourist Information – Bay Area
Information Center, 218-226-3317,
218-226-3143

Where to Stay
Cove Point Lodge, 218-226-3221,
800-598-3221, 4614 Hwy. 61, has suites,
cottages, a fine restaurant and all amenities.

Where to Eat with a Local Flavor
Cove Point Lodge, 218-226-3221, 4614
Hwy. 61, offers fine cuisine and wines.
Lemon Wolf Cafe, 218-226-7225, Hwy.
61, offers handcrafted foods and specials
for kids.

offers a terrific bakery, a Christmas store and the unique
Shipwrecked Gift Shop has a complete collection of
merchandise from Native American to Scandinavian,
including nautical items for those fascinated with the lore of
the lake. Master sausagemaker Bill Jordan will almost
certainly have a specialty item to please your palate at Lake
Superior Sausage Company behind the Holiday Station.
Operated out of East Beaver Bay, Beaver Bay Sports Shop
offers a wide array of outdoor and fishing equipment. Nearby
at milepost 52 on Highway 61, Lake Superior Excursions has
daily narrated boat tours of Lake Superior's north shore in the
summer, as well as special charters aboard the *Grampa Woo
III* offering unique views of shoreline sites from the water.

Beaver Bay, Minnesota,
regional map – page 2.

What's Next
To continue the Circle Tour route, take Highway 61
either southwest to Two Harbors and Duluth or northeast to
Silver Bay heading for Grand Marais.

BERGLAND AND LAKE GOGEBIC, MICHIGAN
Population 440
At the junction town of Bergland, where M-28 is crossed
by M-64 from the north, the nearly 14,000 acres of Lake
Gogebic provide year-round recreation. Lake Gogebic State
Park borders its western shore. The lake sits about 1,300 feet
(400 meters) above sea level. Above the lake, Gogebic Ridge
Hiking Trail offers spectacular views. To the south is the
Sylvania Recreation Area of Ottawa National Forest. A
number of resorts, lodgings or campgrounds are on the lake.

Bergland, Michigan,
regional map – page 28.

What's Next
To the west, Highway M-28 heads for Wakefield,
Bessemer and Ironwood. Easterly lies Bruce Crossing and the
junction with U.S. Highway 45. Depending on your route,

DIRECTORY

B

Tourist Information – Western U.P. Convention and Visitors Bureau, 906-932-4850, 800-522-5657

Where to Stay
Gogebic Lodge, 906-842-3321, N9600 Hwy. 64, is a full-service resort,

with modern lodging, campsites dining and great fall color.
Walleye Lodge Motel and Resort, 906-575-3557, 1497 W. M-28, is open winter and summer for year-round recreation.

we recommend taking Highway 64 north from Bergland to Silver City, the Porcupine Mountains and Ontonagon.

BESSEMER, MICHIGAN
Population 2,145

Bessemer, Michigan, regional map – page 28.

Bessemer is located on M-28/U.S. Highway 2 midway between Ironwood on the west and Wakefield to the east.

Settled when iron ore mining opened on the Gogebic Range in the 1880s, Bessemer experienced the boom of both logging and mining. The logging played out relatively quickly as available stands of timber were depleted, but mining continued until the early 1950s, when many Gogebic Range mines ran out of ores. As the population dwindled in area cities, it seemed the importance of the area would likewise wither, until the development of ski resorts in the nearby mountains resurrected the area.

DIRECTORY

Tourist Information – Bessemer Chamber of Commerce, 906-663-4542, 800-522-5657

With consistently excellent snow, it's no wonder that this became the Upper Peninsular's skiing heartland. Major resorts in the iron mountains include Blackjack, Big Powderhorn and Indianhead ski areas. Several other skiing opportunities are located in close proximity, including Porcupine Mountains and Whitecap Mountains in nearby Montreal, Wisconsin (both discussed elsewhere in listings). Check for combination lift tickets that allow you to ski several or all of the hills. All offer instruction and equipment rentals. Big Powderhorn, a pioneer ski operation in the Midwest, is now in its fourth decade as a major ski area.

What to See and Do
Take County Road 513 from Bessemer to the Copper Peak Ski Flying Hill, the world's highest artificial slide with a 610-foot (188-meter) steel ski-flying tower. Open daily, June 15 through Labor Day, and weekends during fall colors.

Admission fee for chairlift and elevator. The present hill jump record is 512 feet, set by Vasko Stanislav of Czechoslovakia.

Continue on County Road 513, now designated as the Black River Scenic Byway, to Black River Harbor (population 19) and five scenic waterfalls with trails and overlooks, an excellent forest campground, marina, beach and swinging suspension bridge. Fishing charters are available. Beachcombing is a favorite here as is the Labor Day fishing derby.

Hundreds of area streams provide excellent fishing.

Notable Events
• Bessemer holds a Pumpkinfest in October with something for everyone, from pumpkin carving to seed spitting and a pie social. The city also has a nice July 4 celebration.

What's Next
To continue the Circle Tour route, take U.S. Highway 2 either east to Wakefield or west toward Ironwood. At Wakefield, Michigan Highway 28 heads northeasterly toward the Keweenaw Peninsula and Highway 2 bends southeast into the southern Upper Peninsula toward Lake Michigan's north shore.

BIG BAY, MICHIGAN
Population 250

A pleasant 25-mile (40-kilometer) drive north on County Road 550 from Marquette through the forests leads to the village of Big Bay, where delightful Perkins Park has access to Lake Independence, with a boat launch, docks, camping, fishing, swimming and picnic area.

Big Bay, Michigan, regional map – page 22.

The Thunder Bay Inn was once owned by Henry Ford. Built in 1911 as a general store, Ford renovated it in 1940 and used it to house his executives, who visited the Ford Retreat in the Huron Mountains. It was later used in the filming of the movie *Anatomy of a Murder*. Today the inn has been renovated, with charming antique-filled rooms and a friendly tavern/restaurant.

DIRECTORY

Tourist Information – Marquette Country Tourism/Convention and Visitor Bureau, 906-228-7749, 800-544-4321

The Big Bay Point Lighthouse is a 100-year-old bed-and-breakfast inn and an operating lighthouse. The atmosphere is laid-back and casual. Adults only, no pets, but be on the alert for a ghostly encounter that has been reported.

Big Bay Outfitters offers half-day "back country tours" out of Big Bay, as well as longer hiking, fishing or hunting treks through the Huron Mountains, the highest range in Michigan.

B

What's Next

Return on County 550 to Marquette, where you can continue your Circle Tour either east or west on Michigan Highway 28.

BIWABIK, MINNESOTA

Population 910

Biwabik, Minnesota, regional map – page 2.

On the eastern side of Minnesota's Mesabi Iron Range, the alpine-styled town of Biwabik is on Highway 135 a few miles east of Virginia. Through a century, this area has been important in the history of iron mining activity and was the site where the second iron mine was developed on the Mesabi Range. Evidence of mining is almost everywhere, from gaping red-hued holes in the earth to huge mounds of waste rock and overburden stockpiled around the mines.

Today, Biwabik is home to Giants Ridge Golf and Ski Resort, which features "ski or golf from the door" lodging. The resort opened its Quarry course in summer 2003, adding 18 holes of championship golfing to its outstanding original 18-hole Legend course. For about 50 years Giant's Ridge has been a popular ski area that features all the amenities of a major resort.

Sticking with a winter motif, Biwabik offers a lighted sliding hill and skating rink, adding a Norman Rockwell touch to snowy evenings. This is also the hometown of *Honk the Moose*, a popular children's book by Biwabik school teacher author Phil Stong. A life-sized statue of a moose stands in the park at the center of the city to commemorate the story's origin in Biwabik.

What's Next

Leaving Biwabik on Highway 135, you'll travel either west to Gilbert and Virginia-Eveleth or east to Aurora, with Hoyt Lakes a bit farther. A delightful way to return to Minnesota's Lake Superior north shore is to follow the newly paved Superior National Forest Scenic Byway (Forest Highway 11) south from Hoyt Lakes to Silver Bay on Minnesota's north shore of Lake Superior through scenic beauty, overlooks, lakes and forests.

DIRECTORY

Tourist Information – Iron Trail Visitors Bureau, 218-749-8161, 800-777-8497

Where to Stay
Giants Ridge Golf and Ski Resort, 800-688-7669, Cty. Rd. 138, offers suites, villas and room units, Timbers Restaurant/Lounge and most other amenities.

BRIMLEY, MICHIGAN

Area Population 950

Brimley is located a few miles west of Sault Ste. Marie. If traveling M-28 from the west, watch for County 221 north a

few miles before the junction with I-75 at Dafter. From Sault
Ste. Marie, the Lake Superior Circle Tour route that we
recommend takes either Business Interstate 75/County H-63
or Highway 129 south to Six Mile Road and turn right. If
traveling the Circle Tour to the west, this route will take you
closer to the shoreline and cut off several miles of travel.
Information is available on the way out of the Soo at the Soo
Chamber Office on I-75 Business Spur.

Brimley, Michigan,
regional map – page 18.

What to See and Do

Famous at the height of logging days, Brimley is the home
of the Bay Mills Indian Community, which operates the
King's Club Casino, the first tribally run casino in the United
States. The newer Bay Mills Resort and Casino is located on
Waishkey Bay, with two floors of hotel rooms, theme suites,
lounge, restaurant, convention center and the excellent Wild
Bluff Golf Course. The tribe also runs a 75-site RV park, with
30 of those sites offering water, sewer, electricity and cable.

Notable Museums

Wheels of History Museum, operated by the Bay Mills-
Brimley Historical Research Society, displays items from the
early lumbering, fishing, railroading and daily life of the area.
It is located in a rebuilt wooden passenger coach and operates
a gift shop and tourist information center out of the old
Detroit and Port Huron Railroad Caboose *No. 52*.

Parks and Public Areas

Brimley State Park (151 acres) has clean sand beaches,
campgrounds, a picnic area and swimming. Admission by
state park permit.

Point Iroquois Light Station is north of Brimley and has
been on the National Historic Register since 1975, operated by
the Bay Mills-Brimley Historical Research Society and the U.S.
Forest Service. Point Iroquois was named for the Iroquois
warriors massacred there by the Ojibway in 1662. It is one of the
few lighthouses where visitors can climb the 65-foot tower for a
spectacular view of Lake Superior and the bay. There is a museum
inside with a small gift shop, but don't stay too late. Rumors are
a ghost lives at the lighthouse. Open mid-May to mid-October.
Plans have been prepared to expand the parking area at this
popular attraction. No charge; but donations welcomed.

What's Next

Leaving Brimley to the east, a short drive brings you to
I-75 from the south, which leads to Sault Ste. Marie. About a
3-mile trip south from Brimley on Highway 221 leads to
Michigan Highway 28.

B

DIRECTORY

Tourist Information – Sault Ste. Marie (Michigan) Chamber of Commerce, 906-632-3301

Where to Stay
Bay Mills Resort and Casino, 906-248-3733, 888-422-9645, Lakeshore Dr., offers nice lodging, gaming and a full restaurant.

To the west and north, Curley Lewis Memorial Highway (Shore Drive) is Forest Road 3150 and follows a scenic lakeside route from Sault Ste. Marie to Brimley and on to M-123 that takes you to Tahquamenon Falls State Park and Paradise. This is a drive of beauty, especially spectacular in the fall when leaves have achieved their full color. Eastward travelers will take the route described above to Sault Ste. Marie.

Worthwhile stops for westbound visitors include: the Old Mission Indian Cemetery, the U.S. Forest Service Bay View Campgrounds and picnic area at Big Pine and guided, educational tours at Pendills' Creek National Fish Hatchery, where lake trout are reared to replenish stocks in surrounding waters. A scenic overview at Mission Hill Cemetery (watch carefully for the area) is the burial site for the crew of the shipwreck *Myron*, which sank nearby in November 1919. The U.S. Forest Service campground at Monocle Lake has fishing, hiking and swimming. There are private campgrounds in the area.

The forest service road intersects with Michigan Highway 123 about 5 miles (8 kilometers) south of the Rivermouth Unit of Tahquamenon Falls State Park, which includes a campground and Lake Superior access. The eastern Upper Peninsula branch of the North Country Trail enters the area at this point from St. Ignace and extends to Munising in the west, with a number of other segments completed across the region south of Lake Superior. Check with local information centers.

You'll pass the old townsite of Emerson, once home of the Chesbrough Lumber Company and a hub of lumbering famous for pine, but that ceased in the early 1910s. This area is now a center for fishing.

BRUCE CROSSING, MICHIGAN
Area Population 1,115

Bruce Crossing, Michigan, regional map – page 26.

Bruce Crossing is a wonderful crossing of roads where U.S. 45 and M-28 meet almost exactly in the center of the western Upper Peninsula. If you have the hungries or need lodging, check at Tulppo's Restaurant and Motel at the crossroads. During the winter, snowmobilers and cross-country skiers are within one hour of any area in Big Snow Country (see separate listing).

To the south of Bruce Crossing, off Highway 45 at Paulding, you can visit Bond Falls. Nearby are hiking trails, fishing and camping facilities. Paulding is also home to the mysterious Paulding Light, which has gained the burg a great deal of attention. (See details under Paulding listing.)

From Bruce Crossing there are several travel options. M-28 is the east-west route. North on U.S. 45 takes the traveler to Ontonagon.

BRULE, WISCONSIN

Area Population 860

Brule is about midway between Superior to the west and Ashland on Highway 2 and is an entry point to water adventure. Experience the beautiful Bois Brule River, world famous for trout fishing, scenery and exciting rapids. Information and canoe or kayak rentals are available in Brule at Brule River Rentals.

Brule, Wisconsin, regional map – page 2.

Visit the Brule River Fish Hatchery to see how Lake Superior fish are reared. There are guided tours, or you're allowed to roam on your own. Open weekdays year-round and on weekends, June through September. No charge. Handicapped accessible.

The banks of the river from its source at Upper St. Croix to Lake Superior are protected by the Brule River State Forest, 600 acres of which have been designated as the Mott's Ravine Natural Area to foster pine barrens found there. Four different options for canoe or kayak trips are now available. Local outfitters will drop off and pick up paddlers. Below Highway 2 is another day's trip, recommended only for experts. For information and maps, contact the Brule River Forest Station in Brule.

Brule is also one entry point of a side trip that travels south via Highway 27. If you have time, turn east on County Road N to visit Barnes and Drummond, which has an interesting museum of local history. Continuing on Highway 27 leads to Hayward (See separate listing).

What's Next

If traveling west, continue on Highway 2 toward Superior. To the east, you'll pass through several small towns on the way to Ashland.

Calumet - Crystal Falls

CALUMET, MICHIGAN

Population 880

Calumet, Michigan, regional map – page 24.

Calumet, meaning "Reed Pipe" in French Canadian but more widely accepted as meaning "Pipe of Peace," is steeped in history from the copper mining era. Originally named "Red Jacket" in the early years of the copper boom, the village is one of the main focal points of the Keweenaw National Historical Park, authorized in 1992. Historic buildings include the Calumet Theatre, the fire hall and Calumet's magnificent churches. A map of the historic business district is available for walking tours.

What to See and Do

Calumet Theatre opened in 1900 and is still actively used, hosting 60 to 80 events each year. This beautiful showplace was the first municipally owned theater in America. The worthwhile guided tours are given Tuesday through Sunday summer and fall. Self-guided tours are available year-round.

Shute's 1890 Bar has long been a popular Calumet watering hole, next to the Calumet Theatre. It's Michigan's oldest known original tavern with antique fixtures and a magnificent bar.

If you favor the game of golf, try the Calumet Golf Course, 9 holes located just south of town off U.S. 41.

For spectacular sunsets, take State Highway M-203 from Calumet to the west and Lake Superior's shore where you will find the 43-acre Calumet Township Waterworks Park.

Notable Museums

Coppertown USA Mining Museum on Red Jacket Road traces the area's copper mining history through its days of fame as the Calumet and Hecla Consolidated Copper Company. Small admission charge. Open Monday through Saturday (also Sundays in July and August) late May through early October.

Upper Peninsula Fire Fighter's Memorial Museum honors those who have been on the job over the last century. Housed in the historic 1900-era Red Jacket Fire Station, with three floors of historic equipment and other displays. Open early afternoons daily, late June to late September, dependent on availability of volunteers. Small fee.

The Keweenaw Heritage Center is located at St. Anne's Church and contains many interesting displays. It's open daily free of charge from 1-4 p.m. July through Labor Day.

Parks and Public Areas

Italian Hall Memorial Park honors the memory of the many people who lost their lives in 1913 during a bitter miners strike. Someone yelled "fire" while a Christmas party was under way at Italian Hall and people stampeded out. A total of 73 people, mostly children, died. The tragedy created a national sensation and triggered changes in mining labor and free speech laws. The Pine Mountain Music Festival's specially commissioned opera, "Children of the Keweenaw," based on the Italian Hall tragedy, appropriately premiered at the Calumet Theatre, which served as a temporary morgue after the disaster.

Take State Highway M-203 nearly to the Keweenaw Waterway to find the 401-acre F.J. McLain State Park on Lake Superior and Bear Lake. It features modern campgrounds, beaches, an excellent day-use area, refreshments, swimming and agate hunting. Some mini-cabins are available. Admission by park permit.

Notable Events

• Calumet hosts its Great Bear Chase Cross-Country Ski Race in March and a mid-August Heritage Celebration/Boomtown Festival.

Where to Shop

Copper World has copper items, lighthouse collectables, T-shirts and local history books for sale. Next door, check out the stock of goodies and collectables at Calumet Mercantile and General Store on Fifth Street.

Mine Street Station is a development area that houses shopping and lodging facilities. The center is on a parcel of land formerly belonging to the Calumet and Hecla mining company.

DIRECTORY

Tourist Information – Keweenaw Convention and Visitors Bureau, 906-337-4579, 800-338-7982

Where to Stay
AmericInn Lodge and Suites, 906-337-6463, 800-634-3444, 56925 S. Sixth St., offers nice units with many amenities.

Where to Eat with a Local Flavor
Toni's Country Kitchen, 906-337-0611, 79 3rd St., Laurium, has great pasties and other Cornish specialties.

What's Next

If your route is to the north toward Copper Harbor, stay on U.S. Highway 41, but we recommend catching South Shore Drive at Fulton to take a scenic tour of the Keweenaw's eastern shoreline and the small towns of Gay and Lac La Belle (See separate listings). If you're returning from Copper Harbor, continue on Highway 41 to Hancock and Houghton.

CALUMET, MINNESOTA

Population 380

The village of Calumet is the unofficial gateway to the western Mesabi Iron Range and home to the last intact iron ore pit mine in Minnesota that can be toured. Listed on the National Historic Register, the Hill Annex Mine outlines the development of mining from animal use through steam power to modern high-tech equipment. Miners' Day celebrations are held in July. Fossil hunting in the mine is encouraged and pontoon boat rides on the mine pit lake are a nice diversion.

Winter skiers will want to visit Mont Itasca nearby at Coleraine, which is now designated as a U.S. biathlon training center and also offers ski jumping, snowboarding, downhill and cross-country trails.

What's Next

Travelers will take U.S. 169 either northeast toward Hibbing or southwest through Bovey and Coleraine to Grand Rapids.

CASCADE RIVER STATE PARK, MINNESOTA

Cascade River State Park, Minnesota, regional map – page 8.

About midway between Grand Marais and Lutsen, Minnesota, on U.S. Highway 61, Cascade River State Park has 10 streams flowing within its boundaries. Headwater swamps, swift midsections and roaring mouths can be easily explored from hiking trails. Most picturesque is the Cascade River itself, which falls 900 feet (277 meters) in a wispy 3-mile descent to Lake Superior within an easy walk of the highway. Wintertime finds the largest deer yard in the state at Deer Yard Lake.

Historic Cascade Lodge and Restaurant's dining room overlooks the lake and is well worth the stop, even if you can't stay over. The lodge caters to cross-country skiers in winter since it adjoins the 30-mile (48-kilometer) ski trail of the State Park. There's always great food and a welcoming smile.

Traveling on Highway 61 toward Grand Marais, as you approach Good Harbor Bay prepare to stop at the Thomsonite Beach Jewelry Shop, which features thomsonite, one of the gems unique to Lake Superior, set in gold. The gemstones come from a private mine on the Thomsonite

Beach Inn and Suites property, 5 miles (8 kilometers) southwest of Grand Marais. The Good Harbor Scenic Overlook has been upgraded by the Minnesota Department of Transportation, part of the highway improvement going on over several years and in several areas along the north shore. Famed Duluth architect David Salmela designed the "facilities" at this stop. Nearby is Cut Face Falls.

A few miles inland, at the very edge of the Boundary Waters Canoe Area Wilderness, Eagle Mountain is Minnesota's highest peak at 2,301 feet. Ask for directions in either Lutsen or Grand Marais.

Traveling northeasterly leads to Grand Marais. Southward from the Cascade area, you're heading for Tofte.

CASTLE DANGER, MINNESOTA

Castle Danger is 10 miles (16 kilometers) east on Highway 61 from Two Harbors, and the origin of the name is still cloaked in mystery. Once a fishing and logging area, some say it was named for the castle-like formation along the shore, a dangerous area for ships. Another story attributes the name to the ship *Castle*, reputed to have foundered here, although no evidence of that ship has been found.

Castle Danger, Minnesota, regional map – page 2.

Castle Danger is home to the year-round Rustic Inn, a historic log cabin restaurant with delectable homemade pies.

Across the highway, Grand Superior Lodge is the only log resort in the area and occupies the site of the oldest cabin resort on the north shore, Emil Edison's 1920s Campers' Home. A new log lodge opened in 2000 with suites, the Splashing Rock Restaurant and Lounge, meeting and banquet facilities and other amenities. The resort continues its cabin heritage, however, offering nice log guest homes with their own fireplaces (books months in advance, so call early). The same management operates Caribou Highlands Lodge at Lutsen.

Nearby, the coffee is always on at Pioneer Crafts Co-Op, a shop where you will find many works from local artists and craftspeople. For a traditional north shore stay, try Castle Haven Cabins, with its delightful Quilter's Cabin shop.

Castle Danger is only a stone's throw from Gooseberry Falls State Park (see separate listing), one of the most visited spots on Minnesota's north shore.

CHASSELL, MICHIGAN

Population 1,829

On the eastern edge of the Keweenaw Peninsula at Chassell, watch for roadside strawberry stands in season. Strawberries grown here are huge and juicy. Come in July for the Chassell Strawberry Festival.

DIRECTORY

Tourist Information – Keweenaw Convention and Visitors Bureau, 906-337-4579, 800-338-7982

Chassell, Michigan, regional map – page 24.

Amenities in town include a motel, cabins, a bed-and-breakfast inn, bakery and restaurant and a nice bayside park.

What to See and Do

The Sturgeon River Wilderness Area bird sanctuary reaches across the highway east of the village. There is a turnoff and observation platform in the sloughs. The DeVriendt Nature Trail is part of the sanctuary, off U.S. 41. It is a 1.5-mile loop that combines a boardwalk through the slough and chipped trails through the woods. Many waterfowl nest here.

Just south of Chassell, watch for the turn-off to Keweenaw Berry Farm, a fun family stop with a nice farm animal collection for kids to pet and some of the tastiest, piping hot pasties we've found.

On the Portage Entry Road, there is a marina and boat docking area, with boat launch. This is a good spot to see fishing boats up close.

A pleasant way to pass the time is at the Einerlei on U.S. 41, a shop with books, home furnishings, regional art, casual clothing and interesting gardens. They also have a location in Houghton (Einerlei up north). Special events are regularly scheduled.

Chassell has a nice marina – St. Urho's Landing and Swimming Beach.

Notable Museums

Chassell Heritage Center in the old elementary school has museum displays of Chassell Township history and changing exhibits of historic artifacts and modern artworks. The center, home to the Friends of Fashion, houses the most extensive vintage clothing museum collection in the Upper Peninsula. New exhibits continue to gather clothing and accessories dating to the 1860s. On Thursday evenings during summer, local and regional artists, researchers and musicians present programs at the Heritage Center beginning at 7 p.m. In July and August, it's open 1-4 p.m. on Tuesdays and 4-9 p.m. Thursdays.

Notable Events

• In January Chassell hosts the Chassell Bay Ice Fishing Derby and Copper Island Classic X-C Ski Race.

• The Carl Olson Memorial Adventure Trail Run occurs in June.

• July sees the Strawberry Festival and Old Fashioned Christmas in December.

What's Next
If traveling westward, follow Highway 41 along Portage Lake to explore another of Lake Superior's "Twin Cities," the Houghton/Hancock area separated by Portage Lake. If your line of travel is to the east, stay on Highway 41 heading for Baraga and L'Anse.

CENTRAL, MICHIGAN
Central, a small village on U.S. Highway 41 some 25 miles north of Houghton-Hancock on the Keweenaw Peninsula, is a good look at all that remains of a bustling 1800s Keweenaw Peninsula copper mining community. Each July, the town hosts the annual Central Mine reunion of descendants of original settlers in the area at the Central Church.

Just north on Highway 41, plan a stop at the Delaware Mine Tours for an underground copper mine walking tour in one of the oldest mines on the Keweenaw, where you'll see exposed veins of copper. The mine is not handicapped accessible. A variety of friendly animals for the kids has been added at the grounds, which feature rides and exhibits of owner Tom Poynter's extensive collection of scale model railroad equipment. Open mid-May through mid-October. Guided and self-guided tours. Small admission.

North from nearby Phoenix, U.S. 41 approaching Copper Harbor is a designated Scenic Highway and an exceptionally lovely drive, with tunnels of pine and hardwood trees that are especially spectacular in fall color.

Central, Michigan, regional map – page 24.

CHEQUAMEGON NATIONAL FOREST, WISCONSIN
If you're traveling across northern Wisconsin on U.S. 2 between Superior and Ashland, you'll find that the Chequemegon National Forest contains some of the loveliest forested lands in the northland. Hundreds of small lakes deep in the north woods are filled with fishing opportunities.

The forest preserves 850,000 acres of gently rolling terrain and timber, including some pine stands that have been in existence more than 100 years. In autumn, the color along this route is absolutely spectacular. There are numerous hiking and ATV riding trails and more than 500 miles of nicely groomed snowmobile trails through the woods, as well as the Chequamegon Area Mountain Bike Association (CAMBA) Mountain Bike Trail System developed and maintained by CAMBA, which received an award for grassroots development from the U.S. Forest Service. Wintertime activities include cross-country skiing, snowmobiling and snowshoeing.

The Highway is full of recreational opportunities, including the sighting of wildlife around almost every curve.

Chequamegon National Forest, Wisconsin, regional map – page 30.

You'll pass through the blink of a crossroad hamlet Ino (see separate listing), where you can jog south through the scenic Delta Lakes area. The Moquah Barrens Wildlife Area lies about 5 miles (8 kilometers) north of Ino on Forest Road 236. Follow the Moquah Barrens Auto Tour route, using a guide prepared by Chequamegon National Forest personnel.

CHISHOLM, MINNESOTA

Population 6,000

Chisholm, Minnesota, regional map – page 32.

Chisholm, located on U.S. Highway 169 north of Hibbing, is a good stop to experience the history of iron ore mining that was so crucial to the development of this region.

What to See and Do

Both the Minnesota Museum of Mining and the Ironworld Discovery Center, open May through September, will help you understand the heritage of this important mining district. Located on the edge of the Glen Mine, Ironworld's museum, trolley line and historic mining settlement preserve the story of this region's rich history, the life, the work, the place and the people. Ironworld tells the story of how immigrants settled Minnesota's Iron Range in search of their dreams. A 1920s Mesabi Railway trolley takes riders along the edge of the mine for a panoramic view of what mining entailed. Enjoy heritage activities or visit the Iron Range Research Center library and archives, open year-round, to trace your family's roots.

Across the road, the Iron Man Memorial is a statue dedicated to the thousands of miners who have worked in the mines and is the third largest free-standing statue in the United States. The St. Louis County Fair is held at Ironworld Discovery Center in August.

Notable Events

• Chisholm hosts the Range Rock-n-Blues Festival and the National Polkafest at Ironworld, both in June.

COPPER HARBOR, MICHIGAN

Population 100

At the very tip of the Keweenaw Peninsula, Copper Harbor is a beautiful village destination and is more than 150 years old. A marvelous year-round haven that caters to visitors, the village offers an abundance of gift shops, bookstores, marina facilities, great lodging and delicious food. If you're arriving by boat, the marina is a short walk from town. Most businesses in the area belong to the Copper Harbor Information Association and will be happy to provide details on almost anything you might seek.

What to See and Do

Average annual snowfall in the Keweenaw Peninsula is more than 200 inches. A good photo stop en route to Copper Harbor is the tall snowfall measuring gauge, which records annual snowfalls of note. A record 390.4 inches was measured in the winter of 1977-78. Snow means winter fun, and the upper Keweenaw is criss-crossed with more than 250 miles of snowmobile trails. Copper Harbor has 50 miles of cross-country ski trails, most of which become mountain bike and hiking trails when the snow melts.

Copper Harbor, Michigan, regional map – page 24.

Copper Harbor is a hiker's paradise. Although the famous white pine, the Leaning Giant, has fallen, the Estivant Pines still have much to offer. Stroll the paths through 500-year-old towering pines and wilderness forests. This is the last privately owned stand of virgin white pine in Michigan. Follow signs from Copper Harbor. Guide service available from Keweenaw Bear Track Eco-Tours, which provides environmental nature field trips.

Keweenaw Adventure Company conducts kayaking and paddle tours, also offering bicycle rentals, repairs and tours.

Isle Royale Queen III, which offers transportation to and from Isle Royale National Park, welcomes passengers for nightly sunset cruises from July 4 through Labor Day. Operated by the Royale Line Inc.

Copper Harbor's one-room schoolhouse is one of the state's oldest. It has a viewing room, which allows you to see how one teacher oversees students from all the elementary grades, when classes are in session.

The 9.5-mile (15-kilometer) drive over Brockway Mountain has scenic overlooks at regular intervals. The scenic vista at the top is more than 700 feet (215 meters) above Lake Superior, with a view that stretches from Keweenaw Point in the east to Eagle Harbor in the west. The Skytop Inn on the summit offers a nice selection of gifts and souvenirs. Local

BROCKWAY MOUNTAIN, MICHIGAN

From Copper Harbor or Eagle Harbor, take M-26 to experience the 9.5-mile (15-kilometer) drive over Brockway Mountain with many scenic overlooks at regular intervals. The scenic vista at the top is more than 700 feet (215 meters) above Lake Superior, with a view that stretches from Keweenaw Point in the east to Eagle Harbor in the west. The Skytop Inn on the summit offers a nice selection of gifts and souvenirs.

Local bird watchers credit Brockway Mountain as a major viewpoint from which to track the spring and fall migration of hawks and other raptors, since a flyway brings the birds almost directly overhead.

DIRECTORY

Tourist Information – Keweenaw Convention and Visitors Bureau, 906-337-4579, 800-338-7982

Where to Stay
Keweenaw Mountain Lodge, 906-289-4403, overlooks a 9-hole golf course, with individual and duplex log cabins, complete with fireplaces, scattered among the pines with a good restaurant. Open mid-May to mid-October.
Mariner North, 906-289-4637, offers lodging accommodations, a restaurant and lounge with games that make it a nice family choice.
Harbor Hide-A-Way Motel, 906-289-4741, has a Finnish sauna house and two family sized hot tubs that are open to the public year-round, as well as full RV service and tent campsites.
Eagle Lodge Lakeside, 906-289-4294, is three miles west of town and has one- and two-bedroom cabins right on the water
King Copper Motel, 906-289-4214, is close to the harbor and features spectacular sunsets. Parking for those taking the boat to Isle Royale is available across the street from the motel.

Where to Eat with a Local Flavor
Harbor Haus, 906-289-4502, overlooks the beautiful harbor, offers a tantalizing German-American menu and greets the *Isle Royale Queen III* as it arrives in the harbor from Isle Royale with a whistle salute and a "cancan" dance performed by the staff.
Mariner North 906-289-4637 offers a full menu and salad bar for dinner or a casual bar menu for lighter dining.

bird watchers credit Brockway Mountain as a major viewpoint from which to track the spring and fall migration of hawks and other raptors, since a flyway brings the birds almost directly overhead.

Notable Museums

A must stop for history is the Copper Harbor Lighthouse and Museum at the entrance to the harbor facing the village. Emphasis is on Lake Superior maritime history, with access to the keeper's living quarters and the remains of the shipwreck of the *John Jacob Astor*, driven ashore in an 1844 gale. Accessible only by boat (*Spirit of America*), which departs hourly from the Copper Harbor Marina, Memorial Day through mid-October, with limited spring and fall tours. Some evening cruises are offered and a gift shop offers souvenirs.

Another good stop to get a taste of the area's past is the historic Astor House Museum at Minnetonka Resort. Loaded with regional artifacts, including dolls and mining equipment, it is well worth a visit.

Parks and Public Areas

Fort Wilkins State Park is on the 199-acre site of an Army post established in 1844, ostensibly to protect rowdy copper miners from local Indian people. Abandoned in 1870, the fort has been restored, with interpretative actors during the tourism season. Admission by park permit. Camping reservations, mid-May to mid-October. The park was recently expanded to include an additional 498 acres to the south of Lake Fanny Hooe.

Notable Events

• Brockway Mountain Challenge X-C Race in February challenges skiers with some of the most striking scenery around.

• Longest Day Fishing Tournament in June is a chance for anglers to spend the long daylight hours fishing for worthwhile prizes.

• Copperman Triathlon in August establishes bragging rights for winners and non-winners alike.

• Art in the Park in August is an opportunity for artists and craftspeople to show their works to an appreciative public.

• Fat Tire Festival in September challenges mountain bike enthusiasts.

Where to Shop

There are shops galore, some with imaginative names and the gifts to go with them.

Laughing Loon Crafts of the North is loaded with tantalizing gifts, many made from native copper. Nearby, Patchword Books is sure to have interesting reading, no matter the age. Owners Jim and Laurel Rooks are an excellent source of local information.

A second bookstore, Grandpa's Barn, is a delightful shop and owner, Lloyd Wescoat, says her unusual name is an inheritance from her family.

Country Village Shoppes offer gifts, Christmas decorations and interesting food items, including fudge and the local favorite, thimbleberry ice cream sundaes.

Check the offerings of the Sugar Plum Shop for candy and Christmas items, the T-Shirt Gallery or Shea's Tees and Treasures, all located near the historic one-room schoolhouse.

Minnetonka Resort in the middle of town has a well-stocked gift store where you're sure to find just the right souvenir or memento of the area.

What's Next

You'll arrive and depart Copper Harbor by either U.S. Highway 41 or Michigan Highway 26, depending on your

intended route. U.S. 41 is a direct route to Houghton-Hancock, while M-26 follows the Keweenaw's western shoreline through Eagle Harbor and Eagle River, before joining U.S. 41 at Phoenix. Take U.S. 41 to Delaware and turn southeast, if you plan to travel the eastern side of the peninsula back to Houghton-Hancock.

CORNUCOPIA, WISCONSIN

Population 220

Cornucopia, Wisconsin, regional map – page 30.

The village of Cornucopia on Lake Superior's south shore offers both a harbor of refuge for lake boaters and marina services. The old fishing village of "Corny" presents travelers with beautiful sandy beaches and wonderful sunsets over Lake Superior's westerly waters 18 miles (29 kilometers) beyond Red Cliff or 15 miles north of Port Wing on Highway 13 at the junction with County Trunk Highway C.

Cornucopia is the northern-most community in Wisconsin and boasts of having Wisconsin's northernmost post office. It is designated as a harbor of refuge for vessels.

What to See and Do

There are three churches in town, Lutheran and Roman Catholic, but the early Eastern architecture at the Russian Orthodox St. Mary's Church, topped with its three-armed Russian Orthodox cross, is most likely to surprise and charm visitors.

Nearby, the Sea Caves, a popular kayaking and winter snowshoe or skiing destination in Apostle Islands Country, are accessed via Myers Beach Road about four miles east of Cornucopia. The road is also the entry point for a delightful 2-mile summer hike to a grove of ancient pines above the sea caves. Call Apostle Islands National Lakeshore headquarters (715-779-3397) for information on where to put in.

There are two marinas, the Town of Bell Marina and the Siskiwit Bay Marina.

The former home of an Ehlers-family herring processing operation, the "Green Shed," as locals call it, was renovated and developed into a social center and home of the Cornucopia Historic Museum, where a continuous arts, crafts and community flea market operates amidst exhibits of area history. Open Thursdays through Sundays during warm weather months only.

Where to Shop

Ehlers General Store in "downtown Corny," is full of fresh fruits, vegetables and country charm. An institution in the area since its establishment in 1915, it is now in the third generation of Ehlers-family ownership, as son Mark is

DIRECTORY

Tourist Information – Cornucopia Business Association, 715-742-3337; Bayfield County Tourism, 800-472-6338

Where to Stay
The Village Inn, 715-742-3941, Hwy. 13 &. Co. Rd. C, offers beautifully decorated rooms, named after the seasons of the year, with dining room and rustic bar. Fo'c'sle Bed & Breakfast, 715-742-3337, at Siskiwit Marina, provides two modern rooms adjacent to the water.

Where to Eat with a Local Flavor
Fish Lipps North Point Lounge and Restaurant, 715-742-3378, in addition to a good meal, can fix you up with a fishing charter or cruise.
Village Inn, 715-742-3941, offers an excellent menu featuring local fresh fish and a rustic bar. Fish boils Friday and Saturday, June through October (by reservation).

purchasing the store from Harold, who has been a mainstay since joining his father, Herman, at the store in 1946.

Gift shops are located at the Bell Marina, including the Good Earth Shop and the Sea Hag.

A convenience store, laundry and gas station are located in town, as is the Siskiwit Bay Coffee and Curiosities shop, with baked treats, some antiques and other gift items.

Notable Events

• The Community Club Fish Fry in July brings the community and many visitors together for delicious food as a benefit for civic projects.

• Cornucopia Day in August is a celebration of more than a century of Cornie's history and culture, featuring many fun events.

• Community Turkey Feed in November looks toward the holiday season with tasty food and community camaraderie.

CRYSTAL FALLS, MICHIGAN

Population 1,965

Crystal Falls on U.S. Highway 2 in Michigan's southwestern Upper Peninsula is the Iron County seat and a crossroads community where we can catch Highway 141 north to rejoin the Lake Superior Circle Tour as it wends its way to the east or west.

Crystal Falls, Michigan, regional map – page 49.

Crystal Falls was named for a waterfall on the Paint River where a dam now stands. Locals claim that the distinction of being the county seat was moved from Iron River to Crystal Falls in the dark of night during an 1880s poker game. Notwithstanding this questionable origin, the Iron County

Courthouse is a proud structure atop the hill, offering a wonderful vista of the surrounding territory.

Visitors can pick up an Iron County Heritage Route brochure and other informational materials at various businesses in Crystal Falls. There are lodgings in town and an AmericInn Lodge and Suites is located 16 miles west in Iron River.

What to See and Do

Interesting sites worth visiting in town are the Harbour House on Fourth Street (entry fee) and Fortune Pond a couple of miles out of town where nature has healed the scars of mining and turned the former iron ore pit into a lake.

East of Crystal Falls on M-69, take Mansfield Cutoff Road 7 miles north and travel another mile north on Stream Road to a National Historic landmark. Commemorating the 1893 flooding of the Mansfield Mine in which 27 miners lost their lives, the Mansfield Location and Pioneer Church site includes original landmarks and artifacts of that era.

DIRECTORY

Tourist Information – Iron County Chamber of Commerce (in Iron River), 906-265-3822

Parks and Public Areas

West on Highway 2 takes us past Be-Wa-Bic State Park, an entry point to the Pentoga Trail and Larson Park, inviting inspection of their scenic settings. Larson Park was the first roadside picnic site in the state and possibly the country.

What's Next

Staying on U.S. 2 to the west, you're heading for Big Snow Country (see separate listing under Ironwood) in the western Upper Peninsula. Eastward, U.S. 2 heads for Escanaba and an encounter with Lake Michigan's northern shore.

Drummond - Duluth

DRUMMOND ISLAND, MICHIGAN
Population 990

Along with Sugar and Neebish islands, Drummond Island is the largest of the three U.S. islands in the lower St. Marys River and is accessed by ferry from De Tour Village on Highway 134 at the very eastern tip of the Upper Peninsula. The visitor will find a historical museum, plus other good restaurants and lodging. Called the Gem of the Huron, the island offers ample opportunity to photograph another Great Lake. Potagannissing Bay is to the north, but Lake Huron surrounds the rest of the island.

DULUTH, MINNESOTA
Population, 86,920

At the Head of the Lakes, where the St. Louis River, the natural headwaters of the great Gitche Gumee (Kitchi Gami), is located, the cities of Duluth, Minnesota, and Superior, Wisconsin, though in different states, are really the northern Twin Cities, or "Twin Ports," also known as the Head of the Lakes.

The overall Duluth-Superior area, with a population of 243,815, is one of the three largest metro areas beside Lake Superior, each made up of dual cities. Thunder Bay, Ontario, with about 113,000 people, is an amalgamation of the former cities of Port Arthur and Fort William. Sault Ste. Marie, Ontario, and Sault Ste. Marie, Michigan, with a total of about 95,000 people, make up the third metro area. All heavily use the lake for commerce.

> ### DIRECTORY
>
> **Tourist Information –** Drummond Island Information Center, 906-493-5245, Mondays and Tuesdays, 9 a.m.-5 p.m.
>
> **Where to Stay**
> Drummond Island Resort and Conference Center, 906-493-1000, 33494 S. Maxton Rd., is a full service resort with good dining, golf, bowling and shopping.
> Moosehead Lodgings, 906-297-5532, 18354 E., N. Caribou Lk. Rd., De Tour, features cabin lodging near to Mackinac Island ferry service.

Duluth, Minnesota,
regional map – page 2.

A Bit of History

Over the years, Duluth (second largest city on the lake) and Superior (population 27,370) have had a friendly – and in the distant past not so friendly – rivalry, yet it seems almost impossible to mention one city without the other because their history and commerce are so intertwined.

Superior was developed earlier than Duluth by virtue of the fact that all of northeastern Minnesota remained Indian territory until the Treaty of La Pointe was ratified in early 1855, opening up Minnesota's Lake Superior north shore to exploration and settlement. Prospectors immediately flooded to the area, expecting to find a continuation of the fabulous copper ore being mined to the east in Michigan's Copper Country. Traces of copper kept that hope alive, but never led to any substantial mining.

Meanwhile by the 1870s, railroads were being built to the Twin Ports. The promise of shipping huge tonnages of western grain, timber products, freight and passengers was the magnet that led to rapid boom and bust development during the next decade. Although Superior's flat terrain seemed a more logical choice for railroad development, Duluth prevailed in attracting the attention of the rail and shipping developers, becoming the larger city within a few years.

With discovery of iron ore in northern Minnesota, first on the Vermilion Range in the 1860s and later on the Mesabi Iron Range in the early 1890s, a flurry of construction and development kept pace with the explosion of iron ore shipping and a rapidly expanding timber industry that settled sawmill operations along the waterfronts of Duluth and Superior.

By the early years of the 20th century, the Twin Ports were a major force in the economy of Midwest and, indeed, the entire country. Despite the collapse of the timber boom by 1920, the importance of grain and iron ore shipping remained and other enterprises like shipbuilding, commercial fishing, tourism, health and education and, recently, shipping huge cargoes of western coal have each had an impact on the Head of the Lakes and on the lives of people who live here.

Today

Duluth's and Superior's primary products relate to their position on Lake Superior and the Great Lakes. Iron ore, grain, coal and other bulk cargoes are shipped throughout the world from the port, which also receives shipments from many foreign sources via the St. Lawrence Seaway.

But shipping, while important, is not the dominating local economic factor that it once was. Today, health care and the medical field constitute the largest source of employment in Duluth. In addition, three major educational institutions and

several non-degree institutions provide professional and vocational skills to thousands of students each year, making the Twin Ports the regional education center for a large area, as well as fresh-water research and educational facilities that rank it as the fresh-water capital of the region.

This is also the starting point for many people planning a Circle Tour of Lake Superior. The route northeast on Highway 61 along Minnesota's Lake Superior north shore is one of the most popular and scenic routes in the country, being designated as a National Scenic Highway from Canal Park all the way to the international border. For those planning a counterclockwise Circle Tour, Highway 2 east from Duluth through Superior and on into Wisconsin to Michigan's Upper Peninsula is also a scenic and pleasant route to many of the big lake's most attractive destinations.

To find out what's happening in the Twin Ports, pick up a copy of the *Duluth News Tribune, Duluth Budgeteer* or the *Daily Telegram* from the Superior side of St. Louis Bay. Several large shopping complexes and numerous tourist attractions from golf and museums to in-town fishing make these cities one of the most popular tourist destinations in the Midwest. Duluth and Superior each serves as the county seat for, respectively, St. Louis County, Minnesota, and Douglas County, Wisconsin. Each is also a regional center for other governmental entities at both the state and federal levels.

Duluth stretches some 25 miles (33 kilometers) along a mountain bordering the lake, with streams, hills and woodlands distributed throughout the city. The counterpoint of residential, commercial and industrial development sits well on the hillsides, providing an urban wilderness of beauty and comfortable living.

Duluth's neighborhoods all have personalities of their own. And each exhibits an individual style when it comes to shopping. Along East Superior Street from the downtown area, you'll pass through historic neighborhoods with block upon block of magnificent older homes, many qualifying as mansions. This leads to the Lakeside and Lester Park neighborhoods which are the "newer" residential areas that offer their own hometown shopping experiences.

Gary/New Duluth and Morgan Park on the extreme western edge of the city have their company homes and shopping areas. Busy Spirit Valley in West Duluth has a rapidly expanding shopping mall, plus many Grand Avenue and Central Avenue establishments that can provide you with a full day of shopping. In Duluth's Lincoln Park (formerly West End) on Superior Street, the well-designed streetscape affords a pleasant opportunity to visit some of the city's big furniture stores and shops.

D

Canal Park area of Duluth strives to recapture the historical flavor of the city. The area is a popular attraction during the daytime and late into the night with entertainment and restaurants. It has really come alive with the addition of sculptures, other outdoor art and fountains. An Art Walk brochure is available in most information racks with a walking tour of Waterfront Art, listing sculptures and art objects located from Bayfront Festival Park to Lake Place Park and other sites around town.

Park Point, across the Aerial Lift Bridge from Canal Park, is formally called Minnesota Point, a 6-mile-long (9.5-kilometer) sand bar that separates Lake Superior from the sheltered Superior Bay and the Duluth and Superior harbors. At its end, visitors find a 22-acre recreation area, sand beaches with lifeguards (water temperatures near shore can range from 70 to 85 degrees Fahrenheit in the summer, honest), picnic tables, playgrounds, ball fields, a sheltered beach house and Sky Harbor Airport. Windsurfing is a popular pastime on the harbor side. Numerous marinas along the Point harbor private yachts and cruisers. The Duluth Rowing Club often practices and holds races on Superior Bay. A bird sanctuary is maintained beyond the airport at the end of Park Point. Stop at Bay Side Market for the latest information on Park Point happenings.

Despite seemingly long distances in town, visitors without their own transportation will find easy access to transportation by contacting one of several cab companies or boarding Duluth Transit Authority buses that connect to virtually all areas of both Duluth and Superior. Duluth International Airport serves airline passengers or charter and general aircraft arriving in or departing the northland, also offering car rental service. Greyhound Bus Lines provides connections to the Twin Cities from both Duluth and Cloquet.

Duluth serves as the health center for the region and a focal point for educational services, shopping, cultural expression and recreational activities. St. Luke's Hospital operates a 24-hour walk-in emergency care facility on East First Street and also has facilities in the Denfeld neighborhood, Hermantown and Superior. Nearby, the St. Mary's/Duluth Clinic hospitals join St. Luke's in offering a wide range of general and specialized care that have made Duluth a major medical center in the Upper Midwest.

The University of Minnesota-Duluth (UMD) offers both four-year and graduate programs in liberal arts, science and technology, human resources, fine arts and business and is becoming a major center for fresh-water research. It has an excellent medical school. UMD is the home of the Tweed Museum of Art, Marshall Performing Arts Center, Natural Resources Research Institute, the Large Lakes Observatory, a

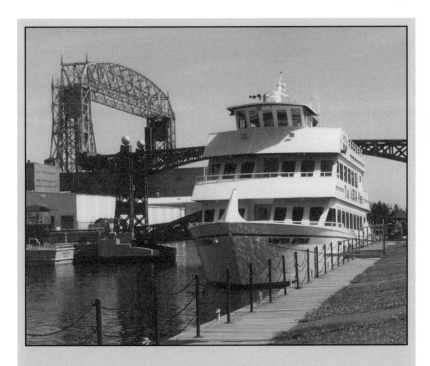

DULUTH'S AERIAL LIFT BRIDGE

Once the Duluth Ship Canal opened in 1871, residents of Minnesota/Park Point needed a connection to the rest of Duluth. For 34 years, ferries provided that connection, transporting people and freight back and forth across the canal, but that service ended after winter freeze-up. Planks were laid across the ice to accommodate traffic and an unsatisfactory suspension bridge was tried, but problems were apparent with those early efforts.

After the channel was widened to 300 feet and concrete piers installed, the city determined that a better solution had to be found. A contest was held and the winning entry was a lift bridge quite similar to the present structure. Officials, however, opted to build an aerial ferry system, with a suspended gondola car moving back and forth on wheels atop the bridge trestle.

It served well for 25 years, but increasing traffic after Henry Ford introduced his Model T in 1908 finally doomed the ferry to obsolescence and in1929-1930 the city rebuilt the superstructure as the Duluth's world-famous Aerial Lift Bridge of today.

One of the most spectacular sites on Lake Superior, the Aerial Lift Bridge rises to a full height of 138 feet (42 meters) in 55 seconds to allow vessels to enter and leave the harbor. Visitors are within yards of foreign ships, giant Great Lakes carriers and spectacular pleasure craft. Well lighted after dark, the bridge is a favorite subject for photographers day or night. Patience is a virtue when the Lift Bridge slightly delays traffic flow.

new library that offers a spectacular lake view to the public, the copper-domed Weber Music Hall and KUMD Radio, offering an interesting variety of programming.

Just a country block away from UMD, the College of St. Scholastica is a startling wonder of majestic Norman Gothic architecture featuring intricately placed stonework. Reminiscent of Olde England, the college offers four-year and graduate programs. Mitchell Auditorium is the home of its renowned Early Music Concert program, among other events scheduled. Lake Superior College offers students up to two years of academic or vocational education.

Smokers should be aware that a city ordinance approved by voter referendum bans smoking in many public facilities in Duluth.

For information on the Superior, Wisconsin, side of the bay, see its separate listing.

What to See and Do

In the harbor area, activity never seems to stop, from gigantic ore carriers moving in and out of their berths, grain ships slipping next to grain elevators or tourist boats scuttling back and forth throughout the harbor, there is much to see and do.

Thompson Hill Information Center and observation area off Interstate 35 near Spirit Mountain not only is loaded with information, it has a breathtaking view of the entire lower St. Louis River basin, the Duluth-Superior harbor and the lake beyond. Visitors and residents always comment on the impact of the vista as they drive over Thompson Hill, day or night.

The Duluth waterfront centers on the refurbished Canal Park at the very tip of Lake Superior. Lake carriers ("lakers") and salt-water vessels ("salties") enter and leave the Duluth harbor through the Duluth Ship Canal. Built in 1871, its piers extend 1,700 feet (525 meters) into Lake Superior. Sightseers can enjoy the plentiful gulls and stroll along the canal's walkways to its lighthouses. And there's a feeling that you can virtually reach out and touch the huge ships towering above you as they pass through the canal.

Next to the Aerial Lift Bridge (see side story), Lake Superior Maritime Visitor Center is one of the most visited sites in Minnesota, offering film shows, model ships and hands-on exhibits featuring commercial shipping on Lake Superior. Former visitors will want to check out this museum again, since many artifacts on display are changed at intervals. Kids love to try their hand at the large ship's wheel. Announcements about shipping activities are made from the museum as traffic moves through the Duluth Ship Canal. Open daily, with shortened hours in the cooler months. There is no fee for this service of the U.S. Army Corps of

Engineers with exhibits from the Lake Superior Marine Museum Association. Boatwatcher's Hotline at 218-722-6489 is a special phone service of the Lake Superior Maritime Visitor Center, U.S. Corps of Engineers and the Duluth Seaway Port Authority, providing up-to-the-minute information concerning the arrivals and departures of ships.

Great Lakes Aquarium is an international facility that focuses on fresh-water issues. The aquarium's $38 million, 62,000-square-foot exhibition building houses huge aquarium tanks with a multitude of species of fresh-water life above and below the surface, in addition to interactive exhibits of environmental significance to Lake Superior and its watershed. The aquarium focuses on Lake Superior as a means to examine fresh-water lakes throughout the world. For the most enjoyment, be sure to be a "hands-on" visitor. The aquarium conducts regular presentations for the public and outreach programs for schools, as well as interesting and entertaining exhibits of lake-related subjects. Aquarium membership allows reduced or free admission.

The city's most popular attraction is the Lakewalk, which hugs the shoreline for more than a mile along the North Shore Scenic Railroad from Canal Park past the Fitger's Brewery Complex to the renovated Leif Erikson Park, home of Duluth's famed Viking Ship and the Duluth Rose Garden, before continuing on to 26th Avenue East for a total of 3.2 miles. The large structure sitting in the water just off the Lakewalk in Canal Park is an old coal-unloading dock from years gone by and is known locally as Uncle Harvey's Mausoleum. It was named for Harvey Whitney of the Whitney Brothers Company from Superior, who had it built in 1919 originally to serve as a receiving facility for Apostle Islands sand and Grand Marais gravel. Within a few years, Lake Superior proved too powerful and Whitney abandoned it. Today, kids dive from it into the cool waters of Lake Superior during the summer. Above the Lakewalk at the "corner" of the lake is Lake Place Park, which covers the interstate highway. This landscaped area is also accessible from downtown. A storm pavilion allows visitors to watch tremendous waves crash into the shore from the protection of its shelter. Flowers and benches provide a pleasant atmosphere at this park in the heart of the city. The Viking Ship celebrates the Vikings' landing in Duluth. The restored Viking Ship sailed from Norway in the early part of the 20th century to celebrate the Nordic tradition. The Rose Garden was rebuilt and restored by the highway department after construction of the interstate highway. More than 3,000 rose bushes and flowering arrangements are maintained. There are many interesting annotated stops along the wide Lakewalk

D

explaining sights and history of the area, including an amazing mammoth mosaic history Image Wall that overlooks the lake. The Vietnam Veterans Memorial and the Korean War Memorial honor area members of the armed forces who served in those wars. Access to the Lakewalk from East Superior Street is made by a wide stairway at Eighth Avenue East near Fitger's or through the historic brewery itself.

Skyline Drive reveals the entire Duluth-Superior harbor and surrounding scenery. The dramatic 30-mile (48-kilometer) drive along the hilltop 600 feet (185 meters) above the shoreline of Duluth is designated as a State Scenic Byway. The route follows the shoreline of ancient Lake Superior when it was much deeper, extending from one end of the city to the other. It offers superb views of Lake Superior, the Duluth and Superior harbors, Hawk Ridge on Seven Bridges Road, rocky canyons and tumbling streams. Frequent observation points and markers help the driver and photographer. Hawk Ridge is a favorite vantage point in September for watching the annual migration of birds of prey. The city has marked the route with signs.

Pause at the Clayton Jackson McGhie Memorial at First Street and Second Avenue East, which honors the lives of three young black men lynched in 1920 by a mob angered by the alleged rape of a white woman. Remembered as one of the most painful events from Duluth's past, the unjust hangings of Elias Clayton, Elmer Jackson and Isaac McGhie from a lightpole in the downtown area lay virtually unacknowledged for six decades. A grassroots committee gained momentum to help the city to face this dark event. Three bronze figures and quotes from a number of civil rights advocates are indelible reminders of brighter future possibilities.

The gigantic Duluth Entertainment Convention Center (DECC) complex offers complete facilities, including an arena, auditorium, curling rink, exhibition halls, meeting space and catering for significant conventions, entertainment and sporting events. Duluth Omnimax Theatre provides IMAX panoramic films on a regular schedule throughout the year. A 10-screen multiplex cinema is adjacent. The DECC's 72,000-square-foot Harborside Convention Center offers 10 meeting rooms and a ballroom with a spectacular view of the Aerial Lift Bridge and harbor. The whole facility is connected to a parking ramp for 601 cars and the downtown area via skywalks.

Bayfront Festival Park is another spectacular waterfront showcase. Located just west of the DECC and Aquarium on the Duluth harbor, the 14-acre park was upgraded with permanent structures, landscaping and special features. Equipped with a 400-foot (123-meter) boardwalk, it's a good spot for ship watching, fishing and frequent summer

Glensheen Historic Congdon Estate

GLENSHEEN HISTORIC ESTATE

A must-visit-more-than-once destination is the Glensheen Historic Estate, a stately home built by Chester and Clara Congdon between 1905 and 1908. Tours explore the 39-room, neo-Jacobean mansion, carriage house and formal gardens on Lake Superior. The estate reflects an elegant way of life that existed in Duluth in the early 1900s. The 22-acre historic site on London Road is operated by the University of Minnesota. It has been featured on A&E's "America's Castles." Tours of the manor house last about an hour; grounds tours are self-guided. An additional tour of the home's third floor "arts and crafts decor" and attic is available, with costumed interpreters present during June through August. The mansion offers daily tours from May-October, with a reduced schedule in winter and spring. It is always best to call first. Tickets are on sale at the Museum Shop. This facility is specially decorated for the holidays, with brunches during December. Concerts are performed on the grounds at Glensheen on Wednesday evenings in July beginning at 6:30 p.m. (1-888-454-GLEN).

entertainment outdoors under the stars, including the annual Bayfront Blues Festival the second weekend each August. Departing ships make their final turn before the Aerial Lift Bridge right in front of the Bayfront area. In one corner of the area, Playfront Park, built entirely with volunteer help and donations, provides skating in winter and an outstanding place for children to enjoy themselves at all times of the year. Additional upgrading of the Bayfront area is planned in the near future so watch for new features.

In addition to regularly scheduled concerts, musical comedies and other entertainment offered at the DECC, Duluth and Superior have numerous other venues for the

performing arts. Renegade Comedy Theatre offers its satiric look at the world and the Duluth Playhouse has regular dramatic and musical comedy performances at The Depot Performing Arts Center. Both offer the opportunity for kids to perform or to attend children's theater events. The four colleges and universities in the metropolitan area also offer a rich blend of musical, dramatic, comedic and dance performances, and independent organizations like Duluth-Superior Symphony Orchestra and Matinee Musicale add to your entertainment choices. Check for schedules of performances for the time you plan to visit.

Cinema enthusiasts will find 33 screens of movie selections in Duluth, with seven more available across the bridge at Mariner Mall in Superior.

Port Town Trolley is a motorized trolley that loops through the downtown business section and Canal Park past attractions along the harbor's edge every half-hour during the summer, enabling riders to explore various points of interest. If your Duluth visit is based in Canal Park, then old-fashioned horse-drawn carriages offer a leisurely, scenic trip through Duluth's downtown and along the city's magnificent waterfront Lakewalk. There are also rental motor scooters and four-wheeled passenger bicycles available.

Duluth-Superior Excursions offer 1³/₄-hour narrated tours of the Duluth-Superior harbor from May through mid-October aboard the 255-passenger *Vista King*, which is moored across Harbor Drive from the ticket office in the Duluth Entertainment Convention Center. Access from Canal Park can be made via the Minnesota Slip Pedestrian Draw Bridge near Bellisio's. Lunch and dinner cruises are available on the 300-passenger *Vista Star*. Excursions include close-up views of the ore docks, Aerial Lift Bridge, Great Lakes cargo carriers, visiting foreign vessels, grain elevators along Rice's Point and other points of interest, all in the comfort of the boat. Private charter cruises and group rates are available. The office also has a gift shop. A complete information counter is operated there by the Duluth Convention and Visitors Bureau from mid May through mid October.

Downtown, the Duluth Skywalk system connects businesses and City Hall to the DECC and the waterfront with a covered, climate-controlled walkway. On inclement days, the skywalk offers a pleasant stroll within the city and its major buildings, including dozens of interesting stores, restaurants and most of the city's downtown multi-level parking lots.

North Shore Scenic Railroad offers 52-mile (84-kilometer) round-trip excursions between Duluth and Two Harbors and shorter 14-mile (23-kilometer) rides between The Depot in downtown Duluth and the Lester River area of Duluth. The

daily historic rail service provides 32-mile (52-kilometer), two-hour dinner and pizza trains from Duluth to Knife River and back. Charters are also available.

SS *William A. Irvin* ore carrier moored in Canal Park was once the flagship of U.S. Steel's Great Lakes fleet. The ship is permanently berthed alongside the DECC as part of the convention facilities. It is one of only two such floating ore boat museums on Lake Superior, the other being SS *Valley Camp* in Sault Ste. Marie, Michigan. The SS *Norgoma*, a passenger liner that is now a museum ship, is located in Sault Ste. Marie, Ontario's Bondar Park. The *Irvin*'s rich staterooms were once used to entertain VIPs as "thanks" for past and future business. Launched in 1938, the "Pride of the Silver Stackers" has been brought back to life as a floating museum. It provides sightseers with a close-up view of a past era of Great Lakes shipping. Open daily during summer with expanded hours Fridays and Saturdays in July and August. The annual Halloween Ship of Ghouls is a ghostly tour that never fails to delight children and others who get a kick out of bumps in the night. Directly aft of the *Irvin*, the retired U.S. Army Corps of Engineers' tug *Lake Superior* offers self-guided tours. Across the Minnesota Slip Pedestrian Lift Bridge in the slip, the retired Coast Guard cutter *Sundew* was opened as the DECC's third floating museum ship in July 2004. Built during World War II a few blocks from its retirement home and serving Lake Superior ports and shipping with distinction during much of its career, Duluth's acquisition of the *Sundew* as an exhibit ship is especially appropriate. Special prices are available to tour all three DECC ships.

Lake Superior and Mississippi Railroad Company near the Lake Superior Zoo on Grand Avenue and Fremont Street behind the Little Store, offers a 90-minute journey from the Zoo area to Gary-New Duluth aboard a vintage train from a bygone era. Ride the rails as travelers did in the 1870s for a 12-mile (19-kilometer) round trip along the scenic St. Louis River. Operated on weekends by an all-volunteer group from mid-June to the Labor Day weekend, the train departs twice each Saturday and Sunday. During the autumn color season, special color trips are operated.

For those who prefer to walk or bike, the Western Waterfront Trail is a 5-mile (8-kilometer) path along the St. Louis River that connects with trails at Jay Cooke State Park. The hiking/biking trail includes picnic areas and boating access sites. It offers cross-country skiing and snowshoeing in the winter. Located at Grand Avenue and 71st Avenue West. Mission Creek Trail is a challenging 3.25-mile (5.2-kilometer) trail, beginning off Highway 23 at 131st Avenue West in Fond du Lac Park. Those seeking a longer route will

want to challenge the 15-mile (20-kilometer) section of the Munger Trail between West Duluth (74th and Grand Avenue) and Carlton. Other hiking/biking opportunities abound, including: the Lakewalk, which begins at Canal Park; Kingsbury Creek Trail, above the picnic grounds at the Lake Superior Zoological Gardens; Lincoln Park Trail, 25th Avenue West and Third Street; Park Point Trail, at Sky Harbor Airport, the farthest point reachable by car past Park Point Recreation Area; Chester Park Trail, 18th Avenue East and Skyline Parkway; Congdon Park Trail, at 32nd Avenue East and Superior Street; Lester Park Trail, 61st Avenue East and Superior Street.

Lake Superior Zoological Gardens in West Duluth features animals from around the world and is one of the most visited paid attractions in the Twin Ports. New exhibits continue to draw visitors again and again. Attractions include Australian kangaroos and kookaburra, and Polar Shores with polar bears, harbor seals and other arctic animals in natural settings. The zoo has a Kodiak and an Alaska brown bear, snow leopards and Siberian tigers. The Contact Corral allows hands-on contact with goats and other gentle species. Picnic areas and campgrounds are nearby. Open daily year-round with reduced winter hours. Grand Avenue at 72nd Avenue West, adjacent to Fairmont Park. Admission, but free with membership. Group rates available.

At the Airport, check out the display of more than 100 inductees into the Minnesota Aviation Hall of Fame. Nearby, the Commemorative Air Force has an aviation museum and a restored pre-World War II PBY airplane on display.

Duluth's public golf courses have had major improvements made within the past few years, rating this area a top golf destination by *Golf Digest*. Enger Park Golf Course on Skyline Boulevard, Grandview Golf Course on the city's west end and Lester Park Golf Course on Lester River Road in the east provide outstanding public access. Private courses include the historic Northland Country Club on East Superior Street and Ridgeview Country Club on Red Wing in the Woodland area of Duluth.

Anglers have plenty of choices for fishing in the Duluth area. A number of charter captains operate from Canal Park next to the SS *William A. Irvin*. River fishing is a popular sport in the spring and fall in a number of rivers along the State Scenic Byway North Shore Scenic Drive, particularly the Lake Superior waters off the Lester and French rivers. North Shore Charter Captains Association provides state-licensed guides for deep-sea sport fishing on Lake Superior. Anglers try for steelhead, chinook, coho, Atlantic salmon and lake trout. All necessary equipment is provided. Half- and

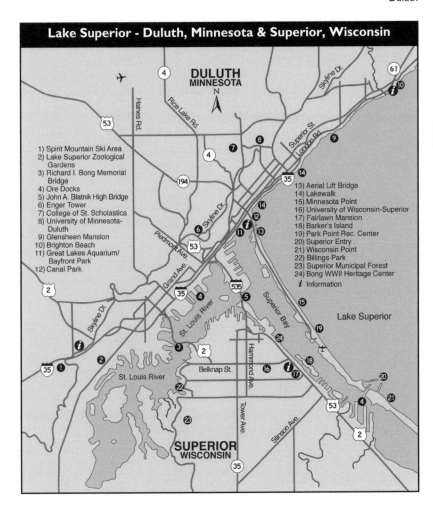

Lake Superior - Duluth, Minnesota & Superior, Wisconsin

1) Spirit Mountain Ski Area
2) Lake Superior Zoological Gardens
3) Richard I. Bong Memorial Bridge
4) Ore Docks
5) John A. Blatnik High Bridge
6) Enger Tower
7) College of St. Scholastica
8) University of Minnesota-Duluth
9) Glensheen Mansion
10) Brighton Beach
11) Great Lakes Aquarium/ Bayfront Park
12) Canal Park
13) Aerial Lift Bridge
14) Lakewalk
15) Minnesota Point
16) University of Wisconsin-Superior
17) Fairlawn Mansion
18) Barker's Island
19) Park Point Rec. Center
20) Superior Entry
21) Wisconsin Point
22) Billings Park
23) Superior Municipal Forest
24) Bong WWII Heritage Center
i Information

full-day charters are available. For a list of charter boat options, contact the Duluth Convention and Visitors Bureau.

Sailing enthusiasts can experience Lake Superior aboard one of the many boats available to rent. Training is offered. Call Lakehead Boat Basin, Duluth, for charter fishing and sailboat rental (experienced sailors only).

The Twin Ports are laced with bikeways, which vary in grade from flat to steep. In addition, the city's buses are equipped with bicycle racks during the bicycling season to help transport riders between locations. A bikeways map has been developed to aid in route selection. It is available in most information locations and at bicycle shops.

Winter sports fans will find many opportunities in Duluth. Cross-country ski trails include Spirit Mountain Ski Area, off Interstate 35 at Boundary Avenue; Magney, off

105

Boundary Avenue near Spirit Mountain; Piedmont, at Adirondack Street and Hutchinson Road; Chester Park, off East Skyline Drive in Chester Bowl; Hartley, at the end of Fairmont Street off Woodland Avenue and the end of Hartley Lane off Arrowhead Road, where the Hartley Nature Center operates an interpretative center offering an interesting schedule of environmental programs; and at Lester-Amity, at Lester River Road and Superior Street. Ski trails are lit for evening skiing at Chester Bowl and Lester Park.

Downhill and cross-country skiing are offered at Spirit Mountain and Mont du Lac at the western edge of Duluth on the Superior, Wisconsin, side and Chester Bowl at Chester Park. Spirit Mountain has several excellent chair lifts and 20 downhill runs. Mountain Villas at Spirit Mountain offers year-round contemporary-styled housekeeping units for extended stays. In the vicinity is AmericInn, which also has lodging south on Highway 35 at Moose Lake. A Country Inn and Suites is located nearby. For a pleasant stay near the zoo and the Willard Munger State Trail, try the Super 8 Motel just off the freeway at 40th Avenue West.

If you'd like a little more adventure, the Outdoor Program at the University of Minnesota-Duluth, offers beginning and advanced instruction in kayaking, canoeing and climbing. They sponsor a variety of trips for folks to test their skills and the program's U.S. Kayak and Canoe Center challenges the skills of paddlers on a stretch of white water below Thomson Dam on the lower St. Louis River, which is operated by Minnesota Power, a major utility and corporate citizen of the area.

Notable Museums

Duluth abounds with museums.

Nine independent organizations make up The Historic Union Depot, a reclaimed 1892 vintage depot in downtown Duluth. Between 1910 and 1920, Historic Union Depot served seven railroads. The Depot was recognized by the U.S. Department of Transportation as one of the best re-uses of a historic railroad depot. The building was listed on the National Register of Historic Places in 1971. Within the Depot, the St. Louis County Heritage and Arts Center preserves the area's rich mining, railway and logging history. The most notable organization is the Lake Superior Railroad Museum, where visitors stroll the streets of a 1910 village, Depot Square, and explore the nationally acclaimed collection of antique locomotives, passenger cars, freight cars and snowplows. There are trolley rides available on a seasonal basis. One of the stars of the collection is Minnesota's first locomotive, *William Crooks*, built in 1860. Other Depot exhibits include four levels of dolls, fashions, furnishings,

industry and art of a bygone era. The Depot also includes the Duluth Children's Museum and the St. Louis County Historical Society. The Depot Performing Arts Center houses the Arrowhead Chorale, Minnesota Ballet, which has its main office and studio at 301 West First Street, Duluth-Superior Symphony Orchestra, Duluth Playhouse, Matinee Musicale and the Duluth Art Institute. Open year-round. Gate fee, group rates. 506 West Michigan Street.

At University of Minnesota-Duluth, the Tweed Museum of Art has five galleries with changing exhibitions drawn from all aspects of contemporary and historical art activity, including a sculpture wing. More than 5,000 objects make up the permanent collection. The 50-year-old museum is closed Mondays and holidays.

Karpeles Manuscript Library houses rare documents, including original handwritten drafts, letters and other historic relics such as the U.S. Bill of Rights and the Emancipation Proclamation. One of seven such private libraries in the country, it is located on the corner of Ninth Avenue East and First Street, across from St. Luke's Hospital. Open daily in the afternoon, except closed Mondays, September through May. Free.

Parks and Public Areas

Duluth is full of parks, picnic and wildlife areas, many of which have been improved and expanded. Chambers Grove in Fond du Lac is on U.S. Highway 23 at the western edge of the city. Fairmont Park is adjacent to the Lake Superior Zoological Gardens. Chester Park houses one of Duluth's ski jumps. Lester Park, on the eastern end of the city, is next to the Lester River, a favorite fishing location. The restful Brighton Beach and its Kitchi-Gammi Park is nearby.

Notable Events

• Duluth annual events include Grandma's Marathon, which features upwards of 6,000 world-class runners competing in a 26.2-mile (42-kilometer) run that follows Lake Superior's scenic north shore from Two Harbors to Canal Park in Duluth. It's been held annually in June since 1977. The Garry Bjorklund Half-Marathon and the *William A. Irvin* 5K Race are held for those folks not up to the full run. The same route is used the second weekend after Labor Day for the NorthShore Inline Marathon, the largest inline skating race in North America and second largest in the world (second only to one in Berlin, Germany).

• Park Point Art Fair is an invitational, juried fair held each June with artists displaying and selling paintings, pottery, jewelry, candle-making and glass-blowing artifacts.

DIRECTORY

Tourist Information Centers –
Duluth Convention & Visitors Bureau,
218-722-4011, 800-4-duluth (438-5884);
DCVB Visitors Center, Harbor Drive
(mid-May to mid-Oct.); Minnesota Tourism,
800-657-3700; Thompson Hill Information
Center, 218-723-4938; Superior-Douglas
County Tourist Information, 715-392-2773,
800-942-5313; Superior-Douglas County
Chamber of Commerce and Convention
and Visitors Bureau, 715-394-7716;
Wisconsin Tourism, 800-432-TRIP (8747).

Where to Stay
Best Western Edgewater, 218-728-3601,
2400 London Rd., offers a wide range of
accommodations overlooking Lake
Superior, pool, sauna, whirlpool, free
breakfast and cocktail party.

Fitger's Inn, 218-722-8826, 600 E. Superior
St., has 62 charming rooms in an 1885
brewery. Great Lake Superior views,
fireplaces, balconies, whirlpools. AAA-
rated 4 diamonds. There are four
restaurants on site.
Hawthorn Suites at Waterfront Plaza,
218-727-4663, 325 S. Lake Ave., offers 107
suites in the heart of Canal Park with
kitchens, pool, hot tub, sauna, Lake
Superior views, 3 restaurants in complex,
free breakfast and cocktails Mon.-Thurs.
Holiday Inn Hotel and Suites Downtown
Waterfront, 218-722-1202, 800-465-4329,
200 W. Superior St., has 350 two-room
suites in downtown and convenient to
everything: Lake Superior views, fitness
center, pool, sauna, whirlpool, 10
restaurants/lounges, kids eat and stay free,
Skywalk to all downtown areas.

• The annual Fourth Fest Celebration is centered at Bayfront Festival Park and its fireworks display over the Duluth Harbor is one of the largest in the region.

• The International Folk Festival is held annually the first Saturday in August at Leif Erikson Park. Sponsored by the Duluth YWCA, it features ethnic foods, dances, crafts, displays and artist exhibits.

• Great Lakes Aquarium hosts an annual Scarium at the Aquarium family Halloween event, which is held in late October, and also offers an annual Valentine's Day event in February. As mentioned, the SS *William A. Irvin* becomes a "Ship of Ghouls" each October.

• Gales of November program, co-sponsored by the Lake Superior Marine Museum Association and *Lake Superior Magazine* is a growing event held early in November in commemoration of shipwrecks, storms and maritime life.

• Christmas City of the North Parade brings Santa to downtown Duluth and starts off the Christmas season. Sponsored by KBJR Television, it's held each year the Friday before Thanksgiving. It also features the lighting of the city's Christmas tree in Lake Superior Plaza.

• On Thanksgiving weekend, Spirit Mountain is the site

DIRECTORY Continued from 108

Inn on Lake Superior, 218-726-1111, 350 Canal Park Dr., features 175 guest rooms and suites on Lake Superior shore, balconies, indoor and outdoor pools, whirlpools, free breakfast bar. Near everything.

Where to Eat with a Local Flavor

Bellisio's Italian Restaurant and Wine Bar, 218-727-4921, 425 S. Lake Ave., Canal Park, serves fine Italian cuisine with an award winning wine list.

Bennett's On the Lake, 218-722-2829, Fitger's Brewery Complex, 600 E. Superior St. An eclectic gourmet menu with a great lake view is offered by owner-chef Bob Bennett.

Grandma's Saloon and Grill, 218-727-4192, 522 S. Lake Ave., Canal Park, With four locations in the Greater Duluth area, these restaurants offer great American casual dining in a one-of-a-kind atmosphere.

Lake Avenue Café, 218-722-2355, 394 S. Lake Ave. In the heart of Canal Park, this restaurant offers a globally influenced menu prepared by the owner/chef Patrick Cross.

Pickwick, 218-727-8901, 508 E. Superior St. A perennial favorite, this eatery has great steaks, seafood and chops. No reservations Fri. or Sat. evenings.

Top of the Harbor Restaurant, 218-727-8981, Radisson Hotel, 5th Ave. W. and Superior St. With a wonderful panoramic view from its revolving rooftop location, this is a good choice for steaks and seafood.

for the Duluth National Snocross Races, the largest on-snow (vs. grass) snowmobile race in the world.

• The Lake Superior Zoo sponsors Zoo Year's Eve in the afternoon on December 31 at the zoo, a family-oriented event that culminates with a gigantic fireworks display in the early evening.

• The Duluth Winterfest presents more than 100 winter activities from January 1 through early March. Centered around the 400-mile (600-kilometer) John Beargrease Sled Dog Marathon that starts at Duluth's Ordean Field and makes a round trip to Grand Marais, ending back in Duluth at Lester Park, it's one of the highlights of the year all along Minnesota's north shore of Lake Superior.

Where to Shop

Duluth is visitor friendly and a mecca for shoppers, be they curio-seekers wanting a souvenir of their visit or serious antique buffs seeking authentic relics of the past.

In Canal Park, you'll find art galleries like Sivertson Gallery, which features a large selection of local, regional and Native art, or bookstores like Northern Lights Books and Gifts with regionally connected offerings. The Duluth Pack

Store offers not only great backpacks, but a wide range of other outdoor gear. Over on Lake Avenue South, Waterfront Plaza houses a hotel, restaurants, and a number of businesses including *Lake Superior Magazine/Lake Superior Travel Guide* and its outlet store on the sixth floor. (Come on up and visit us or contact us for information on joining our Circle Tour Club.) Behind the building, a number of charter captains book half- and full-day angling excursions on the big lake. Across the street, Canal Park Antique Mall has several local dealers who offer the "latest" stuff, antiques and other collectables.

DeWitt-Seitz Marketplace in Canal Park features locally owned shops and restaurants. Many local specialty products add to the shopping fun. The DeWitt-Seitz building, a former warehouse and manufacturing site, is listed on the National Register of Historic Places. Nearby, Lake Superior Nautical offers a nice selection of boat, lighthouse, books and other gift items.

Duluth's Downtown Waterfront offers more than 185 retail businesses, providing a full range of general and specialized merchandise. Along the bricks of Superior Street from Fifth Avenue West to the Fitger's Brewery Complex on Sixth Avenue East, you'll find the heart of downtown shopping. There's a cross section of small shops to be found along the enclosed skywalk system in downtown's concentrated retail area, which extends from Fifth Avenue West to Third Avenue East. Downtown is home to some fine art galleries, all on Superior Street, such as Art Options, Frame Corner Gallery and Lizzard's Art Gallery and Framing. In the 300 block (west), you'll find unique shops like John Marxhausen Jewelry Designer and Goldsmith, one of the most creative Lake Superior designers we've found. In the 200 block from Second to Third avenues west, the Holiday Center houses many shops and restaurants and is the center of the skywalk system. A couple of blocks east at the corner of Lake Avenue, the Duluth Technology Village houses a number of businesses and organizations involved in high tech endeavors, as well as specialty shops and a restaurant, Pizza Lucé, on the street level with a variety of dining throughout the day.

For information on Duluth downtown waterfront merchants, attractions and activities, contact the Greater Downtown Council, which is located at 118 East Superior Street, the Duluth Area Chamber of Commerce at 5 West First Street or the Duluth Convention and Visitors Bureau in Lake Superior Place Suite 100 at 21 West Superior Street.

On East Superior Street, Fitger's Brewery Complex is a renovated 1905 brewery on scenic Lake Superior that features

service and specialty shops and year-round courtyard activities, as well as dining. At Christmastime, reindeer can be found in the courtyard. The complex is listed on the National Register of Historic Buildings and has a free parking ramp for those visiting it. A unique collection of shopping experiences makes Fitger's a must for any visitor. Farther east, merchants along London Road have an overview of Lake Superior while offering many shopping, lodging and dining opportunities. The Wedding Chapel on the Lake is a charmer, should you wish to be married or renew your vows near Lake Superior.

Miller Hill Mall, "over the hill," is the area's major shopping complex, housing more than 100 stores, including three major department stores, bookstores, entertainment, services, restaurants and even a car dealership. It is located at Highway 53 North and Trinity Road. The area also contains many additional smaller malls, stores, theaters and restaurants, including the Village Mall, Burning Tree Plaza, Stone Ridge Shopping Center, with a new development across Highway 53 that houses more shopping and dining opportunities.

Along Central Entrance and the Miller Trunk Highway corridor on the hilltop, many retail businesses have gathered, making the corridor one of the shopping meccas of the lake. Other retail and restaurant spaces continue to be developed in this area. In nearby Hermantown at Haines and Stebner roads, two multiplex theaters feature a wide range of cinema selections for movie buffs. Motorcyclists, of course, will want to check out the Harley-Davidson Sport Center on Stebner Road.

Campgrounds

Campers in the Twin Ports have a wide choice of campground and RV parks from which to choose. Check with Buffalo Valley Camping off I-35 between Cloquet and Duluth, Spirit Mountain Campground or Duluth Tent and Trailer Camp on Scenic Highway 61 east of Duluth. In the Superior area, try Amnicon Acres Campground or Manitou Valley Campgrounds.

What's Next

If your route is northeast, follow Highway 61 heading for Two Harbors and the Scenic North Shore Drive (See Roadtrips at the beginning of this book). If you plan to proceed east along the south shore, catch Highway 2 to cross the bridge into Superior, Wisconsin.

LAKE SUPERIOR
Eagle Harbor - Ewen

EAGLE HARBOR, MICHIGAN

Township Population: 281

Eagle Harbor, Michigan, regional map – page 24.

The small village of Eagle Harbor was once an important port in the early days of the copper boom, but that importance subsided as ships grew larger and the harbor became difficult for the ships to navigate.

What to See and Do

The rules and bylaws for the international charitable, benevolent and fraternal Order of the Knights of Pythias were written in 1858 in this lakeside village by school teacher Justus Rathbone, for whom the schoolhouse was later named. A convention of the Pythian Sisters women's auxiliary still convenes at the Rathbone School each summer.

The oldest Catholic church in use in the Upper Peninsula. is Holy Redeemer Church. Built in 1852, it is still used today, a memorial to Bishop Frederic Baraga. Open daily, mid-June through September.

Notable Museums

The former U.S. Life-Saving Station at Eagle Harbor was once an important facility for maritime safety, but now serves as the public marina. Keweenaw County Historical Museum is housed in the former Eagle Harbor Lighthouse, with many exhibits of earlier times on display including the Signal House. Open daily, mid-June through September.

What's Next

As you travel the west side of the Keweenaw Peninsula stop and search for agates, greenstones and driftwood on the public beaches along M-26.

Heading north from Eagle Harbor on M-26 takes you to Copper Harbor. Heading south, there are nice scenic turnouts and agate beaches between Eagle Harbor and Eagle River, notably Cat Harbor and Great Sand Bay. Be sure to

DIRECTORY

Tourist Information – Keweenaw Convention & Visitors Bureau in Calumet, 906-337-4579, 800-338-7982,

Where to Stay
Eagle Harbor House, 906-289-1039, 256-883-7886, 413 Front Street, Eagle Harbor is an 1845 Michigan Historic home, the oldest on the Keweenaw Peninsula, with a bed & breakfast, cabins and cottages. Eagle River Inn, 906-289-4435, 5033 Front

St., is as near Lake Superior waters as you can get and has a good restaurant.

Where to Eat with a Local Flavor
Shoreline Restaurant, 906-289-4441, M-26 between Copper Harbor and Eagle Harbor, is open daily mid-June through mid-October, serving breakfast, lunch & dinner. Full menu; beer, wine & cocktails. Fitzgerald's Restaurant, 906-289-4435, at Eagle River Inn, has an excellent menu near the lakeshore.

make a stop at Jacob's Creek Falls at Great Sand Bay for a photo. Watch for it from the car window. And while you're there, sample some of the most sumptuous treats imaginable at the Jampot, operated by the good brothers of the Society of St. John. The Jampot is open Memorial Day until mid-October, Monday through Saturday. Visitors cannot help but notice the new onion-domed monastery and church on the lake side of the highway about a quarter-mile from the Jampot.

EAGLE RIVER, MICHIGAN

Township Population 204

Eagle River has the oldest courthouse in Michigan and is the county seat of Keweenaw County. M-26 crosses the Eagle River, with 60-foot (18-meter) Eagle River Falls visible upstream from the bridge. The village's old highway bridge has been turned into a walking bridge, replaced by a modern structure, which is made primarily of wood. On the outskirts of the village is the Evergreen Cemetery, with only weathered headstones left to tell the story of the rough early mining days.

Eagle River, Michigan, regional map – page 24.

In nearby Phoenix, the Phoenix Church, built in 1858 in Cliff, dismantled and reassembled in Phoenix, is operated by the Keweenaw County Historical Society as a museum. The Bammert Blacksmith Shop opens daily, mid-May through early October.

From Phoenix, take Highway 41 to return to Hancock/Houghton. The Circle Tour continues southwest from Houghton on M-26 deeper into Copper Country, winding through Atlantic Mine, South Range, Trimountain and Painesdale, drowsy villages long surviving the closing of their copper mines. The Copper Range Historical Museum is

in South Range in the old bank. Open Monday through Saturday, June to mid-October. Just off M-26 at Painesdale, the restored Painesdale Mine and Shaft offers tours of the hoist and shaft house by appointment. Check in town for the contact.

Twin Lakes State Park (Roland and Gerald lakes) offers 175 acres of heavily wooded wilderness, with campgrounds, swimming, boating, hiking and fishing. Admission by park permit. Play the 9-hole Wyandotte Hills Golf Course, where Wyandotte Hills Resort also offers new resort cabins for visitors. Another quiet place to stay, with a good sand beach, is under the pines at Twin Lakes Resort. Nearby is Krupp's Resort, which also has cottages.

After Winona, the Circle Tour enters Big Snow Country, turning toward the lake and Ontonagon at M-38.

ELY, MINNESOTA

Population 3,840

Ely, Minnesota, regional map – page 4.

The Ely area is entree to the vast Boundary Waters Canoe Area Wilderness and boasts 500 fishing lakes within a 20-mile radius, as well as comfortable lodging and fine dining. Ely is at the far end of Highway 169 from the Mesabi Iron Range or scenic Highway 1 from the north shore Circle Route. As a result of tourism, the city is home to many outfitters and outdoor gear stores and manufacturers.

A Bit of History

Ely owes its existence to iron ore, which was discovered on the shore of Shagawa Lake in 1883 and proved to be so abundant that five mines were eventually developed nearby and a sixth, Section 30 Mine, would operate a few miles northeast in the vicinity of Winton. By 1886, the Pioneer Mine was opened, but did not prove profitable. At that time, the Duluth & Iron Range Railroad connected Two Harbors and Tower and was shipping ore by the thousands of tons, but did not extend beyond Tower-Soudan.

In 1887, when the Chandler Mine began production, the railroad rushed to extend its line to the area and by the 1890s the Ely mines were producing more ore than the original Vermilion Iron Range mine at Tower-Soudan.

Also by the 1890s, lumber companies were active in the area and nearby Winton became a hub for that industry, with two huge mill complexes located on Fall Lake and dozens of logging camps scattered throughout the surrounding forestlands. The populations of both Ely and Winton mushroomed during this period.

While the mines would continue producing ore for nearly a century, the pine forests were logged off before 1920 and Winton's population, which may have reached 500 at its

peak, nosedived as lumberjacks and millworkers moved on and the merchants that catered to their needs closed up shop.

After World War II, iron ore production began declining, as more and more mines scraped bottom and closed. When the last of the Vermilion Range mines, the Pioneer, closed in 1967, the Ely area had already blossomed into a tourist destination city, with dozens of resorts on lakes surrounding the town. It was also known as a premier entry point to the Boundary Waters Canoe Area ("Wilderness" was added to the name in 1978), as thousands of paddlers passed through town on their way to the recreation area – which it remains to the present.

What to See and Do

The winter and summer cabins of Dorothy Molter, long-time BWCAW resident who died in 1986, were moved from her land on Knife Lake to the edge of town as a tribute. Known to thousands of paddlers as the "Root Beer Lady," she offered her homemade brew, wit and compassion to passing paddlers for decades. The cabins reflect her choice for living simply and in contact with nature. Fee.

International Wolf Center offers field trips and information on the timber wolves that live in northeast Minnesota. Fee.

Ely-Winton History Museum at Vermilion Community College is a good place to learn more about the area, from prehistoric to the expeditions of Ely-based polar explorers Will Steger and Paul Schurke. Open Monday through Saturday from Memorial Day to the week after Labor Day. Fee.

To the southwest on Highway 169, be sure to tour the Soudan Underground Mine, located in Soudan Underground Mine State Park between the towns of Tower and Soudan. The only underground iron mine in the world open for tours, visitors are guided to a depth of 2,341 feet where the year-round temperature is a constant 50 degrees Fahrenheit. In the nearby Embarrass area, tours of Finnish farms and homesteads explore the importance of this large ethnic group that pioneered settlement here. Fee.

Visit Lake Vermilion, one of the largest lakes in Northeast Minnesota. Visitors may want to reserve a daylong scenic trip on the boat that delivers mail to waterbound residents.

For gaming fun, take Highway 77 from Tower to Fortune Bay Resort and Casino on the Bois Forte Ojibway Reservation. The tribe also operates its "Legend House" or *Atisokanigamig* heritage museum and its new championship 18-hole golf course, The Wilderness, that opened in summer 2004 on tribal lands.

Boundary Waters Canoe Area Wilderness

More than 1 million acres in size, the Boundary Waters Canoe Area Wilderness (BWCAW) contains hundreds of lakes and rivers, has 1,200 miles of canoe routes and is home to abundant plants and wildlife, including threatened and endangered species. Ely, Minnesota, is the main access point. With over 200,000 people visiting per year, it is one of the most heavily used U.S. wilderness areas.

The U.S. Congress established the special designation in the Wilderness Act of 1964 to "secure for the American People of present and future generations the benefit of an enduring resource of Wilderness."

National Geographic listed the BWCAW as one of 50 sites everyone should see in their lifetime and thousands of paddlers, dog sledders and skiers each year do just that. Park permit required.

DIRECTORY

Tourist Information – Ely Chamber of Commerce, 218-365-6123, 800-777-7281

Where to Stay
Timber Wolf Lodge, 800-777-8457, P.O. Box 147, offers a nice resort experience on Bear Island Lake south of Ely on Highway 21.
River Point Resort and Outfitting Company, 218-365-6607, P.O. Box 397, has a good restaurant and accommodations ranging from log cabins to villa suites where the Kawishiwi River enters Birch Lake.
Blue Heron B&B, 218-365-4720, 827 Kiwishiwi Trail is a nice bed-and-breakfast experience. Has a superb dining room with international gourmet menu.
Grand Ely Lodge Resort, 218-365-6565, 877-472-6335, 400 N. Pioneer Rd., has 61 lakeview rooms and suites, with a good restaurant and many free guest privileges.

Where to Eat with a Local Flavor
Evergreen Restaurant, 218-365-6565, 400 N. Pioneer Rd., kids 10 and younger eating free.
Chocolate Moose, 218-365-6343, 101 N. Central Ave., gourmet food, fine wine and microbrews in a northwoodsy setting.

Where to Shop

This is a good place to stock up on outdoor and winter gear, with a number of local manufacturers like Steger Mukluks and Wintergreen Designs offering outdoor gear tested in the area and on polar expeditions headed by Will Steger and Paul Schurke.

A number of gift stores, galleries and specialty shops make interesting kibitzing and shopping and Ely has a full range of other stores to meet any "necessity."

World renowned outdoor photographer Jim Brandenberg makes his home near Ely and offers his artwork at Brandenberg Gallery in town.

What's Next

To exit Ely, take Highway 1 to the north shore Circle Tour route or travel Highway 169 southwest through Tower and Soudan to continue to other Iron Range cities and sights described elsewhere.

ESCANABA, MICHIGAN

Population 13,660

Although not part of the official Lake Superior Circle Tour route, there is much to recommend a sidetrip or alternate route on U.S. Highway 2 to take in Michigan's southern Upper Peninsula. The highway is the northern leg of the Lake Michigan Circle Tour. Westbound travelers will want to watch for Rapid River at the north end of Little Bay de Noc to follow Highway 2/41 along the shoreline southwesterly to Gladstone (population 4,565) and Escanaba. Eastbound travelers on Highway 2 from Iron Mountain and Big Snow Country in the western U.P. will note the junction where Highway 41 joins U.S. 2 from the south about 20 miles west of Escanaba.

Escanaba, Michigan, regional map – page 49.

A Bit of History

Protected from the storms of Lake Michigan in virtually every direction, Escanaba is a commercial and iron ore harbor and was once the shipping destination for the huge tonnages produced by the many iron mines to the west on the Menominee Range.

Incorporated in 1866, by the early 1880s Escanaba had grown to city status and the waterfront was lined by docks shipping not only iron ore but lumber and other products. It has served as the county seat of Delta County virtually since the county was formed.

Today

Unlike ports on Lake Superior that are dependent on the Soo Locks, this harbor can ship iron ore well into the winter season, making it especially important after the Soo Locks' annual shut down in mid-January. Today, ore cargoes originate on the Marquette Iron Range and are shipped to the Escanaba docks by the Canadian National Railroad.

What to See and Do

A number of parks offer seasonal recreational opportunities.

Five 18-hole and two 9-hole golf courses within a few miles will challenge your skills.

If you're traveling with kids, a stop at the Family Fun Park on Third Avenue North will be welcome, with miniature golf, go-karts, bumper boats and other fun activities.

Art enthusiasts will want to check the schedule at William Bonifas Fine Arts Center in downtown to view exhibits by local, regional and international artists, as well as any performing arts events.

U.P. State Fairgrounds is the site of the Great Lakes Championship Rodeo in June and the U.P. State Fair in August. The fairgrounds are busy throughout the year with a variety of activities like craft sales, sports shows and other events. Information is available at the fairground office.

Chip-In's Island Resort and Casino is about 13 miles (17 kilometers) west of Escanaba at Harris. Offering a 113-room hotel, an RV park, restaurants, convention and banquet facilities, an indoor pool and a wide variety of gaming, it's

DIRECTORY

Tourist Information – Bays de Noc Convention and Visitors Center 906-789-7862, 800-533-4386, in Escanaba, Upper Peninsula Travel and Recreation Association in Iron Mountain, 906-774-5480, 800-562-7134

Where to Stay
Terrace Bay Resort and Campground, 906-786-7554, 800-283-4678, is located on Bay de Noc between the two cities. A year-round recreation and convention facility, the resort offers dining. House of Ludington, 906-786-6300, in

downtown Escanaba opened as an opulent hotel in 1865 and has maintained its reputation as a hotel with class to the present time, with dining and theme rooms.

Where to Eat with a Local Flavor
Hereford and Hops, 906-789-0630, 624 Ludington St., offers a number of house beers brewed on site, pub-style dining, full dinner menu and group dining rooms. House of Ludington 906-786-6300, 223 Ludington St., offers elegant firelight dining with old silver amid charming antiques.

operated by the Hannahville Tribe on the Michigan Potawatomi Reservation.

What's Next

Leaving Escanaba on Highway 2/41, we head either west through a number of towns of the Menominee Iron Range toward Big Snow Country or north and then east on Highway 2 toward St. Ignace and the Mackinac Bridge.

EVELETH, MINNESOTA

Population 3,865

The town of Eveleth was made famous by its iron mines and continues as an important source of iron ore in the form of taconite pellets. However, today it is also noted for the United States Hockey Hall of Fame, open year-round right on Highway 53, that features an extensive display of regional and national hockey artifacts, including a sizable collection from the 1980 "Miracle on Ice" Olympic championship team. In saluting its status as the historic home of U.S. hockey, the city erected the World's Largest Hockey Stick in the downtown. There is a challenging 9-hole golf course open to the public on nearby St. Mary's Lake. The Leonidas Mine overlook provides not only a panorama of several active and abandoned mines, but is the highest point on the Mesabi Iron Range. The Sax-Zim Bog southwest of

DIRECTORY

Tourist Information – Virginia/ Eveleth/Mountain Iron/Gilbert Chamber of Commerce, 218-741-2717; Iron Trail Convention and Visitors Bureau, 218-749-8161, 800-777-8497

town is exceptional for birders and is home to many rare and scarce species.

Businesses seeking economic development assistance or information should contact the Iron Range Resources Agency near Eveleth. The agency's building also houses a nice sampling of area art by the Fine Arts North group. Works are rotated regularly to bring fresh pieces to the ongoing exhibit.

Depending on their itinerary, visitors can travel Highway 53 to the south to return to Duluth, take Highway 37 east to Gilbert, Biwabik and the far eastern Mesabi Range, or travel north a couple of miles on Highway 53 to Virginia.

EWEN, MICHIGAN

Township Population 662

Just west of Bruce Crossing and 15 miles east of Bergland on the Highway 28 Circle Tour route, pause in Ewen, the home of the 1893 World's Fair Load of Logs – a replica of which was displayed here for many years before deterioration forced it to be disassembled. An annual townwide Log Jamboree celebration in mid-September commemorates the logging history of the area.

Ewen, Michigan, regional map – page 26.

If you need a meal or an overnight, check TJ's Restaurant and Motel right on the highway.

Finland

FINLAND, MINNESOTA
Area Population 603

Finland, Minnesota,
regional map – page 2.

To find Finland, take Highway 1 at the intersection with Highway 61 at Illgen City. The village of Finland is perhaps the proudest little village in the Arrowhead. Settled in the early 1900s by many people of Finnish descent, the town took its name when a railroad went through in 1910. The town's designation as Finland actually predates that of the nation by about a decade.

For travelers heading to or from Ely on Highway 1, Finland is one of the only chances to get a bite to eat. Check at Our Place Restaurant for an all-day menu, the Four Seasons Restaurant or West Branch Bar and Grill, which opens at noon. All have full bars. Groceries are available at Finland Cooperative Co.

Surrounded by forest and rugged country, this is a great place to begin snowmobile treks into the woods and there is good fishing in area lakes.

What to See and Do

Finnish Heritage Site, located on County Road 6, features the hand-hewn log home of pioneer John Pine (Petaja) with furnishings and other artifacts from the early 1900s.

Nearby Wolf Ridge Environmental Learning Center is an accredited residential school, with year-round fun and educational programs on the outdoors for school groups, families and adults. Stop for a brochure. There are lots of activities and events year-round, including an Elderhostel summer program.

For a side trip of approximately 10 miles, hikers and backpackers will appreciate the unspoiled beauty of the George Crosby-Manitou State Park east of Finland on Lake County Road 7. The Manitou River flows through the park, then flows southward a couple of miles before plunging into Lake Superior through a deep gorge on privately owned land

along Highway 61. It is the only falls in Minnesota with a straight drop into the lake. A small fee is charged to access the falls. The name is derived from the Ojibway word *manitou*, which most usually means "spirit."

For another treat, continue along County 7 deeper into the hills to visit Crooked Lake Resort and the Trestle Inn for a dandy meal and a drink at a bar built from an old logging railroad trestle. It's an ideal year-round destination and is accessible directly by snowmobile trail during the winter.

Notable Events

• Each year, residents and hundreds of visitors celebrate St. Urho's Day with a fun parade and other antics on the weekend nearest to March 16. St. Urho is a tongue-in-cheek Finnish spoof of Ireland's St. Patrick. The story goes that St. Urho saved the Finnish grape crop by driving out a plague of grasshoppers.

What's Next

If you plan to visit Ely and the Vermilion Iron Range, Highway 1 is the only highway between Two Harbors and the international border that runs inland through Minnesota's Arrowhead.It's a hilly, sinuous track that runs 63 miles (100 kilometers) through the Superior National Forest to Ely. If you hit Highway 1 around sunrise, it's practically guaranteed you'll encounter one or more moose. Be watchful, since many a vehicle has experienced a sudden dangerous encounter with these massive creatures. Some of the region's most spectacular colors can be found along this route in the fall.

To return to the Highway 61 Circle Tour route on Lake Superior, you can backtrack on Highway 1 to Ilgen City or take County Highway 6 and join the route at Little Marais (See separate listing) a bit east of the Highway 1 junction.

DIRECTORY

Tourist Information – Bay Area Information Center in Beaver Bay, 218-226-3317; Two Harbors Area Chamber of Commerce, 218-834-2600, 800-777-7384

Gay - Gunflint Trail

G

GAY, MICHIGAN

Population 36

Gay, Michigan,
regional map – page 24.

This little burg's Gay Bar is has become a must stop on the south shore of the Keweenaw Peninsula on Keweenaw Bay. Opens at lunchtime during the week and Saturdays. Everyone should have a souvenir T-shirt or cap.

To find Gay, catch South Shore Drive from M-26/U.S.-41 out of Fulton-Mohawk. This is an excellent alternate scenic route to Lac La Belle past Point Isabelle.

Gay's annual Fourth of July Parade is a fun event for upward of 4,000 viewers in the area. Lasting from 4 to 15 minutes, the "just for fun" parade starts promptly at 2 p.m. on Main Street. It's reported that the old smokestack nearby actually billows smoke for the event.

What's Next

If you're heading up the Keweenaw, the route from Gay to Lac La Belle along Lake Superior is a marvelous experience, through heavily wooded forests and then, closer to Pt. Isabelle, right beside the water. You'll pass through a nice year-round residential grouping of homes called Little Betsy at Betsy Bay. If traveling southward, you can continue to Highway 26 just north of Lake Linden, or follow South Shore Drive to Fulton-Mohawk to rejoin Highway 26/41.

GILBERT, MINNESOTA

Population 1,847

At Gilbert, visitors find an international welcome at two entries to town. Featuring flags of many nations and welcoming signs in a variety of languages, the international motif is accented by The Whistling Bird, a restaurant featuring awesome Caribbean specialties.

Like most Iron Range towns, Gilbert owes its existence to the early 1900s mining activity. An earlier townsite called Sparta was originally planned to hold the populace, but had

to be abandoned when iron ore was discovered under the site. Gilbert grew nearby and was incorporated in 1909. Through its history, it has boomed at times and ebbed at others, but has maintained an active business district and residential area.

Gilbert is home to the Iron Range Off-Highway Vehicle Recreation Area, the state's first designated system of trails on abandoned mine land designed for ATVs, dirt bikes and 4x4 trucks. With typical Iron Range tongue in cheek, local folks have dubbed the body of water in the abandoned mine as Lake Ore-Be-Gone.

What's Next

There are three routes to exit Gilbert. Take Highway 37 westerly toward Eveleth to Highway 53 to visit other Iron Range towns. Highway 135 heads eastward toward Biwabik, Aurora and Hoyt Lakes or west heading for Virginia.

GOOSEBERRY FALLS STATE PARK, MINNESOTA

Gooseberry Falls State Park is a must stop between Two Harbors and Beaver Bay-Silver Bay on Minnesota's north shore of Lake Superior and provides lessons in history, geology and beauty. Seven other state parks are located along this stretch of Minnesota's north shore, offering natural beauty at every turn.

Gooseberry Falls State Park, Minnesota, regional map – page 2.

Gooseberry is Minnesota's most visited state park. The Gooseberry River is said to have been named for explorer/fur trader Sieur des Groseilliers, whose French name means "gooseberry bush." The river drops through a series of spectacular falls and rapids to the rocky shore of Lake Superior.

A Bit of History

From the time the highway first passed through this area and a bridge across the river was built in 1924, efforts were undertaken to preserve the scenery around the falls on the Gooseberry River. In 1933, those efforts bore fruit, about 660 acres of land along the river were acquired by the state. In the 1930s, a Civilian Conservation Corps (CCC) camp at Gooseberry laid out the various areas and built the stone buildings.

Today the park encloses 1,662 acres of natural north shore beauty and wildlife. Numerous trails through conifer, aspen and birch take the more adventurous to each of the cascading falls and the homes of the wildlife. Some trails are difficult. Allow one to five hours to see the park.

The new Gooseberry River Bridge over the gorge allows for safe pedestrian traffic to view the falls and surrounding scenery. This construction also opened most of the nearby walking paths for easier access.

123

DIRECTORY

Tourist Information – Park Information Center, 218-834-3855

Where to Stay
Castle Haven Cabins, 218-834-4303, 3067 E. Castle Danger Rd., Two Harbors 55616, is a traditional north shore resort. Grand Superior Lodge, 218-834-3796, 2826 Hwy. 61, is a new log lodging with grand views of Lake Superior and a good restaurant and lounge.

Gooseberry Trail Side Suites, 218-834-3905, 3317 E. Hwy. 61, Two Harbors 55616, is an option to cabin occupancy.

Where to Eat with a Local Flavor
Rustic Inn Cafe and Gift Shop, 218-834-2488, 2773, Hwy. 61, has a good menu and awesome dessert items. Splashing Rock Restaurant at Grand Superior Lodge, 218-834-3796, serves fine cuisine with great Lake Superior views.

What to See and Do

Among the highlights of the park are the upper and lower falls, the Gooseberry River, the mouth of the river and adjoining lakeshore, trail hikes up to the fifth falls, a segment of the Gitchi-Gami State Trail and the cliffs along Lake Superior.

A beautiful visitor center and highway information stop is on the lakeside of Highway 61 just before the bridge. The striking building contains an excellent interpretative center and gift shop.

The delightful Gooseberry Falls State Park Campground is located at the water's edge. It's always full, so book early. There's also wonderful cross-country skiing here.

What's Next

If your route takes you northeast, about a mile from Gooseberry Falls State Park is a boat launch, paved parking space and nice trails to beach areas. The former site of Twin Points Resort, the site was acquired by the Sugarloaf Cove Interpretive Center Association and traded to the state for the site of that organization's property near Schroeder, Minnesota. The boat launch and parking areas are handicapped accessible, but some trails will prove difficult for the handicapped.

GOULAIS RIVER, ONTARIO

The village of Goulais River is situated on Lake Superior's eastern shore about 25 kilometers (16 miles) north of Sault Ste. Marie or 40 kilometers (25 miles) south of Batchawana Bay, just off Trans Canada Highway 17.

What to See and Do

Shop at one of the area antique, flea markets or gift stores. There are also several Canadian craft stores.

Goulais River, Ontario, regional map – page 18.

In 1862, Bishop Frederic Baraga, the "Snowshoe Priest," built a church here that's still in use.

Buttermilk Alpine Ski Village, off Highway 552, has a 90-meter (270-foot) vertical drop and a double chairlift. A number of chalet rental units are available. Try the Austrian and German specialties at their Schnitzel Haus Dining Lounge, which is listed in "Where to Eat in Canada."

Cross-country skiers will want to check Stokely Creek Lodge and Ski Touring Center for either day skiing or a longer stay with all the comforts of a first-class resort. The many miles of groomed trails are friendly to skiers of various skill levels and the center sponsors several special ski events during the winter.

DIRECTORY

G

Tourist Information – Tourism Sault Ste. Marie, 800-461-6020; Algoma Kinniwabi Travel Association, 800-263-2546

What's Next

Traveling south, the Goulais River Valley is the entry point into the Sault Ste. Marie area. Here, the granite hills of the Canadian Shield rise from the lowlands. It's a zone of lakes, waterfalls and streams, many stocked with trout. Due to the swamps, marshes, fens and bogs, a wide variety of waterfowl and shorebirds, as well as moose and beaver, inhabit the area. On the high ground stand maple forests, while white birch and pine dominate the remaining landscape.

The Lake Superior Circle Tour cuts through the heart of the valley via Highway 17, crossing the Goulais River about 24 kilometers (15 miles) north of Sault Ste. Marie. The Queen lady's-slipper grows wild in the nearby swamp, an orchid with a large three-inch blossom. It is found only in the Lake Superior region in midsummer.

North on Trans Canada Highway 17 and at the extreme southern end of Batchawana Bay is Havilland Bay and the small Gitchee Gumee Marina, which serves as one of the few refueling stops for boats between Michipicoten Harbour and Sault Ste. Marie. Although somewhat shallow, good services are provided and there's a boat ramp for access to the lake. Boat rentals are available. The marina serves meals in its bar/restaurant. For a lake cruise or charter fishing, try Swan Charters at the marina.

GRAND MARAIS, MICHIGAN

Population 450

The quaint village of Grand Marais (Mah-ray) is snuggled in a natural harbor. You'll find it by taking Michigan

Grand Marais, Michigan, regional map – page 20.

Highway 77 north from M-28 at Seney. An alternate route preferred by many travelers is to catch Highway 58 to the west in Munising and travel about 40 miles through Pictured Rocks National Lakeshore (see listing under Pictured Rocks).

There are docks, a lighthouse, a park and a scattering of shops and delicious restaurants. The site first served as a harbor of refuge for early voyageurs and was settled as a fishing village. It later served as the sawmill headquarters site for the huge Alger Smith Lumber Company, which logged as far away as Seney, Germfask and Curtis and operated the 78-mile Manistique Railroad to serve its camps and mill. The county is named for General Russell Alger, a partner in the company, who served as governor and senator for Michigan and was Secretary of War during the Spanish-American War.

This small town is a hotbed of journalistic efforts, with two newspapers. The *Grand Marais Gazette* (focusing on "harder" news) and the *Great Lakes and Grand Marais Pilot* (with more of an eye to history and human interest stories) compete for readers. With Grand Marais, Minnesota, this is one of the most competitive newspaper markets on Lake Superior.

DIRECTORY

Tourist Information – Grand Marais, Michigan, Chamber of Commerce, 906-494-2447

What to See and Do

Grand Marais sports a historic Pickle Barrel House, sometimes used as an information center – a gift from Bill Donahey, creator of the "Teenie Weenies" syndicated comic strip, popular in the 1920s and '30s. An effort is under way to restore and repair the structure.

Notable Museums

Adjacent to the Grand Marais Historical Museum, which features local history, Grand Marais Historical Society has erected a bronze memorial to commercial fishermen next to the pier.

The Grand Marais Maritime Museum is run by the Pictured Rocks National Lakeshore.

Notable Events

• The town hosts the Great Lakes Sea Kayak Symposium and its annual Fly-In in July and the Grand Marais Music Festival in August.

Campgrounds

Woodland Township Campgrounds provides a base for fishing, swimming, hiking and agate hunting.

What's Next

To leave Grand Marais, take either M-77 south to pick up
M-28 at Seney or catch H-58 to the west and the Pictured Rocks.

GRAND MARAIS, MINNESOTA

Population 1,355

In describing the harbor village of Grand Marais (Mah-
ray), overused adjectives like quaint, casual and charming are
often offered. But here they are entirely appropriate and the
city's cultural, recreational and comfortable facilities make it a
year-round destination. Located on Highway 61 about 45
miles (72 kilometers) south of the international border or 52
miles (85 kilometers) northeast of Silver Bay on Minnesota's
north shore, you'll want to consider an overnight or longer
stay to see the town at all times of the day. There are plenty of
lodging choices in Grand Marais, although in the busy season
even this multitude of rooms can fill up fast.

Grand Marais, Minnesota,
regional map – page 8.

A circular harbor is the centerpiece of this tourist-oriented
town with a reputation for hospitality. The harbor provides
one of the few safe refuges for boaters along Minnesota's Lake
Superior shoreline. Artist Point, a Presque Isle, Michigan,
style point of rocks to the eastern end of the harbor, is the
perfect place to watch sunrises and is loaded with trails and
points of inspiration. Access is behind the Coast Guard station.

For a great way to capture the local feel, pick up a copy of
the *Cook County News-Herald* or *Cook County Star*. These two
newspapers make this small town a hotbed of journalistic
competition.

Much of this part of the north shore is within the Superior
National Forest, 3 million acres of original America. A U.S.
Forest Service district ranger office is in Grand Marais and
another is maintained in Tofte. Both provide walk-in
information centers about the forest. Handicapped fishing
piers are located throughout the forest.

What to See and Do

With its excellent harbor and breakwater, Grand Marais is
often crowded with sailing yachts and the deep-sea fishing
boats. To plan an adventure trip, check with Bear Track
Outfitting. Eco-tours aboard the North House Folk School's
Hjordis leave the school's dock four times daily.

Arrowhead Center for the Arts, a multi-use facility on the
campus of Cook County Schools, offers a variety of visual and
performing arts productions. It centralizes the focus of fine arts
groups like the Grand Marais Art Colony, Playhouse, WTIP-FM
radio and North Shore Music Association, also serving as a site for
workshops, exhibits, art classes and performances for the entire
community. There are also facilities for conferences and meetings.

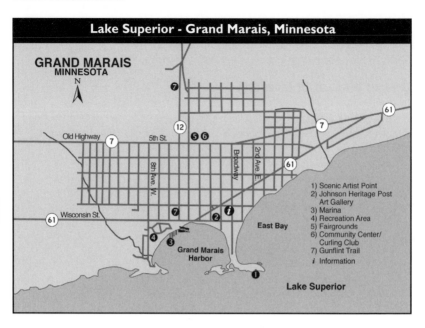

Lake Superior - Grand Marais, Minnesota

GRAND MARAIS
MINNESOTA

Old Highway 5th St.

Wisconsin St.

East Bay

Grand Marais
Harbor

1) Scenic Artist Point
2) Johnson Heritage Post
   Art Gallery
3) Marina
4) Recreation Area
5) Fairgrounds
6) Community Center/
   Curling Club
7) Gunflint Trail
i Information

Lake Superior

North House Folk School on the harbor provides classes in kayak and boat building, sailing, sledding and many traditional crafts. From preparing herbs to building a kayak (or casket) or making a fur hat, this is where you can learn.

Just east of Grand Marais is the small, but historic, village of Croftville. Visit the Indian burial grounds and the historic St. Francis Xavier Church, listed on the National Register of Historic Places.

Notable Museums

Cook County Historical Society Museum will be of great interest. Open daily May to October. The society features a historically accurate fish house museum on the waterfront that displays the society's collection of fishing artifacts and exhibits. Also at the site and almost on the spot where it was built 70 years ago by the Scott family, the historic tug *Neegee* is part of the fishing exhibits, nestled beneath a roof that shelters it from weather damage. The tug set nets and harvested fish for many years in the waters around Grand Marais. No fee, but donations welcome

Johnson Heritage Post Art Gallery shows works of art representing local pioneer and contemporary artists. Open year-round, it is devoted largely to the paintings of Anna Johnson, dating back to 1907. Special exhibits and displays of area artists change during the year. Open daily May to October, with restricted hours on Sundays and November through April. No fee, but donations welcome.

Notable Events

• Fishermen's Picnic has been held in Grand Marais since the 1920s. It's a complete package of festivities, held the first weekend of August.

• An Arts Festival in early July adds to the appeal of summer in Grand Marais.

• The Cook County Historical Society Fishcake Contest and Dinner is held in early October.

• Moose Madness Weekend is held in later October.

Where to Shop

In the downtown area, there are many gift and other shopping opportunities. A few special locations are:

Lake Superior Trading Post is loaded with clothing and gifts. This is one of the best shopping experiences around the lake. Linda Zenk has assembled a wonderfully eclectic collection, from snowshoes to crystal pitchers.

Drury Lane Book Store has a nice eclectic collection of titles and authors. It's down the road from The World's Best Donuts.

Sivertson Galleries houses one of the largest collections of Lake Superior paintings in the country. Sivertson also has a gallery in Duluth's Canal Park. Howard Sivertson, the late George Morrison, Liz Sivertson, Betsy Bowen and Hazel Belvo are some local artists of note whose works are featured.

Campgrounds

The Grand Marais Recreation Area is modern and convenient to the downtown, offering facilities for boaters, RVers and campers. It has a playground, indoor pool, sauna and whirlpool.

What's Next

Before leaving Grand Marais, we recommend a 60-mile side trip on the Gunflint Trail, which is described in its own listing.

If your route of travel is south on Highway 61, you'll pass through Lutsen, Tofte and Schroeder. If you're headed to Grand Portage and the International Border, there are several sites of interest. The tiny settlement of Colvill has an interesting Civil War tie. It was named after a colonel in the war, who took his "R&R" here. A marker tells the whole tale. One of the quietest "towns" on the shore, you can match the colonel's quest to rest frazzled nerves with a stay at a local establishment. Nearby is the Kadunce River, which offers a wading trek of less than a mile past several low falls and through a spectacular narrow, high gorge. Here, hikers will be able to climb relatively easily to the Superior Hiking Trail bridge and return to the highway via the SHT. Rated: moderate to difficult.

Gunflint Trail

An attractive diversion from the Circle Tour route on Highway 61 at Grand Marais, Minnesota, is the Gunflint Trail. The trail tracks some 60 miles inland past hundreds of lakes and forested areas. It is also an eastern entry to the Boundary Waters Canoe Area Wilderness and a number of resorts can outfit visitors with whatever is needed to make a day or longer trip into BWCAW. Wilderness along the way doesn't mean roughing it on this trail, however. The Gunflint offers excellent lodging and dining at many resorts or restaurants. Gunflint has also become a major cross-country skiing destination in the Upper Midwest and most of the resorts in the area actively promote outdoor winter sports and groom trails for guests.

Those wishing more information will want to stop at the Gunflint Information Center on Highway 61 in Grand Marais. (See separate Gunflint Trail listing.)

DIRECTORY

Tourist Information – Grand Marais, Minnesota, Visitor Center, 218-387-2524, 888-922-5000

Where to Stay
Best Western Superior Inn & Suites, 218-387-2240, Hwy. 61 E., has six luxury suites with fireplaces.
East Bay Hotel and Restaurant, 218-387-2899, is a historic hotel right on the waterfront.
For a B&B stay, ask about Dreamcatcher, Snuggle Inn, MacArthur House or Jägerhaus German B&B, a few miles up Highway 61 at Colvill.

Where to Eat with a Local Flavor
Angry Trout Cafe, 218-387-1265, 416 W. Hwy. 61, has great dining right on the waterfront.
Birch Terrace Supper Club and Lounge, 218-387-2215, 601 W. Hwy. 61, offers summer deck dining.
Harbor Lights Supper Club, 218-387-1142, 1615 W. Hwy. 61, has a hillside view of town.
Sven and Ole's Pizza, 218-387-1713, 7 W. Wisconsin St., specializes in Italian foods ala Norwegian.
Gun Flint Tavern, 218-387-1563, 111 W. Wisconsin St., offers eclectic and ethnic foods, fine wine, 40 microbrews and live music.

Fourteen miles (22 kilometers) up the shore from Grand Marais, at the mouth of the Brule River, is another historic Minnesota resort, Naniboujou Lodge and Restaurant. It's a much-photographed attraction due to its brilliantly colored interior designs, which are of Cree origin, and its history as a private club of the Prohibition era. After June, be sure to schedule your arrival to savor afternoon high tea. Drop-ins are welcomed for this special afternoon event. Reservations for non-lodgers at dinner are recommended for groups of five or more.

Unusual lava flows make for unusual rapids in the Brule River as it seeks Lake Superior. Judge C.R. Magney State Park offers a ridge-line hike to the spectacular Devil's Kettle Falls, a boiling cauldron of hellish proportions that mysteriously disappears into the bedrock. Named after Clarence Magney, once mayor of Duluth and a Minnesota Supreme Court justice, the preserve has fishing and 5 miles (8 kilometers) of cross-country ski trails.

The Arrowhead Trail starts at Hovland, another Scandinavian immigrant fishing settlement. This most northeasterly of the trails in Minnesota ends on McFarland Lake within sight of Canadian territory.

GRAND PORTAGE, MINNESOTA

Area Population 560
Named by the early voyageurs, the "Grand Portage" consists of an 8.5-mile (13-kilometer) uphill trek around a

series of waterfalls and rapids. Rising some 600 feet from Lake Superior's shoreline, at the top of the incline it intersects the Pigeon River and the inland canoeing routes leading to Lake of the Woods and the important fur-trading posts to the west.

On Ojibway reservation land, the community of Grand Portage lost its early importance after the land where the reconstructed fur outpost now sits was abandoned by the North West Company in 1803 under terms of the Treaty of Paris that ended the Revolutionary War. Before then it was the mid-continent hub for voyageur activity. The Chippewa name Kitchi Onigum ("Great Carrying Place") reflects this heritage. At the foot of Mt. Josephine, the modern village of Grand Portage sits snuggled on Grand Portage Bay, with Isle Royale floating mirage-like on the horizon, 26 miles (34 kilometers) away.

You'll reach Grand Portage on Highway 61 either from the International Border at Pigeon River or from the southwest via Grand Marais.

What to See and Do

The reconstructed Grand Portage National Monument is a replica of the first white settlement in Minnesota, originally constructed in 1731. The stockade, kitchen, the great hall, canoe warehouse and other re-creations of the early fur-trading settlement make for an interesting morning or afternoon. Interpretive and special events are scheduled during the months of operation, including historic cooking and baking, Native American craft demonstrations and walking tours. It has an on-site gift shop and more than adequate parking.

The Grand Portage Band of Lake Superior Chippewa reached agreement to take over maintenance and construction work at the monument, the first such agreement between Native Americans and the U.S. Park Service. The park is open mid-May to mid-October. Summer tours are available daily with a nominal admission. Average visit is one to two hours.

The 8.5-mile (13-kilometer) Grand Portage Trail can be hiked from the stockade to the site of Fort Charlotte on the Pigeon River, where the voyageurs were able to begin their marathon portaging/paddling trip to the far-flung wintering posts to the west.

The cream of this area's lodging, dining and hospitality is Grand Portage Lodge and Casino, a good place to settle for snowmobiling in the winter and hiking and nature programs in the summer. The lodge has an active casino, with bingo and other gaming. It also offers two dining areas. The tribe operates Grand Portage Marina and Campground adjacent to the lodge.

Isle Royale

Isolated by 20 miles of open water, the only way to reach Isle Royale National Park without your own boat is by taking a ferry from Grand Portage, Minnesota, or Copper Harbor and Houghton, Michigan. The island is the site of annual moose and wolf research conducted by Michigan Technological University at Houghton in one of the longest wildlife studies in the world. It is also rated as a National Biosphere, which bans pets, a provision that protects the dynamic wolf packs that prey on the moose population.

Most of the island is camping territory, but Rock Harbor Lodge at the northeast corner offers lodging and a good restaurant. Reservations are required. Several good harbors give boaters safety if the weather turns nasty. (See separate Isle Royale listing.)

DIRECTORY

Tourist Information – National
Monument Visitor Center, **218-475-2202**

Where to Stay
Grand Portage Lodge and Casino,
218-475-2401, 800-543-1384, Hwy. 61,
offers 100 rooms, and gaming with walk
out access to Lake Superior.

Where to Eat with a Local Flavor
Island View Dining Room at Grand
Portage Lodge and Casino,
218-475-2401, Hwy. 61, has good food
with a nice view of the Susie Islands.

Grand Portage, Minnesota,
regional map – page 8.

At the tip of Hat Point near Grand Portage, growing from
an outcropping of rock hanging over the lake, the gnarled and
tenacious Spirit Little Cedar Tree (Witch Tree) has watched
Lake Superior for at least 300 years. Important spiritually to
the Ojibway, the tree seems to create reverence within all who
visit it. There is restricted land access to protect the tree and
the old trails have been closed off. In the meantime, it is easily
visible from the water to kayakers and boaters and on
Wenonah cruises to Isle Royale.

Grand Portage is the closest access from the mainland to
Isle Royale National Park, Michigan. See the listing for Isle
Royale for more information. Providing passage from
Minnesota are the *Voyageur II,* May through October, and
the *Wenonah,* mid-June to Labor Day, operated by the Grand
Portage-Isle Royale Transportation Line, still owned by the
famous Sivertson fishing family. They operate out of Grand
Portage Marina, which offers full facilities for boaters,
including fishing licenses, charts, launch and pumpout services.
Charter service available. Advance reservations required.

A must stop is the Grand Portage Bay Rest Area just above
Highway 61 and 5 miles (8 kilometers) from the border. The
overlook offers a view of Lake Superior that is spectacular and
a visitor information center operates year-to-year, dependent
on annual funding.

Another get-your-camera-out stop is the view of the Susie
Islands from Mt. Josephine to the northeast of Grand
Portage. A group of three large and several small islands, the
Susies lie just south of the Canadian border near Pigeon
Point. A pulloff for safe stopping has been provided on Mt.
Josephine. This is the last easily accessible view of Lake
Superior's shoreline before passing into Canada, where the
highway moves inland several miles. Ryden's Border Store on
the U.S. side of the border features money exchange, customs
information and a Duty Free Store.

Grand Portage State Park on the U.S.-Canadian border is the only park in the United States being operated jointly by the state and a tribe. Acquired from private hands by the Minnesota Parks and Trails Council, the land is held in trust for the Grand Portage Band of Chippewa and dedicated for use as a state park. The park encompasses more than 300 acres and includes the site of an Indian trading post, as well as an old logging flume that was used in the late 1800s and early 1900s. Hiking and ski trails have been developed. Featured is a trail (rated intermediate) to the spectacular Pigeon Falls (High Falls) on the Pigeon River, nearly 100 feet (31 meters) high. The entrance to the state park is just before the U.S. Customs gate above Highway 61. The turn is hard to catch if you're not watching carefully. Ontario's Pigeon River Provincial Park borders the park to the north.

Notable Events

• The Grand Portage Great Rendezvous is held each year the second weekend in August, a traditional powwow sponsored by the band. The Friends of Grand Portage have nationally known speakers as a Rendezvous event.

What's Next

You'll exit Grand Portage either southwesterly bound for Grand Marais or northward to the International Border with Canada.

GRAND RAPIDS, MINNESOTA

Population 8,000

On the western edge of the Mesabi Iron Range where Highway 2 from the east and west intersects Highway 169 from the south or north is Grand Rapids. Best known for its thriving wood products industry through its history, that heritage is carried on by Blandin Paper Company, which supplies coated paper for many magazines and catalogs. Grand Rapids has ample lodging, good dining and many activities throughout the year that will appeal to visitors.

Grand Rapids, Michigan, regional map – page 32.

What to See and Do

Old Central School is a prime example of Romanesque Revivalist architecture. It houses the Itasca County Historical Society Museum, a children's museum and the Judy Garland Museum.

For a golf outing, check out the "grand slam" that includes Sugarbrooke, Pokegama, Wendigo and Eagle Ridge golf courses in the area.

Tours of Blandin's paper mill are offered from June through Labor Day.

DIRECTORY

Tourist Information – Grand Rapids Chamber of Commerce, 218-326-6619; Convention and Visitors Bureau 218-326-9607, 800-355-9740

Where to Stay
AmericInn Lodge & Suites, 218-326-8999, 888-950-8999, 1812 Pokegama Ave. S, has 59 rooms with indoor pool and enhanced continental breakfast.
Rainbow Inn, 218-326-9655, 888-248-8050, 1300 E Highway 169, offers 80 rooms, pool, two restaurants and a game room.
Sawmill Inn, 218--326-8501, 800-667-7509, 2301 S. Hwy. 169, has 124 double, king and suite units, a good restaurant and welcomes pets.

Where to Eat with a Local Flavor
Sawmill Inn Dining Room, 218-326-8501, 2301 S. Hwy. 169, offers fine cuisine and local favorites like walleye pike.

Minnesota Forest History Center also fosters the area's timber heritage and includes an interpretative building displaying themes of forest history, including a realistic 1900 lumber camp. Special events are scheduled throughout the summer. For winter opportunities, call ahead for information.

Notable Events
• The annual Judy Garland Festival is held in June, celebrating the star's origins in this town.

What's Next
Visitors seeking a wider range can travel west on Highway 2 to Deer River, at the eastern edge of the Leech Lake Reservation. The Leech Lake Band of Ojibwe operates the White Oak Casino there, the Palace Hotel Casino farther west at Cass Lake and the Northern Lights Gaming Casino, Hotel and Events Center near Walker. Leech Lake is at the center of Minnesota's Heartland tourism area and offers great muskie and other fishing.
From Grand Rapids, travelers can return to Duluth and the Lake Superior Circle Tour via U.S. Highway 2 or travel northerly to other Mesabi Iron Range cities and sites.

GREENLAND, MICHIGAN
Population 160

At the junction of M-38 with M- 26 southeast of Ontonagon, pause at the community of Greenland for an excellent tour of one of Copper Country's historic underground mines. Adventure Copper Mine has been the site of mining activity for 5,000 years or more, but hit the big

time during the mid-1800s copper boom. This popular site offers extensive guided underground and grounds tours, with a wide panorama of forests and countryside from one of the mine's adits (openings) high on a "backdoor" hillside as a bonus during the tour. New owners have incorporated added areas of the mine to the tour and knowledgeable guides bring the history and 1800s' mining technology to life as they lead the way through the drifts (shafts) and stopes (rooms) of the mine. A gift shop offers handcrafted copper items and there are 25 forest campsites available on the site for those seeking a place to stay.

Greenland, Michigan, regional map – page 26.

GROS CAP AND PRINCE TOWNSHIP, ONTARIO

Combined Population 1,325

Translated as Big Cape from the French, Gros Cap is where Lake Superior is said to end or begin (depending on your orientation) and the St. Marys River begins. Along the 26-kilometer-long (16-mile) Highway 550 to the village of Gros Cap, take Marshall Drive to find several lookouts rising as much as 200 meters (656 feet) above the lake. All ships entering and leaving the locks at Sault Ste. Marie must pass this huge rock ridge, the base of the Canadian Shield rising to the north. Down at the hamlet of Gros Cap (population 350), rock hounds will want to search the bayfront for agates.

Gros Cap, Ontario, regional map – page 18.

On the way to and from Gros Cap, Prince Township (population 973) offers a community center and a museum in the form of Prince United Church, built in 1885. The yard outside the church holds well-preserved farming artifacts. The township fathers and mothers have reconstructed a pioneer home on the premises. It's worth a brief stop even if you can't get into the buildings.

These two worthwhile stops off Trans Canada Highway 17 north of Sault Ste. Marie, Ontario, and westward on Highway 550 about 20 minutes take you to the point that the earliest voyageurs recognized as the beginning of Lake Superior's uncertainties, after their relatively peaceful passage through the St. Marys River. It's a sight that visitors long remember.

The Sault Ste. Marie Airport is located off Highway 550, turning at Prince Township. Located at the airport is the Provincial Fire Centre, one of the largest centers of forest fire information and research in the world.

GULLIVER, MICHIGAN

Population 840

A must-stop just a bit off the highway at Gulliver and past McDonald Lake is the 1895 Seul Choix Point Lighthouse Museum, which marine historian Frederick Stonehouse rates

DIRECTORY

Tourist Information – Schoolcraft
County Chamber of Commerce,
906-341-5010

Gulliver, Michigan,
regional map – page 49.

G

in his book *Haunted Lakes II* as one of the
most haunted sites on the Great Lakes.
Once dilapidated but now restored, Seul
Choix (locally pronounced SIS-Shwa) is
said to be haunted by a cigar-smoking
ghost of a former keeper, along with other
"shades of the past." Museum personnel
are quick and comfortable discussing their
ghosts and can point to any number of phenomena and
recordings documenting the haunts.

What's Next

Gulliver is in the central southern Upper Peninsula on
U.S.Highway 2, which follows an east-west track around Lake
Michigan's northern shoreline. Traveling Highway 2 west
from Gulliver, the shoreline city of Manistique offers a good
selection of lodging facilities, including several state or private
campgrounds, motels, resorts and bed-and-breakfast inns, and
dining for whatever your taste may be. If traveling east, you'll
pass through a number of small towns heading for St. Ignace
and the Mackinac Bridge.

GUNFLINT TRAIL, MINNESOTA

Gunflint Trail, Minnesota,
regional map – page 8.

The Gunflint Trail, which begins in Grand Marais, is a
58-mile long (94-kilometer) Minnesota Scenic Byway that
runs to the Canadian border.

The Trail is a major resort area, with accommodations
varying from camping to rustic housekeeping cabins, bed-
and-breakfast inns and elegant lodges. On a drive up the trail,
you'll see signs for Bearskin Lodge, Golden Eagle Lodge,
Poplar Creek Guesthouse, Moosehorn B&B, Old
Northwoods Lodge, Clearwater Canoe Outfitters and Lodge
and perhaps the most well-known resort on the trail, the
Gunflint Lodge. Founded by Justine Kerfoot in the 1920s,
the Gunflint Lodge has been operated by her family ever
since.

The Gunflint is home to hundreds of miles of groomed
cross-country ski and snowshoe trails, as well as snowmobile
routes. You'll find both the silent sport enthusiast and the
snowmobiler here.

Most lodges offer packages of instruction, guided treks
and equipment rental. Specialty trips such as those offered by
Boundary Country Trekking (cross-country ski treks with
overnight stops at Mongolian yurts) have been featured in
national magazines. You may ski or hike lodge-to-lodge, with
your bags and car transported for you.

The Gunflint Trail is a major entry point to the Boundary
Waters Canoe Area Wilderness (BWCAW) and fishing rarely

gets much better. In summer, hikers may explore hundreds of miles of trails, many of which offer spectacular views. The Trail is home to several outfitters who will supply everything you need for a weeklong trek into the BWCAW or an afternoon paddle on one of the many surrounding lakes. Most resorts also provide canoes and kayaks for guests' use.

Because it's the wilderness, visitors might be surprised to find fine gourmet dining here. The Gunflint Lodge has long been known for its fine dining. Old Northwoods Lodge, with its enormous stone fireplace, offers superb dining as well as an excellent wine and beer list. For more casual dining, try the Trail Center for a burger. The Trail Center is also one of the only spots to pick up provisions and gasoline on the Trail.

At the end of the Gunflint Trail, you'll find Trail's End Café, a tiny spot in the middle of the wilderness where you can get a burger or a cup of good homemade chili. It's definitely worth the trip.

DIRECTORY

Tourist Information – Gunflint Trail Information Center, 218-387-3191, 800-338-6932

G

Hancock - Hurley

Hancock, Michigan,
regional map – page 24.

HANCOCK, MICHIGAN

Population 4,325

Hancock is on the hillside over the Portage Lift Bridge that connects the city to Houghton. In a nod to Hancock's sizable Finnish community, some street signs are in both English and Finnish.

Hancock is smaller than its twin across Portage Lake, but has interesting shopping on Quincy Street. Part of the downtown is listed on the National Register of Historic Places. A brochure, available at many locations, will guide you along historic streets and past significant buildings and classic homes.

This is the home of Finlandia University, the only Finnish college in America. The school is home to the Finnish-American Heritage Center, which is housed in a remodeled Catholic church built in 1885. It houses a museum, art gallery and theater. Open weekdays. North Wind Books, is also located at the university. Open Mondays through Saturdays.

All of the shopping is within walking distance from the 54-slip, full-service Houghton County Marina on the Waterway in Hancock, however lovers of copper artworks will want to visit Eric Walli's Copper Arts Studio just north of the Quincy Mine Hoist on U.S. 41.

What to See and Do

Copper Country Community Arts Council on Quincy Street features three galleries with monthly exhibits and classes. Open Tuesday through Saturday.

In the winter, take advantage of Mont Ripley Ski Hill, which long served as the only alpine ski facility in the Keweenaw, but is now joined by Mt. Bohemia at Lac La Belle.

Quincy Hill is on U.S. 41 heading north, overlooking Hancock, Houghton and the deep valley of the Keweenaw Waterway.

Quincy Mine Site is the complex on U.S. 41 just north of town and has tours of the Nordberg, the largest steam hoist

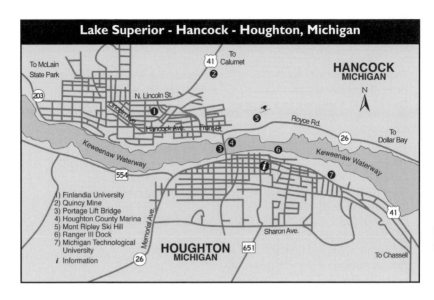

Lake Superior - Hancock - Houghton, Michigan

1) Finlandia University
2) Quincy Mine
3) Portage Lift Bridge
4) Houghton County Marina
5) Mont Ripley Ski Hill
6) Ranger III Dock
7) Michigan Technological University
i Information

ever manufactured. It operated from 1921 to the mid-1930s, lowering and raising men and copper from the 9,260-foot-deep (2,850-meter; 1.5 mile) shafts, at a maximum speed of 3,200 feet (985 meters) per minute, or 36.4 miles per hour. There is an inclined cog-railway tram to shuttle visitors to one of the old copper mines for visits to the underground diggings. Also displayed on the site is a 17-ton copper boulder discovered in Lake Superior off the Keweenaw and a G-scale model railroad. Incredibly detailed, it won the Bert Boyum Historic Preservation Award. Open late April through late October, with limited spring and fall tours. Fee.

Notable Museums

Pewabik House and Museum on Hancock Street is a resource on the history of the area and the life and work of potter Mary Chase Stratton (founder of Pewabic Pottery).

Notable Events

• Hancock hosts the Heikinpaiva Mid-Winter Finnish Festival and Maasto Hiihto Cross-Country Ski Race in mid-January.

• Bridgefest and the Keweenaw Chain Drive Festival are held in mid-June.

• Keweenaw Trail Run challenges competitors in wonderful surroundings in June.

• Keweenaw Lighthouse Celebration in July celebrates the numerous lights existing on the peninsula.

• Houghton County Fair occurs near the end of August.

DIRECTORY

Tourist Information – Keweenaw Peninsula Chamber of Commerce, 906-482-5240; Keweenaw Convention and Visitors Bureau, 906-337-4579, 800-338-7982

Where to Stay

Ramada Inn Waterfront, 906-482-8400, 877-482-8400, 99 Navy, is on Portage Lake with boat docks and dining at the The Upper Deck.
Best Western Copper Crown Motel, 906-482-6111, 800-528-1234, 235 Hancock, has large rooms with queen beds and other amenities.

Where to Eat with a Local Flavor

Kaleva Café, 906-482-1230, 234 W. Quincy, has a good home-cooked menu and especially fine pasties.
North Shore Grill and Pub, 906-482-46778, 2131 Jasburg Rd., features steaks, seafood, game and Italian, with a separate pub menu.
Gemignani's Italian Restaurant, 906-482-2920, 512 Quincy, features handmade lunch and dinner fare.

Campgrounds

Hancock Recreational Boating and Camping Facility is located 1 mile (1.6 kilometers) west of downtown Hancock on M-203. It has a free swimming beach, campground with full facilities (fees), boat launch and picnicking area. Open mid-May through September.

What's Next

Beyond Houghton/Hancock, the Keweenaw Peninsula offers hikers numerous trails of varying length and degree of difficulty in nature sanctuaries owned and managed by the Michigan Nature Association.

Heading north on U.S. 41 from the Quincy Hill park you'll pass numerous abandoned mine sites and some ghost towns. The area is designated as the Keweenaw National Historical Park, established to preserve the history and traditions of the Keweenaw's mining past. For more specific information, contact the park office (906-337-3168) in Calumet on Red Jacket Road or check with the Keweenaw Convention and Visitors Bureau on U.S. Highway 41 between Calumet and Laurium.

Going north from Hancock, there's an alternate route heading into the Keweenaw Peninsula proper. Take M-26 to the east as it passes through Ripley, Dollar Bay, Hubbell and Lake Linden on the way to Laurium. Dollar Bay is home to Horner Flooring, the top producer of wooden basketball and dance floors in the world. Tours for groups can be arranged. At Hubbell, where the famed Calumet and Hecla Copper Company processed its copper ore, take Sixth Street and several turns to Upper and Lower Hungarian Falls. Trails rated: moderate.

HAYWARD, WISCONSIN

Population 2,130

Traveling south from Brule on Highway 27 from U.S. Highway 2 leads to Hayward, the home of the National Fresh Water Fishing Hall of Fame, documenting the exploits of noteworthy anglers and their prize-winning catches. This is also home to the World Lumberjack Championships. Just east of Hayward is the Lac Courte Oreilles Casino and Convention Center, operated by the Lac Courte Oreilles Band of Lake Superior Ojibway. If your route is easterly, you can reconnect to the Circle Tour route by taking U.S. Highway 63 northeasterly toward Hurley. If traveling to the west from Hayward, catch Highway 77 through areas dotted by inland lakes and interesting towns to reconnect to the Circle Tour via Highway 35.

Hayward, Wisconsin, regional map – page 50.

HELMER, MICHIGAN

Township Population 900

South on H-33 from Seney on the M-28 Circle Route, Helmer is home to a fascinating historic bed-and-breakfast inn and restaurant that you'll want to put on your agenda. Originally the Helmer House was the home of a Presbyterian minister and eventually became a general store and hotel. After renovation in 1982, it has become a favorite destination for those who want to escape the cares of the world. Five rooms are available. The restaurant specializes in fresh-caught whitefish. One of Lake Superior's Best. Open May through October.

Helmer is also the gateway city to the Manistique chain of lakes, with plenty of recreational opportunities.

Helmer, Michigan, regional map – page 46.

HERBSTER, WISCONSIN

Population 195

The western Bayfield Peninsula towns of Herbster and Port Wing are accessed via Highway 13 from either Cornucopia to the north or off Highway 2 about five miles east of Superior.

Like its neighboring community of Port Wing, the small Lake Superior village of Herbster captures the spirit of the commercial fishing industry of old. Herbster offers overnight camping and an excellent sand beach. Try trout fishing in the Cranberry River. The town has in-room lodging and restaurant dining available. Northern Lights Gifts and Craft Shop offers items all made by local artists and crafters. The Raindrop Garden Gallery also makes a pleasant stop or take nearby Bark Point Road to find Bark Point Studio and Gallery. A few miles from the crossroad center of town on

Herbster, Wisconsin, regional map – page 30.

H

DIRECTORY

Tourist Information – Bayfield
County Tourism, 800-472-6338

Where to Stay
Willow Motel, 715-774-3385, offers the
only in-room lodging in town.

Where to Eat with a Local Flavor
Cranberry Inn, 715-774-3557,
Hwy. 13 and Lenawee Rd., offers great
Italian cuisine and pizza.

Lenawee Road, check the historic log
gymnasium, built by the Works Progress
Administration in 1940 from local timber.

The Apostles' famous caves are
accessible from Herbster, offering
spectacular ice formations in the winter
and kayaking nooks and crannies in the
summer.

What's Next

Depending on your route, up or down
the road a bit, Port Wing has a claim to
fame with its annual fish boil, which sounds
strange but is absolutely enticing. (See
separate listing)

HERMANSVILLE, MICHIGAN

Township Population 1,050

On Highway 2 about midway between Escanaba and Iron
Mountain, keep an eye out for Hermansville to visit the IXL
Historic Museum, housed in the 1882 headquarters building
of the Wisconsin Land and Lumber Company. Rooms of
elegant period furnishings, wonderfully elaborate woodwork,
pictures, records and tools of the 1880s document the time
when IXL Hardwood Flooring Company revolutionized the
lumber industry and became the largest hardwood flooring
manufacturer in the country. A National Register of Historic
Places site, it's open Memorial Day through Labor Day, with
group tour arrangements during the off-season. Fee.

HEYDEN AND SEARCHMONT, ONTARIO

Combined Population 600

Searchmont, Ontario,
regional map – page 18.

In the winter, ski hills around the communities of Heyden
and Searchmont, to the north of Sault Ste. Marie, come to life
as excellent winter havens. The Heyden Adventure Base Camp
sports a 65-meter (250-foot) vertical drop with five runs and
5 kilometers of cross-country trail. Searchmont Resort is east of
Heyden on Highway 556 and has a drop of 230 meters (700
feet), making it the largest of this region's ski hills. The town has
a tourist association, several bed-and-breakfast inns, a groomed
snowmobile trail to Wawa and a dog sled business that gives rides.
Mountain Ash Inn offers a nice lodging choice in the area.

Buttermilk Alpine Ski Village is just north of Heyden at
Goulais River off Highway 552, with a 90-meter (270-foot)
vertical drop and a double chairlift. A number of chalet rental
units are available. Try the Austrian and German specialties at
their Schnitzel Haus Dining Lounge, which is listed in
"Where to Eat in Canada."

At this point, you have reached the eastern-most part of Lake Superior, where its waters empty into the downstream currents of the St. Marys River rapids and flow south to Lake Huron and the rest of the Great Lakes.

HIBBING, MINNESOTA

Population 17,070

Hibbing, located almost exactly in the heart of the Mesabi Iron Range on U.S. Highway 169, boasts a number of attractions of interest to travelers of the Iron Trail. Here are manmade canyons and hills of waste reflecting the city's history as "the iron ore capitol of the world." Here, too, are beautiful lakes in the surrounding area, perfect for recreation and relaxation. The city is a shopping center for the area, offering virtually anything a shopper needs. There are good lodgings, fine dining and many other amenities.

Hibbing, Minnesota, regional map – page 32.

A Bit of History

Hibbing takes its name from Frank Hibbing, a timber cruiser and prospector who first discovered iron ore in the region in the mid-1890s. A village was platted and grew almost overnight as miners and others moved in to look for their bonanza. Unfortunately for the town, iron ore lay directly under it and the original townsite had to be abandoned in 1918, with all of its buildings being either demolished or moved to the present site. That move was completed by 1921 and mining progressed into the former city site, which came to be known as North Hibbing. Vestiges of that townsite still exist and are described below.

What to See and Do

Hull-Rust-Mahoning Mine is the world's largest open pit iron mine and a historic landmark. At the edge of the mine and townsite, a viewpoint provides a full view of the mine. Exhibits of massive equipment used in iron mining are located nearby and allow close up examination of the machinery that keeps mines working.

A few blocks from the mine viewpoint, markers denote all that remains from the original village, which was moved to allow mining of iron ore under parts of the location.

Also near the mine viewpoint, the Greyhound Bus Origin Center commemorates the beginnings of this important company to the growth of the country.

Paulucci Space Theater has daily programs about the heavens and an Omnimax presentation on the campus of Hibbing Community College.

Hibbing is the hometown of Bob Dylan (known locally as Bob Zimmerman) and the Hibbing Public Library has an

DIRECTORY

Tourist Information – Hibbing
Chamber of Commerce,
218-262-3895, 800-444-2246; Iron Trail
Convention and Visitors Bureau, 218-
749-8161, 800-777-8497

interesting collection of memorabilia that exhibits photos and other material relating to the star's life and work. In late May, the city takes note of its famous son with a Bob Dylan Days celebration.

Hibbing High School auditorium was designed after New York's old Capitol Theatre and has long been a showplace of the area.

Golfers will find a real bargain at the 9-hole Hibbing Municipal Golf Course or may want to check out the private Mesaba Country Club.

Notable Museums

Hibbing Historical Society Museum is located in the Memorial Building at 23rd Street and Fifth Avenue East. Open May 15 through September. Fee.

What's Next

Dependent on your route of travel, you can take U.S. 169 northeasterly to the eastern Mesabi Range or west through several smaller cities to visit Grand Rapids. Another choice is to catch Highway 37 east to U.S. 53 which will take you to Duluth.

HOUGHTON, MICHIGAN

Population 6,630

Houghton, Michigan, regional map – page 24.

Houghton is the largest city of the Keweenaw Peninsula and all of Copper Country. It is accessed on highways U.S. 41 or Michigan 26 north from Highway 28.

A Bit of History

The word "Keweenaw" is said to mean "portage" in Ojibway. Portage Lake always provided a natural water pathway across most of the Keweenaw Peninsula, but the complete water path was blocked at the north end by a rocky highland that required a portage. This is what was called Keweenaw. In the late 1800s, a canal was opened through this area, connecting Lake Superior with itself and creating a shortcut for lake vessel shipping. In essence, most of the Keweenaw Peninsula became an island above the completed waterway.

Here in the heart of Copper Country, King Copper as they call it, copper has been found throughout the western end of Upper Michigan and into the Keweenaw from earliest times. There's a copper color in almost everything. Copper has been responsible for much of the prosperity that the region has experienced. From 1870 to 1910, this was considered one of

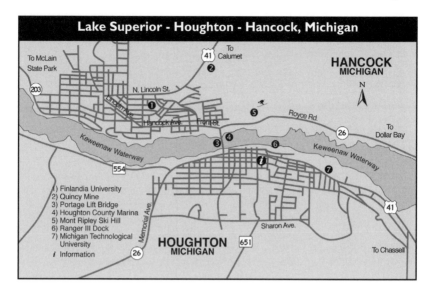

Lake Superior - Houghton - Hancock, Michigan

To McLain State Park
To Calumet
41
2
HANCOCK
MICHIGAN
N
203
N. Lincoln St.
1
5
Royce Rd.
Lincoln Ave.
Hancock Ave.
Front St.
3
26
To Dollar Bay
Keweenaw Waterway
4
6
Keweenaw Waterway
554
i
7
41
1) Finlandia University
2) Quincy Mine
3) Portage Lift Bridge
4) Houghton County Marina
5) Mont Ripley Ski Hill
6) Ranger III Dock
7) Michigan Technological University
i) Information
Memorial Ave.
Sharon Ave.
26
HOUGHTON
MICHIGAN
651
To Chassell

the wealthiest regions of North America. All copper mining activity, with the exception of the Copper Range Company at White Pine to the southwest, ceased decades ago. Today, tourism is a major economic factor in the area.

What to See and Do

Houghton is home to the 7,000-student Michigan Technological University. U.S. 41 cuts through the campus. MTU's world-class A.E. Seaman Mineral Museum displays more than 30,000 specimens of rocks and gemstones from around the world. It has excellent exhibits and an extensive archive of minerals located on the fifth floor of the Electronic Energy Resources Center building. Handicapped accessible.

Come in the winter for Michigan Tech's Winter Carnival with snow statues in early February. The Keweenaw Symphony Orchestra is located at the university and provides concerts throughout the year in the $20 million Rozsa (Roh-zay) Center for the Performing Arts. Featuring the largest stage north of Midland, Michigan, the center can seat a full symphony orchestra on its stage. It is a major addition for the performing arts for the entire region, with a full schedule of nationally recognized performers. Also at Michigan Tech, J.R. Van Pelt Library houses the Copper Country Archives, an important resource for scholars of the area.

The double-decker, quarter-mile-long Portage Lift Bridge joins Houghton and the Circle Tour with Hancock and the rest of the peninsula at Portage Lake. Completed in 1959, it is believed to be the heaviest lift bridge in the world and is certainly the largest lift bridge on Lake Superior, surpassing

145

Isle Royale

Isle Royale National Park, which has its headquarters in Houghton, Michigan, can be accessed by water or air from the city. The Ranger III, operated by the National Park Service, makes two round trips a week, staying overnight on Tuesdays and Fridays and returning the following day. Passengers on the 165-foot double decked boat are dropped at Rock Harbor Lodge, which is the only lodging and dining facility on the island. Reservations are required for boat and lodging.

The second means of accessing the island from Houghton is by seaplane, operated by Royale Air Service. Passengers choosing this service can opt to be landed at either Rock Harbor on the northeast side of Isle Royale or at Windigo on the south side. Flights take about 30 minutes. (See separate Isle Royale National Park listing.)

even the Duluth Aerial Bridge. In Michigan, it is second only to the Mackinac Bridge for largest bridge honors. The upper level is a four-lane highway, and the lower level is a rail bridge. The span is raised and lowered like an elevator for passing watercraft. Average openings per year is 700. A Bridgefest Celebration is held annually on Father's Day weekend, complete with parade, races, dances, seafood and more.

Michigan's Upper Peninsula is the place to be for musical immersion in June and July. Featuring opera, symphonic and chamber music, the Upper Peninsula's annual Pine Mountain Music Festival engages world class artists to perform in the communities surrounding Houghton/Hancock, Iron Mountain, Marquette and Land O' Lakes. The festival has been feted in articles in major newspapers, including London's *Financial Times*, and has won Michigan's top arts awards.

The 110-foot *Keweenaw Star* cruise ship offers tours on the Keweenaw Waterway. Offering an assortment of cruise packages, the operator of *Keweenaw Star* has daily departures from Dee Stadium and various charter options. In late July, the cruise service offers special lighthouse tours in conjunction with the Keweenaw Lighthouse Celebration and the last weekend in September the excursion operator also offers a special Keweenaw Peninsula fall color and lighthouse tour. Reservations recommended for special cruises. The fall color season is from mid-September through mid-October. Do plan a color-filled trip.

Houghton is headquarters for Isle Royale National Park and home of the *Ranger III*, which twice weekly ferries visitors to Rock Harbor on the nation's first island national park. Information and books concerning the park are also located in the Isle Royale Natural History Association Visitor Center. (More details on Isle Royale are included in the Copper Harbor, Michigan, listing.)

The Keweenaw Water Trail Association has developed maps and associated information for silent watercraft boating along the waterway and around the Keweenaw Peninsula. For information, contact the association through the Keweenaw Convention and Visitors Bureau (KCVB) in Calumet.

Portage Lake Golf Course is located on U.S. 41 south of Houghton, offering an 18-hole challenge.

Where to Shop

Shopping in downtown Houghton is a bit of fun, moving past quaint shops, always a surprise a few steps on. The Houghton downtown is easily accessible in all kinds of weather through its skyways, which bridge between buildings.

Stop in at Down Wind Sports on Shelden Avenue for great outdoor accessories. Surplus Outlet has something for the

DIRECTORY

Tourist Information – Keweenaw Peninsula Chamber of Commerce, 906-482-5240; Keweenaw Convention and Visitors Bureau, 906-337-4579, 800-338-7982

Where to Stay
Best Value King's Inn, 906-482-5000, 888-482-5005, 215 Shelden Ave., is near everything and has a large indoor pool. Best Western Franklin Square Inn, 906-482-0146, 820 Shelden Ave., has conference facilities and its Northern Lights Restaurant offers a wonderful view of the Keweenaw Waterway.

Budget Host Inn, 906-228-7494, 2603 W. U.S. Hwy. 41, has recently updated rooms, family units and kitchenettes.

Where to Eat with a Local Flavor
The Ambassador, 906-482-5054, 126 Shelden, has an old world bar and interior decorating.
Suomi Home Bakery and Restaurant, 906-482-3220, 54 Huron, has ethnic dishes to die for.
The Library, 906-487-5882, 62 Isle Royale St., is a popular eatery serving a delicious meal in a casual atmosphere and features craft beers from its microbrewery.

adventurer in you. Einerlei up north has more of the same quality gifts and crafty merchandise found at their Chassell location.

On Memorial Drive, the Keweenaw Gem and Gift shop has marvelous examples of local gemstones placed in interesting settings. Its building simulates a "headhouse," the structure covering the top of a mine shaft. The Copper Country Mall has a collection of stores for those who feel the urge to splurge.

What's Next

Across the Portage Lift Bridge, Hancock sits nicely on the hill overlooking Houghton and the waterway. North on U.S. 41, the Keweenaw Peninsula beckons travels for wonderful scenery and interesting activities for visitors. Southbound travelers can take U.S. 41 to a junction with Michigan Highway 28 to travel either east or west. Southwest from town, M-26 is the logical route for those traveling westerly on the Circle Tour.

HOYT LAKES, MINNESOTA

Population 2,280

Hoyt Lakes is the site of mining pioneer E.J. Longyear's first use of a diamond drill to test for iron ore. The Longyear Drill Site is commemorated a few miles beyond Hoyt Lakes on Highway 110.

Built in the mid-1950s as a self-contained town to house Erie Mining Company employees, Hoyt Lakes is located

DIRECTORY

Tourist information – Iron Trail Convention and Visitors Bureau, 218-749-8161, 800-777-8497; Hoyt Lakes Chamber of Commerce, 218-225-2209, 800-224-4802

Where to Stay Country Inn of Hoyt Lakes, 218-225-3555, 866-444-3555, offers nice lodging on a hill overlooking town.

Hoyt Lakes, Minnesota, regional map – page 32.

adjacent to Colby and Whitewater lakes. Here is a nice municipal campground (reservations strongly recommended), a challenging 9-hole golf course and a paved hiking, biking and skating trail that weaves its way through town and surrounding scenic areas. Forest Highway 11/Superior National Forest Scenic Byway is a nice drive from Hoyt Lakes south toward Lake Superior, making an easy connection between the Iron Range cities and Minnesota's north shore.

Hoyt Lakes hosts a Water Carnival each summer in late July.

HURLEY, WISCONSIN

Population 1,820

Hurley, Wisconsin, regional map – page 28.

Hurley is the twin of Ironwood, Michigan, and an integral part of the region's winter playground, Hurley is the western gateway to Big Snow Country and the ski area at Whitecap Mountains in nearby Montreal. It's the eastern gateway to Wisconsin for westbound travelers and is also home to some nice restaurants, as well as the Red Light Snowmobile Rally held in early December each year. Named for Hurley's more boisterous past during early lumbering days, the Red Light Rally celebrates the area's access to more than 450 miles (720 kilometers) of snowmobile trails in northern Wisconsin through Hurley.

A Bit of History

Hurley's early days as a center of logging gave the town a reputation for having streets lined with bar rooms, vice and wrongdoing. So notorious was the city that old-time lumberjacks often referred to northern Wisconsin's logging centers as being "Hurley, Hayward and Hell." Today, the city is much tamer and boasts fine cultural and recreational activities.

What to See and Do

Visitors in the area with an interest in Finnish culture and history will want to visit nearby Little Finland, home of the National Finnish American Festival, with many artifacts and curios that came from Finland when their owners

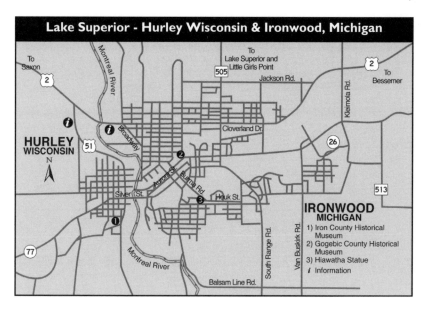

Lake Superior - Hurley Wisconsin & Ironwood, Michigan

immigrated. A gift shop offers a large selection of items and is open 10 a.m. to 2 p.m., Wednesdays and Saturdays, April through December.

Just west of Hurley via U.S. 2, be sure to stop at Eagle's Bluff Golf Course for a panoramic view of the territory. Michigan's Copper Peak and the Porcupine Mountains are easily visible to the east, while, with a little imagination and a clear day, you can spot Lake Superior and the Apostle Islands to the west.

A couple of miles west beyond Eagle's Bluff on Highway 2, watch for a sign to Kimball Town Park. Turn left for a short drive to a delightfully pleasant little park and waterfall. You'll find a one-lane wood-decked bridge, a relaxing picnic area, toilets, a small playground with swings and basketball court for the kids and a rustic pavilion. The West Branch of the Montreal River gently cascades over a series of ledges in the riverbed, called Kimball Park Falls.

Mountain bikers will want to try the more than 200 miles of trails of the Pines and Mines Mountain Bike Trail System, which is accessible from Highway 77 near Hurley.

Kayakers and canoeists will be interested in paddling the "Rivers Through Time" route that follows the historic trek taken by native people, voyageurs and early pioneers along the Flambeau Trail and other waterways. A cooperative effort of Iron County Development Zone, the Wisconsin Humanities Council and National Endowment for the Humanities, there are "Rivers Through Time" maps and written descriptions available from the Information Center or the Development Zone office in Hurley.

DIRECTORY

Tourist Information – Hurley Chamber of Commerce, 715-561-4334; Western U.P. Convention and Visitors Bureau, 906-932-4850, 800-522-5657

Where to Stay
Days Inn, 715-561-3500, 850 N. 10th Ave., has good rooms, indoor pool and ample parking, with continental breakfast.

Hurley Inn, 715-561-3060, 1000 10th Ave. N., offers 100 units.
Anton-Walsh B&B, 715-575-2065, 202 Copper St., is a restored 1890s-era house with a pleasant breakfast menu.

Where to Eat with a Local Flavor
Liberty Bell Chalet, 715-561-3753, 109 5th Ave. S., has delectable Italian fare.

Notable Museums

Iron County Historical Museum recalls Hurley's colorful past. The museum is in the old county courthouse, complete with bell tower. In downtown Hurley, the museum is open Monday, Wednesday, Friday and Saturday year-round. Closed holidays. Fee.

Notable Events

• In August, Hurley hosts the annual Paavo Nurmi Marathon, named after one of the greatest distance runners in the 1920s, and among the older marathons in the country.

• Iron County Heritage Festival is held townwide in early August.

• Red Light Snowmobile Rally celebrates Hurley's rowdier past in mid-December.

What's Next

Before leaving the Hurley area, those heading west who have a bit of extra travel time will want to consider a side trip southward that takes an interesting and entertaining circular route to Ashland. If the southern routes sound interesting, see listing for Wisconsin's Lake Country.

The Circle Tour Route follows Highway 2 east through Ironwood into the Michigan Upper Peninsula or west to Ashland within 5 miles (8 kilometers) of Lake Superior's shoreline, which can be accessed by turning north at the village of Saxon.

Ino - Isle Royale

INO, WISCONSIN

Area Population 860

On Highway 2 in northern Wisconsin, you'll pass through the blink of a crossroad hamlet Ino, where you can jog south to visit the scenic Delta Lakes area. Hundreds of small lakes deep in the north woods are filled with fishing opportunities. This lovely forested and scenic area is well worth an hour side trip off Highway 2 south at Ino on County Highway E to County H, which angles northwest back to Highway 2 in Iron River. Several resorts do offer visitors a chance to stay in the Delta Lakes area.

The Moquah Barrens Wildlife Area lies about 5 miles (8 kilometers) north of Ino on Forest Road 236. Follow the Moquah Barrens Auto Tour route, using a guide prepared by Chequamegon National Forest personnel.

Ino, Wisconsin, regional map – page 30.

IRON MOUNTAIN, MICHIGAN

Population 8,525

Iron Mountain snuggles into a large bend of the Menominee River that forms the boundary between Michigan and Wisconsin. Like a mother hen with chicks, a number of smaller towns in both Wisconsin and Michigan surround Iron Mountain.

The city offers a good selection of lodging and dining and is interesting for the number of good museums and visitor sites.

You are well away from the shores of both Lake Superior and Lake Michigan at this point on Highway 2 in the southern Upper Peninsula. Nearby iron ore mines once fostered an abundant economy here, but that boom ended decades ago. Although the mines are long since depleted, many of the smallish communities you pass were mining locations where the families of employees lived, worked and did most of their day-to-day business.

Before leaving Iron Mountain, shoppers should check out the various antique, gift and specialty stores for that perfect gift from the north country.

Iron Mountain, Michigan, regional map – page 49.

DIRECTORY

Tourist Information – Dickinson Area Partnership/Chamber of Commerce, 906-774-2002; Upper Peninsula Travel and Recreation Association, 906-774-5480

Where to Stay
Best Western Executive Inn, 906-774-2040, 1518 S. Stephenson Ave., boasts the area's largest guest rooms, suites and deluxe continental breakfast. Pets welcome.
Comfort Inn, 906-774-5505, 866-774-5505, U.S. 2/141, 1555 N. Stephenson, is near to everything with free continental breakfast.

Pine Mountain Hotel and Resort, 906-774-2747, N3332 Pine Mountain Rd., is a full service lodging and resort a couple of miles from downtown and near golfing and skiing.

Where to Eat with a Local Flavor
Dobber's Pasties, 906-774-9323, 1400 S. Stephenson Ave., specializes in the U.P.'s favorite meal.
The Blind Duck Inn, 906-774-0037, Cowboy Lake, Kingsford, offers Mexican, Italian and American specialties with a lakeside view across from the airport.

What to See and Do

The city is home to the Festival of the Arts for eight weekends of music, drama, art and dance from mid-June to mid-August. Some of the events are sponsored by Pine Mountain Music Festival and scheduled at the Community Performing Arts Center on East B Street. The Dickinson County Council for the Arts is an umbrella for many artistic and performing events.

Pine Mountain Ski Jump is ranked as the "world's highest artificial ski jump" (as opposed to Copper Peak's claim as the highest artificial ski slide, where ski flying is performed).

Timber Stone Golf Course is ranked as a premier 18-hole challenge by *Michigan Golfer Magazine* and offers golf packages through a number of local lodging facilities. There are nine other golf courses of varying degrees of difficulty within easy commuting distance.

Notable Museums

The Cornish Pump Museum houses the largest mine pump ever built. Located west of U.S. 2 on Kent Street, it is open daily, Memorial Day to Labor Day, with reduced hours in spring and fall. Small entry fee.

Menominee Range Historical Foundation Museum has more than 100 exhibits that document mining and other aspects of early days in the area. Monday-Saturday, Memorial Day to Labor Day. Entry fee.

What's Next

Continue on your southern Upper Peninsula trip either to the west by departing on Highway 2/141, which enters Wisconsin for a brief sojourn just west of Iron Mountain and passes through two small towns, the interestingly named Spread Eagle and Florence, before re-entering Michigan in Iron County. If traveling east on Highway 2, you'll quickly spy Kingsford, Norway and Vulcan on your way to Escanaba and an encounter with the northern leg of the Lake Michigan Circle Tour route.

Just east of Iron Mountain on Highway 2, a roadside park with tables, water and toilets at Quinnesec gives a nice view of Fumee Falls.

If time allows, pause in Norway at the Jake Menghini Historical Museum, housed in a historic log cabin that once served as a carriage stopping point. Displaying artifacts from Jake's personal collection, as well as exhibits that change yearly, the museum is free of charge, although donations are accepted, Open Memorial Day through the Saturday prior to Columbus Day in October. Also at Norway, waterfalls aficionados can check out Piers Gorge, where white water tumbles over a 10-foot falls and roars wildly through canyon walls. It is among the fastest moving water-flows in the state.

In Vulcan, plan to take an underground train tour at the Iron Mountain Iron Mine, where you'll travel 2,600 feet (800 meters) through the drifts and stopes (tunnels and roomlike areas) of the mine.

IRON RIVER, MICHIGAN

Population 2,425

Another hen-and-chick community on Highway 2 in the southwestern Upper Peninsula along with the Iron Mountain area, Iron River is surrounded by the former mining locations of Gaastra, Caspian, Stambaugh and Mineral Hills. Here winter travelers will find wonderful terrain for snowmobilers, cross-country skiers and other outdoor cool weather recreationists.

Iron River, Michigan, regional map – page 49.

Accommodations range from camping to deluxe American-plan resorts.

What to See and Do

Downhill skiers will want to check out Ski Brule. A number of year-round resorts and lodging facilities are located on trails or within minutes of a good starting point for a day of outdoor fun.

Iron River is the home of the U.P. Championship Rodeo, which has been held each July since 1967.

West of Iron River is the Ottawa National Forest, a huge area of the western U.P. set aside for multiple-use. The

Ottawa Visitor Center in Watersmeet can provide full information on its 27 campgrounds, hiking and biking opportunities, canoeing, fishing, hunting or any other recreational activity within this wonderfully scenic area.

Southwest of Watersmeet, the 19,000-acre Sylvania Wilderness Area and Sylvania Recreation Area provide more opportunities for outdoor recreation. The Recreation Area was once the province of the rich and famous, but is now open to the public with a 48-unit campground with showers, beach and picnic areas and boat launches on Clark, Crooked and Long lakes.

Lac Vieux Desert, a large lake south of town, is nestled between Michigan's Ottawa Forest and Wisconsin's Nicolet National Forest. This headwaters of the Wisconsin River, home of the World Record Tiger Musky, is great for walleye, muskies, bass, northern pike and panfish.

Also in the area is the Cisco Chain of Lakes with 15 lakes interconnected to offer more than 270 miles (360 kilometers) of scenic shoreline and wonderful fishing.

Lac Vieux Desert Resort Casino is a couple of miles north of nearby Watersmeet on U.S. 45, offering full amenities and gaming fun.

Golfers will want to try Gateway Golf Club, a public 9-hole course with lounge and pro shop in the border town of Land O' Lakes, Wisconsin.

DIRECTORY

Tourist Information – Iron County Chamber of Commerce, 906-265-3822; Upper Peninsula Travel and Recreation Association, 906-774-5480

Where to Stay
AmericInn Motel and Suites, 906-265-9100, 800-634-3444, 40 E. Adams, offers 46 units right on Highway 2 with continental breakfast.

Notable Museums

Iron County Historical Museum in nearby Caspian features 20 pioneer buildings reflecting logging, mining, transportation and other aspects of settling the area. The home of Carrie Jacobs-Bond, who wrote "I Love You Truly" and "Perfect Day" is one of the exhibits. Nearby, the Lee LeBlanc Wildlife Art Gallery features more than 200 works. The oldest steel headframe (the structure sitting above the mine shaft to which the mine's lifting equipment was attached) in the Midwest towers over the site, which includes 100 major exhibits and the largest miniature logging exhibit in the world. Open June through September daily. Fee.

IRON RIVER, WISCONSIN

Area Population 2,085
Iron River calls itself the "Blueberry Capital of the World" and proves it annually with a festival the fourth weekend of July. Wild blueberries grow on low bushes along roadsides

and throughout the Chequamegon National Forest. For many, searching for the small sweet berries is as much fun as eating them.

DIRECTORY

Tourist Information – Iron River Area Chamber of Commerce, 715-372-8558, 800-345-0715

What to See and Do

Iron River's 9-hole par 37 Northern Pine Golf Course is located on Airport Road just west of town.

Hikers will find a 60-mile (96-kilometer) section of the North Country National Scenic Trail traversing the northern half of the Chequamegon National Forest. The trail crosses the Brunsweiler and Marengo rivers as well as several smaller, good quality trout streams. The trail begins at County Highway A near Lake Ruth, approximately 5 miles (8 kilometers) south of Iron River. For other hiking opportunities, check with local information centers.

Iron River, Wisconsin, regional map – page 30.

In downtown Iron River, the White Winter Winery provides a good sample of honey-based mead wines, which are made from the product of local bees. Visit the Iron River Co-op to stock up at one of the few remaining co-op grocery stores. Scandia offers gifts and other items from the Norse traditions.

Notable Museums

A block south of the junction of Main Street and Highway 2, the Western Bayfield County Museum has exhibits of early photos, artifacts from early life in the area, a collection of wedding gowns, family Bibles, one dating from the 1700s, and a complete collection of a pioneer newspaper. Fee.

Notable Events

• Sled Dog Races have teams of dogs and humans vying for honors in February.

• Summer Fest in June celebrates the full blush of the warm season.

• Blueberry Festival at the end of July gives everyone ample opportunity to sample this favorite regional fruit, while enjoying many other events.

What's Next

West from Iron River on Highway 2, the small outpost of Blueberry goes by in a blink, but slow down and pause to check out the antique shops, if they're open. Heading east on U.S. 2, you pass through the tiny hamlet of Ino on your way to Ashland. Two interesting sidetrips off Highway 2 at Iron River follow county highways. County A heads north and picks up Highway 13 at Port Wing for a tour of the western Bayfield Peninsula. South from Iron River, Highway H angles

southeasterly through the beautiful Delta Lakes region, then picks up County E northward to reconnect to Highway 2 at Ino.

IRONWOOD, MICHIGAN

Population 6,295

Ironwood was founded on iron mining. Called the Western Gateway City to the Upper Peninsula, Ironwood sports a Michigan Visitor Center on the U.S. 2 Circle Tour route at the state border with Wisconsin at the Montreal River, with tons of brochures, travel information and complete rest facilities.

What to See and Do

Downtown on Houk Street, a 52-foot (16-meter), 16,000-pound fiberglass statue of Hiawatha in formal headdress holds his peace pipe, extending a hand of welcome over the city and the great "Gitche Gumee." In an area near the statue are several mining artifacts, with an informational plaque describing them.

Ironwood Theatre (circa 1928) and the Gogebic Range Players offer community theater productions throughout the year. The theater also offers a schedule of varied entertainment. It is on the National Register of Historic Places.

Notable Museums

Old Depot Park Museum is located in the railroad depot in downtown Ironwood, operated by the Ironwood Area Historical Society. Open afternoons, Memorial Day through Labor Day. No fee, but donations welcome.

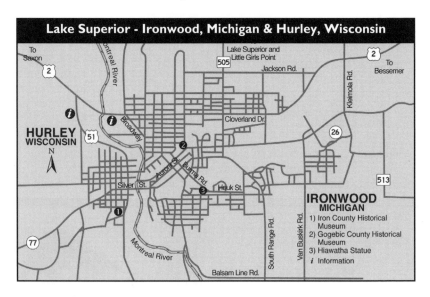

Lake Superior - Ironwood, Michigan & Hurley, Wisconsin

IRONWOOD
MICHIGAN
1) Iron County Historical Museum
2) Gogebic County Historical Museum
3) Hiawatha Statue
i Information

BIG SNOW COUNTRY, MICHIGAN

When it comes to snow, Big Snow Country in the western Upper Peninsula is well named. It annually receives 200 to 300 inches of the white stuff. For many, it means hours of shoveling. But for those seeking recreation, it means snowmobiling, skiing and other winter activities beyond expectations, with five major facilities concentrated between the Porcupine Mountains Ski Area to the northeast and Whitecap Mountains Ski Area southwest of Ironwood-Hurley, Wisconsin. Other major Big Snow Country resorts include Indianhead, Blackjack and Big Powderhorn, clustered near Bessemer. Nearby national and state forest areas also present many other winter recreational opportunities, from snowmobiling to cross-country skiing and snowshoeing.

DIRECTORY

Tourist Information – Western U.P. Convention and Visitors Bureau, **906-932-4850, 800-522-5657;** Ironwood Chamber of Commerce, **906-932-1122**

Summer is also a grand time in Big Snow Country. The natural wilderness conditions are a huge attraction. More than 900,000 acres of the Ottawa National Forest are spread through the area. Nearly 400,000 visitors annually touring the Ottawa by auto may sound busy, but it's not. Close to 600,000 others come to hike trails, hunt, canoe and fish its rivers and lakes and to enjoy other summer outdoor activities. More than 35 waterfalls are accessible by roads and woodland trails.

Notable Events

• Gogebic County Airport Fly-In in June gives non-pilots a chance to see neat airplanes and get to know the pilots.

• Upper Lakes Renaissance Faire in July is a fun event based on the middle ages.

• Festival Ironwood in July celebrates the heritage and history of the city.

• Gogebic County Fair is held in August at the fairgrounds in the western edge of the city.

• Jack Frost Festival of Lights Parade is the traditional kickoff of the holiday season in early December.

Campgrounds

There is camping and a playground at Curry Park on Highway 2 at the west edge of the city.

What's Next

Ironwood's twin city, across the state border of Wisconsin and Michigan, is Hurley, Wisconsin, (see separate listing)

DIRECTORY

Tourist Information – Ironwood
Tourism Council, 906-932-1000;
Ironwood Chamber of Commerce,
906-932-1122; Western U.P. Convention
and Visitor Bureau, 906-932-4850

Where to Stay
AmericInn Motel and Suites,
906-932-7200, 866-476-4796, 1117 E.
Cloverland, offers 49 units with whirlpools
and complimentary continental breakfast.
Super 8 Motel - Ironwood, 906-932-3395,
106 E. Cloverland Dr., is a good family
lodging.

Where to Eat
Don and G.G.'s Food and Spirits,
906-932-2312, 1300 E. Cloverland Dr., is
sure to have something to please.
Elk and Hound, 906-932-3742,
200 Country Club Rd., has a good menu,
two nice fireplaces and overlooks the
Country Club.
Joe's Pasty Shop, 906-932-4412,
116 W. Aurora St., has famously good
pasties.
Pizza King Joe, 906-932-0989,
400 Silver St., has homemade Italian fare.

Ironwood, Michigan,
regional map – page 28.

which is part of Big Snow Country, and just over the
Montreal River Bridge on Highway 2. If your route takes
your east, you'll follow U.S. 2 through Bessemer to
Wakefield, where you have the option of following the Lake
Superior Circle Route on Michigan 28 or continuing on
Highway 2 for a trip through the southern Upper Peninsula.

A more interesting and attractive route is to follow the
alternate Lake Superior Circle Tour sign located at Lake
Street, traveling 17 miles (27 kilometers) north of Ironwood
on County Road 505 to Little Girls Point, which was named
for an Ojibway girl who died there in the 1800s. It is also the
site of native burial grounds. A sweeping view of the lake and
surrounding shoreline can be seen from this elevated
viewpoint, which is in County Park and Campgrounds. Just
before the border on the Michigan side (5.5 measured miles
from the County Park at Little Girls Point), an unmarked
cutoff toward the lake affords a spectacular view of Superior
Falls on the Montreal River as it falls toward the lake.
Especially in the morning when the sun is right, this overlook
is ideal for pictures. A lower trail leads one-quarter mile to a
cliff overlooking Lake Superior. A rather steep trail takes
hikers to the river's mouth, but it's tough to climb back up.
Rated: difficult.

From here you can continue west on County Road 505,
which joins Wisconsin 122 near Saxon Harbor and picks up
Highway 2 at the town of Saxon, or you can backtrack to
Ironwood to continue east.

ISHPEMING, MICHIGAN

Population 6,685

In Ojibway, the name of the iron mining city Ishpeming means "on high ground" or "in heaven." This is the heart of the Marquette Iron Range, the only range in the Upper Peninsula still producing iron ore. Architecture reflects the days of mine captains and miners.

Ishpeming, Michigan, regional map – page 24.

What to See and Do

Tilden Iron Ore Mine offers tours each June through August, Tuesday-Saturday, leaving from the Marquette Chamber office at noon, and the Ishpeming-Negaunee Chamber office at 12:30 p.m. Advance reservations.

A cast-iron statue of a Native American man stands on an island at converging streets in the small downtown business district. Known locally as "Old Ish," the statue is a favorite of residents, keeping careful watch over the city since 1884.

Al Quaal Recreation Area in North Ishpeming offers year-round outdoor activities, with a 1,500-foot (460-meter) iced toboggan run, downhill and more than 18k of cross-country skiing, some lighted for night skiing or snowshoeing. Summer choices of tennis, hiking, swimming or canoeing on Teal Lake are offered.

Notable Museums

Ishpeming is the appropriate site for the U.S. National Ski Hall of Fame and Museum. This is where skiing in America was born. Miners from Scandinavia brought the sport along when they came to work the mines. Inductions are held annually. On U.S. 41 between Second and Third streets. Open Monday through Saturday year-round free of charge. This is also home to the Ishpeming-Negaunee Chamber of Commerce Information Center.

Iron Range Mining Heritage Theme Park is located in a former mine building on Euclid Street. Among many exhibits, a 2,660-pound flat slab of native copper standing 6 feet tall and 3 feet wide will catch your eye.

Where to Shop

Ishpeming-Negaunee offer virtually anything a shopper needs, from groceries, convenience items, gifts and souvenirs to gas and vehicle servicing. Nearby Marquette to the east is certain to be able to fill all needs.

In the Ishpeming downtown area, the historic Butler Theatre has been extensively renovated and now hosts antique dealers that each feature a distinct line of products. The interior of the 90-year-old Butler Theatre Antique Mall building replicates the art-deco wall flowers and retro floor of

DIRECTORY

Tourist Information – Ishpeming-Negaunee Chamber of Commerce, 906-486-4841, 888-578-6489

Where to Stay
Best Western Country Inn, 906-485-6345, 800-528-1234, 850-U.S. 41 W., offers 60 standard and king units, with a new RV park nearby.
Best Western Jasper Ridge Inn, 906-485-2378, 866-875-4312, 1000 River Pkwy., has 26 standard, king and suite units with continental breakfast.

Where to Eat
Country Kitchen, 906-485-1074, 850 U.S. Hwy. 41 W., offers all-day family dining and a separate bar/lounge.
Jasper Ridge Brewery, 906-485-6017, 1035 Country Lane, serves lunch and dinner with steak and pizza specialties and craft beers brewed on-site.

the original theater and the products will entice antique enthusiasts.

Da Yoopers Tourist Trap outside of Ishpeming will improve any frame of mind you may be in. Recording artists Da Yoopers are headquartered at You Guys Records in Ishpeming. Their satirical, bawdy hits include "Second Week of Deer Camp," "Rusty Chevrolet" and "Smelting U.S.A." Their gift shop and separate rock shop reflects their "different" outlook on life and questionable taste, but we love it.

Notable Events
• Noquemanon Cross-Country Ski Race in latter January challenges skiers in the area where American skiing was born.
• Pioneer Days in early July celebrates the history and heritage of this multi-ethnic area.
• Renaissance Festival in late July is a romp that celebrates fun in the Middle Ages.
• Ore to Shore Mountain Bike Epic in early August has pedallers vying for honors in awesome surroundings.

ISLE ROYALE NATIONAL PARK, MICHIGAN

Copper Harbor and Houghton, Michigan, and Grand Portage, Minnesota (see individual listings), are the three departure points to Isle Royale National Park, the largest island in Lake Superior. The *Isle Royale Queen III* leaves Copper Harbor daily with round trips to the island from mid-May to late-September. Reservations are required. The National Park Service operates the double-decked *Ranger III* from Houghton, departing on Tuesdays and Fridays and returning the following day.

Isle Royale National Park is 50 miles (75 kilometers) from Upper Michigan's Copper Country and 18 miles (29 kilometers) from the nearest point on the Minnesota shore. The island is about 45 miles long (68 kilometers) and 9 miles wide (14 kilometers), a land area of 210 square miles (544 square kilometers). It became a National Park in 1940.

Isle Royale is classified as a National Biosphere, so no pets are allowed because they may interfere with native wildlife. This is strictly enforced. There are no roads or cars on the island, but parking is available at embarkation points on the mainland.

Isle Royale National Park charges user fees. Children 12 and younger are free. Isle Royale can be a day trip, but plan to stay for at least a few days. Most people hike and camp. There are more than 160 miles of trails and many campgrounds. Sturdy hiking shoes and rain gear are a must for any trip to Isle Royale. And bring a camera. The island's population of moose, wolves, beaver, fox and other wildlife is sure to make your visit worthwhile. Trout fishing among Isle Royale's reefs will certainly yield some big ones.

Unless you intend to camp or are arriving in your own boat, you will need to stay in accommodations at Rock Harbor on the northeast side of Isle Royale. Rock Harbor Lodge also has a gift shop and marina store, with laundry and showers available, as well as fishing tackle, fishing charters, sightseeing tours, camping and hiking accessories from the concessionaire, Forever Resorts.

Lake Superior - Isle Royale National Park, Michigan

DIRECTORY

Tourist Information – Isle Royale National Park Headquarters, 906-482-0984; Isle Royale Natural History Association, 906-482-7860

Where to Stay
Rock Harbor Lodge, 906-337-4993 summer, 270-773-2191 winter, has the only lodging and dining on Isle Royale, offering 60 motel-type lodges and 20 housekeeping rooms with private baths. Open late May through early September. Check with park headquarters for campground information or reservations.

Boats up to 65 feet (20 meters) can be accommodated at the Rock Harbor Marina with 450 feet (140 meters) of dock space. Fuels, AC electrical, pump-out and fresh-water hookups are available. Also boat and canoe rentals by the day or week and fishing charters.

Windigo, located at the head of Washington Harbor at the southwestern end of Isle Royale, is the perfect starting point for camping and hiking tours of the island and offers trout fishing. There are no overnight facilities at Windigo, but campsites are available on Washington Creek. A grocery store has cold sandwiches, freeze-dried foods, canned goods and soft drinks. Fishing tackle, licenses, laundry and showers are available.

Royale Air Service offers flights from Houghton to Rock Harbor and Windigo by float plane.

Interpretive cruises and walks will take you to Lookout Louise, Daisy Farm, Rock Harbor Lighthouse and Edisen Fishery, Passage Island and Raspberry Island.

Isle Royale is a popular destination for scuba divers. Among the more noteworthy wrecks in this underwater preserve are the *America, Emperor, Cox, Kamloops, Algoma, Congdon* and *Monarch*. Superior Diver conducts dive excursions June through September, weather permitting. They operate out of Grand Portage, Minnesota. Information and books concerning the park are available through the Isle Royale Natural History Association, co-located at the park headquarters on the waterfront in Houghton.

Kakabeka Falls - Knife River

KAKABEKA FALLS, ONTARIO

Township Population 600

At Kakabeka Falls, 29 kilometers (18 miles) west of Thunder Bay on Highway 11/17, the most spectacular waterfall on the Circle Tour route attracts vast numbers of falls fanciers each year. Though small, the town has lodging and dining and businesses able to meet most travelers' needs.

Kakabeka Falls, Ontario, regional map – page 8.

Amethyst fanciers in the area will want to check the Kakabeka Falls Gift and Amethyst Shoppe, which features "blueberry amethyst" from a vein of the mineral bearing the deep purple coloring of the fruit. Try tubing on the Kaministiquia River at Stanley between Kakabeka Falls and Thunder Bay. River Rat Rentals will provide the tubes for a three-hour relaxing trip down the river.

DIRECTORY

Tourist Information – Park Information, 807-473-9231; Ontario Parks, 888-668-7275

At 39 meters (128 feet) high, Kakabeka Falls is called the "Niagara of the North." Within Kakabeka Falls Provincial Park, numerous viewing platforms surround the falls. The site is friendly to the physically challenged. Interpretative programs are offered at the park's visitor center during summer months. The park also contains some of the world's oldest fossils in the 2-billion-year-old rocks of this area. Camping is available mid-May to mid-September. Winter activities available include 13 kilometers of cross-country ski trails.

KNIFE RIVER, MINNESOTA

Population 260

You can easily identify when you cross the county line between St. Louis and Lake counties on Scenic North Shore Drive, since you'll pass beneath the bridge of the North Shore Scenic Railroad just before you enter or as you leave Knife River. The town's name comes from the Ojibway words *makomaani ziibing*, literally "Knife River," referring to sharp rocks in the riverbed.

A Bit of History

Settled in the 1880s by commercial fishermen, the town survived a few years on fish and farming, but from 1898 to 1919, a logging operation was active here and Knife River boomed. Alger Smith Lumber Company also operated a 100-mile logging railroad nearly to Grand Marais. Until 1929 the area was the scene of attempts to mine copper. None of the veins proved commercially viable.

Only a few fishermen continue the long tradition of catching and peddling fish from this rural community. It is still one of the north shore's most active sport fishing areas. The Knife River Marina is home to several dozen Lake Superior pleasure vessels and charter fishing operations.Many boats work full time out of the Knife River Marina to take fishing enthusiasts approximately one mile from shore in several different directions to try their luck at hooking onto a large lake trout, coho or chinook salmon and to view the shoreline from a waterborne perspective. Lake Superior deepens to more than 500 feet (166 meters) within a mile of shore, so it is no more than 15 minutes from the time the boat leaves the marina until customers can be fishing. The charter boats work from the Knife west to the French River and east as far as Two Harbors.

Fresh and smoked fish are available locally, as are good cheeses. If your appetite is more immediate, Emily's 1929 Eatery offers a nice menu and your favorite beverages in a setting that has been the town's social center since it opened in 1929 as a general store and post office. They also have rooms in a B&B style.

DIRECTORY

Tourist Information – Two Harbors Area Chamber of Commerce, 218-834-2600, 800-777-7384

Knife River, Minnesota, regional map – page 2.

Lac La Belle - Lutsen

LAC LA BELLE, MICHIGAN

Township Population 175

Although technically not on the Circle Tour route, we recommend taking wonderfully scenic South Shore Drive at Mohawk through Gay and Point Betsy to visit Lac La Belle. If you're driving U.S. 41 farther north on the Keweenaw Peninsula, turn east just north of Delaware for the 5-mile (8-kilometer) trip to Lac La Belle.

Lac La Belle, Michigan, regional map – page 24.

Nearby are the remains of an old stamp mill used to crush copper-bearing rock from nearby mines in the 1800s. It is here that the first electricity in Keweenaw County was used – to light the Lac La Belle stamp mill. This is a major bird migration flyway in April and May.

In the winter, the area is a favorite destination for skiers and snowmobilers and more than 200 inches of average snowfall per winter nearly guarantees excellent conditions for any type of outdoor winter activity.

What to See and Do

Lac La Belle is especially scenic in autumn, when the multicolored hillsides around the lake catch the sun and reflect in the water.

At Lac La Belle, stop at the easily accessible Haven Falls in Haven Park, with a drop of 38 feet (11.5 meters).

Near Lac La Belle, Mt. Bohemia has been developed into a major midwestern downhill ski facility that is billed as "the Rocky Mountains of the Midwest." Featuring a 900-foot vertical drop, Mt. Bohemia includes 42 runs of the longest and steepest expert terrain in the Midwest and a radical snowboard park. Slope difficulty ranges from intermediate to expert, but with no beginner hill. A resort offers lodging on site.

DIRECTORY

Tourist Information – Keweenaw Convention and Visitor Bureau, 906-337-4579, 800-338-7982

Where to Stay
Lac La Belle Lodge Resort, 906-289-4293, has lakeside accommodations and dining. Mount Bohemia, 906-289-4105, 6532 Lac La Belle Rd., offers limited trailside lodging.

Parks and Public Areas

Three miles beyond the village of Lac La Belle is Bete Grise (BAY-ta GREE), location of the breakwater and harbor entrance to Lac La Belle (the lake) through the Mendota Ship Canal. The old Mendota Lighthouse has been extensively restored and is privately owned.

Keystone Bay is part of the Keweenaw Underwater Preserve, a 103-square-mile area that protects the waters and shipwrecks around the Keweenaw Peninsula.

In December 1989, the U.S. Coast Guard cutter *Mesquite* went aground off Keweenaw Point. In July 1990, the 180-foot (55-meter) vessel was removed from the hazardous reefs, moved about 2 miles to the southeast of Keweenaw Point and then sunk in Keystone Bay in 80 to 120 feet (24-37 meters) of water. Today, the vessel is an underwater attraction, the perfect shipwreck for the curious scuba diver.

Other vessels in the Keweenaw Underwater Preserve include the *Langham* at Bete Grise, *Scotia* at Keweenaw Point, *Wasaga* at Copper Harbor, *City of St. Joe* at Little Grand Marais Harbor, *Traveller* at Eagle Harbor and the *Moreland* at Sawtooth Reef, Eagle River.

To depart Lac La Belle, travel either westerly five miles to pick up U.S. 2 or take South Shore Drive to rejoin Highway 41 at Mohawk.

DIRECTORY

Tourist Information – Western U.P. Convention and Visitor Bureau, 906-932-4850, 800-522-5657

Where to Stay
Gogebic Lodge, 906-842-3321, N9600 Hwy. 64, Marenisco, is a full service resort with modern lodging, camping and dining.
Walleye Lodge, 906-575-3557, 1497 W. M-28, Bergland 49910, is a popular summer and winter lodging.

LAKE GOGEBIC AND BERGLAND, MICHIGAN

Area Population 440

Bergland is at the junction of Michigan highways 28 and 64 in the western Upper Peninsula. The town sits on the north end of the nearly 14,000-acre Lake Gogebic, which provides year-round recreation. Lake Gogebic State Park borders its western shore. The lake sits about 1,300 feet (400 meters) above sea level. Above the lake, Gogebic Ridge Hiking Trail offers spectacular views. To the south is the Sylvania Recreation Area of Ottawa National Forest and there are a number of resorts, lodgings and campgrounds on the lake.

LAKE MICHIGAMME, MICHIGAN

Population 290

The M-28/U.S. Route 41 Circle Route follows the forested shoreline of Lake Michigamme (Mich-i-GAW-mee), with blue water and pristine islands visible from vistas and through the trees. Van Riper State Park is a 1,044-acre park system. The headquarters, off U.S. 41 and M-28 at Lake Michigamme's eastern end, has modern and rustic campgrounds, excellent beach facilities, picnic area, a boat launch site and information on rental of a limited number of cabins. One-half mile west on the Peshekee River is a rustic campground.

Lake Michigamme, Michigan, regional map – page 24.

The quaint village of Michigamme, located on the west end of the lake, offers diverse and unique shopping with casual dining. For lodging in the area, contact Three Lakes Motel (906-323-6101).

What's Next

About 5 miles (8 kilometers) east of the M-28/U.S. 41 junction at Tioga Creek at a fork in the road, Tioga Park is scenic, with a low waterfall, bridge, picnic tables and a pathway with signage explaining the logging history of this early town and sawmill site. By continuing east, you head for Ishpeming, Negaunee and Marquette.

West of Michigamme is the intersection of U.S. 41 and M-28. If you wish to enter the Keweenaw Peninsula, turn north on Route 41. This will take you to the lakeshore and an area of Lake Superior that is a playland unto itself, full of enticing history and year-round activities. This is also the easterly boundary of the Western Upper Peninsula Heritage Trails network to more than 70 historic sites, described in a guide available at Western Upper Peninsula infocenters.

By proceeding west on M-28, visitors can bypass the Keweenaw on a direct route into the Western Upper Peninsula and Big Snow Country through Bruce Crossing. This section of the Circle Tour takes you past farms and rolling hills that give way to forested lands. In Big Snow Country, any time of year is full of grandeur and excitement, but more on that later.

LAKE NIPIGON, ONTARIO

From the city of Nipigon on Lake Helen, Trans Canada Highway 11 heads northeastward toward Lake Nipigon, which at 100-by-70 kilometers (62-by-43 miles) is the largest inland lake entirely within Ontario. This northeast-bound route is called the Frontier Trail.

The trip opens the north to thousands of anglers, hunters and other outdoor enthusiasts who seek vast wild areas in wonderful scenery to pursue their adventures. This area is also the watershed that provides the greatest source of flow into the big lake via the Longlac Water

DIRECTORY

Tourist Information – North of Superior Tourism Association, 807-887-3333, 800-265-3951

Where to Stay
Royal Windsor Lodge, 807-887-5291, P.O. Box 276, Nipigon, has housekeeping cabins and RV sites on Lake Nipigon's Orient Bay, with access to great fishing and hunting and all the supplies needed for the perfect outdoor adventure.

Lake Nipigon, Ontario, regional map – page 45.

Diversion and the Nipigon River. For beachcombers, many of the Lake Nipigon beaches consist of black sand that has been eroded from Lake Nipigon's basaltic cliffs and gathered by wave action on the shorelines. Some contain good rockhounding possibilities.

The southeast corner of Lake Nipigon at Orient Bay has many waterfalls that freeze in the winter and attract hearty visitors interested in climbing the icy precipices. It's a sport practiced in few other areas of the world and involves using mountaineering equipment to scale the icy surfaces.

For a map of the Frontier Trail route and a brief description, see separate listing under Recommended Drives.

LAKE LINDEN, MICHIGAN

Population 1,080

Lake Linden, Michigan, regional map – page 24.

At Lake Linden north of Houghton/Hancock on M-26, stop at Lindell's Chocolate Shop, an old-fashioned ice cream parlor, for a trip into the past. For campers, the Lake Linden Village Park and Recreation Area is located on Torch Lake, with a picnic area, tennis, horseshoe and basketball courts. It is open Memorial Day through September.

Houghton County Historical Society's Museum Park is a 15-acre historic mill site of the Calumet and Hecla Copper Company, including the historic red schoolhouse, church and museum building, the Copper Country Railroad Heritage Center and the Lake Linden & Torch Lake Railroad, 3-foot gauge railroad located on the grounds. Open daily mid-June through September. Fee. The Copperland Arts and Crafts Shop is next to the museum, specializing in handcrafted copper gifts and artworks.

DIRECTORY

**Tourist Information – **Keeweenaw Convention and Visitors Bureau, 906-337-4579, 800-338-7982

LAKE SUPERIOR PROVINCIAL PARK, ONTARIO

Lake Superior Provincial Park, Ontario, regional map – page 18.

South of Wawa, Ontario, Trans Canada Highway 17 passes through Lake Superior Provincial Park, getting travelers to a number of points of adventure and interest. Established on the same day in 1944 that Sibley Provincial Park (now Sleeping Giant Provincial Park near Thunder Bay) was set aside, the park preserves 1,540 square kilometers (602 square miles) of wild country and a large section of the eastern Lake Superior shoreline.

The sights and activities in this park are worth a full day or more. The park's flora and fauna are mixes of southern and northern species. Moose with big racks are common. Other animals such as wolves, bears and woodland caribou have been reintroduced. There is a good variety of birds, too.

What to See and Do

There are 11 hiking trails, walking trails to waterfalls and scenic lookouts and eight canoe routes ranging from several hours to several days in length, which access secluded places made even more beautiful by the extra effort required to reach them. The most rugged hiking trail is the Lake Superior Coastal Trail, which follows 55 kilometers (33 miles) of the park's shoreline and takes almost a week to hike in its entirety. Rated: difficult.

The park offers interpretive programs in July and August and camping, fishing, hunting, boating and picnicking on the shore of Lake Superior. Canoe rentals are available at all campgrounds during peak summer months.

Passing through the park, be sure to stop and put your feet in Lake Superior at the various bays along the way. Old Woman Bay on the northern end of the park offers excellent photo opportunities at an interesting picnic area. The Nokomis Hiking Trail is adjacent.

Pinquisibi Trail passes several waterfalls on the Sand River. If you're a camera enthusiast, you're sure to come away with fine memory photos.

Once Highway 17 returns to the shore of Lake Superior, a stop at Katherine Cove is an absolute must. Some of the most unusual rock striations extend from the land into the crystal-clear waters of the lake, a guaranteed breathtaker for any photo album. The clean sand beach will captivate you. There's a picnic area and easy hiking around the cove.

Although the pictographs on Agawa Rock are a highlight of the Lake Superior Circle Tour at Lake Superior Provincial Park on the eastern shoreline, they are not easy to visit. In fact, visitors are advised to avoid attempting a visit if weather is inclement, since the path can be slippery and treacherous. The current paintings are believed to be about 100-150 years old.

Although due to the natural formation they are unfortunately not handicapped or easily accessible for many visitors, the pictographs at Agawa Rock are the park's high point. You descend to the water's edge via a rugged 400-meter (one-quarter-mile) trail, spectacular in its own right. On a cliff face directly on Lake Superior's shore, the extensive native paintings include canoes, caribou, horse and rider, and *Michipeshu*, the Horned Lynx spirit of the lake. These pictographs can be viewed when the lake is calm. *Extreme caution* (we can't stress it enough) is necessary when visiting the site. The barriers that used to protect you are no longer in place. Do not proceed beyond the trail, as the rocks and ledge are slippery and waves are unpredictable and dangerous. Native people may have painted at this site for as long as 2,000 years, yet the paintings that remain visible today are likely only 150 to 400 years old.

DIRECTORY

Tourist Information – Lake Superior Provincial Park Headquarters, 705-856-2284

A beautiful new visitor center was opened at Agawa Bay Campground about midway between Wawa and Sault Ste. Marie in 2004. A must stop for families, it offers themed multi-media exhibits featuring "The Power of the Lake" and a wealth of information on all aspects of the park. The audio-visual displays include models that capture the era of logging, local shipwrecks and disasters, bushplane history, commercial fishing, works of the Group of Seven artists, stories of voyageurs and early settlers, Hudson's Bay Company, sculptures, art of pictographs and an enlargement of the Lake Superior map that was developed by *Lake Superior Magazine*.

Campgrounds

There are 274 camping sites at the three campgrounds in the park: Rabbit Blanket Lake Campgrounds, Agawa Bay Campground and Crescent Lake Campground. Rabbit Blanket Lake Campgrounds at the north end of the park has flush toilets, showers and laundry facilities and is open late May to early October.

On the south end of Lake Superior Provincial Park, Agawa Bay Campgrounds is the largest of the three campgrounds with modern rest-rooms, showers, laundry facilities, the new park Visitor Center and is open late May to early September, and Crescent Lake Campground, more primitive and open late June to early September.

L'ANSE, MICHIGAN

Population 2,110

L'Anse (Lahnze) was named from the French word meaning "bay." It lies at the head of Keweenaw Bay on Lake Superior.

The reservation of the Keweenaw Bay Band of Chippewa is located here and the Village by the Bay Marina and park is a highlight of the waterfront. Many years of planning and work resulted in revitalization of the L'Anse waterfront with new marina and park facilities, a pavilion and playground, making the city accessible to waterborne visitors. Tie-ups for eight to 10 boats. Another waterfront attraction is Indian Country Sports store, with a 44-foot working lighthouse that shines a welcoming "aid to navigation" beam to fishermen and other boaters up to 5 miles away in Keweenaw Bay.

In L'Anse, Curwood Park has picnic tables and playgrounds. Also historical displays, including L'Anse's first post office.

The Huron Mountains are to the northeast, remote and mysterious. Among the peaks are Mount Arvon and Mount Curwood. For many years, Curwood was recognized as the highest point in Michigan, but a 1982 U.S. Geological Survey found that Mt. Arvon measured 1,979.28 feet above sea level, while Curwood measured only 1,978.24, a bit less than a foot lower. The Visitor Information Center has information for those wishing to visit Mt. Arvon. It entails about a half-mile walk from a parking lot to the summit, from which there is only a limited view, but qualifies hikers for the Highpointers' Club for those reaching the highest peak in each state. The Info Center will also be able to direct you to a viewpoint off Golf Course Road for a great vista of the area and the bay beyond.

L'Anse, Michigan, regional map – page 24.

An interesting side trip is to Pequaming. (see separate listing.)

DIRECTORY

Tourist Information – Baraga County Tourism and Recreation Association, 907-524-7444, 800-743-4908

Where to Stay
Hilltop Motel, 906-524-6321, U.S. Hwy. 41, features a nice panorama of town and Keweenaw Bay.
L'Anse Motel & Suites, 906-524-7820, U.S. Hwy. 61, offers nice amenities and nearby dining.

Where to Eat with a Local Flavor
Hilltop Restaurant, 906-524-7858, U.S. Hwy. 61, offers all-day dining and is legendary for it's sweet rolls and pastry.

LARSMONT, MINNESOTA

Population 280

A few miles between Two Harbors and Knife River on the North Shore Scenic Drive is Larsmont, once important in the fishing and timber industries. Larsmont's Little Red Schoolhouse, which is on the Register of Historic Places, is used as a community building. The Larsmont area is now popular for its cabin resorts and private campgrounds right on the lake.

Larsmont, Minnesota, regional map – page 2.

Just before you get to Two Harbors, you pass the traditional starting line for Grandma's Marathon. More than 6,900 runners cue up each June to make the 26.2-mile (42-kilometer) run that follows the scenic north shore to Canal Park in Duluth.

171

Among the top running events in the nation, the race also features several related shorter races on the same weekend. Nearby is the starting line for the NorthShore Inline Marathon, the third-largest inline race in the world, held in September.

Near these two start lines on the expressway is Adventure Mall, a large antique store.

DIRECTORY

Tourist Information – Keweenaw Convention and Visitors Bureau, 906-337-4579, 800-338-7982

Where to Stay
Laurium Manor Inn, 906-337-2549, 420 Tamarack, offers charming B&B amenities in the mansion of a copper baron.

Where to Eat with a Local Flavor
Toni's Country Kitchen, 906-337-0611, 79 Third St., offers all-day family dining with an emphasis on Cornish pasties and baked goods.

Laurium, Michigan, regional map – page 24.

LAURIUM, MICHIGAN
Population 2,125

Laurium was an active, booming copper capital when Copper Country produced the red ore. It was the home of George Gipp, the original "Gipper" football star of Notre Dame immortalized in a performance by Ronald Reagan in a movie with a coach's famous pleas to his team to "Win one for the Gipper." A memorial to the Gipper stands along the highway. He is buried in the town's cemetery and the George Gipp Recreation Area commemorates his athletic prowess.

Self-guided walking tours of the town of Laurium are available. Most homes on the tour were built in the early 1900s. There are also maps available for a self-guided walking tour of the Calumet and Hecla Industrial Core. On the tour, Laurium Manor Inn, one of the largest mansions in the western Upper Peninsula, especially offers a glimpse of the wealth in the Copper Country at the turn of the century.

LES CHENEAUX ISLANDS, MICHIGAN
From the very eastern tip of Michigan's Upper Peninsula at De Tour, M-134 takes us to Cedarville and Hessel in the Les Cheneaux Islands area in the southern U.P. There are 36 islands in the group, with marinas, beaches and waterfront walks to delight the visitor. Visit the Les Cheneaux Historical Museum for insight into the lake-oriented culture of the region. On the second Saturday in August, attend the Antique Boat Show, Art Festival and Regatta in Hessel. Cedarville's annual Les Cheneaux Snowfest in February is also famed for its festive nature. Golfers will want to try out Hessel Ridge Golf Course. From here, we head for a junction with I-75 to visit St. Ignace, Mackinac Island (see separate listing) and the Mackinac Bridge, described in the St. Ignace listing. If you plan to continue your explorations along the south part of the Upper Peninsula, take U.S. Highway 2 from St. Ignace toward Wakefield in the western U.P. If this is your choice, you'll be

traveling the northern leg of the Lake Michigan Circle Tour route, with many interesting places to poke around.

LITTLE MARAIS-
TACONITE HARBOR, MINNESOTA

On the Minnesota Circle Route along Highway 61, the county line between Lake and Cook counties intersects the Lake Superior shore at Morris Point near the Caribou River, where prehistoric lake beaches can be seen near the highway.

Little Marais, Minnesota, regional map – page 2.

This section of Highway 61 is one of spectacular scenery. The area was settled by Scandinavian fishermen drawn by the craggy beauty so like their homeland fjords. The communities along the way – Schroeder, Tofte, Lutsen, Grand Marais and Hovland – all retain some of this fishing village charm. Net drying reels, double-ended dories and fish sheds with their front doors opening into the lake can still be seen in many of the rocky inlets.

One such inlet, Sugarloaf Cove, once served as an important timber rafting site and has subsequently been acquired by the Sugarloaf Interpretive Center Association, which has expended a good deal of energy and investment in restoring natural features and construction of an interpretative center on the site. The center is open weekends from May through September and a hiking/snowshoe trail is signed for self-guided tours. Guided tours with specific topics commence at the center on the second Saturday of each month. Watch for the sign just past milepost 73 on the lake side of the highway.

Where to Shop

Eagle's Nest Gifts offers a nice stop to pick out a memorable gift item.

Spirit of Gitche Gumee features a gourmet coffee bar, a bed-and-breakfast inn and a gift store that carries a wide variety of locally produced gifts, art and craftwork, specializing in north shore cedar and other wood items.

DIRECTORY

Tourist Information – Two Harbors Area Chamber of Commerce, 218-834-2600, 800-777-7384; Lutsen-Tofte Tourism Association, 218-663-7804, 888-616-6784

Where to Stay
Fenstad's Resort, 218-226-4724, 6572 Hwy. 61, has lakeshore cabins with nice lake access and a boat ramp. Stone Hearth Inn, 218-226-3020, 6598 Lakeside Estates Rd., is a great B&B experience in a historic pioneer building.

Where to Eat with a Local Flavor
Satellite's Country Inn, 218-663-7574, Schroeder, offers local fish and homemade pies amidst artifacts of the area.

Fish Out of Water spotlights wood-crafted Scandinavian items, but also has many other lines of arts and crafts available. There's bound to be something that appeals to you. With flags and a large area for parking, you can't miss it.

What's Next

Traveling northeasterly on Highway 61 brings you to Schroeder, where the former LTV Steel Mining Company facilities at Taconite Harbor remain a visible part of this stretch of lakeshore. Minnesota Power now operates the large electric generating plant. The future of the harbor and railroad facilities has not been announced, although Cleveland Cliffs acquired them at the time the power plant was sold. A state harbor of refuge for boaters is now complete at the site.

Traveling southwest on Highway 61 from Little Marais, you'll soon come to Silver Bay on the way to Duluth.

LUTSEN, MINNESOTA

Area Population 250

Lutsen, Minnesota, regional map – page 8.

At Lutsen stands a year-round recreational complex built in 1894 by C.A.A. Nelson, a commercial fisherman who became Minnesota's "Pioneer in Pleasure." Lutsen Resort and Sea Villas was the north shore's first resort. Designed by renowned architect Edwin Lundie, the current lodge is classic "north shore," but totally modern.

What to See and Do

The area's predominant claim to fame is winter activities, including excellent downhill and cross-country skiing. Once the home of former Olympic skier Cindy Nelson, the area is a part of the extensive North Shore Trail System. Lutsen is the perfect point to start your winter trail exploration. All-season trail maps, with information on cross-country skiing and snowmobiling, canoeing, camping, hiking, mountain biking and fall color touring, are available along the shore.

In addition to the 90 downhill runs for which Lutsen Mountains ski resort is famous, a summer attraction at Lutsen Mountains is the Alpine Slide, an iceless sled track that winds down Eagle Mountain (this one a mere 1,660 feet/415 meters high). There are tram rides across from mountain to mountain that are a must for fall color seekers. If you like mountain biking, Lutsen Mountains offers nearly 50 miles (75 kilometers) of marked bike trails in its Mountain Bike Park.

The scenic Caribou Trail runs north inland from Lutsen to Brule Lake. The road is 20 miles (32 kilometers) long. Also in this area is the North Shore Mountain Ski Trail, a 130-mile (200-kilometer) groomed cross-country system from

DIRECTORY

Tourist Information – Lutsen-Tofte Tourism Association, 218-663-7804, 888-616-6784

Where to Stay
Lutsen Resort and Sea Villas, 218-663-7212, Hwy. 61, offers a wide range of lodging choices with many amenities.
The Mountain Inn at Lutsen, 218-663-7244, 800-686-4669, provides a range of accommodations with whirlpool, sauna and recreation packages.

Caribou Highlands Lodge, 218-663-7241, 13 Bridge Run Rd., offers lodge rooms, condominiums and townhomes, with good dining and spectacular views.

Where to Eat with a Local Flavor
Lutsen Resort Dining Room, 218-663-7212, Hwy. 61, has great fish and other entrees with the perfect view of Lake Superior.

Temperance River to Bally Creek north of Cascade River State Park near Grand Marais, much of which is right on the Lake Superior shore. Maintained by Solbakken Resort, Cascade River State Park and Cascade Lodge and Restaurant, information is available at area resorts and the North Shore Commercial Fishing Museum in Tofte.

What's Next

Traveling northeast on Highway 61 takes you to Grand Marais. Southwesterly points the visitor toward Silver Bay, Two Harbors and Duluth.

Cascade River State Park

Cascade River State Park is a lakeside park with 10 streams flowing lakeward through it. Overlooking Lake Superior, Cascade Lodge is privately owned and a history lesson in itself, with lodging, food and access to miles of ski trails. Most accessible of the streams is Cascade River, where the water runs a series of rapids on its descent to the lake. Hiking trails access most of the other streams as well. The largest herd of deer in Minnesota winters at Deer Yard Lake within the park's borders. (see separate listing.)

Mackinac Island - Munising

MACKINAC ISLAND, MICHIGAN

Population 460

A short ferry ride from St. Ignace in Michigan's southeastern Upper Peninsula takes you to world renowned Mackinac Island. Time all but stands still on this 3.5-mile-long (5.6-kilometer) island. Automobiles are banned. Transportation is by bicycle, horseback and horsedrawn carriages, which clop past shops, hotels, museums and Victorian mansions. Highlights include a lilac festival in June. Most of the island is a state park, with Fort Mackinac offering exhibits and demonstrations of blacksmithing, cooking and spinning – a living-history museum with interpreters on site. The ancient muskets and cannon are fired with regularity.

Golfers will want to challenge the 1898-era Wawashkamo Golf Club links on the island, with beautiful scenery punctuating the distinction of being Michigan's oldest continuously played 9-hole course. It is also listed as a state and national historic site.

Food is available in many gourmet restaurants and also in the Fort Tea Room overlooking the Straits of Mackinac.

While on the island, you can take narrated carriage tours, visit fudge and souvenir shops and enjoy the finest of hotels – the Grand Hotel. The 286-room hotel has the world's longest porch (880 feet). Reservations are a must, and there's a fee to simply enter the grounds.

After your visit, another ferry ride gets you back to your car to continue your Circle Tour by whatever route you choose. Return to the Lake Superior Circle Tour by traveling I-75 north from St. Ignace toward Sault Ste. Marie. For a trip along Lake Michigan's northern Circle Route, take Highway 2 west from St. Ignace. A number of highways travel north from Highway 2 to allow you to rejoin the Lake Superior Circle Tour on M-28 wherever you choose.

DIRECTORY

Tourist Information – Mackinac Island Tourism Bureau, 906-847-6418, 800-454-5227

MADELINE ISLAND, WISCONSIN
Population 180

Historic Madeline Island is the only one of the 22 Apostle Islands not in Apostle Islands National Lakeshore. The island is 14 miles long (22.5 kilometers) and 3 miles wide (5 kilometers). It is the only island with commercial development. It has sandy beaches, wooded trails, good fishing and sailing and breathtaking views no matter which way you turn. Plus outstanding food and shopping opportunities. The village of La Pointe is the primary developed area of the island. (See separate listing).

You can reach the island via a ride on one of the car ferries that carry passengers across 2.5 miles (4 kilometers) of Lake Superior to the island. The Madeline Island Ferry Line offers regular service between Bayfield and La Pointe on one of four boats, *Madeline, Nichevo, Island Queen,* or the latest and largest addition to the fleet, the *Bayfield*. Take your vehicle or bicycle, or simply walk on board. There are more than two dozen 20-minute round trips daily between late June and Labor Day.

During the winter after freeze-up, residents drive back and forth between the island and mainland on the thick ice. In the winter, an ice road freezes and is plowed between Bayfield and La Pointe which has an official highway designation and is marked by recycled Christmas trees. In the season between ice formation and break-up, a windsled transports passengers.

For pilots, Madeline Island has an uncontrolled, lighted 3,000-foot (915-meter) paved runway, Madeline Island Airstrip, 1.5 miles (2.5 kilometers) east of La Pointe.

What to See and Do
The 18-hole Madeline Island Golf Course was designed by Robert Trent Jones and offers breathtaking lake views, pine forests and the perfect challenge to any golfer. Sometimes dubbed "the Saint Andrews of the North."

Snow Ryder Dogsled Adventures organizes various adventure packages that teach mushing and offer visitors outdoor excitement as they mush a dog team around the island, on the lake ice and areas of the National Lakeshore. Check with Island Inn for details (715-747-2000).

A two-hour Madeline Island Bus Tour of sites is available twice daily from the end of June to early September, offering not only a narrated tour, but music, with a stop at Grants Point for a hike at Big Bay State Park, which also has a nice campground. Located a half block from the island ferry landing.

Many visitors arrive in their own boats and Madeline Island Yacht Club offers full service and transient dockage, with a launch ramp, fuel, pumpouts and a complete ship's store. Sail and power bare-boat or captained charter rentals

Getting There By Boat

Lying a tantalizing 2.5 miles (4 kilometers) across open water from Bayfield, La Pointe and Madeline Island is a magnet that seems to demand the attention of visitors. For those who arrive in their own boats, getting to the island is a matter of less than a half-hour trip. For those without a boat, the crossing can be made on one of the ferries operated by Madeline Island Ferry from docks in Bayfield and La Pointe. You simply walk, bike or drive your car aboard, relax and enjoy the scenery. More than 2 dozen crossings are made per day in the busy summer season. In winter, an ice road is maintained after freeze-up, with a wind sled providing service when ice conditions warrant.

There is a lighted, paved, uncontrolled air strip for visitors arriving by air. It's located 1.5 miles east of La Pointe. See separate listing.

3

177

DIRECTORY

Tourist Information – Madeline Island Chamber of Commerce, 715-747-2801, 888-475-3386; Bayfield County Tourism, 800-472-6338

Where to Stay
Inn on Madeline Island, 715-747-6315, offers excellent accommodations with a pool and manages numerous other island rental properties.
Madeline Island Motel, 715-747-3000, is a two-story, 11-unit facility with an 18-hole miniature golf course and game room.

Woods Manor, 715-747-3102, is a bed-and-breakfast inn that can handle groups up to 10 people.

Where to Eat with a Local Flavor
Ella's Island Cafe, 715-747-2400, a favorite of locals, serves breakfast and lunch.
Lotta's Lakeside Cafe, 715-747-2033, in Lakeview Place features bistro-style dining.
Tom's Burned Down Cafe, 715-747-6100, is a unique island experience, with good beer, live music and entertainment.

Madeline Island, Wisconsin, regional map – page 30.

are available at Apostle Islands Yacht Charters at the marina. It is in easy walking distance of all La Pointe attractions.

From early June to late July, the island is a magnet for musicians and budding performers, as Madeline Island Music Camp attracts students and master musicians who not only study, but perform regular concerts open to the public.

A map showing attractions and service facilities is available at the Chamber office. Points of interest include St. Joseph's Catholic Church, built on the site of Bishop Frederic Baraga's third church; the La Pointe Post Office, which was part of the Old Mission built by Protestant missionaries in 1834; and the burial site of O-Shaka, son of Chief Buffalo and a chief speaker of the Ojibway on Lake Superior.

For those who choose not to walk, mopeds or bicycles in a variety of styles can be rented from Motion to Go, which has a gift shop. If you choose this mode of travel, be aware that some roads are narrow, although most are paved, mainly flat and easy to ride. Blacktop shoulders on the Big Bay road make for safer navigation.

Notable Museums

Discover La Pointe's varied history at the Madeline Island Historical Museum, with a wonderful 20-minute historical, musical video by Warren Nelson of Lake Superior Big Top Chautauqua. The Wisconsin Historical Society operates this museum that is located on the site of an early American Fur Company post, displaying lumbering, fur trading and fishing artifacts spanning three centuries that will fascinate visitors of all ages. The important role of the Native Americans, who have influenced the development of this largest of the Apostle Islands, is also told. The museum houses the Capser Center. Fee charged. Open June through early October.

A block east of the Madeline Island Museum is the Lake View Schoolhouse, a restored one-room school, and the Madeline Island Historic Preservation Association Heritage Center. Open May through October on a limited schedule.

Parks and Public Areas

Drive or bike across Madeline Island and enjoy a day or an overnight at Big Bay State Park. Contact the Wisconsin Department of Natural Resources for campground openings during the busy tourist season in July and August. Park sticker is required. The park provides a 5-mile (8-kilometer) loop for cross-country skiers in the winter.

Big Bay Town Park, operated by the town of La Pointe, has 44 rustic campsites, four with electricity, and a picnic area. Overlooking a lagoon, a wooden walking bridge leads to a sandy beach.

Ojibwa Memorial Park is located next to the marina in La Pointe. The most famous people buried in the ancient Indian burial grounds are Ojibway Chief Buffalo and fur trader Michel Cadotte.

Where to Shop

Visitors searching for unique treasures of the island should stop at Island Thyme, near the ferry landing. Waterfront Gallery & Gifts displays works by many local artists and has a unique selection of gifts. Woods Hall Craft Shop is three blocks from the landing with hand-woven rugs, original designs, jewelry, pottery and more. Other "gifty" stops include Essential Elements, La Pointe Provisions, the Inn's Rendezvous Gift Shop or the Ships Store at the Marina. Weavers, knitters and others who are into needle arts will want to check out the many supplies and items at Mad Island Weavers.

MANISTIQUE, MICHIGAN

Population 3,580

Traveling Highway 2 in Michigan's southern Upper Peninsula, the shoreline city of Manistique offers a good selection of lodging facilities, including several state or private campgrounds, motels, resorts and bed-and-breakfast inns, and dining for whatever your taste may be. The city's commercial harbor is now mainly used by fishing boats, but provides full amenities for recreational boaters.

Manistique, Michigan, regional map – page 49.

What to See and Do

The historic "Siphon Bridge" on Old Highway 2 was once

DIRECTORY

Tourist Information – Schoolcraft County Chamber of Commerce, 906-341-5010; Manistique Area Tourist Council, 800-342-4282

Where to Stay
Manistique Kewadin Inn, 906-341-6911, 800-539-2346, is a full service lodging, dining and camping facility with shuttle service to the casino.

a subject of Ripley's "Believe it or Not," being the only roadway in the world that was 4 feet below water and partially supported by the water under it. Different use of the river's water by the paper mill makes it no longer true, but motorists thus looked out nearly eye level from their car windows at the surface of the water. Today, the bridge is still in place and a 73-year-old historic water tower and museum are adjacent to it.

Near the downtown, the Lakeshore Boardwalk is a good place for a stroll.

Other sites in the general area worth considering are Thompson Fish Hatchery, Wyman Forest Nursery, the iron furnace relics at the ghost town of Fayette on the Garden Peninsula and the southern entry to the Seney National Wildlife Refuge, which we discuss in a separate listing.

What's Next

To continue your Circle Tour of the southern Upper Peninsula, continue on Highway 2. To the east, you're heading for St. Ignace and the Mackinac Bridge through a string of smallish towns. To the west, you'll also pass through several small towns to Rapid River, where U.S. 2/41 bends southward for Gladstone and Escanaba.

MARATHON AND HEMLO, ONTARIO

Population 4,450

Marathon, Ontario, regional map – page 14.

Marathon is a dual-industry town on the lakeshore at the end of Peninsula Road (Highway 626), 5 kilometers (3 miles) from Trans Canada Highway 17 and the Marathon Airport. An Information Centre and Scenic Lookout are located on Highway 17 another 5 kilometers (3 miles) beyond the intersection to Marathon. The facility is used in the winter as the Superior Slopes Ski Hill, operated by the township. Wintertime attracts snowmobile enthusiasts by the thousands, since the hills around Marathon are ideal for the sport.

Hemlo, about 20 kilometers (12 miles) inland on Highway 17 primarily owes its existence to gold mining in the immediate vicinity. Three active mines are 2 kilometers (1.5 miles) beyond the intersection of highways 17 and 614. These are the largest gold mines in the country. Two of them, David Bell Mine and Williams Mine, make Marathon their headquarters. The third, Golden Giant Mine, is located in Hemlo. If you visit, you'll find yourself driving down the Yellow Brick Road – really!

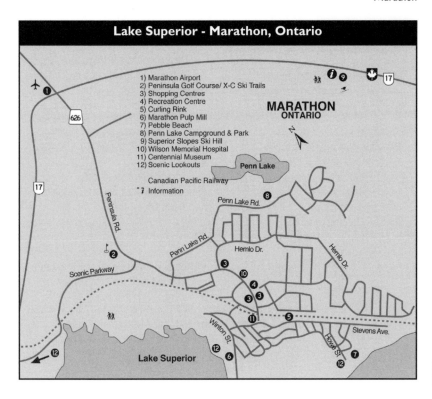

Lake Superior - Marathon, Ontario

1) Marathon Airport
2) Peninsula Golf Course/ X-C Ski Trails
3) Shopping Centres
4) Recreation Centre
5) Curling Rink
6) Marathon Pulp Mill
7) Pebble Beach
8) Penn Lake Campground & Park
9) Superior Slopes Ski Hill
10) Wilson Memorial Hospital
11) Centennial Museum
12) Scenic Lookouts

Canadian Pacific Railway

? Information

MARATHON
ONTARIO

Penn Lake

Penn Lake Rd.

Peninsula Rd.

Hemlo Dr.

Hemlo Dr.

Scenic Parkway

Winton St.

Stevens Ave.

Howe St.

Lake Superior

A Bit of History

Rail building and lumbering fueled a city of 12,000 people in the last decades of the 1800s, when it was called Peninsula. The town was renamed for the Marathon Paper Mill, which was constructed in 1944. Now Marathon Pulp Inc., the mill is involved in various modernization programs.

Tales of gold have always circulated in the region. Prospecting started as early as 1869, but a huge ore body was not discovered until 1981.

As a result of new investment in gold, Marathon has seen the addition of houses, apartments, businesses, recreation facilities and several shopping malls like Marathon Centre Mall along Peninsula Road.

Golfers will want to try the scenic 9-hole Peninsula Golf Course, designed by Stanley Thompson, C.G.A.

Notable Events

• A Figure Skating Show in early April showcases the skills of area skating students.

• The Chamber of Commerce Trade Show in late-April/early May lets merchants display the latest goods and merchandise.

181

DIRECTORY

Tourist Information – Marathon Community Services Department, 807-887-3188, 800-621-1029

Where to Stay
Best Western Airport Motor Inn, 807-229-1213, 800-528-1234, Hwy. 17, has comfortable rooms convenient for travelers.
Marathon Harbour Inn, 807-229-2121, 888-729-3404 (reservations), 67 Peninsula Rd., has nice units and the Prime Cut Restaurant.

• A Fishing Festival in June celebrates the excellent angling in the area.

• Marathon Music Festival in early June is a chance to catch up on musical entertainment.

• The Children's Festival in July gives kids a chance to have a great time.

• Nostalgia Days at Neys Provincial Park celebrates the heritage and history of the area in August.

• The Pic Mobert and Pic Heron Bay Powwow in August is a celebration of First Nations people and culture.

What's Next

Traveling southward from Marathon, Highway 17 bends inland away from Lake Superior for a considerable distance, providing views of new and exciting scenery, wildlife and possible new adventures. The wild land and lakeshore that the highway skirts is occupied by Pukaskwa National Park. Westward from Marathon, the highway heads for Terrace Bay, Schreiber, Rossport and Nipigon.

MARQUETTE, MICHIGAN

Population: 19,660

Marquette, Michigan, regional map – page 22.

A beautiful harbor city on Lake Superior's south shore in Michigan's Upper Peninsula, Marquette (Mar-KETT) serves as both a bustling commercial port for outbound shipments of iron ore from mines near Negaunee and Ishpeming as well as for incoming coal cargoes destined for the large electric generating plant, and is also a comfortable setting for recreational boaters who dock there permanently or for transitory stays in pleasant surroundings.

Convenient to the harbor, Marquette's downtown offers nearly everything that visitors might be seeking. From art to convenience items, most can be found within walking distance of the harbor.

Depending on your direction of travel, Marquette is accessible on Michigan Highway 28 from either the east or west and northbound visitors can pick up U.S. 41 at Escanaba or M-35 at Gladstone in the southern U.P. to travel to the city. Airline service is provided at Sawyer International Airport at Gwinn, south on M-553. Area bus service is operated by the Marquette County Transportation Authority (Marq-Tran) at West Spring Street and taxi service is also available.

A Bit of History

Marquette is named for Father Jacques Marquette, the early French Jesuit missionary-explorer who ministered to the Ojibway and other native people in the area from 1669 until his death in 1675. A statue of Marquette stands on a boulder in a small rock garden adjacent to the Marquette Chamber of Commerce at 501 Front.

Although Native American and French voyageurs used the sheltered waters of Marquette harbor for rest, fishing and transport of furs and other cargo, no significant settlement existed at the site until the late 1840s. The 1844 discovery of iron ore at Teal Lake was the spur that led to development of the harbor and the city starting in 1849. The Marquette Iron Range took on the city's name, despite the fact that the iron mines exist closer to the cities of Negaunee and Ishpeming, about 10 miles inland from the harbor.

Following the discovery of iron, it was clear that a harbor was vital to the efficient transportation of the product to eastern steel making facilities. Early prospectors and mining people had landed at the Marquette site and picked it as the ideal location for such shipping facilities. With that in mind, clearing of the waterfront began, with a young Peter White credited for felling the first tree in that effort. Thus was the foundation laid for one of the area's legendary pioneer businessmen – one who wrote the bill of lading for the first iron ore shipment from Marquette and whose name years later would grace an ore freighter and remains etched today on the public library in Marquette.

3

The bright red Marquette Harbor Lighthouse always makes a good photo and has marked the way to Marquette for mariners since 1866. Contact the Maritime Museum to visit the light.

– *Lake Superior Magazine*

Within two weeks of the start of clearing, a dock was built of the downed timber filled with sand and rocks from the area, but was immediately washed away by one of Lake Superior's legendary storms.

Undaunted, the founding fathers used manual labor to land everything necessary for sustenance, mining and construction of an iron forge on the beach until a second dock could be built. Ore was transported by teams of draft animals during winter freeze up from the Teal Lake mines to the Marquette forge for smelting into iron "blooms." The iron blooms were shipped the spring of 1851, but the endeavor did not prove economical, with the iron selling for much less than the cost of production and transportation. Thereafter, iron ore became the main commodity that the docks at Marquette handled and that remains true to the present.

Through the years, other influences like commercial fishing and timber production would have an impact on the history of the city, but it remains a city dominated by waterfront activity and by the shipments of iron ore and, today, large coal cargoes to serve the Presque Isle Power Plant. It's waterfront is also a haven for many recreational boaters using Lake Superior waters.

Today

The largest city in the Upper Peninsula, Marquette is the regional shopping, medical, banking and service center of the U.P., as well as an important iron ore shipping port. The downtown has resisted the "malling" effect and remains vibrant and vital, preserving many historic aspects of its past.

Work in the downtown is turning a sizable area of abandoned property into an ambitious $2 million development called "Marquette Commons," a heritage and cultural complex with more and reconfigured parking, a new building with a skating surface, fountain and inviting green spaces. The city also acquired former railroad property that includes 3,500 feet (1,075 meters) of lakeshore that is being developed.

The 9,300-student Northern Michigan University (NMU) contributes to the quality of life with a wide variety of programs: education, arts, sports, music, entertainment, lectures and other recreation, including changing exhibits at the new NMU DeVos Art Museum, which opened in early 2005. Guided campus tours can be arranged. Marquette and NMU are home to the U.S. Olympic Education Center. At NMU, training is offered in four of the Olympic sports, with negotiations in progress to add others. Tours are offered 3-5 p.m. Tuesday through Friday. The Superior Dome at NMU is an 8,000-seat domed stadium made of 781 Douglas fir beams and more than 100 miles of fir decking. It is the largest

wooden domed stadium in the Western Hemisphere and second only to a dome in Japan that is two feet larger.

Marquette Regional Hospital is the regional center for medical and health care. A major employer in Marquette, it also affiliates with many associated health care providers, specialists and clinics that serve a wide range of needs in the area.

What to See and Do

An extensive calendar of artistic, cultural and other area activities is published in *Marquette Monthly*, a free distribution tabloid found in many newsstands. The daily *Mining Journal* provides the latest news and information about the area.

One of our favorite pastimes is walking the breakwater to the lighthouse and watching arriving ships. Rockhounding is great! In the winter, there's ice watching, snowshoeing and cross-country ski trails. But guard against inclement weather.

The courtroom drama *Anatomy of a Murder* was a fictional account of an actual event in nearby Big Bay. Author Robert Traver (in reality attorney John Voelker) was from Ishpeming and served for many years as county prosecutor, as well as a period as a state Supreme Court justice. Voelker's many original manuscripts and memorabilia are permanently on display in the exhibits at the Superior Dome on the campus of Northern Michigan University, which also features U.P. history, environmental displays and athletic memorabilia of interest to visitors. The city celebrates the anniversary of Voelker's birth in June each year and his hometown, Ishpeming, renamed a local pond "Voelker Lake" to honor his memory as both a bestselling author and an avid trout angler.

The Marquette area is known for its creative bent, with many artists in residence and it's one of several Upper Peninsula venues where the Pine Mountain Music Festival holds performances during the months of June into July. Check the info centers for the local schedule.

Shiras Planetarium at the high school has been called one of the best in the country. Public shows are Monday evenings (unless Monday is a holiday, when it is closed).

Marquette County Courthouse on West Washington in the downtown is a lovely old building with first-floor marble and mahogany paneled walls. It was the setting for the courtroom drama *Anatomy of a Murder*. The late John Voelker was heard for many years as county prosecutor in this courtroom.

Ojibwa Casino II is located at Kawbawgam Road and M-28 East, providing Las Vegas-style action with progressive slots, craps, blackjack and other gaming.

Two large marinas serve boaters in the Marquette area. Cinder Pond Marina is at Lower Harbor Park near

downtown and offers 112 slips and a playground for the kids. Charters for fishing trips, a cruise to the Huron Islands and a Lake Superior lighthouse cruise are especially recommended. The 95-slip, full-service Presque Isle Marina is north on Lake Shore Boulevard, as is a quaint shopping area with arts and crafts. For hikers, bikers and inline skaters, there are 17 miles (27 kilometers) of paths which extend from Presque Isle through the city along the Lake Superior shoreline.

For golfers, there are four 18-hole courses in the area: Marquette Country Club, Chocolay Downs near Harvey, Red Fox Run in Gwinn or Wawonowin Country Club in Ishpeming. The area's newest course, Homestead, offers a 9-hole challenge on County Road 480.

Moosewood Nature Center is a nice family stop at Presque Isle Park, offering a variety of nature programs for kids of all ages.

Marquette Fish Research Station (hatchery) in Harvey is a good family stop. Open daily, year-round on Cherry Creek Road, near routes 28 and 41. No charge.

Step in the footprints of the famous in front of the downtown Book World Bookstore, formerly the Nordic Theatre. Jimmy Stewart, Lee Remick and other stars were filmed in the historic downtown area for the movie version of *Anatomy of a Murder*.

For on-the-water activity, Uncle Ducky's Cruises offers charters for groups up to six people and also welcomes fishing charters. Their charter service is located at the Ellwood A. Mattson Lower Harbor Park.

Tour services in the Marquette area include: Great Northern Adventures, offering outdoor adventure vacations; Big Bay Outfitters, with wilderness and waterfall tours; Marquette Country Tours, specializing in historic and cultural tours, as well as outdoor treks; Superior Adventures, with charter fishing and hunting guide services.

Mid-February visitors to the Marquette/Munising area should consider taking in the races at the Trenary Outhouse Classic. In this fun competition, two people push "outhouses" 500 feet along a snowy road. It attracts more than 3,000 spectators to the downtown area of the city, located at the junction of highways 41 and 67 southeast of Marquette.

Notable Museums

On Front Street, the Peter White Public Library includes the Marquette Arts and Culture Center for public use for classes, exhibits, performances and other cultural events. Its Gallery offers works by area artists.

Marquette Maritime Museum specializes in Great Lakes maritime history with emphasis on the Marquette area.

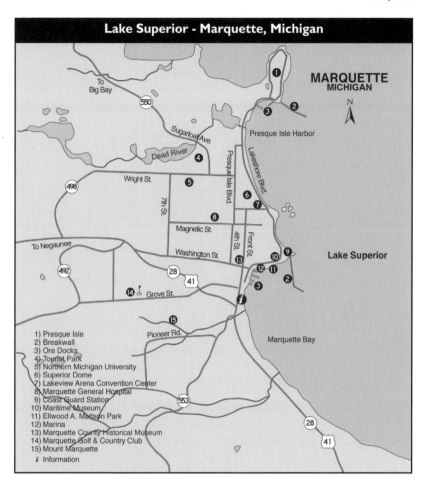

Lake Superior - Marquette, Michigan

To Big Bay

MARQUETTE
MICHIGAN

N

Sugarloaf Ave.

Presque Isle Harbor

Dead River

Presque Isle Blvd.

Lakeshore Blvd.

Wright St.

7th St.

498

To Negaunee

Magnetic St.

4th St.

Front St.

Washington St.

Lake Superior

492

28

41

Grove St.

Pioneer Rd.

Marquette Bay

1) Presque Isle
2) Breakwall
3) Ore Docks
4) Tourist Park
5) Northern Michigan University
6) Superior Dome
7) Lakeview Arena Convention Center
8) Marquette General Hospital
9) Coast Guard Station
10) Maritime Museum
11) Ellwood A. Mattson Park
12) Marina
13) Marquette County Historical Museum
14) Marquette Golf & Country Club
15) Mount Marquette

553

28

41

i Information

Evinrude developed and tested the first outboard motor in Marquette Harbor, which a display commemorates. Also on display is the birch-bark canoe that Charles T. Harvey used while building the first lock at Sault Ste. Marie in the 1850s. The museum exhibits the giant Second Order Fresnel lens that shone from Stannard Rock Lighthouse, in addition to two other lenses in its collection. A memorial to World War II submariners features a conning tower (bridge) honoring Marquette native Capt. David McClintock and the crew of the USS *Darter*'s heroic action in the Battle of Leyte, Philippines. Small charge. Gift shop. Open seven days a week Memorial Day to October.

Marquette County Historical Society Museum in the downtown area on Front Street tells a good overall story of the area's history with exhibits on pioneer life, mining and lumbering, as well as special programs from time to time.

Monday to Friday. Small charge. Closed weekends and holidays.

Upper Peninsula Children's Museum on West Baraga Avenue is a great stop for families and offers interactive education displays and outreach services throughout the U.P. Open daily 10 a.m.-6 p.m., except noon to 5 p.m. Sundays. Fee, although reduced with membership.

Parks and Public Areas

Presque Isle, an almost-island of 328 acres at the end of Lakeshore Boulevard, offers picnicking, hiking, biking, tennis, a swimming pool with 160-foot (49-meter) water slide, playground and Thursday night summer band concerts. Black Rocks and Sunset Point at the park are especially nice to view sunsets. Be careful near the cliff edges. Along Lakeshore Boulevard, visitors may still see the aftermath of a May 2003 flood that washed out a bridge, shut down the Presque Isle Power Plant, washed out the dam impounding the lake at Tourist Park and isolated businesses and residents from the rest of the town for several weeks.

Elwood Mattson Lower Harbor Park is just out of the downtown, with beautiful grounds, a range of amenities and the Cinder Pond Marina for boaters.

McCarty's Cove and Shiras parks occupy about a mile of lakeshore on Lake Shore Boulevard from Lighthouse Point going north toward Presque Isle Harbor.

Notable Events

• Noquemanon Ski Marathon occurs in mid- to late January and attracts thousands of competitors from the upper Midwest.

• U.P. 200 Sled Dog Race/Winterfest takes place in mid-February, stimulating sled dog teams with a challenging trail and a nighttime start. Winterfest is a fun family event featuring outdoor activities.

• Mid-February visitors should consider taking in the races at the Trenary Outhouse Classic. In this fun competition, two people push "outhouses" 500 feet along a snowy road. It attracts more than 3,000 spectators to the downtown area of the city, located at the junction of highways 41 and 67 southeast of Marquette.

• Superior Bike Fest is a chance to explore area trails in early June.

• John Voelker Birthday Celebration in late June commemorates the local ties of the award-winning author (pen name Robert Traver) and local prosecuting attorney.

• International Food Festival in early July features scrumptious foods in a beautiful waterfront setting.

• Fourth of July Festival features a huge parade and many other events for family fun.

DIRECTORY

Tourist Information Centers –
Marquette Area Chamber of Commerce,
906-226-6591, 888-578-6489; Marquette
Country Tourism/Convention and Visitors
Bureau, 906-228-7749, 800-544-4321;
Michigan Tourism, 800-5432-YES (937)

Where to Stay
Landmark Inn, 906-228-2580, 230 N.
Front St., is a four-star hotel, with
excellent dining and a great view from its
upstairs lounge. Each room is decorated in
a different theme, many with views of Lake
Superior.
Nordic Bay Lodge, 906-226-7516, 800-
892-9376, 1880 U.S. 41 South. In addition
to having charming rooms and a chapel,
there is an on-site restaurant and licensed
bar across U.S. 41 from the Lake Superior
shore.

Where to Eat with a Local Flavor
Vierling's Restaurant and Marquette
Harbor Brewery, 906-228-3533, 119
S.Front St., is a turn-of-the-century
barroom-style restaurant with historic
pictures and prints on the walls and a
microbrewery offering a nice selection of
craft beers.
Upfront & Company, 906-228-5200,
102 E. Main, is a large facility that features
wood-fired pizzas, a full menu, a complete
bar and a special area for entertainment acts.
Heritage Room, 906-228-2580, 230 N.
Front St. (Landmark Hotel). Casual to
gourmet dining are featured here and in
the hotel's Northland Pub or North Star
Lounge.
Casa Calabria, 906-228-5012, 1106 N.
Third St., offers good Italian cuisine from
gourmet to pizza, with steaks and other
entrees on the menu.

3

• Blueberry Festival occurs in late July with many activities
celebrating and eating food using the area's favorite wild fruit.
• Art on the Rocks is a giant exhibit and sale of regional
arts and crafts in the special landscape of Presque Isle Park.
• Seafood Fest serves sumptuous fish and other seafoods
on the waterfront in early August.
• Ore to Shore Mountain Bike Epic in early August is a
tough biking challenge for riders of all skill levels.

Where to Shop
The Studio Gallery on Lakeshore Boulevard features
works by local artists Maggie Linn, Kathleen Conover, Vicki
Allison Phillips and metalsmith artist Yvonne LeMire.
Nearby, is an outlet that rents bicycles to pedal along the
lakeshore and through the city.
Historic Downtown Marquette is a vital, growing area
offering many opportunities for the shopper. Michigan Fair
features Michigan-made products. Art of Framing, Art UP
Style and Screened Image and Graphic Design offer a variety
of gifty items. Town Folk Gallery has antiques, beading and
hand-crafted women's wear and the Hotplate is a paint your

own pottery shop. Needleworks carries yarns, fabrics, quilting supplies and looms and spinning wheels. Mole Hole has charming service and quality gifts. Wattsson & Wattsson Jewelers carry a line of items made from 14 karat gold and feature an underground mine experience right in the store. Photographer Jack Deo's Superior View Historic Photo & Art Gallery is on the street level at the corner. There are bookstores, restaurants and clothing stores. Down the hill on Front Street, Getz's offers three floors of clothing and footwear for men, women and children.

The shopping district around the university is known as The Village, full of restaurants and nifty gifty shops. A stop at Scandinavian Gifts or Habitat will definitely fulfill your gift list.

Westwood Mall is a major shopping center. Marquette Mall also houses a number of businesses, including an indoor miniature golf course. Both are located on U.S. 41 West, where there are also a number of restaurants. Along the way in that area, watch for the Touch of Finland to find a wide variety of Finnish items, including an extensive supply of sauna products.

Campgrounds

Tourist Park on the Dead River on the north end of town once featured a lovely little lake where the river was impounded. A 2003 flood destroyed the dam and the river now flows unrestricted through the park. There is a playground, showers, space for picnicking and electrical service to all 110 campsites, with 38 offering full hookups.

What's Next

Sugarloaf Mountain, 8 miles (13 kilometers) north on County Road 550 toward Big Bay, is a good hike with a spectacular view from the top of the mountain.

Explore Little Presque Isle along Lake Superior in the Escanaba River State Forest off County Road 550 on the way to Big Bay.

Take an interesting side trip to Gwinn to see the historic display in the terminal of Sawyer International Airport, which offers air service from the former Air Force Base. Here, the Marquette County Aviation Wall of Fame honors both military and civilian local airmen who made significant contributions to flight. And as long as you're in the neighborhood, take a ride through the Gwinn townsite, an early model townsite designed and built for employees of Cleveland Cliffs Iron Co. The entire town is listed in the National Register of Historic Places.

Follow Highway M-28 east toward Munising or Highway U.S. 41/M28 west from Marquette headed for Negaunee and Ishpeming.

MICHIPICOTEN ISLAND PROVINCIAL PARK, ONTARIO

The Ojibway name of Michipicoten refers to high bluffs. Michipicoten Island Provincial Park, 60 kilometers (37 miles) out in Lake Superior from Wawa, is one of the most mysterious and remote of Ontario's provincial parks. Michipicoten Island is the third largest island in the lake, sparking myths of mirages for generations because, viewed from the mainland, it seems to float above the water and is often obscured by fog, which is frequent in this area of the lake.

> ### DIRECTORY
>
> **Tourist Information –** Wawa Ministry of Natural Resources District Office, 705-856-2396; Ontario Parks, 888-668-7275

On the island's south shore, Quebec Harbour is the site of a row of fishing huts and summer cottages. It also houses a Coast Guard station. Michipicoten Island is accessible only by float plane or large boats, remaining undeveloped with no commercial tourist facilities. It has no park facilities or campgrounds, but visits are permitted.

MINNESOTA'S IRON RANGES

No exploration of northern Minnesota's wonders would be complete without a visit to to the Mesabi and Vermilion iron ranges. We recommend that visitors venture about an hour north on Highway 53 from Duluth, take Forest Highway 11/Superior National Forest Scenic Byway at Silver Bay from Highway 61 on Minnesota's north shore or catch Highway 1 at Illgen City or Highway 6 at Little Marais to visit Minnesota's Mesabi and Vermilion iron ranges. Here you can find museums, overlooks of active and inactive iron mines, interpretation of the area, entertainment, recreation, great accommodations, melt-in-the-mouth ethnic foods and the opportunity to descend into an underground iron mine for a one of a kind tour.

Minnesota's Iron Ranges, regional map – page 32.

3

If traveling on Highway 53 directly from Duluth or you choose the Superior Scenic Highway/Forest Road 11 from Silver Bay to the Mesabi Iron Range, be sure to stop at the Mineview in the Sky at the edge of Virginia from May through October for excellent help in planning your visit. As the name indicates, it also provides an outstanding viewpoint over an abandoned iron mine located almost in the middle of town.

Once you're on the Iron Range, there are several directions of travel on what has come to be called the Iron Trail, which opens the way to many experiences and is home to 35 sites listed on the National Register of Historic Places.

While the Iron Range is world famous for its huge iron ore mines, it is an area with more than 2,000 miles of scenic groomed snowmobile trails, is surrounded by the beauty of

Superior National Forest and offers wildlife watching, silent sports adventure and a wide range of fishing – some in depleted mine pits that have filled with water and been stocked with game fish.

The 132-mile (198-kilometer) paved Mesabi Trail from Grand Rapids to Ely is progressing by 10 to 15 miles per year, and will eventually go all the way to Ely. It provides wonderful opportunities for hikers, bikers and inline skaters to get close to the land and see many sites not available by highways.

For information on individual Iron Range sites, see descriptions in the listing for the city where they are located.

MOHAWK, MICHIGAN

Population 200

Mohawk, Michigan, regional map – page 24.

Mohawk offers two shopping opportunities while traveling U.S. 41 and the Circle Route north on the Keweenaw Peninsula from Houghton/Hancock through several ghost mining towns. Here Superior Wood Works Inc. makes and sells rustic indoor and outdoor furniture and the showroom of Bird's-Eye Creations Inc. sports a nice selection of specialty items crafted from bird's-eye maple. From here you can continue to follow Highway 41 toward Copper Harbor at the tip of the Keweenaw, but we recommend turning southeast on South Shore Drive from Fulton-Mohawk to Gay. This route hugs the eastern edge of the peninsula and travels several miles right on the shore of Keweenaw Bay. See listings for Gay and Lac La Belle for information.

MONTREAL, WISCONSIN

Population 810

Montreal on Wisconsin 77 a few miles southwest of Hurley is an old mining community that hasn't changed much over the years. The restored village with its quaint homes is listed on the National Register of Historic Places.

Whitecap Mountains Resort in Montreal is located on Lake Weber and offers 200 acres of alpine skiing terrain ranging from novice to expert slopes and trails. This is an especially attractive area in the summer. Located 11 miles (17.5 kilometers) west of Hurley on State

Highway 77, the resort offers hotel accommodations with all
the amenities and Skye Golf Course with 18 holes of high
caliber challenges. An additional 9 holes of championship golf
is scheduled to open in 2007. The resort also participates in
the Big Snow Country "wild card" program that makes all the
hills in the area available to participating skiers.

Montreal, Wisconsin,
regional map – page 28.

MONTREAL RIVER HARBOUR, ONTARIO
Population 21

As the southern gateway to Lake Superior Provincial Park,
the tiny townsite of Montreal River Harbour is about midway
between Wawa and Sault Ste. Marie on Trans Canada Highway
17. Here is a gorge that is simply breath-taking in its own
right. If you park on one of the side roads on either end of the
highway bridge over the Montreal River, you can walk back
to the bridge to look down into the gorge. This is an
unprotected view, so watch the traffic carefully.

Montreal River Harbor,
Ontario, regional
map – page 18.

The road to the north across from Twilight Resort will
take you closer to the river. The view at the mouth of the
river is spectacular. In various seasons, large runs of salmon,
trout and smelt spawn at the mouth. The view at the mouth of
the river is spectacular and rock collectors will be more than
sorely tempted by the treasure trove of washed pebbles. In
mid-summer, look for blueberries and raspberries. Montreal
River Harbor is also home to Mad Moose Lodge, a premier
destination for hikers, rock and ice climbers, boaters, nature
lovers and other outdoor adventure types.

3

South from Montreal River, watch for the scenic pullout
at Alona Bay, location of important exploration for copper
and silver since the late 1700s. This site
offers a unique sunset experience. In the
late 1940s, pitchblende, an indication of
the presence of uranium, was rediscovered
at Theano Point and an abandoned
uranium mine is nearby.

Farther south on Highway 17, Pancake
Bay Provincial Park and Pancake Bay take
their names from the voyageurs, who would stop their canoes
here on their way east to Montreal. Only one day away from
Sault Ste. Marie and fresh provisions, they would make
pancakes with their remaining flour. The modern Pancake Bay
offers a long sand beach on the big lake. Swimming, hiking and
camping. Open early May to early October.

DIRECTORY

Tourist Information – Batchawana
Bay Tourism Association, 705-882-2235

For gift buyers of souvenirs and native collectables, visit
Agawa Indian Crafts and the Canadian Carver at Pancake Bay
for unique wood carvings and other treasures. This popular
stop offers a campers' grocery, packaged goods,
fishing/hunting licenses and great service at the filling station.

Attractions include hand-carved wooden statues of bear, moose, wolf and other bush animals. Be sure to click a picture of their famous Weather Rock. Guaranteed to accurately tell you what the weather is at any moment.

If your route is north from Montreal River, you soon enter Lake Superior Provincial Park and are on your way to Wawa at the north end of the park. See listings for information on both the park and Wawa.

MOUNTAIN IRON, MINNESOTA

Population 4,000

Mountain Iron is where iron ore was first discovered on the Mesabi Range by the famous "Seven Iron Men" of Duluth's Merritt family in 1890. This is also the home of the largest taconite plant and one of the largest taconite mines in the world. The plant atop its mountainous site is visible for miles as you travel toward Mountain Iron/Virginia. The Mountain Iron Mine Viewpoint overlooks the massive mine. If you seek lodging, an AmericInn is located in the Virginia/Mountain Iron area.

DIRECTORY

Tourist Information – Virginia/ Eveleth/Mountain Iron/Gilbert Chamber of Commerce, 218-741-2717

Σ

To visit the western Mesabi Iron Range area, take U.S. 169 west from Mountain Iron toward Chisholm and Hibbing. To return to the Circle Tour, take Highway 53 south toward Duluth or Highway 135 east from Virginia through Biwabik, Aurora and Hoyt Lakes to catch Forest Highway 11/Superior National Forest Scenic Byway to Silver Bay on Lake Superior's north shore.

MUNISING, MICHIGAN

Population 2,580

Munising, Michigan, regional map – page 22.

The century-old Munising (MEW-ni-sing) may be one of the best kept "secrets" on Lake Superior for visitors. From friendly dining and lodging to wonderful hiking and interesting tours, this is a stop that may tempt visitors to spend a day or two longer than they originally planned.

Located on a natural Lake Superior harbor, the town and harbor are protected by Grand Island, the second largest of the U.S. islands in Lake Superior. The original Chippewa name for the island was Kitchi minising (literally, great or grand island), which was altered and later transferred to the town on the mainland.

A concerted, collaborative effort between public and private groups in Alger County to promote "heritage tourism" has resulted in an emphasis on historical and cultural information and sites within Munising and the county.

Information is available at the visitors centers or the County Historical Society (906-387-4308).

What to See and Do

Ferry-and-barge service to Grand Island, which is protected by the U.S. Forest Service, is located at Grand Island Landing. Camping, hiking and biking are available. Private vehicles are not allowed on the island. The island has been the site of major archaeological effort to explore the earliest inhabitation, said to have occurred about A.D. 1200 at a village the Ojibway people later called Geta Odena (Kay-tay O-day-na).

A number of waterfalls are found within the city limits.

Alger County All Veterans Memorial stands at the head of Munising Harbor in Bayshore Park.

Pictured Rocks Boat Cruises leave regularly from Munising docks mid-May through the early October color season. The 2¹/₂-hour cruises are subject to weather. Skylane Air Tours offers aerial views of the area.

Alger County Historical Society Museum includes a fur trader's cabin on grounds overlooking Lake Superior. It is located on Washington Street near the Pictured Rocks National Lakeshore Munising Falls Interpretative Center.

Golfers can try the Pictured Rocks Golf and Country Club, an 18-hole par 72 course located 4 miles east of Munising on Highway H-58.

The original iron blast furnace has been restored at Bay Furnace Recreation Area. The furnace was used for production of pig iron in the 1870s when the town was known as Onota. The U.S. Forest Service campground and picnic area now occupies that spot on Lake Superior to the west of the village of Christmas located just west of Munising. You'll also find good agate hunting, sandy beaches and a talking "snowman." The village post office holds holiday cards until December for mailings, with a hand-stamped Christmas, Michigan, postmark. Do shop in the gift shops, where it's Christmas any time of year. Kewadin Casinos operates a gaming facility in the village.

Parks and Public Areas

Pictured Rocks National Lakeshore is headquartered 4 miles northeast of downtown Munising at a former Coast Guard Station. On display is an old U.S. Coast Guard Lifesaving self-righting rescue boat. The park shares a visitor center with Hiawatha National Forest at the junction of State Road M-28 and County Road H-58. Open year-round Monday through Saturday. From mid-May through October,

Pictured Rocks

Visitors to Munising will certainly want to consider taking a water level tour of Pictured Rocks National Lakeshore aboard a Pictured Rocks Boat Cruises vessel, which arrive and depart on a regular schedule from the waterfront dock. We also recommend an automobile tour of the park by taking County Highway H-58 from Munising to Grand Marais. The 42-mile route, a bit less than half of which is paved, gets travelers close to most of the park's major attractions and campgrounds and is the only land access to the entire park. The western 15 miles is marked by the multi-colored limestone formations for which the park is famous. The remaining 27 miles are marked by sandy beaches, sand dunes and varied landscapes. See separate listing.

3

DIRECTORY

Tourist Information – Visitor
Information Center, 906-387-3700

Where to Stay
Pair-a-Dice Inn, 906-387-3500,
866-387-3500, E7889 W. M-38, offers 48
standard and suite units with continental
breakfast and nearby gaming.

Where to Eat with a Local Flavor
Dogpatch Restaurant, 906-387-9948,
E. Superior St., has a good steak and
seafood menu and a fun "L'il Abner"
atmosphere.

the center is also open Sundays and can provide the latest on
the area and the National Lakeshore.

The National Lakeshore operates an interpretative center
at Munising Falls, located about 2 miles (3 kilometers)
northeast of downtown.

Alger Underwater Preserve includes 113 square miles (293
square kilometers) of Lake Superior shoreline at Munising.
Scuba divers regularly descend to view major shipwrecks in
the harbor. The public can view the wrecks of the Alger
Preserve on the Glass Bottom Boat shipwreck tour.
Reservations are suggested at Shipwreck Tours Inc. of
Munising.

A large section of the 860,000-acre Hiawatha National
Forest encompasses much of the area around Munising, with
forest trails, hiking and mountain bike trails and
campgrounds. Some of the best snowmobile trails in the
Upper Peninsula are in this area, as well as some of the best
cross-country skiing in the region. Lodging is available within
the forest at a number of motels in Munising.

Negaunee - Norway

NEGAUNEE, MICHIGAN

Population 4,500

Negaunee (Na-GAW-nee) is an iron mining town on M-28 and U.S. 41 a short way west from Marquette. More than 150 years ago, the first iron on the Marquette Range was discovered in the roots of an upturned tree on the shores of Negaunee's Teal Lake, which offers the best walleye and trout fishing in the area.

Negaunee, Michigan, regional map – page 22.

What to See and Do

An Iron Ore Monument is located just east of Negaunee on U.S. 41.

Lucy Hill is the site of the first naturbahn luge (loozh) course in the United States that meets International Luge Federation standards. What is luge? Basically, it's hurtling down an icy course on a small sled while lying on your back. For the winter visitor, national and international competitions are held each year between late December and early March. Open to spectators every weekend. The bottom one-sixth is open to the public for instruction and "trial sliding" on weekend afternoons when no competitive event is scheduled. Lucy Hill is just south of Negaunee on old M-35.

There are 17 miles (25 kilometers) of cross-country ski trails in the area that offer beautiful vistas. An annual snowshoe race and the Guts Triathlon, a rare combination of snowshoeing, cross-country skiing and running, are held here.

The area celebrates winter in January with the Heikki Lunta WinterFest and hosts Pioneer Days in July.

Notable Museums

Follow the signs to the Michigan Iron Industry Museum at 73 Forge Road. It's a good stop for children. Open daily, May through October. Free.

Negaunee Historical Museum is located in the old American Legion Building at Main Street and Brown Avenue.

Daily and Sunday afternoons Memorial Day through August. Antique enthusiasts will want to visit the Old Bank Building, a three-story triangular 1874 building with 25 rooms displaying antiques and collectables representing the lifestyle and tastes of the people who settled the Upper Peninsula.

DIRECTORY

Tourist Information – Ishpeming/
Negaunee Chamber of Commerce,
906-486-4841, 888-578-6489

What's Next

To either the east or west, the Circle Tour route follows Highway M-28/U.S. 41. To the west lies the Keweenaw Peninsula and a world of interesting sights and experiences. About 10 miles east, Marquette beckons.

NEWBERRY, MICHIGAN

Population 1,917

Newberry, Michigan, regional map – page 20.

Newberry is located on M-123 just off M-28 about halfway between Sault Ste. Marie and Marquette. Designated by the state legislature as "Michigan's Moose Capital" and the southern gateway to Tahquamenon Falls State Park, Newberry also opens the way to a number of attractions like the Manistique lakes and Seney National Wildlife Refuge to the south and west. It is an old lumbering town that holds an aura of the past and still contributes to the timber industry, with several mills and logging operations. There are a number of good lodging and eating establishments in the area. The weekly *Newberry News* is a great source of what's currently happening in the area.

What to See and Do

Golfers can play the Newberry Country Club just south of the village. It's been there since 1928 as a 9-hole course and was expanded to an 18-hole par 71 course.

You can take a ride on a narrow-gauge train and a riverboat cruise, with destination Tahquamenon Falls. Drop down through Newberry to M-28 and back east to catch the Toonerville Trolley at Soo Junction. The longest 24-inch narrow-gauge railroad now operating, the train takes you to the Tahquamenon River where you board a river boat to the falls. An attractive alternative to this 6.5-hour trip is a 1.75-hour round trip on the train.

Ask directions to Oswald's Bear Ranch, where you can see native black bears in natural environs. The largest bear ranch in the United States, the compound includes three walk-about bear habitats to explore, with newborn and yearling cubs cavorting near a small lake. Open Memorial weekend through September 30.

Notable Museums

Luce County Historical Museum is located in the old sheriff's residence on West Harrie Street.

Tahquamenon Logging Museum houses a collection of lumbering artifacts. The 29-acre camp is on the banks of the Tahquamenon River at the outskirts of Newberry.

Notable Events

• Woodchoppers' Ball celebrates the logging heritage of the area in March.

• Music Festival in June brings a variety of musical styles to town.

• Old Time Music Jamboree in July harkens back to the days of unamplified music.

• Lumberjack Days in August pulls out all the stops to remember the time when white pine was king.

• Michigan Fiddlers Jamboree in August gives bragging rights to the best of the state's fiddlers.

Campgrounds

Luce County Park and Campground has 28 sites on 33 wooded acres on the south shore of Round (also known as North Manistique) Lake to the north of Curtis. An excellent place to plant yourself for full access to inland lake swimming, fishing and hiking opportunities. Open Memorial Day to early October.

What's Next

From Newberry, you can stay on Highway M-28 in either direction, with the Circle Tour eastern route toward Sault Ste. Marie and the western leg heading to Munising through Seney and Shingleton. A more scenic – though rustic – path westward is to turn north on M-77 (recently repaved) at Seney to Grand Marais.

Another off-the-beaten path locale is the village of Deer Park, a lumbering town of the late 1800s. Take County Road 37 north of Newberry off M-123. You'll be in Big Two-Hearted River country which has excellent fishing, agates, driftwood and seascapes. This is the region made famous by Ernest Hemingway. His Nick Adams fished and canoed here. Muskallonge Lake State Park and campgrounds are located just above the Lake Superior shoreline.

From Deer Park to Grand Marais on Forest Road H-58, most of which is not paved, you'll count off 13 miles (21 kilometers)

DIRECTORY

Tourist Information – Newberry Visitor Information Center, 906-293-5562, 800-831-7292

Where to Stay
Best Western Newberry, 906-293-4000, 800-528-1234, Hwy. 28.
Days Inn Newberry, 800-293-3297, Hwy. 28.

Where to Eat with a Local Flavor
Pickleman's Pub and Pantry, 906-293-3777, M-28 & M-123.

of washboard road, all hard sand, surrounded by sand lots, forest and Lake Superior beach. The going is slow (30 minutes of travel time), but most interesting with beautiful views.

NEYS PROVINCIAL PARK, ONTARIO

Neys Provincial Park, Ontario, regional map – page 12.

Neys Provincial Park occupies the Coldwell Peninsula about midway between Marathon and Terrace Bay on Lake Superior's Canadian north shore. Neys is naturally significant as a habitat for woodland caribou and historically significant as a World War II prisoner of war camp. German officers captured in Europe were impounded at what is now the site of the park's campground. Remains of the camp and old logging booms are everywhere.

Other activities in the park are hiking, boating, picnicking, swimming, attending interpretative programs and enjoying the beach. Neys is the site of an interesting shipwreck, old ore-carrying Whaleback *#115*, with artifacts exhibited in the park's interpretative center, where programs are provided during summer. There is ample campground space, with access to Lake Superior and the Little Pic River, where there are some boat docks and a launch area. Nostalgia Days are held the second weekend in August. The park is open mid-May to mid-September.

This striking landscape has served as the subject of many paintings by A.Y. Jackson, Lawren Harris and other members of Canada's early 20th century Group of Seven artists fraternity from Toronto. They visited a vibrant Coldwell in the early 1920s. Now it is nearly a ghost village.

A must stop in the area is the pulloff at the Little Pic River above the gorge to the east on the south side of Highway 17. A spectacular view of the highway bridge over the river offers an excellent and famous photo opportunity. You can see the Canadian Pacific Railway bridge and the tracks as they round the Coldwell Peninsula. The pulloff is quick, however, so keep a careful watch for it.

On the small stream of Angler Creek between Coldwell and Marathon, not far from the Highway 17 bridge, was another World War II prisoner of war camp.

DIRECTORY

Tourist Information – Neys Provincial Park Headquarters, 807-229-1624

Where to Eat with a Local Flavor
Neys Lunch and Campground, 807-229-1869, across from Park Visitor Center.

NIPIGON, ONTARIO

Population 2,500

A town of junctions, Nipigon, called the "Crossroads of Canada," is where highways 11 from the northern regions and 17 from the east connect, where the Canadian National and Canadian Pacific rail lines cross and where the waters from Lake Nipigon tumble into Lake Helen and then the most northerly waters of Lake Superior.

The timber products industry is an important part of Nipigon's economy and Columbia Forest Products is one of the largest employers in the area.

Nipigon, Ontario, regional map – page 10.

Nipigon is known as a sportfishing haven and holds the world record for the largest speckled trout, caught in the Nipigon River below Rabbit Falls in 1916.

What to See and Do

Nipigon Marina is located in the downtown area on the Nipigon River. A well-marked channel leads to a beautiful harbor and the marina can accommodate vessels of all sizes. The marina sports 30 slips, plus full facilities, and is the only port on the Great Lakes where you can reach the 49th parallel by water.

Nipigon River Recreation Trail extends from the marina along the west bank of the Nipigon River for 8.2 kilometers (5 miles) to Red Rock. Average hiking time is $2^1/_2$ to $3^1/_2$ hours. The middle section of the trail is rated difficult but the stretch from the Nipigon Marina to Stillwater Creek is quite easy and provides good access to the shoreline habitat. From the Red Rock end, the first kilometer to Lloyd's Lookout is a steady uphill, but can be rated: moderate. Its reward is a panoramic view of Nipigon Bay and Red Rock from the bench at the lookout – and a handful of wild blueberries, in season.

Three building-sized murals grace the downtown streets. Painted by Dave Sawatzky, they represent the historic heritage of Nipigon.

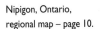

The 9-hole North Shore Golf Club lies nestled among the cliffs surrounding the towns of Nipigon and Red Rock, offering plenty of challenge on a championship course.

Winter visitors will find cross-country skiing nearby at the privately owned Karhu Ski Trails on Maata Road, where the longest loop is 7.1 kilometres.

The nearby Lake Helen Indian Reserve houses St. Sylvester's Historical Church, built in 1870, and the Lake Helen Powwow Grounds that is home to an annual traditional powwow each July.

Notable Events

• Blueberry Blast in late July is an opportunity to sample the delectables possible from the popular fruit.

• Fall Fair and Fish Derby in early September gives everyone some favorite activity to indulge in.

• Hike for Health in later September is a nice hike and benefit between Red Rock and Nipigon.

Campgrounds

Campers will enjoy the Stillwater Tent and Trailer Park,

DIRECTORY

Tourist Information – North of Superior Visitor Center, 807-887-3333, 800-265-3951

Where to Eat with a Local Flavor
Normandie Hotel, 807-887-2448, 20 Front St., has a good German menu.

which includes an amethyst gift shop and mineral museum.

What's Next

The Circle Tour Route heads either east on Trans Canada Highway 17 toward Rossport, Schreiber and Terrace Bay or southward on Highway 11/17 bound for Thunder Bay. If time allows, an interesting side trip following Highway 11 northward is described in the listing for Lake Nipigon, Frontier Trail.

NOLALU, ONTARIO

Township Population 700

Nolalu, Ontario, regional map – page 22.

Nolalu is west and south of Thunder Bay on Highway 588. Here, Artesian Wells Resort has housekeeping cabins close to fishing and winter activities. The Farmers' Mercantile Gift Gallery is a neat stop, with six retail outlets offering a variety of gifty and specialty products. It's one of 40 studios and galleries on a 40-stop self-guided, mapped tour called "Handmade in Thunder Bay." Ask for a brochure at information centres.

If you're after a little leisure summer sport, try tubing on the Kaministiquia River. Backtrack a bit from Nolalu and take Highway 588 to Stanley between Kakabeka Falls and Thunder Bay. River Rat Rentals will provide the tubes for a three-hour relaxing trip down the river.

NORWAY, MICHIGAN

Population 2,910

In the southwestern Upper Peninsula on Highway 2 at Norway, the Jake Menghini Historical Museum is housed in a historic log cabin that once served as a carriage stopping place. Displaying artifacts from Jake's personal collection, as well as exhibits that change yearly, the museum is open free of charge Memorial Day through the Saturday prior to Columbus Day in October, although donations are accepted.

Waterfalls aficionados can check out Piers Gorge in Norway, where white water tumbles over a 10-foot falls and roars wildly through canyon walls. Plan to stop at nearby Vulcan east of Norway for an underground tour by train of the Iron Mountain Iron Mine, where you'll travel 2,600 feet (800 meters) through the drifts and stopes (tunnels and roomlike areas) of the mine. On the western side of Norway, a roadside park with tables, water and toilets at Quinnesec gives a nice view of Fumee Falls.

DIRECTORY

Tourist Information – Dickinson County Chamber of Commerce in Iron Mountain, 906-774-2002.

Ontonagon - Oulu

ONTONAGON, MICHIGAN

Population 1,770

Ontonagon (On-toe-NAH-gun) is a historic port that had early significance in the copper boom years. This is the terminus of historic U.S. 45, which extends from Lake Superior's shore to the Gulf of Mexico. The historical sign in the downtown explaining the highway's importance is a great place to take a memory picture. To find Ontonagon, follow U.S. 45 northward from M-28 at Bruce Crossing. The *Ontonagon Herald* will bring you up to date on the area and give you leads to meet your needs.

Ontonagon, Michigan, regional map – page 26.

What to See and Do

The five-acre Riverfront Park provides waterfront access with picnic facilities and a playground.

Ontonagon Marina has space for 49 boats, including six transients.

Notable Museums

Ontonagon County Historical Museum on River Street has mining exhibits, the Fifth-Order Fresnel lens from the Ontonagon Lighthouse, the switchboard from Michigan's first telephone system at Rockland and a replica of the famous Ontonagon Boulder, a 3-ton mass of pure copper that was discovered nearby in the Ontonagon River and now is housed at the Smithsonian Institute. Daily tours of the lighthouse start at the museum. The lighthouse was acquired by the historical society and is undergoing restoration. Open year-round Monday through Friday, Saturdays from Memorial Day to Christmas. Small fee.

DIRECTORY

Tourist Information – Ontonagon Area Chamber of Commerce, 906-884-4735

Where to Stay
Superior Shores Resort, 800-344-5355, 1823 M-64, has nice lakeside cabins and a great beach.

Where to Eat with a Local Flavor
Harbor Town Cafe, 906-884-4727, 409 River St., is a local favorite for pasties.

Notable Events
• On Labor Day weekend, Ontonagon has a dandy celebration, with a parade.

Ouimet Canyon Provincial Park, Ontario, regional map – page 10.

Campgrounds
Campers and RVers will want to contact River Pines RV Park and Campground.

What's Next
The Circle Tour passes westward along M-64, a soothing shoreline drive which offers easy Lake Superior beach access. To travel the route to the east, take M-38 heading for Baraga, but watch for the intersection with M-26, where you'll want turn left if you plan to visit the Keweenaw Peninsula.

OUIMET CANYON PROVINCIAL PARK, ONTARIO

A huge rift in the diabase caused by erosion or faulting, the canyon walls of Ouimet Canyon Provincial Park stand 165 meters (500 feet) apart and 115 meters (350 feet) high and face each other for 3 kilometers (2 miles). On the floor of the canyon, plants native to the arctic tundra grow where the lower temperature and shadows blot necessities of indigenous regional plants. No travel is allowed to the bottom of the canyon.

Ouimet is a day-use only park, with hiking trails along the canyon rim. A boardwalk to viewing platforms makes this area more accessible for visitors. Two spectacular viewing pods overlook the canyon's edge and feature interpretative signs. An impressive standing rock formation is nearby. Visitors should remain on designated trails. A visit here is well worth the trip. Rated: easy. Facilities are available at the canyon and a small souvenir shop is adjacent to the parking lot, which is 11 kilometers (7 miles) off Highway 11/17. Open mid-May to early October. Provincial Park day-use fees apply.

Nearby on Valley Road, Eagle Canyon Adventures features a recently opened campground with 30 full-service RV sites, shaded tenting and picnic sites and Ontario's longest suspension bridge high above the canyon. A shop has food items, supplies, souvenirs and crafts.

OULU, WISCONSIN
Township Population 540

Oulu, a small hamlet just off Highway 2 east of Superior near Brule, is noted for its entry sign – a large painted rock with the name of the town on it. Visit the Oulu Glass Gallery and Studio for a display of blown, stained and fused glass. Jim and Sue Vojacek have made this a real family affair, one that will amaze you. Open daily, May through New Year's. Glass blowing

demonstrations during November and December. Follow the signs off Highway 2. You'll get there, and the drive is worth it. Backtrack to Highway 2 to continue the Circle Tour either to the west or the east.

Oulu, Wisconsin, regional map – page 30.

Paradise - Pukaskwa Park

PARADISE, MICHIGAN
Population 500

Paradise, Michigan, regional map – page 18.

The aptly named small village of Paradise along Lake Superior on M-123 is known as a jumping-off point for scuba divers exploring shipwrecks in Whitefish Point Underwater Preserve and a destination for honeymooners. It's also the nearest town and the northeast entry to Tahquamenon Falls State Park (see separate listing). Paradise offers fishing, hiking and extensive sandy beaches as well as rockhounding opportunities. It's a popular location for kayakers. It overlooks Whitefish Bay, infamous for its treacherous waters and many shipwrecks.

At the end of Tom Brown Sr. Memorial Highway, which winds past the ghost town of Shelldrake 10 miles (16 kilometers) north of Paradise, is the Whitefish Point Harbor, offering safe refuge, a boat launch and parking next door to the former Brown Fishery (which is not open to the public). About 5 miles farther on the road brings you to Whitefish Point Lighthouse, Bird Observatory and the Great Lakes Shipwreck Museum. (See separate listing for Whitefish Point.)

DIRECTORY

Tourist Information – Paradise Area Tourism Council, 906-492-3927

Where to Stay
Curley's Paradise Inn, 906-492-3445, M-123 at Whitefish Point Rd., has nice, recently renovated lodgings.
Best Western Lakefront Inn & Suites, 906-492-3770, 8112 N. M-123, is a newer lodging facility in the area.

Notable Events
• Mardi Gras de Snow Festival in January celebrates winter activities of the area.
• Annual Blueberry Festival in August continues the area's long reputation as a treasury of this favored fruit.
• Halloween Fun: "The Haunted Trail" is a scary romp for kids of all ages at Halloween time in October.

PAULDING, MICHIGAN

Paulding is 9 miles south of Bruce Crossing on U.S. Highway 45. Here you can visit Bond Falls Park for a view of the falls. There are hiking trails, fishing and camping facilities in the area.

Paulding is famous for the Paulding Light, a mysterious reddish glow that appears almost every evening once darkness has fallen. Not an official attraction, the phenomenon does attract dozens of people each night who observe this bright light rise out of the forest to the north, hover low in the sky, grow in intensity, change hue toward red and eventually disappear. A real mystery light, many claim it is the ghost of a railroad brakeman, others the lights of distant cars or even "swamp gas." First sighted about 20 years ago, no one has the real explanation. South of Paulding, watch for signs to take the Robbins Pond Road (a Forest Service road) for about a mile. The cars parked along the way will tell you when to stop. Then you decide what creates the light.

There is no lodging in Paulding, but if your night encounter with the mysterious light detains you longer than planned, lodging is located a few miles south in Watersmeet, where you can pick up Highway 2 as an alternate route to Wakefield, Bessemer and Ironwood. Farther east on Highway 2 at Iron River, AmericInn welcomes travelers.

Paradise, Michigan, is the nearest town and the northeast entry to Tahquamenon Falls State Park. Home to the second largest waterfall east of the Mississippi River, the park features a stairway and viewing deck that puts visitors close to the water as it rushes over the 48-foot-high, 200-foot wide waterfall.

P

DIRECTORY

Tourist Information – Western U.P. Convention and Visitor Bureau, 906-932-4850, 800-522-5657

Paulding, Michigan, regional map – page 26.

What's Next

To return to the Circle Tour Route, catch Highway M-28 at Bruce Crossing. To the west is Wakefield, Bessemer and Ironwood. To the east, you're heading for Marquette, but will want to consider taking U.S. 45 north toward Ontonagon and the Porcupine Mountains country. This route also opens the Keweenaw Peninsula for a visit.

PEQUAMING, MICHIGAN

Pequaming, Michigan, regional map – page 24.

In the 1940s, the Huron Peninsula. northeast of L'Anse, was the center for Ford Motor Company Upper Peninsula enterprises, which produced millions of board-feet of lumber each year for use by the automaker. Henry and Clara Ford had a summer home in Pequaming called The Bungalow, which is listed on the National Register of Historic Places, but privately owned. Pequaming also has a marina and some residential cottages.

Continue to the northeast to visit Skanee (See separate listing), or backtrack to return to L'Anse. Point Abbaye, at the tip of the peninsula, offers a view of the expansive Lake Superior. The Huron Islands rise above the waves to the east, the Keweenaw Peninsula to the west. Limited camping at the mouth of the Huron River.

DIRECTORY

Tourist Information – Baraga County Tourist Association, 906-524-7444, 800-743-4908

PICTURED ROCKS NATIONAL LAKESHORE, MICHIGAN

Pictured Rocks, Michigan, regional map – page 20.

From either Grand Marais or Munising, a drive through Pictured Rocks National Lakeshore is highly recommended, but take into account that a bit less than half of the 40-mile route is paved, with the remainder being dirt.

The Lakeshore is open 24 hours daily year-round, but the Grand Sable Visitor Center a mile west of Grand Marais on County Road H-58 operates Memorial Day to Labor Day to provide the latest information about the park. The Munising Visitor Center is open year-round.

For this listing, the route is described westerly from Grand Marais to Munising.

This is Hiawatha Country, made famous in Henry Wadsworth Longfellow's epic poem, "The Song of Hiawatha." Multicolored sandstone cliffs, beaches, sand dunes, waterfalls, inland lakes, wildlife and the forests of Lake Superior's shoreline beckon visitors to explore the 73,000-plus acre park, which is only 3 miles wide and hugs the shoreline for more than 40 miles.

Hike along the 5-mile (8-kilometer) stretch of sand dunes which reach up to 85 feet (26 meters) in height. The dunes sit on top of 275-foot-high (85-meter) glacial deposits of the Grand

Sable Dunes along Lake Superior, reaching inland to form Grand Sable Lake. It's a good spot for children to play. A path with wooden steps and overlooks follows Sable Falls to its base. It offers an ideal opportunity for photographs of the vistas.

Keep an eye out for signs pointing to the Log Slide parking lot and viewpoint, where the towering dunes meet Lake Superior. In heavy logging days, logs were hauled to the lip of the sand dunes and slid down the 500-foot (154-meter) log chute to be rafted to market. A scenic overlook and wayside exhibits make for a pleasant experience. If you decide to shoot-the-chute, keep in mind that it may take less than five minutes to descend, but more than an hour to climb back up the steep slope.

DIRECTORY

Tourist Information – Visitor Information Center, 906-387-3700 (Munising), 906-494-2660 (Grand Marais, summer)

The Au Sable Light Station is visible from this overlook. The 87-foot-high Au Sable Lighthouse is being restored. The original six-foot-high Fresnel lens that once warned mariners away from the rocky coast has been returned to the lighthouse.

The park has three campgrounds that are accessible by vehicle (with fee): Hurricane River, Twelvemile Beach and Little Beaver Lake. Thirteen back-country campgrounds and eight group sites are spaced along a 42-mile section of the North Country National Scenic Trail. There is no entrance fee, but a paid permit is required for overnight camping.

You should watch for the signs at Melstrand to Chapel Beach, which doesn't have camping facilities. For other lake-shore sites, take Miners Castle Road north to Miners Castle, a unique sandstone formation that is possibly the most photographed natural feature on Lake Superior.

Winter enthusiasts will enjoy the Pictured Rocks areas. Two systems of cross-country ski trails offer spectacular views of Lake Superior, waterfalls and the Grand Sable Dunes.

See the Munising listing for information on boat cruises along the Lakeshore.

POPLAR, WISCONSIN

Population 550

Poplar is the hometown of Richard Ira Bong, "America's Ace of Aces," a title he earned by shooting the most enemy aircraft, and World War II veteran. A museum honoring Bong and all World War II veterans is located in nearby Superior. Also in Poplar, golfers will want to test their mettle against the 18-hole Poplar Golf Course and Campground on County Road D.

Poplar, Wisconsin, regional map – page 2.

What's Next

On Highway 2 just east of Poplar is the small town of Maple, where you'll catch your first or last glimpse of the lake and Superior-Duluth in the distance from high along one of the ancient shorelines of Lake Superior. Night or day, the view is impressive.

A village and resort area about 5 miles (8 kilometers) south of Poplar on County Road P, Lake Nebagamon boasts a depot and post office that were built at the village site in 1896. The area is well-known for its summer recreation, which includes Botten's Green Acres Golf Course, a 9-hole par 35 course south of the townsite. Nearby at Lake Minnesuing is Norwood Golf Course, another 9-hole par 34 course. A few miles south at Solon Springs, Hidden Greens North offers an 18-hole par 72 challenge amid tranquil, tree-lined splendor. It's worth asking directions to get there. The clubhouse offers a bar and lounge for relaxation after the round.

Port Wing, Wisconsin, regional map – page 2.

PORT WING, WISCONSIN

Population 430

The harbor at Port Wing opens the waters to prolific fishing opportunities. A boat launch and transient slips are available at the Port Wing Marina and Holiday Pines Resort. The marina has gas (no diesel), a mechanic shop, showers, a snack bar and added 14 slips recently. Charter service is located at the harbor for anglers wishing to get out on the big lake with an experienced captain. The drive from the marina east of town goes through the Port Wing Boreal Forest. There are two city parks.

A reclaimed church houses local art and pottery at Port Wing Pottery and across the highway Hoth Lee Gallery offers commissioned and consignment artwork for sale. Other outlets offer lovely crafted gifts, most made by local artisans.

Port Wing's claim to fame is its annual fish boil, which sounds strange but is absolutely enticing. The smells, outdoor ambiance and flavors of fish make it worth a special late summer trip. Held each year the Saturday before Labor Day.

If your route takes you north, Highway 13 passes through Herbster, Cornucopia and Red Cliff on the way to

---

DIRECTORY

Tourist Information – Superior-Douglas County Tourist Information, 715-394-7716, 800-942-5313; Wisconsin Tourism, 800-432-8747

DIRECTORY

Tourist Information – Bayfield County Tourism, 800-472-6338

Where to Stay
Anchor Inn and Campground, 715-774-3658, 8875 Hwy. 13, has cabin lodging and campsites.
Holiday Pines Resort, 715-774-3555, 9130 Beach Rd., offers lakeside lodging.

Where to Eat with a Local Flavor
Cottage Cafe, 715-774-3565, 8805 Hwy. 13, offers homemade soups, pizza and good pies.

Bayfield. To the south and west are charming farms and farmland. This route offers occasional glimpses of Lake Superior and the Minnesota coastline over the trees. You'll pass through the small dairy communities of Cloverland and Lakeside. A bit farther along Wisconsin 13 at the Brule River, rest a bit at the canoe launch area or watch the river from the bridge. It's a chance to get right to the river's edge without having to forage through the brush. Take the Brule River Road into the Brule River State Forest for beach access and fishing opportunities. Handicapped accessible. See details in listing for Brule.

PUKASKWA NATIONAL PARK, ONTARIO

If any stretch of coast on Ontario's shore could be deemed the wildest and most undeveloped, it would be in the Pukaskwa National Park. Pukaskwa (pronounced PUK-a-saw) was opened in 1983. It is Ontario's largest national park and the only Canadian national park on Lake Superior. The park offers vistas of Lake Superior, with a rugged landscape carved out of the Canadian Shield and northern forests. The wilderness is one of the reasons visitors choose Pukaskwa as their destination.

Only one road penetrates the boundaries. Highway 627 leads 12 kilometers (7.5 miles) from Highway 17 to Hattie Cove, which is 42 kilometers (26 miles) from Marathon, yet is in the extreme northern tip of the 1,880-square-kilometer (720-square-mile) preserve. The vast interior is accessible only by trail, river or lake. Rated: difficult. A campground with 67 sites, some with electricity, is near the visitor center. Short walking trails and access to three sand beaches on Lake Superior, plus a picnic area, are located at Hattie Cove. Handicapped accessible. Fees charged. Reservations for the back country are recommended.

Although the park is open year-round, the road into Hattie Cove is not maintained during the winter. However, visitors may walk, ski or snowshoe in.

The Canadian Boreal Shield, Lake Superior shore and boreal forest are combined within the park. Nowhere else is the resulting environment so striking. Here are jagged mountain crests (some rising 460 meters or 1,500 feet above the lake's surface), moose, wolf, caribou and bear and subarctic flora. Within Pukaskwa is a small herd of woodland caribou, the farthest south that these animals can still be found naturally in Ontario.

Visitors with good doses of curiosity and adventurous desire, along with extensive wilderness experience, can backpack the trails deep into the park. From the trail head at

DIRECTORY

Tourist Information – Pukaskwa National Park Headquarters, 807-229-0801

P

Lake Superior - Pukaskwa National Park

Hattie Cove, the trail follows the coast 60 kilometers (37 miles) to the North Swallow River. The Coastal Trail, with its marvelous suspension bridge over White River Gorge, suits hikers' needs well. It is the route most often traveled if you have limited time. Canoes on interior rivers, as well as power boats and sailboats on Lake Superior, are common means of seeing such sites as Otter Island Light and Cascade Falls, where the Cascade River ends its trek to Lake Superior in the grand flourish of a 15-meter (49-foot) plummet.

Back country visitors must register in and out with the park office, either in person or by phone. Group size limit is eight people per party. Kayak and canoe rental is available in Marathon.

Red Cliff - Rossport

RED CLIFF, WISCONSIN

Reservation Population 924

Red Cliff and the Red Cliff Indian Reservation are home of the Red Cliff Band of Lake Superior Chippewa. Nearby, Native Spirit Gifts and Indian Museum shop offers a delightful selection of Woodland Native crafts. The reservation, located 3 miles north of Bayfield on Highway 13, operates the Red Cliff Fish Hatchery, where advance reservations allow visits.

Red Cliff, Wisconsin, regional map – page 28.

The Red Cliff Entertainment Complex offers a variety of gaming fun at the Isle Vista Casino, as well as live entertainment, bar and restaurant. The complex is open seven days a week, year-round. It's worth a stop just to see the beautiful wall-sized mural on Native American life that was created by Rita Vanderventer. With recent completion of a new wastewater treatment facility, the tribal council approved contracts for a new $20-$22 million casino, hotel, restaurant and marina complex to replace the present facility.

The view of the islands from the area around the center is spectacular. The 45-slip Buffalo Bay Marina provides services for those traveling by boat.

Sea kayakers will want to check on packages of instruction, full-day or half-day tours of nearby sea caves, shipwrecks and Bass Island offered by Living Adventures.

Red Cliff's annual Fourth of July Powwow is a festival of traditional dance, song, food, arts and crafts. An outdoor concert in September is also a popular attraction.

Campers will find several options in the area. The Point Detour Campground has updated facilities and looks out on the Apostle Islands. The Russell Town Park at Little Sand Bay, the Ranger Station and Hokenson Fishery also offer campsites.

DIRECTORY

Tourist Information – Bayfield Chamber of Commerce, 715-779-3335, 800-447-4094; Bayfield County Tourism, 800-472-6338. Camping information, 715-779-3743

What's Next

Just west of the Red Cliff reservation is a National Lakeshore visitor center, with camping, boat launch and the restored Hokenson Brothers Fishery. Well worth the stop, you'll find it by taking County K to Little Sand Bay Road.

To the west 18 miles on Highway 13, Cornucopia has the state's northernmost post office. South on the highway takes you to Bayfield, Washburn and Ashland.

RED ROCK, ONTARIO

Population 1,260

Red Rock, Ontario, regional map – page 10.

No traveler can fail to notice the rusty red layers of stone that give this region and the town of Red Rock its name. A ruddy hematite-bearing strata of rock called Red Rock Cuesta is sandwiched between a granite base and younger diabase that flowed into the red layer and was exposed by erosion. The picturesque cuesta is evidence of the direction of glacial movement and is at the end of Highway 628 on Nipigon Bay.

Red Rock, the home of a large packaging mill owned by Norampac, offers the lakeside Pull-a-Log Park on the bay. A 50-slip Red Rock Marina combines a breakwall with fish and wildlife habitat, boat docks, full fuel and pumpout facilities, fishing ramps and a park with a boardwalk along the beach within this most northerly town on the big lake. Hiking and cross-country ski trails extending to Nipigon have been developed.

Red Rock annually holds a June fishing derby, a Canada Day celebration with fireworks over the marina on July 1, the Paju Mountain Run in early August, "Live from the Rock" Folk Festival in August and a winter carnival in February.

DIRECTORY

Tourist Information – North of Superior Tourism Association, 807-887-3333, 800-265-3951

What's Next

As we leave Red Rock and turn north on Highway 11/17 for Nipigon or south toward Thunder Bay, we're now truly north of Lake Superior.

ROCKLAND, MICHIGAN

Population 267

Rockland is just west of the junction of U.S. 45 and M-26. It is well worth a slow drive through the streets of this small town to view the interesting and well-decorated Victorian homes. At the Rockland Historical Museum, there are photographs, antiques and documents of the town's past. A park and playground are located in the center of town, a communitywide effort that is open to the public. Incidentally, Rockland is the site of the first telephone system to operate in

the state of Michigan. The original switchboard for the phone system is housed in the Ontonagon County Historical Society in Ontonagon.

DIRECTORY

Tourist Information – Ontonagon Area Chamber of Commerce, 906-884-4735

From Rockland, take a quick side trip southwest onto the Victoria Road to the old restored ghost mining village of Victoria, about 5 miles (8 kilometers) off Highway 45. Here, 4 of 10 log homes constructed in the early 1900s as homes for the miners working at Victoria Mine have been restored and are open for guided tours from Memorial Day through mid-October. Ongoing work by volunteer workers can be seen on a fifth home that will be opened for tours in the future. Daily tours of the homes or interesting surrounding sites are offered. Fee.

The famous three-ton pure-copper Ontonagon Boulder, which is now housed in the Smithsonian Institution in Washington, D.C., was discovered on the Ontonagon River at the site where Victoria Dam was later constructed.

ROSSPORT, ONTARIO

Population 113

Founded as a stop on the Canadian Pacific, Rossport first developed into a fishing village known as McKay's Harbour. It was a port instrumental in delivery of supplies for the building of the railroad in the mid-1880s and trains still pass day and night. New highway signage makes it less likely that Rossport will be missed, but it does sit slightly off Highway 17. A stop is well worth the time.

Rossport, Ontario, regional map – page 12.

What to See and Do

The many islands of Schreiber Channel dot Lake Superior's face, and you may well find beautiful yachts anchored in the harbor.

If you want to sightsee from water level, kayaks and canoes can be rented from Superior Outfitters, which sponsors a Sea Kayaking Festival the last weekend in June each year.

Walk quiet Church Street and visit the Rossport Cemetery, where many a historic figure lies in peace. The Catholic and Protestant cemeteries lie side-by-side.

Rossport continues to be an important starting point for lake divers, although no charter boats are available for either divers or anglers who do not have their own craft. The marina facilities continue to be improved as part of an update program that includes permanent fuel and pumpout facilities.

Casque Isles Hiking Trail begins or ends in Rossport, depending where you start. The trail runs 52 kilometers (31

DIRECTORY

Tourist Information – North of Superior Tourism Association, 807-887-3333, 800-265-3951

Where to Stay
Rossport Inn, 807-824-3213, 6 Bowman St., is a historic lodge offering seven guest rooms and good dining.

The Willows, 807-824-3389, is a nice B&B inn occupying the former schoolhouse.

Where to Eat
Serendipity Gardens Cafe and Guest House, 807-824-2890, Main St., has gourmet dining in a lovely setting.

miles) in length from Rossport through Schreiber to Terrace Bay. The trail, divided into five sections for day hikes, is maintained by the Casque Isle Hiking Club, which provides guided tours during the summer. This trail is rated difficult, but a favorite of avid hikers who also do much of the maintenance and improvements on the trail.

Notable Museums

Rossport Caboose Museum is loaded with local historic artifacts, including a plethora of railroad photos.

Parks and Public Space

Rainbow Falls Provincial Park has two campgrounds in the Rossport area. The lakeshore campground has 36 sites, with showers, laundry facilities, a picnic shelter and a sand beach on Lake Superior.

Rainbow Falls, located farther up above the highway, encompasses the hills around Whitesand Lake and the Whitesand River as it tumbles over Rainbow Falls. From a wooden hiking bridge over the river, sunlight can be seen refracted in rainbows by the mist from the cascades. There are an additional 97 tent and trailer sites at the Rainbow Falls campground. Hiking trails (which include a section of the Casque Isles Hiking Trail) run throughout the park. Rated: difficult. Open mid-May to mid-September.

What's Next

From Rossport, follow Highway 17 either to the east toward Schreiber or west bound for Nipigon.

St. Ignace - Superior

ST. IGNACE, MACKINAC AREA, MICHIGAN

Population 2,570

St. Ignace is a gateway to Mackinac Island. It is also considered the gateway to the Upper Peninsula from Lower Michigan, as well as being the junction where we join two other Great Lakes Circle Tours: the Lake Huron and the Lake Michigan Circle Tours. A city full of good eating and lodging options, St. Ignace and its surroundings are good for several days of sightseeing, if you have the time.

St. Ignace, Michigan, regional map – page 46.

What to See and Do

The massive, awe-inspiring Mackinac Bridge is a dominant feature of this area. At 8,614 feet (2,650 meters) including anchorages, it's the world's longest suspension bridge. Twin towers rise 552 feet (170 meters) above the Straits of Mackinac, which join Lake Huron with Lake Michigan. Maximum water depth at midspan is 295 feet (90 meters). The "Mighty Mac" is closed to pedestrian traffic except on Labor Day, when the two east lanes are open to walkers. More than 45,000 people annually make the walk from St. Ignace to Mackinaw City on the Lower Peninsula, beginning at 7:30 a.m.

To the north of St. Ignace, you'll find Castle Rock, an interesting and accessible example of several similar rock formations in the area called "sea stacks." A stairway takes visitors to a viewing platform 195 feet (65 meters) above water level atop the rock which native people once used to scan the surrounding area. Other sea stacks are St. Anthony's Rock, also in St. Ignace, and Arch Rock on Mackinac Island.

Named for and honoring the life of French missionary Father Jacques Marquette, the Marquette National Memorial is located off U.S. Highway 2 in Straits State Park. It offers a magnificent view of the Mackinac Bridge. No charge. Open June to Labor Day.

Walk the waterfront on the Huron Boardwalk, with a view of the many bay activities and the island. Historic events

S

DIRECTORY

Tourist Information – St. Ignace
Area Chamber of Commerce,
906-643-8717

Where to Stay
Days Inn of St. Ignace Suites,
906-643-8008, 1067 N. State St., offers
nice rooms close to most things to do.
Holiday Inn Express, 906-643-0200,
800-906-0201, 965 N. State St., has
whirlpool rooms, indoor pool and
continental breakfast.

are described on the signs along the way.
For boaters, the city operates a 100-slip
marina with full fuel, water, pumpout and
dockside power service.

Mackinac Island (population 469) has
three ferry lines regularly making the trip
across the 7-mile (11-kilometer) span of
Lake Huron from St. Ignace. See separate
listing for Mackinac Island.

Notable Museums

Visit the Museum of Ojibwa Culture
at Marquette Mission Park, which
preserves the culture and folkways of the
Huron and Ojibway people who first
inhabited this important route to the
west. No charge to enter the park, but
there is a fee for the museum.

Notable Events

• The annual Straits Area Auto Show and St. Ignace Car
Show Weekend is at the end of June and includes a parade
and cruising, concerts and Mackinac Bridge Rally.

ST. JOSEPH ISLAND, ONTARIO

St. Joseph Island, Ontario,
regional map – page 18.

On the Ontario side of the St. Marys River is St. Joseph
Island, about 45 kilometers (30 miles) southeast of Sault,
Ontario. Accessed by bridge on Highway 548 off Highway 17
(Trans Canada Highway), the towns of Richards Landing and
Hilton Beach welcome visitors.

At the southeastern end of the island (51 kilometers or 34
miles), Fort St. Joseph National Historic Site contains the
remains of an important outpost of the fur
trade from the late 1700s to early 1800s,
with walking trails, a bird sanctuary, a
reception center and displays of artifacts
from this historic era. Open daily mid-
May to mid-October.

DIRECTORY

Tourist Information – St. Joseph
Island Economic Development Office,
705-246-1780

Boaters will find three marinas
(Richards Landing Municipal, Hilton
Beach and Whiskey Bay) along with other
areas amenable to anchoring.

At Echo Lake, about midway to St. Joseph Island on
Highway 17, a handicapped accessible 340-meter (1,100-
foot) boardwalk and viewing platform is located in the Lake
George Marsh. The 647-acre wetland is used by migrating
waterfowl for feeding and rest. It is a Living Legacy Heritage
site designated by the Ontario government.

SAULT STE. MARIE, MICHIGAN

Population: 14,500

Sault Ste. Marie offers history, shopping, a variety of
waterborne commerce to watch, nightlife, fine dining and all
of the other amenities of an international metropolitan center.

Sault Ste. Marie, Michigan,
regional map – page 18.

A Bit of History

At Sault Ste. Marie, you're in Michigan's oldest city and
the third oldest in the United States. The rapids of the St.
Marys River had been, for regional Indian people, a spring
meeting place for generations (and, yes, St. Marys without the
apostrophe is the proper spelling in this case). They would
come to talk and to spear and eat whitefish. This traditional
fishing and gathering place of the Chippewa and other Great
Lakes tribal people first saw Europeans when voyageur
Etienne Brule passed this way in 1620. A Jesuit mission was
established by fathers Jacques Marquette and Claude Dablon
by the year 1668. After establishing the mission, Marquette
and Dablon named the city to honor the Virgin Mary and the
nearby rapids. It is home to the Sault tribe of Chippewa, also
known as Ojibway. Before the white men came to the area,
the Ojibway, who lived nearby, portaged their canoes around
the *bahweting* (rapids) to reach Lake Superior. In the three
centuries since, the two cities of Sault Ste. Marie (nicknamed
Sault on the Ontario side and Soo on the Michigan side) have
been divided by the St. Marys River and an international
boundary, but gained worldwide shipping importance after
the first Soo Lock was opened on the Michigan side in 1855.
The 2-mile (3-kilometer) span of the International Bridge
opened in October 1962, improving transportation between
the two Sault Ste. Maries. Prior to the bridge, ferries taxied
automobiles and passengers across the St. Marys River. There
are now more than 3.5 million vehicular crossings of the
bridge annually. Travel time from downtown to downtown is
generally 15 minutes. Today, together, this is the third largest
metropolitan area on Lake Superior, behind Thunder Bay
and Duluth-Superior.

Today

The economy of Soo, Michigan, is closely tied to Great
Lakes and international shipping via the St. Marys River.
Much of the commercial activity on the river has historically
depended on cargoes passing between Lake Huron and Lake
Superior. In earlier times, when the rapids made marine
passage impossible, that included unloading ships,
warehousing cargo, moving the cargoes past the rapids that
stopped interlake transportation, then reloading it on other
ships to continue its journey. Much of that effort ended in

1855 when the first Soo Lock opened. Today, the Soo Locks remain important to local commerce by employing many skilled workers, and passing ships continue to contribute to the economy by contracting for some supplies from merchant firms in the city. In addition, the Soo Locks attract thousands of visitors to the city each year to watch the locks in operation, making tourism an important ingredient in the city's economy.

Soo is also a regional education center. Lake Superior State University occupies the site of old Fort Brady, with some historic buildings still intact. The 115-acre campus is a good spot to photograph the International Bridge to Ontario. The university offers many interesting programs like a robotics laboratory, criminal justice, nursing, fisheries and wildlife and many professional degrees. The LSSU hockey team is a consistent contender on the national collegiate hockey scene.

What to See and Do

Four American navigational locks make the Michigan Soo a major center of marine transportation, as well as a center of tourism and the most visited site on Lake Superior. With the opening of the St. Lawrence Seaway in 1959, foreign flagged vessels, known on the Great Lakes as "salties," are now much in evidence, giving the Soo Locks a truly international flavor. Poe Lock is the largest lock in the St. Lawrence Seaway and is the only one that can handle the super freighters, which are more than 1,000 feet (308 meters) long and 105 feet (32 meters) wide. In about 45 minutes from entry into a gate, the locks raise and lower lakers and ocean-going vessels 21 feet (6.5 meters) between Lake Superior and Lake Huron. More than 95 million tons of cargo pass through the locks annually. Parks parallel the locks, with three observation platforms and a U.S. Army Corps of Engineers Information Center. From the platforms, visitors are within feet of the vessels going through the locks. There are good exhibits at the info center, explaining exactly how the lock system works. Once a year in June the Corps allows visitors to walk out to the locks for a closer inspection. Portage Avenue runs parallel to the lock and has a row of souvenir and gift shops (ranging from touristy to artistic), restaurants and attractions.

Beginning at the information center in the upper Locks Park, take a stroll along the city's one-mile (1.6 kilometer) Historic Waterfront Pathway, extending through Brady Park and the lower Locks Park, past four major historic buildings and to the SS *Valley Camp* museum ship. The pathway has been signed with information describing the history of the St. Marys River. Stop at the John Johnston House, the oldest

Soo Locks

No matter what else catches your attention in Sault Ste. Marie, it's a fact that you cannot ignore the waterfront and maritime activity on the St. Marys River. Central to that fact are the famed Soo Locks, four of which are on the Michigan side, with one on the Ontario side.

A visitor center operated by the United States Army Corps of Engineers is a vital stop for Soo, Michigan, visitors, with detailed information about the operation of the Soo Locks, which raise and lower ships and recreational craft more than 20 feet to compensate for the different water levels of Lake Superior and Lake Huron.

While the raising or lowering of up to 1,000-foot (308-meter) ships carrying upward of 60,000 tons of cargo seems awesome, the concept of the locks is relatively simple. Gates enclose the ship in the lock and water is admitted or discharged, depending on whether the ship is being raised or lowered. When the water level reaches the level of that beyond the gate, it is opened and the vessel glides away at the new elevation.

The Canadian Lock on the Ontario shore once handled commercial shipping traffic, but was damaged in 1987 and rebuilt to handle smaller boats and recreational traffic. The new Canadian Lock was constructed inside the original and is surrounded by beautiful grounds and buildings. that give visitors access to walk out on the structure for close up views.

Tour services are available on both sides of the river to get visitors close to the shipping and locking activity.

In 2005, Michigan celebrated the 150th anniversary of the opening of the first lock in 1855. The task of constructing that first lock was herculean. Most of the needed work was completed with man and horsepower, explosives and sheer willpower, but resulted in much more efficient transportation on the Great Lakes.

S

house in Michigan, built in 1793. A plaque marks the site of the restored 19th century homes of Bishop Frederic Baraga and Henry Schoolcraft. Another historic spot is the Kemp Commercial Building, long influential in the city's affairs through shipping and commercial fishing.

Museum Ship SS *Valley Camp* is a retired 550-foot (170-meter) Great Lakes freighter and maritime museum, one of only two such floating ore boat museums on Lake Superior, the other being in Duluth, Minnesota. See the gleaming stainless steel galley, dining rooms, the crew's quarters and bridge, authentically maintained. The two recovered lifeboats from the *Edmund Fitzgerald* are on display. There is also a large aquarium with Lake Superior fish. The Ship's Store has gifts and many nautical items for sale and is a must stop on your visit. Open daily from mid-May to mid-October. Operated by Le Sault de Ste. Marie Historic Sites.

Tower of History takes visitors up 21 floors for a 20-mile (32-kilometer) panoramic view of the city, locks, the lakes and Sault Ste. Marie, Ontario. There's a video depicting the history of the Great Lakes and Sault Ste. Marie. Open mid-May to mid-October.

Although the city's oldest church, the majestic twin-towered United Presbyterian Church, was destroyed by fire in 2000, it was rebuilt and is again open. History buffs can walk past Sault Ste. Marie's four remaining historic churches as well as the new United Presbyterian edifice by following a pathway marked on the sidewalks. Visitors can get maps and information at the Tourist Information Center.

Soo Locks Boat Tours leave from two docks for narrated two-hour cruises through the Soo Locks alongside huge ships, up river to the Algoma Steel Mill and past the St. Marys Rapids. Docks are at two locations east on Portage Avenue. Tours run daily May 15 to October 15. Also there are $2^{1}/_{2}$-hour dinner cruises including the locks tour. The company offers $4^{1}/_{2}$-hour Saturday morning St. Marys River lighthouse cruises with water level views of Point Iroquois, Gros Cap Reef and the remains of Round Island lighthouses, as well as many other sites. Boarding at 7:45 a.m. with continental breakfast. Reservations recommended for dinner and lighthouse cruises. A nice added service is free kenneling for your pets during the tour.

Another interesting way to sightsee is aboard Soo Locks Train Tours. With new and refurbished equipment, the rubber-tired trains offer a fun way to tour the area from the depot in the downtown area.

Linksters will want to sample the pleasures of Sault Ste. Marie Country Club or Tanglewood Marsh, both with 18 holes.

Visitors to the city using boats can use the Charles T. Harvey Marina on Riverside Drive near the golf course. It has

DIRECTORY

Tourist Information – Sault Ste. Marie, Michigan Convention and Visitors Bureau, 906-632-3366; E.V. Erickson Michigan Travel Center, 906-632-8242

Where to Stay
Ramada Plaza Ojibway Hotel, 906-635-8125, 240 W. Portage is a historic lodging right on the waterfront. Super 8, 906-632-8882, 3826 I-75 Business Spur, has nice lodgings with many extras. Lockview Motel, 906-632-2491, 327 W. Portage, offers waterfront lodging close to everything. Kewadin Casino Hotel, 906-635-1400, 2186 Shunk Road, provides comfortable lodgings with Las Vegas gaming excitement and regular performances by nationally known artists.

Where to Eat with a Local Flavor
Freighter's Restaurant, 906-632-4211, 240 W. Portage St., is right on the waterfront. Great shipwatching while you dine.
The Antler's, 906-632-3571, 804 E. Portage, creates its atmosphere combining hunting and a speakeasy past. Expect a few speakeasy raids! Its good pub menu includes huge burgers.

a rest station and provides fuel and other services. Adjacent to the *Valley Camp* in Mariners' Park, the city-owned George Kemp Downtown Marina features 62 slips for transient boat traffic. For camping next to the river, try Aune-Osborn Campground on Riverside Drive. It has one hundred sites and is across from the Country Club golf course. Open mid-May to mid-October.

Kewadin Casinos (key-WAY-den) is a Vegas-style casino with all the games and entertainment that go with it. Located on Shunk Road within the city limits, the casino is operated by the Sault Band of Chippewa Indians. A Clarion Hotel is attached to the casino and the Dreammakers Amphitheater, which seats 1,500, is home to headliners from the entertainment industry. Shuttle bus and limousine service from area hotels are available.

S

Notable Museums

Art lovers will love to visit Alberta House Arts Center and its Olive M. Craig Gallery and Gift Shop. They feature Upper Peninsula arts and crafts, exhibits that change regularly through the season and workshops. Open February through November, Tuesday through Saturday. This is also the de facto headquarters for much of the artistic efforts in the area.

The River of History Museum is located on Portage Avenue in the Federal Heritage Building, also called the Old Post Office. It is operated under the auspices of the Sault Ste.

Marie Foundation for Culture and History. The museum documents 8,000 years of the region's Native American, early missionary, pioneer and marine history. Open with no fee seven days a week, except November and December, when it's open Tuesday through Saturday.

Archeology fans will want to stop by the Federal Heritage Building to see artifacts from archeological digs on the original site of Old Fort Brady. Dating from 1822, the fort is the scene of an encampment of more than 100 re-enactors in July. It is also the site of a history and culture camp for kids during the summer.

Notable Events

• I-500 Snowmobile Classic is a challenging race for snow sledders on an oval track in early February.

• Soo Locks Festival is a yearly June celebration of the importance of the four American locks to commerce on the Great Lakes and includes the International Bridge Walk and Engineers Day described below.

• International Bridge Walk/Engineers Day is a yearly June opportunity for visitors and residents to stretch their legs by hiking across the International Bridge as well as walk out on the locks to examine them at close range.

• Great Tugboat Race is an annual July competition to determine the fastest boat in the twin Saults' tug fleets.

• Summer Arts Festival is an August celebration of the region's artistic skills on the Michigan waterfront.

• Sault Salmon Derby in September challenges anglers each year to vie for the biggest fish for a nice prize.

What's Next

If your Circle Tour Route crosses into Canada from Soo, you'll cross the International Bridge to Sault, Canada, where you'll want to explore a while before picking up Trans Canada Highway 17 heading north. Be aware that non-residents older than 17 must have a Crown Land Camping Permit to stay overnight on Crown Land. Permits are available from most Ontario license issuers and Ministry of Natural Resources offices. We also suggest you review material on border crossing in the front of this volume.

If your itinerary is across Michigan's Upper Peninsula, we suggest leaving the Soo area south on Interstate 75/U.S. 2 toward St. Ignace. About 10 miles south you'll pick up Michigan Highway 28 and head west. However, if you intend to stop at Brimley, you can take either Business Interstate 75/County H-63 or Highway 129 south and turn west at Six Mile Road, which will take you closer to the shoreline and cut off several miles of travel. Either way, you'll be traveling into

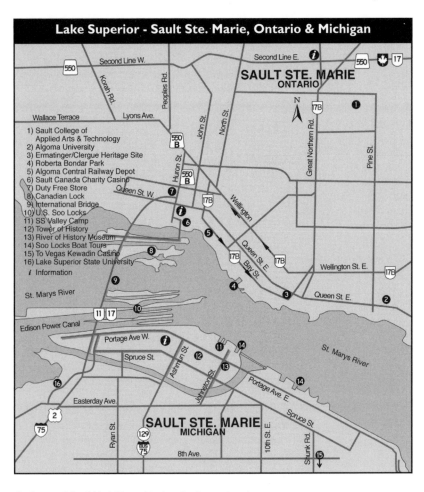

Lake Superior - Sault Ste. Marie, Ontario & Michigan

SAULT STE. MARIE
ONTARIO

SAULT STE. MARIE
MICHIGAN

1) Sault College of
   Applied Arts & Technology
2) Algoma University
3) Ermatinger/Clergue Heritage Site
4) Roberta Bondar Park
5) Algoma Central Railway Depot
6) Sault Canada Charity Casino
7) Duty Free Store
8) Canadian Lock
9) International Bridge
10) U.S. Soo Locks
11) SS Valley Camp
12) Tower of History
13) River of History Museum
14) Soo Locks Boat Tours
15) To Vegas Kewadin Casino
16) Lake Superior State University
i Information

the heart of the fabled Upper Peninsula. An option that we
strongly recommend is to visit the eastern and southern U.P.
by traveling south to St. Ignace to take in the mighty
Mackinac Bridge and a number of other interesting sights and
experiences on the north shoreline of Lake Michigan.

SAULT STE. MARIE, ONTARIO

Population: 78,000

Whether entering the city from Soo, Michigan, or via
Highway 17 from the north, the Ontario Sault has a wealth
of sites, shopping, dining and cosmopolitan charm deserving
a generous period of exploring and poking around by visitors.
Although the younger of Lake Superior's only international
metro area, Sault, Ontario, managed to become the larger of
the twin cities by mixing an interesting blend of early fur
trade wealth with later industrial production, importance as a

Sault Ste. Marie, Ontario,
regional map – page 18.

225

shipping center and as the regional center for a wide range of other activities.

An enticing array of ethnic dining will tempt you to indulge in all your favorite foods, then walk away the calories by hiking along the river front or shopping for a nice assortment of Canadian and international goods. There is also a great assortment of lodging options that allow you to relax in whatever atmosphere you desire after a day of exploring.

A Bit of History

Despite being on a marshy flood plain, the Canadian Sault Ste. Marie became the larger of the two cities after 1783, when a treaty made the river the boundary between Canada and the new United States. The fur companies were headquartered in Montreal, so business needed to be conducted on Canadian soil.

The early history of this Sault is firmly tied to the fur trade and the exploits of the voyageurs. From the mid-1600s until the mid-1800s, huge volumes of beaver and other pelts were trapped and shipped from the northern United States and Canada to England via both the Great Lakes waterways and Hudson's Bay in the northern territory.

A canal for canoes was dug on Canadian soil in 1799. It included an 11.7-meter (38-foot) lock, used to raise and lower boat traffic between Lake Huron and Lake Superior. It was destroyed by U.S. troops during the War of 1812. By the mid-1800s, development in the Lake Superior region and the need to carry resources to the populous down-lake markets on larger ships pressed for a new canal. Prior to the opening of the American canal and lock in 1855, a few ships, some weighing up to 400 tons, were laboriously portaged around the rapids with lots of mules, logs, men and grease. The Canadian canal and lock opened in 1895, was damaged in 1987, rebuilt for recreational craft and re-opened in 1998.

Soon after the Canadian Lock opened, Francis H. Clergue, a Maine entrepreneur, implemented a grand plan to reap the benefits of the river's hydroelectric power, regional lumber and iron ore from Michipicoten. Although he went bankrupt, his Algoma Steel Corporation has been successfully producing steel ever since and remains a significant Sault employer despite recent economic difficulty. Besides shipping and steel, the Sault boasts chemical, paper, lumber and veneer plants.

In the latter 20th century, the Sault waterfront was beginning to show deterioration, and a plan was put in place to reclaim and rejuvenate areas where tank farms and tired industrial buildings dominated. That effort, years in the implementation, has resulted in one of the most attractive,

ST. MARYS
RIVER BOARDWALK

First time visitors to Sault, Ontario, may find it hard to believe, but the waterfront area was once the scene of deteriorating industrial sites, large tank farms and other eyesores. Decades of planning and construction have resulted in renovation of that area into what can arguably called the centerpiece of the city.

A vital part of that waterfront rejuvenation is the St. Marys River Boardwalk, which stretches along the waterfront from the Civic Centre to Canadian Canal and Lock, offering a chance stretch the legs and see many interesting sights along the way. There are fishing platforms, cute statues of wildlife, the Roberta Bondar Tent Pavilion, which often has interesting events scheduled, and the Roberta Bondar Marine Park and Marina, where visiting boaters can tie up. Named for the Sault native, the Bondar sites honor Canada's first female astronaut.

If you have time, be sure to visit the Penthouse Observation Gallery atop the Civic Centre for a grand panorama of the entire St. Marys waterfront area, as well as the interactive exhibits and artwork in the lobby of Roberta Bondar Place where the Ontario Lottery and Gaming Corporation is headquartered.

vibrant waterfronts on Lake Superior, attracting thousands of shoppers, tourists, strollers, anglers and others seeking an up close lake experience. This helps to make a strong tourism economy in the Sault.

Today

In addition to producing a wide range of industrial products, the Sault serves as the regional shopping mecca for a large surrounding area. It also supports a strong cultural heritage that includes museums, performing arts, music and drama.

An educational center for the region, Sault Ste. Marie is home to Algoma University College, strong in undergraduate arts and music courses. Affiliated with Laurentian University in Sudbury, Ontario, Algoma has a historically interesting campus, architecturally blending the old with the new and Native Canadian culture with European. The Old Shingwauk

School, an early boarding school for First Nations students, is the base for the University's library/resource center. A 150-year-old cemetery on the grounds is regularly maintained. The campus overlooks the St. Marys River. Tours are available.

The Sault College of Applied Arts and Technology on Great Northern Road operates the Northern Ontario School of Hospitality, along with many other technical and vocational programs.

Sault serves as the medical and health care center of the Ontario Algoma area, with smaller outlying practices and facilities referring patients to medical personnel and facilities in Sault Ste. Marie, where Sault Area Hospitals and physicians in a wide range of specialties provide services to clients. The hospitals are a major employer in the city.

What to See and Do

The primary areas of interest to the visitor in the Sault, Ontario, are along the waterfront. The most visible and romantic thing about the Sault is the movement of lakers, salties, cruisers and pleasure boats along St. Marys River, but there is much else in this third largest Lake Superior city to see and do.

After being damaged in 1987, the new Canadian Lock was re-opened in 1998 to serve small craft. Built inside the walls of the original commercial lock, which was 277 meters (900 feet) long, the new lock is 77 meters (250 feet) long, 15.4 meters (50 feet) wide and 13.5 meters (44 feet) deep, with a below-water draft of 3 meters (9.8 feet) and is surrounded by park land. Stroll around the grounds or visit the interpretative center. You can walk across the gates and view the rapids. The lock now serves recreational navigation from May through October. The adjacent area is operated as Sault Canal National Historic Site by Parks Canada. The heritage buildings in the lock area are constructed of red sandstone, excavated during the construction of the canal.

Perhaps the Sault's most popular attraction is the St. Marys River Boardwalk, which extends from the Civic Centre to the Canal. In addition to paths for biking and running, the pathway has viewing stations and a fishing platform that's guaranteed to produce a "big one." Interpretive signs and cute statuary are situated along the path.

The provincial charity Casino Sault Ste. Marie offers more than 450 slot machines ranging from a nickel to $5, as well as 16 table games. It's adjacent to the Boardwalk next to Station Mall.

On Foster Drive, the Civic Centre houses the municipal government. Fine art and sculptures are evident within the building and on the grounds. Tours of the facility are available. The Penthouse Observation Gallery at the top gives a panorama of the St. Marys River region.

The Ontario Lottery and Gaming Corporation headquartered in Roberta Bondar Place overlooks the waterfront. The computerized building houses some of the equipment that maintains the lottery operations. There are a number of exhibits in the main lobby which include interactive displays and works of art. The building also contains other governmental offices.

Kiwanis Community Theatre Centre is the major venue for concerts, theater productions, touring performances and other entertainment in Sault, Ontario. Other sites where performances may be scheduled include Verdi Hall and various churches.

The Arts Council of Sault Ste. Marie oversees many community events associated with the fine and performing arts. The Sault Symphony Orchestra, Sault Opera, Algoma Conservatory of Music and local dance schools give regular performances in many locations. In addition, local theater groups present occasional staged productions and college and university groups schedule numerous performing groups that contribute to a rich cultural atmosphere on both sides of the St. Marys River.

Retired in 1974, the 85-meter (188-foot) *Norgoma* was the last passenger ship built to cruise the Great Lakes. The ship serves as a museum, located in the Bondar Marina area. Open daily late May to October 1.

Take a two-hour narrated tour of the canal and locks from the water aboard the *Chief Shingwauk*, a 70-foot Lock Tours Canada vessel. The captain will get you right up to some of the big lakers coming through the locks. Boats leave from the Roberta Bondar Park dock, off Foster Drive. Several daily departures from mid-June until mid-October.

No visit to the Sault area would be complete without devoting a day to the Agawa Canyon Train Tours of the Algoma Central Railway. The rails that connect Sault Ste. Marie with Hearst pass through strikingly beautiful country. A daylong excursion through the Agawa Canyon area is offered seven days a week from early June through October and Friday through Sunday year-round. Most popular is the 174-meter-deep (575-foot) Agawa Canyon tour, traveling about four hours to the canyon area just east of Lake Superior Provincial Park. After a two-hour exploratory layover, the train returns to the station on Bay Street in the late afternoon. A second, longer trip leads to Hearst for an overnight, six days a week (not on Monday), returning the next day or later if you choose. No reservations on the Hearst trip, although reservations at one of three Hearst motels (Companion, Northern Seasons or Queens) or two bed-and-breakfast inns are necessary. During the autumn, the railroad regularly conducts daylong fall color tours into the region. On

S

DIRECTORY

Tourist Information – Algoma Kinniwabi Travel Association, 800-263-2546; Ontario Tourism, 800-ONTARIO [668-2746]; Sault Ste. Marie Chamber of Commerce, 705-949-7152; Tourism Sault Ste. Marie, 800-461-6020

Where to Stay
Waterfront Holiday Inn, 705-949-0611, 208 St. Marys River Dr., is right on the boardwalk with outside seating in nice weather.

Quality Inn Bay Front, 705-949-9264, 180 Bay St., offers waterfront views near the Algoma Central depot and Station Mall.

Where to Eat with a Local Flavour
New Marconi Restaurant, 705-759-8250, 480 Albert St. West, is a fully licensed establishment whose Italian cuisine has earned raves for years. Also offers a full Canadian menu.

weekends, January until March, the Snow Train plows north through the canyon on another daylong excursion. These trips offer the only transportation for sleds and snowmobilers seeking the best wilderness trails and accommodations north of the Sault. Dining car service en route. Advanced reservations should be made the day before travel.

Spruce Haven Petting and Wildlife Zoo features miniature horses, African pygmy goats, Vietnamese pot-bellied pigs, bunnies and other animals friendly to kids. Highway 550 and Carpin Beach Road, then follow the signs.

Both federal and provincial forestry centers are located in Sault Ste. Marie. The Great Lakes Forestry Centre on Queen Street is one of the most advanced forestry research institutes in the world. Operated by the Canadian Forestry Service, weekday self-guided tours are available July and August only. Tours feature greenhouses, laboratories and live insect displays. Next door is the Ontario Forestry Research Institute, a state-of-the-art, high-tech research facility which studies climactic effects on tree species. Complete with cold rooms and greenhouses, the Institute can "cheat the tree" by creating summer in winter and vice versa.

St. Mary's Ukrainian Church on St. George's Avenue East has no tours, but is open for viewing.

The world's tallest free-standing cross stands regally on the campus of St. Mary's College, off Wellington Avenue East.

For golf, try one of the area courses: Maplewood Golf Course, Queensgate Greens, Root River Golf Club, Sault Ste. Marie Golf Club, Superior View Golf Course and the city's newest championship golf course, Crimson Ridge.

In town fishing is available at various locations and the St.

Marys River Boardwalk features a fishing platform that allows anglers to wet a line right downtown.

Winter visitors and hockey enthusiasts will want to check the schedule of the Sault Greyhounds, a Junior A class amateur squad that showcases top talent heading for Olympic and National Hockey League action. Playing a 34-game home schedule, the Greyhounds compete with 20 other league teams.

Boat visitors can use the Bondar Marina, a full-service facility with 38 transient slips for boats up to 100 feet long, which greets boaters at the Captain "Skipper" Manzutti Welcome Centre, named for a longtime, prominent local businessman. The marina is a registered Canadian Customs check-in point and is the local outlet for Canadian and U.S. navigational charts. The marina is part of the Roberta Bondar Marine Park, named for Canada's first woman astronaut, who was born and grew up in Sault Ste. Marie. Downtown near the Civic Centre and adjacent to the boardwalk, the park features the 14,500-square-foot Roberta Bondar Park Tent Pavilion for concerts, special events and farmers market. The "tent-like" structure dominates the waterfront.

Notable Museums

Sault Ste. Marie Museum, housed in the old post office in Queenstown, interprets Algoma District's history. Prehistoric and pioneer artifacts, a re-creation of Queen Street in 1912 and relics of industrial development let the visitor investigate lifelike history. Open daily year-round. A few blocks away in front of the courthouse, a 22-foot-tall World War I "cenotaph" sculpture dedicated in 1922 by the Governor General of Canada honors those who gave their lives in World War I.

Built in 1814 by a wealthy fur trader, the Ermatinger Old Stone House is the oldest stone house in Canada west of Toronto. The house on Queen Street East was the early social and business focal point of the Sault. Fully restored and decorated with authentic artifacts. You'll meet interpreters in costume during self-guided tours. Also on the site is the Clergue Blockhouse, where industrialist F.H. Clergue, who established the rail, pulp and paper and steel industries in the area, once lived. Open mid-April through late November.

Located on Pim Street, the Canadian Bushplane Heritage Centre is the only facility of its type in North America, a museum that preserves the heritage of bush flying and aerial forest fire fighting. The building is the site where the science of water bombing of forest fires was developed. It was recently named Canada's best indoor attraction by Attractions Canada. A new object theatre "Wings over the North" opened in 2004. Open daily year-round. In the historic hangar at the end of Bay Street on the waterfront

Art Gallery of Algoma has an important permanent collection and regularly hosts exhibits from across the continent. It sits on the waterfront at East Street. Open Monday through Saturday.

Stop in at the Sault Ste. Marie Public Library and check out the Indian Pictograph mosaic by Jean Burke in the lobby, donated in 1967 by the Canadian Federation of University Women. Open daily.

Parks and Public Areas

Fort Creek Conservation Area is a getaway reserve for hiking and picnicking located at Second Line West and People's Road. Bellevue Park, on the eastern waterfront at Queen Street East and Lake Street, has a greenhouse, plenty of green lawn and extensive flower gardens.

Kinsmen Park on Landslide Road has historic trails and Crystal Falls. It's home to Sault Trails and Recreation, with some of the finest cross-country trails in the district. There are more than 40 kilometers (25 miles) of marked and groomed trails. Pointe Deschenes Park has hiking, picnicking and camping. The Forest Ecology Trail offers self-guided nature hikes.

Across the Canadian lock from the Canal Historic Site and on South St. Marys Island, is the Attikamek Wilderness Trail, which offers recreational activities like hiking and cross-country skiing. Whitefish Island, the third island in this area, located immediately south of South St. Marys Island, has been returned to the Batchawana First Nations and is designated as a national historic site.

Notable Events

• Ontario Winter Festival "Bon Soo" at the end of January into February is more than two weeks of winter fun that includes fireworks, outdoor recreation and family activities at the Bondar Pavilion.

• Gardening Festival in March gets a head start on the growing season by showcasing the latest in garden tools and products.

• Great Outdoor Show and Sale is an April opportunity for outdoor recreationists to put together or to satisfy their wish lists.

• Rotary Dragon Boat Races is a charitable June competition in which teams of paddlers vie in brightly colored boats on the waterfront.

• International Bridge Walk and Great Tugboat Race in late June is a chance to hike the 2-mile bridge spanning the St. Marys River and catch the excitement of tugs vying to be the fleetest of the fleets.

• Canada Day Celebrations celebrate the July 1 establishment of the nation.

• RotaryFest Summer Festival in mid-July is a celebration of family summer's joys.

• Can/Am Salmon Derby in mid August pits top anglers and would be anglers for nice prizes.

• Algoma Fall Festival takes place from September into November and includes a wide variety of entertainment and other events on a nearly daily basis.

• Santa Parade in November gives kids of all ages a chance to celebrate jolly old St. Nick's arrival.

Where to Shop

The downtown area of Sault Ste. Marie has more than 60 independent shops in a five-block area that are sure to meet virtually any need, from souvenirs to toiletries.

In addition, the Station Mall on Bay Street has 120 outlets and the Cambrian Mall on Great Northern Road has more than 70 stores.

What's Next

If you're leaving the Sault to continue your Circle Tour route, you'll cross into the Michigan Soo over the International Bridge and will want to check the Crossing the Border section in the front of the volume for information on customs and other requirements. If your journey is destined to go deeper north into Ontario, you'll take Trans-Canada Highway 17, which is also designated in town as Great Northern Road. Either way, the Circle Tour has much more of interest along your route of travel.

SAXON AND SAXON HARBOR, WISCONSIN

U.S. 2 between Ashland and Hurley travels within 5 miles (8 kilometers) of Lake Superior's shoreline, but it's possible to access the lake directly at Saxon Harbor via Wisconsin 122 approximately 12 miles (19 kilometers) west of Hurley, 5 miles (8 kilometers) north of Saxon off Highway 2.

Saxon, Wisconsin, regional map – page 30.

Several charter fishing captains dock their boats in the harbor, offering a day of fishing or a cruise on the lake. Saxon Harbor offers fuel for visiting boaters. Saxon is also located on good snowmobile and cross-country ski trails.

SCHREIBER, ONTARIO

Population 1,447

Nestled in a valley surrounded by rugged hills, Schreiber is one of the oldest communities on the north shore of Lake Superior, traditionally serving as a railroad center with some of the most vibrant railway history in all of Canada.

Schreiber, Ontario, regional map – page 12.

Known as "Little Italy" for its sizable Italian population, the town boasts several excellent restaurants and and shoppers will find a number of craft and gift shops to explore.

S

DIRECTORY

Tourist Information –Township of Schreiber, 807-824-2711 ext. 28, 877-247-3423

Where to Stay
Circle Route Motel, 807-824-2452, Hwy. 17, offers 31 modern units, with a restaurant, convenience store and gasoline on the premises.

Where to Eat with a Local Flavor
Rosie & Josie Restaurant, 807-824-2031, 99 Ontario, has a good menu of Italian and Canadian selections.

What to See and Do

Visitors will want to visit two plaques in the downtown area that commemorate Sir Collingwood Schreiber, one of the builders of the Canadian Pacific Railway, and the Japanese Canadians who were relocated to the town in 1942. Also, view the rail yard, the historic Canadian Pacific Depot, a restored 1955 yard engine and an authentic railway motor car in which to sit.

Near the underpass on Highway 17, turn immediately south to descend to adventure. Hike, bike or drive down Isbester's Drive, the rail heritage route, to a handicapped-accessible gazebo featuring exhibits and amenities at Schreiber Beach, Lake Superior's northernmost beach opening directly onto the the big water from the mouth of Schreiber Channel. Examine the gazebo's interesting display panels, bring a picnic lunch, lounge on sand, pebbles or rocks and listen to the sound of the surf. Nearly $1 million in provincial funds were invested to improve the access road to the lakeshore and visitors are likely to appreciate this investment in access to the beach and its amenities.

If you're up to it, explore the Casque Isle Hiking Trail, part of the Trans Canada Trail System. To the east, follow the creek trail past a one-person suspension bridge to ascend to spectacular views, rugged terrain and, eventually, Mt. Gwynne. Beachside to the west are flowing formations of ancient, surf-smoothed rocks that lead immediately to a route to more distant conservation reserves.

Another point of interest is Worthington Bay Beach, accessible on the rugged Casque Isles Trail east past Mt. Gwynne or by following long and aging trails from town or off the highway. This secluded, lovely site has remnants of the generating and milling site for the old Northshore Mines, including an engine block said to be from a captured submarine.

The Trans Ontario Provincial Snowmobile Trail (TOPS) is immediately available and excellent fishing and hunting adventures are found in the surrounding wilderness area. At the corner of Winnipeg and Scotia streets in downtown, Schreiber is working on a display of Canadian Pacific Railway exhibits, including the city's rail, cultural and natural heritage.

Notable Events

Heritage Days townwide celebration in mid-July features special meals, games and a townwide yard sale, as well as other fun events. The cooler season "Peel Off Winter" Carnival toward the end of February is a chance to celebrate winter.

Campgrounds

Campers will want to check out the Travel Rest Tent and Trailer Park, where they'll find a heated outdoor pool.

What's Next

To continue on the Circle Tour, take Trans Canada Highway 17 either west toward Rossport and Nipigon, or east heading for Terrace Bay and Marathon.

SCHREIBER CHANNEL, ONTARIO

The trip between Nipigon and Rossport offers many pullouts for rest, picnicking and sightseeing. Cast your eyes upon the multitude of islands in Nipigon Bay and the Schreiber Channel. You're looking at a group of 59 islands, designated as "Nirivia" by some locals, covering 583 square kilometers (225 square miles), the largest of which is St. Ignace, blessed with inland lakes, waterfalls and Mount St. Ignace with an elevation of 568 meters (1,863 feet) and one of the tallest peaks contained within Great Lakes waters. St. Ignace is the second largest island on Lake Superior after Isle Royale. More than 120 kilometers (75 miles) of hiking trails cut through island forests literally crawling with wildlife. Boaters who visit these islands find many with black sand similar to that found on Lake Nipigon. It is loaded with geodes and collectable rocks like agates and other semiprecious stones. Wilderness excursions into Nirivia are conducted by Nirivian Island Expeditions of Thunder Bay with biking, kayaking, camping, fishing and cruises.

Schreiber Channel, Ontario, regional map – page 12.

Stop at the pullout overlooking Kama Bay. Here you are seeing the northernmost waters of Lake Superior. In the distance, you can see the town of Red Rock.

East of Kama Bay, you'll see a road (a quick turn) toward the lake to a picnic area. This area overlooks the lake from high atop the cliffs with the tracks of the Canadian Pacific running below. A wonderful spot for overview pictures, but don't get too close to the edge of the cliffs!

The Pays Platt Indian Reserve about midway between Rossport and Schreiber usually offers charter fishing, with access to some of the best trout fishing on the lake.

SCHROEDER, MINNESOTA

Population 190

Schroeder, Tofte and Lutsen on Lake Superior's Minnesota north shore are rapidly growing in popularity as year-round tourist destinations. They are villages with

populations of several hundred each a few miles apart, with parallel histories as Scandinavians came in the late 1800s and settled. These immigrants lumbered, mostly in Schroeder, and fished, more so at Tofte and Lutsen, to feed their families.

Near Schroeder, Taconite Harbor is a large industrial complex housing a coal-fired power plant operated by Minnesota Power and iron ore docks that formerly served the needs of LTV Steel Mining Company. A state harbor of refuge for boaters is located at the west side of the complex on the lake, with parking and a boat ramp that give a great view of the docks, which are occasionally visited by large freighters delivering coal for the power plant.

DIRECTORY

Tourist Information – Lutsen-Tofte Tourism Association. 218-663-7804, 888-616-6784

Where to Stay
Lamb's Resort and Campground, 218-663-7292, 19 Lambs Way, offers summer cabins and often has spaces when public campgrounds are full.

Where to Eat with a Local Flavor
Satellite's Country Inn, 218-663-7574, located a few miles southwest of town, has fish and other local entrees.

Schroeder, Minnesota, regional map – page 2.

What to See and Do

In the spring, the Cross River, normally a quiet stream falling through the rocks, becomes a raging torrent of water on its way to the lake. The spectacular falls pass directly under Highway 61 at "downtown" Schroeder, well worth a 20-minute stop. Highway upgrading in this area has made it much more visitor-friendly, so pull over, park and grab the wide-angle lens for the camera. Visit at different times of the year for varying flows over the falls.

It was in Schroeder that Father Frederic Baraga (BEAR-a-ga), the legendary Snowshoe Priest from the Upper Peninsula of Michigan, landed after struggling through a terrific storm on the lake in 1846. As a tribute, he erected a wooden cross at dawn the next day. A symbolic granite cross now stands in recognition at the site on the mouth of the Cross River, named after the event. Follow the road to the boat ramp and park in the little paved lot. A well-worn but ill-marked path toward the river across private land will take you to the cross and a wonderful beach with direct access to the lake. Not easily accessible for the handicapped. There are facilities at the boat launch. During summer, there is a Lutheran Church service at 7:30 a.m. Sunday mornings on the rocks near the cross.

Cross River Heritage Center occupies the former Cross River General Store building on the south side of the highway. The building serves as a museum/interpretative center with many displays and exhibits. Handicapped accessible, this facility is headquarters of the Schroeder Area Historical Society.

A bit east of Schroeder on Highway 61 is Temperance River State Park. Legend has it that the Temperance River was playfully named because it – unlike every other river along the north shore – has no "bar" at its mouth. In a steep gorge just up from the mouth, the water drunkenly falls 160 feet (49 meters). Along the rim are potholes and cauldrons visible from the many hiking trails and cross-country ski trails. An observation deck overlooks the beach. Nearby, on the upper side of the highway, Temperance Traders features unique, locally crafted gifts, as well as offering newly constructed, modern one- and two-bedroom cabins.

Campgrounds

Lamb's Resort, Cabins and Campground is a relaxing location, often with spaces when public campgrounds are full.

What's Next

Continue the Circle Tour on Highway 61 heading either northeast toward Tofte, Lutsen and Grand Marais or southwest to Silver Bay, Two Harbors and Duluth.

SENEY, MICHIGAN
SENEY NATIONAL WILDLIFE REFUGE

Township Population 180

The Lake Superior Circle Tour follows M-28, shooting straight as an arrow eastward for 23-plus miles (37 kilometers) between Shingleton and Seney – known to locals as the "Seney Stretch." If approaching on M-28 from the east, Seney is about 20 miles west of the junction with M-123 near Newberry. A quiet village of fewer than 200 residents and one saloon today, Seney was known as the "Sin City of the North" or "Hell Town in the Pine" during heavy white pine lumbering days of the late 1880s.

Seney, Michigan, regional map – page 20.

South of town on M-77, the Seney National Wildlife Refuge acts as the magnet that draws visitors to the area. The 96,000-acre refuge and visitor center on M-77, 5 miles (8 kilometers) south of Seney and 2 miles (3 kilometers) north of Germfask in the Great Manistique Swamp, is one of the larger U.S. wildlife refuges east of the Mississippi. During summers, a posted schedule of programs is offered at the refuge. The refuge has hiking and auto tours, many species of birds and other wildlife to see and is a pleasant way to stretch the legs in wonderful surroundings.

DIRECTORY

Tourist Information – Newberry Area Chamber of Commerce, 906-293-5562, 800-831-7292; Seney Wildlife Refuge, 906-586-9851

S

SIBLEY PENINSULA, SLEEPING GIANT PROVINCIAL PARK, ONTARIO

Basking in the massive protection of Sleeping Giant Provincial Park on Sibley Peninsula east of Thunder Bay, Ontario, Tee Harbor is a favored subject for photographers, and for boaters seeking dockage in sheltered waters. Actually two harbors are formed by the rocky natural "breakwall" that projects from the mainland at upper right of this photo. A short trip from Tee Harbor brings boaters to Silver Islet, a favored destination of locals who have maintained the historic log cabins with loving care as summer homes.

Traveling either north from Thunder Bay or south from Nipigon and Red Rock on Trans Canada Highway 11/17, keep an eye out for signs pointing the way to Pass Lake, the gateway to Sibley Peninsula and Sleeping Giant Provincial Park.

Sleeping Giant Provincial Park offers more than 70 kilometers (43 miles) of hiking and backpacking trails taking you to the park's interior and to vistas atop the Sleeping Giant 300 meters (900 feet) above Lake Superior. Coastal kayaking and biking within the park are also popular activities. Swim in Marie Louise Lake. Camping is available. The Visitor Centre is located in the Marie Louise Lake Campground and features displays, slide shows and lectures, with a family activity area and gift shop. Open mid-May to early October. Cross-country skiing (both classic and skate styles) is available on more than 60 kilometers (40 miles) of groomed trails during the winter and it is the site of the Annual Sibley Ski Tour, the largest such event in Northwest Ontario.

Return to the Circle Tour by backtracking to Pass Lake. and Trans Canada Highway 11/17.

SILVER BAY, MINNESOTA

Population 2,060

Silver Bay is nestled in the Sawtooth Mountains northeast of Two Harbors and Duluth and just a short distance off Highway 61. Growth of the town primarily provided homes

S

and other amenities for employees of the former Reserve Mining Company, Minnesota's first large-scale taconite operation.

Sitting in a natural, scenic amphitheater, Silver Bay is a "company town" that has many recreational facilities including tennis courts and the scenic 9-hole public Silver Bay Country Club with adjoining driving range. The city also operates a municipal business park for businesses seeking space.

Silver Bay, Minnesota, regional map – page 2.

Silver Bay's amenities include a municipal airport, business park and great snowmobile, hiking and ski trails, including the Red Dot Trail, a 27-mile ATV and snowmobile route through Tettegouche State Park connecting Silver Bay and Beaver Bay.

This is the beginning (or end, depending on your plan of travel) of Forest Highway 11/Superior National Forest Scenic Highway (Lake County Highway 15). It connects the lakeshore with the Iron Range.

Many of the town's businesses are located in the shopping mall at the center of the townsite, including two banks, a well-stocked grocery store and restaurant Other shopping opportunities are located along Outer Drive that leads from the highway.

> ## DIRECTORY
>
> **Tourist Information –** Ontario Parks 888-668-7275; Terry Fox Information Center 800-667-8386
>
> **Where to Eat with a Local Flavor**
> Karen's Kountry Kitchen, 807-977-2883, Hwy. 587, Pass Lake, is open summers 11 a.m.-7 p.m., with limited scheduled in spring and fall.

A Bit of History

Originally homesteaded by fisherman Oscar Pederson in 1920, the location gained its name when Pederson asked the captain of the steamship *America* what he should call his place. The captain suggested "Silver Bay" because he thought the rocks along the shoreline of the bay had the appearance of silver. When the town was incorporated in 1956, it kept the name.

Today

Northshore Mining currently operates the large taconite plant, which can produce more than 7 million tons of iron ore pellets per year at full capacity. The ore is moved down the Great Lakes by giant ore ships, which call regularly in Silver Bay. Visitors can view a mining equipment display at the plant. Cleveland Cliffs Company, which owns and operates the facility, has created a series of three scenic overlooks along a mile-long loop of hiking trail on a hillside offering vistas over the big lake, the plant site and the city. A different theme is presented and interpreted at each site, identifying landmarks and explaining what is seen. Paved parking areas are available for cars and RVs. Tours of the

plant are offered Tuesdays, Thursdays and Saturdays. Check with the Information Center, operated along Outer Drive by the Bay Area Historical Society. It also has a nice display of artifacts from the society's collection.

In 2003, a pilot plant located on North Shore's property successfully produced the first run of direct-reduced iron nuggets. With more than 96 percent pure iron content, compared with 65 percent in taconite pellets, the iron nuggets are worth about six times the value of taconite pellets. Subsequent trials proved the process and generated so much interest that the Minnesota Legislature passed legislation to speed construction of a commercial plant at the former Erie Mining Company in Hoyt Lakes, which is likely to be important to the Minnesota's Iron Range and the American iron industry.

What to See and Do

Silver Bay Marina, west of Northshore Mining's plant, offers a harbor of refuge and a 61-slip, full-service facility for north shore boaters. Adjacent to the marina is Bayside Park, with picnic facilities, a nice beach and a scenic overlook of the lake and the iron ore processing facilities.

On the way along Outer Drive, be sure to notice the statue of Rocky Taconite, as well as the award-winning landscaping that blossoms from spring into fall.

Campgrounds

If you need camping space, check at Northern Exposure Campground a short way east of town.

What's Next

Depending on your travel plans, you'll take Highway 61 either northeasterly toward Grand Marais or southwesterly toward Two Harbors and Duluth. About three miles to the southwest, Beaver Bay makes an interesting stop.

A few miles east of town on Highway 61, a narrow lakeside road at milepost 57 takes tourists to the top of a high coastal bluff known as Palisade Head, much like those extending easterly for 40 miles (64 kilometers). Watch closely for the right turn, which is on a slight downgrade of Highway 61. The road to the top is steep but safe.

The face of the 350-foot (108-meter) cliff is sheer rock

DIRECTORY

Tourist Information – Two Harbors Area Chamber of Commerce, 218-834-2600, 800-777-7384

Where to Stay
AmericInn Lodge and Suites, 218-226-4300, 150 Mensing Dr., offers a range of units and a large waterslide in the pool area.

Where to Eat with a Local Flavor
Northwoods Cafe, 218-226-3699, Shopping Center, offers family dining in a hometown atmosphere.

and can be viewed safely from a stone wall at the top. This is a popular spot for blueberry picking and is also especially popular with rock climbing enthusiasts, who have adopted several such locations on Minnesota's north shore. White-tailed deer are often seen quietly eyeing visitors from protective foliage, and dedicated birders may catch a glimpse of peregrine falcons that nest in the area. You'll want to bring your camera for the excellent views of Shovel Point to the northeast and other vistas. Open daily.

Indian archers are said to have tried to shoot their arrows to the top of the 350-foot cliff from their canoes on the surface of the lake, with few achieving such a feat. The rugged coastline along Palisade is often likened to that of Maine and Oregon. The site has been used by Hollywood filmmakers for such movies as "The Good Son," with Macaulay Culkin.

SILVER CITY, MICHIGAN

Population 120

Silver City has a rich traditional seaside feel and plenty of accommodations to make any vacation pleasurable. Silver City's main claim to fame is a primary entrance to Porcupine Mountains Wilderness State Park, Michigan's largest. The town is about 18 miles north of Bergland on M-64 from the M-28 Circle Tour Route or 13 miles southwest along Lake Superior from Ontonagon on M-64.

Silver City, Michigan, regional map – page 28.

There are several interesting shops in Silver City, including Silver City General Store, offering local arts and crafts, Great Lakes Trading Company, with art, antiques and woolens, and Wilderness Artisans, with unique art pieces and a shop full of surprises.

Parks and Public Areas

One of mid-America's highest mountain ranges (1,958 feet or 600 meters above sea level) contains the 58,332-acre Porcupine Mountains Wilderness State Park. Route 107 takes you to the park's Visitors Center, just off the main road on South Boundary Road. Oft-photographed Lake of the Clouds has an escarpment overlooking the incredibly blue lake and forest that guarantees a vivid memory and a perfect picture. A handicapped-accessible boardwalk and viewing platform offers easier access and another viewpoint for visitors.

The Porcupine Mountains Ski Area is 1 mile (1.6 kilometers) west of the park headquarters on Union Bay. A

DIRECTORY

Tourist Information – Porcupine Mountains Area Chamber of Commerce, 906-885-5399; Western U.P. Convention and Visitors Bureau, 906-932-4850, 800-522-5657

Where to Stay
AmericInn Lodge and Suites, 906-885-5311, 120 Lincoln Ave., offer full service lodging with an assortment of units and a good restaurant.

S

section of the National Scenic Trail cuts through the park. Admission by park permit.

The Porcupine Mountains Chamber offers a brochure for people who want to experience the mountains, but aren't up to a deep wilderness backpack excursion.

What's Next

To travel toward Ontonagon and the Keweenaw Peninsula, take M-64 easterly from Silver City. To return to M-28, take M-64 south from Silver City through White Pine to Bergland. About 2 miles from Silver City, Greenwood Falls (also known as Bonanza Falls) on the Iron River is a local favorite. The adjacent lands were donated by Copper Range Company to the local government to preserve the site when the company ceased operations.

If your route is west to Wakefield, a scenic and interesting way to get there is to take South Boundary Road from Silver City through the state park to County Road 519, then south. Along the way, visit the Summit Peak Observation Tower above Mirror Lake. Cut back to the lake to see the waterfalls on the Presque Isle River, where there are modern private campgrounds and access to backpacking trails that criss-cross the park.

SILVER ISLET, ONTARIO

Silver Islet, Ontario, regional map – page 10.

Thirty kilometers (20 miles) beyond Pass Lake is the tip of the Sibley Peninsula where a mere rock sticks above Lake Superior's waters. It's called Silver Islet. From 1869 until 1884 this tiny island was blanketed with buildings and docks so it covered 10 times its natural area. The men on the island were silver miners. In total, they extracted $3 million worth of the precious metal. If you can get out on the water around the still privately held islet (namesake of the village), you can see pilings and deep shafts just below the surface which descend to the remaining treasure below. On the mainland, a few original cottages from the miners' village of the same name remain, although they're now private summer homes.

DIRECTORY

Tourist Information – Terry Fox Information Center, 800-667-8386

This is a favorite vacation destination, especially for residents of Thunder Bay. All have to generate their own power, and generally get their water directly from the lake. The historic Silver Islet General Store opens for summer business on Victoria Day weekend in late May and offers tea, pizza, soups, desserts and a pool table in the back. Moonlight teas on Saturday nights are a reservation must. A store has been in this location since 1871. Mountain bike rentals are available. After Labour Day, drop-in visitors should not

assume they'll find the store open. Gift items are available nearby in the former assay office, now a gift store. Sibley's historic Sea Lion rock formation (in Sleeping Giant Provincial Park) can be accessed from the Kabeyon trailhead, where parking is available. Park fees apply.

A full service marina dock is planned for Silver Islet, however transient tie-ups are still allowed on the government dock at moderate fees. To make arrangements stop at the store.

What's Next

The return from Silver Islet to Highway 11/17 is along the same route followed on the way in, although there are occasional short side roads to allow exploration. Once on Highway 11/17, you've headed either southward for Thunder Bay or the northwest corner of Lake Superior to the north, with many miles of scenic beauty to lure us and a wealth to see and do along the way.

SKANEE, MICHIGAN

Township Population 480

Skanee is a dot of a town that offers the Joyce Witz Marina, which has good facilities for boats and anglers, but the area is tight for large vehicles. There is a free launch at Arvon Township Park.

> **DIRECTORY**
>
> **Tourist Information –** Baraga County Tourist Association, 906-524-7444, 800-743-4908

Skanee, Michigan, regional map – page 24.

Skanee Town Hall dates to 1895. The Skanee Historical Museum has artifacts from the late 1800s to early 1900s. Twelve miles (19 kilometers) from L'Anse on the way to Skanee, stop at Silver River Falls, where the river cuts its way through slate rocks on the west end of the Huron Mountains. There are facilities in the parking area. You'll return to the Circle Tour route by backtracking.

SLATE ISLANDS PROVINCIAL PARK, ONTARIO

The Slate Islands are an archipelago of eight isles, which together form a circle of land that rises sharply out of Lake Superior about 13 kilometers (8 miles) off Terrace and Jackfish bays. It has been designated Slate Islands Provincial Park. Geological studies indicate that the islands were formed by a meteor or asteroid impact more than a billion years ago. Scientists estimate the "rock" was as much as 30 kilometers (18 miles) wide when it struck the earth, burying itself 3 kilometers (2 miles) under the surface. The islands were logged in the 1930s, but have regained natural splendor and are now a favorite for pleasure boaters,

Slate Islands, Ontario, regional map – page 12.

S

> **DIRECTORY**
>
> **Tourist Information –** Terrace Bay Tourist Information Centre, 807-825-9721, 800-968-8616; Ontario Parks, 888-668-7275

kayakers and anglers. They even support a herd of woodland caribou, the densest population of caribou in North America.

Boaters will want to photograph the lighthouse sitting on the southern tip of Patterson Island. Landlocked visitors can check at the Terrace Bay Information Centre for a list of charter boat operators.

Twelve miles east of Terrace Bay on Highway 17 is the ghost town of Jackfish where Jackfish Lake Motel Efficiency Cabins offers one or two bedroom fully equipped units with TVs, a coffee shop and a gift store. Set in nearly ideal fishing and hunting habitat, Jackfish Lake is in fact a beautiful bay off Lake Superior. Jackfish is thought to be the site of the first gold mine in Northwestern Ontario, dating from about 1871.

SOUTH GILLIES, ONTARIO
Township Population 590

South Gillies, Ontario, regional map – page 8.

If you have the time, make a reservation and stop at Rose Valley Lodge and Restaurant in South Gillies, 16 kilometers (10 miles) to Rose Valley Road, then turn right for a half mile. The lodge, a remodeled Finnish farmhouse on 440 acres, is an ideal place to sample gourmet meals and country living. Owners refurbished the dining room and offer lodging in two bed-and-breakfast rooms and two cottages. A sauna was added. Reservations are a must.

DIRECTORY

Tourist Information – Thunder Bay Tourism and Economic Development, 807-625-3960, 800-668-9360; Ontario Tourism, 800-668-2746

A short jaunt on Highway 590 leads to the Kakabeka Falls area. See separate listing.

Several other small towns can be explored in the immediate area, offering goods and services for visitors who take this trip inland.

What's Next
The direct route to Thunder Bay is to backtrack to Highway 61, but can also go a few miles north to catch Highway 588 and enter the southwestern edge of the city.

SPLIT ROCK LIGHTHOUSE STATE PARK, MINNESOTA

Split Rock Lighthouse, Minnesota, regional map – page 2.

One of the most photographed lighthouses on the Great Lakes, Split Rock Lighthouse was built in 1910 in response to six shipwrecks within a dozen miles of the Split Rock River. A number of them were ore carriers whose compasses were rendered useless by the nature of their cargo and masses of iron under the lake. Fog and dangerous reefs made travel unusually treacherous under such conditions.

The construction of the lighthouse was a heroic feat, since there were no roads in the region at that time. All of the materials

down to the last brick had to be shipped in and hoisted up the 130-foot (43-meter) cliff by a derrick, which itself had to be lifted by rope and pulley to the top of the cliff. Split Rock Lighthouse State Park and the Split Rock Lighthouse Historic Site give tourists triple their money in historical detail, entertainment and nostalgia. A sizable recent addition to the visitor center adds much more space for interesting displays about the lighthouse and the area (including a wall-sized replica of the *Lake Superior Magazine* Travel Map).

Visitors to the 25-acre Historic Site are guided by staff through the lighthouse and invited to climb the winding stairs to the top where they can get a close-up view of the multi-crystal-lensed beacon that was made in France. They will hear stories about problems that threatened the lighthouse keeper and nearly caused the beacon to fail from time to time. The view from the lamproom is unparalleled. Picnic facilities are available.

Each November 10, the light shines across Lake Superior in commemoration of the 1975 wreck of the *Edmund Fitzgerald* and also may mark other memorable events through the year.

The operation of the 2,500-acre park and the interpretative center are the result of a joint venture of the

Split Rock Lighthouse near Beaver Bay, Minnesota, has stood sentry duty on its 130-foot cliff for nearly a century. Built to guide navigators past a particularly dangerous section of Minnesota's north shore that claimed six ships within a dozen miles during a 1905 storm, Split Rock was at first only accessible by boat. The 1924 passage of the roadway brought instant popularity to the picturesque site and its imposing lighthouse structure. The 25-acre historic site is now enclosed by the 2,500-acre Split Rock Lighthouse State Park,

S

DIRECTORY

Tourist Information – Split Rock
Lighthouse Historical Site,
218-226-6372; Split Rock Lighthouse
State Park, 218-226-6377

Minnesota Historical Society and the state park system. Open normal hours mid-May to mid-October daily, limited winter hours Friday-Sunday, history center only. Closed in December. State park sticker required for park use, but not the lighthouse, although there is a small fee for touring the lighthouse and grounds. Hiking and picnicking in the park are included in the lighthouse admission fee.

The popular Split Rock Lighthouse State Park Campground offers an excellent opportunity for camping with families. Cart-in camping is available for those with young children.

Just beyond Split Rock is Gold Rock, another jut of land into Lake Superior. This 80-acre property was acquired in 1998 and was incorporated into Split Rock Lighthouse State Park.

SUPERIOR HIKING TRAIL, MINNESOTA

The Superior Hiking Trail parallels Scenic Highway 61 from Two Harbors to the Canadian border and is planned to eventually connect to Duluth. Earning high praise from hikers and hiking organizations, additional sections of the trail are being completed by volunteers, allowing free and easy access from many places of lodging along the way. More than 240 miles (350 kilometers) of trail are well-signed and maintained by volunteers to provide hikers with challenges at whatever level they desire. In fact, the Superior Hiking Trail has become a part of a lodge-to-lodge hiking system on the shore. Superior Shuttle service is available on Fridays, Saturdays and Sundays at many of the participating lodges, as well as numerous pickup and drop-off points along the trail from May to late October.

DIRECTORY

Tourist Information – Superior
Hiking Trail Association, 218-834-2700

SUPERIOR, WISCONSIN

Population 27,370

Superior, on the Wisconsin bank of the St. Louis River, was originally planned to be the primary city at the Head of the Lakes, but commerce and happenstance allowed Duluth to dominate in size. However, Superior's heritage is longer established.

This Wisconsin city exerts a strong influence on transportation. As part of the world port, its iron ore, coal facilities and grain elevators supply ships from around the world. With a much flatter terrain than its sister, Superior has captured many of the rail yards that serve the region. It is also a trucking center.

Superior has several neighborhoods with homes of classic design, including Billings Park, which overlooks the St. Louis River on the city's west end. Each neighborhood offers small shops with a friendly welcome to all visitors.

Superior, Wisconsin, regional map – page 2.

A Bit of History

The first trading post in the region was established in the 1790s on Conner's Point in Superior. The city was well established by 1855 and seemed sure to be the commercial center of the Upper Midwest, with the only entry to the protected harbor. The signing of the Treaty of La Pointe with the Ojibway opened northern Minnesota for settlement and exploration and Duluth came into existence. The 1871 opening of the Duluth Ship Canal removed Superior's dominance as a port and Duluth soon supplanted Superior and the major settlement at the Head of the Lakes.

Today

Superior was one of the busiest ship construction ports on the Great Lakes. Today, Fraser Shipyards continues to repair and modify huge lake ships in its facilities on the waterfront near the Blatnik Bridge. Its operations can be seen up close during a tour on the Vista Fleet tour boats.

The University of Wisconsin-Superior (UWS) is a major employer and has an outstanding curriculum of education with full four-year and advanced degrees in all major areas of concentration, including business, music, fine and applied arts and sciences. The university is also involved in major Lake Superior environmental research. Through the Lake Superior Research Institute, it sponsors ecology cruises on the *L.L. Smith Jr.* out of Bayfield, Wisconsin, and Duluth and Two Harbors, Minnesota. UWS is also home to Wessman Arena, a year-round facility that hosts hockey and skating in winter and numerous community events during the rest of the year.

Wisconsin Indianhead Technical College offers nearly five dozen courses ranging from short term to two years for students seeking vocational skills that will give them entree to careers.

S

What to See and Do

Osaugie Trail, a paved pathway, offers a pleasant 5-miles for summer hiking, biking, boarding and blading along the Superior waterfront eastward to Moccasin Mike Road. At the halfway point at Loonsfoot Landing, the trail is also open for motorized recreationists to connect to the unpaved Tri-County Corridor multi-use trail through Douglas, Bayfield and Ashland counties. In winter, the entire trail is open for snowmobile traffic. Plans call for the Osaugie to be extended to Wisconsin Point and Connor's Point.

Barker's Island is a recreational focal point of Superior. Here, picnicking, shore fishing, a boat-launching site and shopping are part of the Barker's Island scene. It's possible to watch huge ships heading in and out of the port on a Vista Fleet tour boat sightseeing cruise of the Duluth-Superior harbor, which has a boarding stop at the island. Barker's Island is home to the Superior Charter Captains Dock Association, with a number of fully licensed captains who'll be happy to take you where the big fish lurk.

Barker's Island Marina is a 420-slip facility which includes a ship's store, new boat showroom, charter service, sailing instruction and rental. The marina is one of the largest in the Midwest.

Vista Fleet runs a regular schedule of two-hour tours of all Duluth-Superior harbor sites and facilities, with a bonus of a trip onto Lake Superior under the Duluth Aerial Lift Bridge. In Superior, the boarding dock is at Barker's Island.

The impressive Superior Public Library is located in a modern structure on the corner of Tower Avenue and Belknap Street. The library is home to 27 beautifully wrought wall-sized murals painted by well-known regional artist Carl Gawboy depicting early area history.

A favorite weekend destination of locals is the Lake Superior beach along Moccasin Mike Road, offering rustic picnicking spots, beach walking and driftwood gathering. Watch out for the occasional poison ivy plant. The road extends from the east side of the city at Highway 53 to Wisconsin Point and the Superior entrance of Lake Superior, then to the Superior Harbor, where a lighthouse stands guard. We're told this is a favorite "submarine race" watching locale. Shortly before reaching the Superior Entry, watch for a 17th century Fond du Lac Ojibway Burial Ground beside the road, marked by a plaque 4.5 miles from Highway 2. Although the remains were moved many years ago, native people still honor the location with ceremonial objects placed at the marker.

Burlington Northern Santa Fe Ore Docks in Superior are the largest in the world, loading taconite ore onto 1,000-foot (308-meter) lake vessels. Nearby, a good stop is an Observation Platform at 30th Avenue East at Loonsfoot Landing off U.S. Highway 2/53 in the Allouez area.

At the junction of highways 2 and 13 east of town, be sure to check out the unusual Finnish Windmill. Constructed by Jacob Davidson in the northern European style, the mill's arms had large "sails" to catch the wind. The mill no longer operates, but the building was preserved by Davidson's descendants, who presented the unique structure and grounds to the Old-Brule Heritage Society in 2001 for use as a public exhibit of early life and enterprise in the area. A turnout allows you to stop, take photos and learn a bit of local history.

Courtesy Superior Public Museums

FAIRLAWN MANSION

Fairlawn Mansion faces Barker's Island and overlooks Superior Bay from across Highway 2/53. Built in 1889 as a private residence, this 42-room Victorian-style mansion is now open year-round and epitomizes the lifestyle of early lumber-mining baron and former Superior Mayor Martin Pattison and his wife, Grace. It recalls the early days of maritime commerce, mining, Indian lore and elegance that seemed out of place in the rugged frontier country. Once again an opulent showplace on Superior waterfront, Fairlawn Mansion had fallen into considerable disrepair before being rescued by Superior and Douglas County preservation groups. Extensively restored during 1998, the exterior and first floor display the elegant character of its early life. The third floor is also complete and is devoted to displays from the period when the mansion was a children's home. After restoration, the home was featured on the A&E's "American Castles" series. The McDougall Garden is the first of three planned garden projects to restore the grounds. Fee for entry and open only Thursday-Sunday during winter.

S

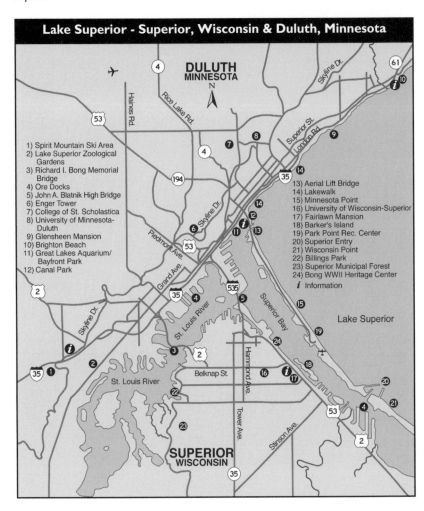

Lake Superior - Superior, Wisconsin & Duluth, Minnesota

1) Spirit Mountain Ski Area
2) Lake Superior Zoological Gardens
3) Richard I. Bong Memorial Bridge
4) Ore Docks
5) John A. Blatnik High Bridge
6) Enger Tower
7) College of St. Scholastica
8) University of Minnesota-Duluth
9) Glensheen Mansion
10) Brighton Beach
11) Great Lakes Aquarium/ Bayfront Park
12) Canal Park

13) Aerial Lift Bridge
14) Lakewalk
15) Minnesota Point
16) University of Wisconsin-Superior
17) Fairlawn Mansion
18) Barker's Island
19) Park Point Rec. Center
20) Superior Entry
21) Wisconsin Point
22) Billings Park
23) Superior Municipal Forest
24) Bong WWII Heritage Center
i Information

Notable Museums

Richard I. Bong World War II Heritage Center on Highway 2/53 near Barker's Island includes many personal belongings of WWII vintage donated by veterans who served along with America's Ace of Aces Richard Ira Bong. A P-38 fighter plane similar to the plane flown by Major Bong is displayed, along with his many awards, including the Medal of Honor. Major Bong was a native of nearby Poplar, Wisconsin, and earned the Ace of Aces distinction in the Pacific Theater for shooting down the most enemy planes of any U.S. pilot either before or since WWII. The center is open daily from 9 a.m. to 5 p.m. Fees apply. The Superior and Douglas County Visitor Information Center at the Bong Heritage Center is a dandy.

SS *Meteor* Museum on Barker's Island displays the only remaining whaleback ore carrier, which looks more like a submarine than anything else. These vessels were developed and built in Superior. Guided tours are offered through the *Meteor*. The museum includes displays and a collection of pictorial history on turn-of-the-century whaleback shipping. Open daily mid-May through mid-October.

Adjacent to the *Meteor* are a playground, miniature golf course and quaint shops. A Seamen's Memorial is dedicated to the 29 crew members of the *Edmund Fitzgerald*, which sank in 1975 after leaving Superior. The Boathouse Restaurant is adjacent to the *Meteor* with a menu specializing in Lake Superior fish prepared on a wood grill. In summer, the 80-seat establishment gains additional seating on a nearby docked 55-foot wooden sailboat.

After serving for 30 years as the family residence for Grace and Martin Pattison, who earned a fortune by prospecting and securing title on iron ore properties in northern Minnesota, Fairlawn Mansion (see side story) was donated to the Superior Children's Home and Refuge Association and would house unfortunate children for 42 years. Renovations changed the original building, and by the early 1960s the association disbanded and abandoned the structure. The city assumed ownership and Douglas County Historical Society did considerable restoration and needed repair work, culminating in a 1997-98 yearlong massive restoration of the exterior and the first floor interior. Once again the late 1800s elegance of Fairlawn wows visitors to the museum operating there. Groundswork is restoring gardens and landscape. Fee.

Historic and present-day firefighting equipment and police memorabilia are displayed at the Old Fire House and Police Museum. It is also a state Hall of Fame for those professionals. It is open to group tours and has family rates. At Highway 2/53 and 23rd Avenue East. Open Wednesday through Sunday in summer.

S

Parks and Public Areas

The city of Superior maintains 19 parks within its boundaries, as well as the Superior Municipal Forest, the third largest city-contained forest in the United States. The 4,000-acre forest has 19 miles (30 kilometers) of hiking and cross-country ski trails over beautiful rolling terrain, including the 1.6 mile paved Millennium Trail and the 6-mile Pokegama Multipurpose Trail, which was developed in wonderfully natural surroundings and opened by the Cyclists of Gitchee Gummee Shores for hikers, bikers and snowshoers. There is also an archery course with 39 shots at 14 targets. (Jefferson Memorial Forest in Louisville, Kentucky, is the

DIRECTORY

Tourist Information – Superior and Douglas County Visitor Center, 715-394-7716, 800-942-5313; Wisconsin Travel Information Center, 715-392-1662

Where to Stay
Barker's Island Inn and Conference Center, 715-392-7152, 300 Marina Dr., offers full-service lodging, with good rooms, a good restaurant, lounge and more.
Days Inn-Superior/Bayfront, 715-392-4783, 888-515-5040, 110 Harborview Pkwy., has 111 units, with a restaurant co-located on the site.
Holiday Inn Express Hotel & Suites, 715-682-7121, 303 2nd Ave. E., has 84 queen and king units, with continental breakfast.

Super 8 Motel-Superior, 715-398-7686, 800-800-8000, Hwys. 2 & 53 S., offers 40 units with continental breakfast.
Superior Inn, 715-394-7706, 800-777-8599, 525 Hammond Ave., has 69 units, welcomes pets and has continental breakfast.

Where to Eat with a Local Flavor
Hammond Bar and Steak House, 715-392-3269, 1402 N. 5th St., has a nice menu and good a view of the Blatnik Bridge.
Gronks Grill and Bar, 715-398-0333, 4909 E. 2nd Ave., has a full menu and some rate their burgers as the best in town.

largest municipal forest with 5,504 acres and Forest Park in Portland, Oregon, has nearly 5,000 acres.)

Other hiking and cross-country ski opportunities can be found in Brule River State Forest and in Solon Springs.

At Pattison State Park, you can visit Wisconsin's highest waterfall, "Big Manitou," as the Black River plunges 165 feet (50 meters). The park, donated by and named after former Superior Mayor Martin Pattison, includes campsites, hiking trails, a picnic area and swimming beach, as well as ski and snowshoeing trails. A total of 9 miles of nature trails includes a 2-mile (3-kilometer) labeled trail. Interpretative programs and checklists of the park's birds and mammals are available. Brown and brook trout are native to the river, while rainbow are stocked each year. Located 12 miles (16 kilometers) south of Superior on Wisconsin Route 35 and County B, Pattison Park is open all year. Many facilities, including two campsites, are handicapped accessible.

Farther east, the Amnicon River is the focus of the 825-acre Amnicon Falls State Park. Named from Ojibway words meaning "where fish spawn," the Amnicon flows over a series of spectacular waterfalls and rapids within the park on the way to its mouth at Lake Superior. Interesting geologic formations along the riverbed are the result of an earthquake that occurred a half billion years ago. Another attraction in

the park is the 55-foot (17-meter) covered "bowstring"
bridge, one of only five such bridges remaining in the United
States. The bridge allows visitors to cross to an island in the
Amnicon River. There are campsites, a 2-mile nature trail, a
shelter in the picnic area and a playground. Anglers can catch
trout, walleye and muskellunge. Located southeast of the city
and 1 mile east of the junction of Highways 2 and 53 off U.S.
Highway 2 on County U.

Downhill skiing is nearby at Mont du Lac Ski Area.

Douglas County offers a total of 325 miles of winter
snowmobile/ATV trails.

If you're traveling with skateboarders, check out the free
use of the skateboard park at 28th Street and Hammond
Avenue near the Mariner Mall.

Superior offers summer recreation at Nemadji Golf
Course, a 36-hole full-service facility at 58th and Tower that
has earned a 4-star rating by *Golf Digest*. Lessons are available.

Nearby 9-hole courses are located at Pattison Park, two in
the town of Gordon and two at Lake Nebagamon, with 18-hole
courses at Poplar and Solon Springs, where it's worth asking
directions to the excellent 18-hole Hidden Greens North
Golf Course, which also offers a lounge and bar services.

About 20 miles east of town on Highway 2, the Brule
River is excellent for canoeing/kayaking and fishing. It is
known as the "River of Presidents" because Presidents Grant,
Cleveland, Coolidge, Hoover and Eisenhower all cast lines
there. President Calvin Coolidge, in fact, spent considerable
summer time near the Brule in northwestern Wisconsin.
During his presidency, the senior high school in Superior was
called "the Summer White House" because he sometimes did
business from there.

Notable Events

• Gitchee Gumee Brewfest draws craft brewers from
throughout the Midwest in April.

• Fourth of July Parade and Festival is a traditional,
spectacular celebration of independence.

• Head of the Lakes Fair in July is one of the larger such
expositions in the Upper Midwest.

• Lake Superior Dragon Boat Festival in August involves
paddling and is an exciting event benefitting local causes.

• Great Northern Rodeo in September brings the western
tradition to Lake Superior.

Where to Shop

Superior Antique and Art Depot houses a collection of
constantly changing antique and art dealer displays. The
historic building served as Superior's main railroad depot

until the railroad yards were relocated out of the city. Situated at Oakes and Broadway, just off Tower Avenue and the downtown area. Open seven days a week.

Mariner Mall presents a variety of stores, including a department store, specialty shops, food and services and a multi-screen movie theater located on the corner of Hill Avenue and North 28th Street.

Downtown Superior offers a tremendous variety of dining and shopping opportunities and is home to the Business Improvement District and the Development Association of Superior & Douglas County. The main thoroughfare has recently been upgraded along Tower Avenue. The South Tower shopping district has a number of large and smaller retail outlets.

If you're looking for sporting or outdoor gear, Northwest Outlet on Belknap can supply nearly any need.

What's Next

If you're traveling from east to west on Highway 2, your next stop will be Duluth across either the Blatnik or the Bong bridges. If you're eastbound, follow Highway 2 through a series of small towns heading toward Ashland. If you plan to visit the Bayfield Peninsula, watch for the junction with Highway 13 east Superior or just west of Ashland.

Tahquamenon Falls
State Park - Two Harbors

TAHQUAMENON FALLS
STATE PARK, MICHIGAN

Michigan Highway 123 makes a northerly loop from and to Michigan Highway 28 in the eastern Upper Peninsula, giving access to Paradise (see separate listing) and Tahquamenon Falls (Ta-KWAH-meh-non), one of the largest U.S. waterfalls west of Niagara Falls and second largest east of the Mississippi River. Tea-colored water approaches the 48-foot-deep (15-meter), 200-foot-wide (61-meter) sandstone cliff in low rapids, then plunges over the edge into a pool of boiling bubbles. More than 50,000 gallons of water per second flow over the edge. Handicap-accessible paths lead from the parking area to overlooks. A 94-step stairway continues down to the overlook at the edge of the falls. Other steps wind down to the river's edge below the falls.

Four miles (6.5 kilometers) downstream, the river wraps itself around an island in a series of smaller falls and rapids. The island is accessible by rowboat from a Lower Falls riverside concession. There's a small fee. There are separate entrances for both falls, part of the nearly 40,000-acre Tahquamenon Falls State Park, second only in size to Michigan's largest state park, Porcupine Mountains Wilderness State Park in the Western U.P. A vehicle permit is required.

Tehquamenon Falls State Park, Michigan, regional map – page 18.

DIRECTORY

Tourist Information – Newberry Area Tourism Council, 906-293-5562, 800-831-7292; Paradise Area Tourism Council, 906-492-3927; Tehquamenon Falls State Park Headquarters, 906-492-3415

Where to Eat with a Local Flavor
Tahquamenon Falls Brewery & Pub, 906-492-3300, Camp 33, offers a pub menu and their own craft brews right in the park.

What's Next

If your Circle Tour is west to east, M-123 heads straight south from Paradise, but if your route is east to west you can reconnect with M-28 at Newberry through Lake Superior

State Forest. If that's your choice, watch for a turnoff on County 500 toward Little Lake and the old Two-Hearted River Life-Saving Station. Little Lake affords boaters a harbor of refuge from Lake Superior, although it is subject to shoaling activity. There are few remains of the original station at Two-Hearted River, but a historical marker commemorates the exploits of the lifesaving team that served so well in this remote locale, 17 miles from the main road.

Once completely isolated but now accessible on a seasonal extension of County Road 412 on the shoreline to the east of Little Lake is the Crisp Point Lighthouse. Considered to be among the most threatened lighthouses in the United States, it is now being restored by the Crisp Point Light Historical Society in an admirable rescue effort. The society received the 2000 *Lake Superior Magazine* Achievement Award for its accomplishments.

TERRACE BAY, ONTARIO

Population 2,400

Terrace Bay, Ontario, regional map – page 12.

Made famous by Louis Agassiz in an 1850 lithograph, Terrace Bay is named for three levels of glacial sand and gravel deposits that step up from the lake. In total, they rise more than 100 meters (325 feet). The town, inland and to the east, was built more than 50 years ago for employees of a giant Kimberly-Clark (now Neenah Paper Inc.) pulp mill. At that same time, the Ogoki and Longlac rivers to the north were dammed by Ontario Hydro for a power-generating plant. The diversions direct water into Lake Superior rather than Hudson Bay. The flow from these diversions almost equals the flow of either the St. Louis or the Nipigon river, the two major natural tributaries to Lake Superior.

What to See and Do

Just west of town, a half mile off the highway, an accessible boardwalk can be followed to an observation deck at the 30-meter-tall (100-foot) Aguasabon Falls and Gorge. The view is spectacular, and additional unprotected footpaths are nearby if you wish to hike down to the lakeshore. The river follows deep fractures in the bedrock, which is about 2,600 million years old. The exposed rock is called granodiorite. The turnoff to this attraction is at the Aguasabon Falls Campground and signs are posted.

DIRECTORY

Tourist Information – Terrace Bay Tourist Information Centre, 807-825-9721, 800-968-8716

Where to Stay
Red Dog Inn, 807-825-3285, Highway 17, offers lodging, a restaurant and lounge.
Imperial Motel and Drifters Roadhouse, 807-825-3226, Hwy 17, is near to everything, with nicely renovated rooms, a good restaurant and lounge.

Lake Superior - Terrace Bay, Ontario

TERRACE BAY
ONTARIO

N

Aguasabon Gorge Rd.

Aguasabon River

17

Mill Rd.

17

Selkirk Ave.

Ridgewood Rd.

Kenogami Rd.

Beach Rd.

1) Aguasabon Falls & Gorge
2) Aguasabon Beach
3) Aguasabon Falls Campground
4) Golf Course
5) Recreation Centre
6) Centennial Park
7) Shopping Centre
8) Kimberly-Clark Pulp Mill
9) Pumphouse Beach
- - Canadian Pacific Railway
i Information

Lake Superior

The Trestle Ridge Ski Area is located just above the town, offering five ski runs from beginning to intermediate-advanced, plus a snowboarding area and instruction.

If you are interested in snowmobiling, the Lake Superior Family Snowgoers groom and maintain about 210 kilometers (130 miles) of snowmobile trails going west, east and north from town. They're part of the TOPS (Trans Ontario Provincial Snowmobile) trail system running throughout Ontario.

Terrace Bay is a favorite of golfers and waterfall lovers. The 9-hole Aguasabon Golf Course scenically overlooks Lake Superior.

If you feel the need for a workout, ask about using the community center's facilities.

Behind the visitor center, there's a path to the top of the hill for a breathtaking, panoramic view of the area or you can follow the caribou tracks to the downtown shopping centre. The Information Centre is open mid-May to mid-October.

The Casque Isles Hiking Trail, a 52-kilometer (31-mile) stretch, begins in Terrace Bay, passes through Schreiber and ends in Rossport. Along this trail, hikers see glacial terraces, Indian pictographs and remnants of an old prospectors' mining camp. Rated: difficult. The total trail takes three to five days to hike, but is broken into five sections for easier day

hikes. For more information and maps of the local trail system, contact the Information Centre.

Notable Events
- Terrace Bay hosts a well-attended Fish Derby in June.
- Canada Day Celebrations on July 1 are held in most Canadian towns.
- Terrace Bay's Annual Drag Races take place in early August
- The Annual Fall Fair is celebrated in September.

What's Next
To the west, Trans Canada Highway 17 heads for Nipigon, but watch for signs pointing you to Rossport. To the east, Highway 17 leads to Schreiber and the northeast corner of Lake Superior near Marathon.

TETTEGOUCHE STATE PARK, MINNESOTA

Tettegouche State Park, Minnesota, regional map – page 2.

A few miles northeast of Silver Bay on U.S. Highway 61 is Tettegouche State Park (formerly Baptism River State Park). Tettegouche almost doubled its size through a land exchange program and offers extensive hiking covering an area of more than 14 miles (22 kilometers). No vehicles are permitted. Rugged, mountainous terrain, one mile of Lake Superior shoreline, four inland lakes, cascading rivers and undisturbed northern hardwood forest highlight this pristine area.

Access to the park is by foot trail from the Baptism River highway rest area, where there are a state park headquarters, information center and small gift shop. Hikers and campers can load their gear onto two-wheeled pull carts and move it to their site. Leave plenty of time to explore here, and bring hiking shoes. Included in the park is Tettegouche Camp, unique in architecture with log constructed buildings, including a main lodge, kitchen and a number of cabins. The camp dates from the late 1800s and is an uphill walk from a parking area of the park. Inquire at the main office.

Inland, three waterfalls on the Baptism River include Minnesota's highest waterfall, which drops 80 feet (25 meters). Pigeon Falls on Pigeon River at the international border is higher, but is technically listed as being in both Minnesota and Ontario. The hike to the high falls of the Baptism is 1.5 miles (2.5 kilometers) and takes about 45 minutes one way. The waters of the Baptism River were used to anoint new converts to the Christian faith.

Along the trail you'll find Conservancy Pines, a stand of Norway pines that has been standing since the early part of the century.

From the park's upper parking lot, the three-quarter-mile Shovel Point Trail goes toward the lake for almost a quarter of

a mile, then turns. The remaining route to Shovel Point can be somewhat hazardous due to the cliff-type terrain, but the result is a perfect viewing platform from which you can see the palisade shoreline. Do be careful in this unprotected area during your walk. These trails are generally open in the winter for cross-country skiing and snowshoeing and the cliffs are another of the north shore's preferred rock-climbing destinations.

Just to the east a bit, Whispering Pines Motel in Illgen City is on land originally owned by 3M Company. Over the years the highway passed through the property, another inn burned down and buildings were moved. Today, it's a quiet resort at the intersection with Highway 1 heading inland and is close to the lake and state park.

DIRECTORY

Tourist Information – Tettegouche State Park Headquarters, 218-226-7676; Two Harbors Area Chamber of Commerce, 218-834-2600, 800-777-7384

What's Next

You can continue your Circle Tour either northeast or southwest by following Highway 61. To the east, you're heading for Grand Marais through Schroeder, Tofte and Lutsen. Westerly takes you to Silver Bay, Beaver Bay and Two Harbors.

THUNDER BAY, ONTARIO

Population: 113,000

Thunder Bay presents a multitude of sights, sounds and scents to greet the traveler. It ranks as the 14th most populous city in Ontario and the largest city on the 2,080-kilometer (1,300-mile) Lake Superior Circle Route. The 156-square-mile metropolitan area is located almost exactly in the center of Canada, 2,980 water kilometers (2,235 miles) from the Atlantic Ocean and 2,530 land kilometers (1,900 miles) from the Pacific. It is 280 kilometers (175 miles) from Duluth, Minnesota, and 690 kilometers (430 miles) from Sault Ste. Marie, Ontario.

Thunder Bay, Ontario, regional map – page 10.

The city is situated on a magnificent natural harbour (it's spelled "harbor" in the United States) and is a worthy destination that adds to the delight of driving one of the most beautiful routes on the continent. If you arrive by air, the Thunder Bay Airport Terminal affords you panoramic views of the Sleeping Giant and Thunder Bay (the body of water to the east and the Nor'wester Mountains to the west. A metropolitan transit system provides service throughout the city and about a dozen taxi companies also offer transportation.

Thunder Bay has many attractions. If you need any questions answered or want hints about Thunder Bay, stop by any of the Visitor Information Centres. In the downtown, the

Pagoda is the oldest tourist bureau in Canada (open mid-May through September). For information on the wider area contact the Terry Fox Information Centre and monument (open year-round) east on Highway 11/17.

For travelers entering the area from the north and east, Trans Canada Highways 11 and 17 join at Nipigon and give an easy drive southward to Thunder Bay. (See the listing for Nipigon for detail.) This Canadian Lakehead section of the trip through Northwestern Ontario extends from the international border at Pigeon River to the Sibley Peninsula-Sleeping Giant east of Thunder Bay. The entire Circle Tour route in Ontario is in the Eastern Time Zone.

Visitors traveling southwest of the city on Highway 61 toward the international border may be surprised to find a fertile valley that sustains a variety of agricultural endeavors in these northern latitudes. Tidy farms dot the roadside and herds of livestock can be seen grazing in summer pastures against the rugged backdrop of stone mountains that hem in this farming area both to the east and west.

A Bit of History

A fort was erected by the French in 1717 at the mouth of the Kaministiquia River (locally called "the Kam"). When the North West Company moved its mid-continent operations from Grand Portage, Minnesota, to Fort William in 1803, the fort became the site of the annual rendezvous, where goods from Montreal and furs from the wilderness traded hands. The trading remained steady until the mid-1800s and made this the world's largest fur trading post.

The importance of the area to lake and rail shipping made it prime for development. When the railroad arrived from the east in the 1870s and continued pushing westward, Port Arthur grew a bit to the north of Fort William, but the twin cities, which came to be called the Lakehead, became a crucial link in commerce between the agricultural west and ports to the east. Until relatively recent times, Thunder Bay ruled supreme as the largest grain handling port in the world.

For a century, the two cities vied in all aspects of business before Port Arthur and Fort William amalgamated in 1970 into a modern industrial center with paper and lumber mills, grain elevators and port facilities. The grand result is the city of Thunder Bay, which took its name from the body of water to its east.

Today

Thunder Bay is a working city, teeming with activity. It's a port city lying in the shadow of the legendary Sleeping Giant Provincial Park on the Sibley Peninsula, which protects

SLEEPING GIANT & OUIMET CANYON

Near Thunder Bay are two of the most intriguing Lake Superior region parks noted for beautiful scenery and geologic formations.

Sleeping Giant is immediately noticeable from almost any hillside in the city, but requires about a half-hour drive northward on Trans Canada Highway 11/17 to Pass Lake to take Highway 587 into the park. The townsite of Silver Islet is at the end of road and nearly the end of the park. The only route is to backtrack on H-587. (See separate listing.)

Ouimet Canyon Provincial Park is about 65 kilometers (40 miles) north of Thunder Bay and consists of a 115 meter (350 feet) deep canyon in the rock formation. At 3 kilometers (2 miles) in length, the canyon walls face each other at a distance of 165 meters (500 feet) and create an ecoclimate at the bottom totally different from that at the surface. There are good viewing platforms, boardwalks and two viewing pods right on the canyon's edge. (See separate listing.)

the harbor to the east. Today, its shipping economy is bolstered by papermaking, forest products, major industrial and manufacturing facilities and tourism. With a large new Regional Health Center, the city serves the health needs of a broad area of northwestern Ontario.

Thunder Bay is the home of two institutions of higher education: Lakehead University, with a beautiful campus in the heart of the city and, a few blocks away, Confederation College, site of Thunder Bay Art Gallery and a diverse range of technical, academic and Native courses.

261

As with other Lake Superior cities, tourism is an important part of the economic mix in Thunder Bay. With many must-see sites from the busy waterfront to its many attractive and interesting parks and public spaces, this is a city that most visitors will want to take time to explore.

What to See and Do

A must stop in the western part of Thunder Bay and close to excellent cross-country skiing is Fort William Historical Park, which has been reconstructed on an oxbow, 14 kilometers (9 miles) upstream on the Kam and has been named one of Canada's Top 10 Attractions. Inside the stockade you are returned to life as it was in 1815. Craftsmen, voyageurs, company officials and native people interact and converse as they would have two centuries ago. The summer is filled with special events at Fort William, along with some special events in the winter. Among the notable celebrations are the Great Rendezvous on the second weekend in July, Ojibwa Keeshigun that celebrates First Nations culture in August and various programs that allow guests to dress as voyageurs and camp at the Fort. The Fort's Learning Wigwam is great for kids. Open mid-May to mid-October, with a number of special holiday events during winter.

The Sleeping Giant is clearly evident from any east-facing bluff in Thunder Bay. Some say Ojibway legend tells how Naniboujou, both spirit and human, watched over his people as they explored Lake Superior's waters, warning them that he would turn to stone if they revealed the presence of a fabulous island of silver. The legend is that he laid down in Thunder Bay and turned to stone after white men discovered the silver lode at Silver Islet, becoming the southern tip of the Sibley Peninsula, which juts into Lake Superior and displays his crossed-armed silhouette as a reminder. The majority of the peninsula is protected by Sleeping Giant Provincial Park.

Thunder Bay Art Gallery has a fine collection of native art and is northwest Ontario's largest public gallery. A bit difficult to locate at the edge of the Confederation College campus, the gallery is well worth the effort. Open afternoons Tuesday through Sunday. Nominal fee, but free on Wednesdays.

Kakabeka Falls, 29 kilometers (18 miles) west on Highway 11/17, is one of the most spectacular waterfalls on the Circle Tour. Located within Kakabeka Falls Provincial Park, at 29 meters (128 feet) the falls is nicknamed "Niagara of the North" and the Canadian Shield rock formation that forms the base of the cataract is said to be 2 billion years old, containing some of the world's oldest fossils. Handicapped friendly, there are a number of viewing platforms around the falls. The park visitor center offers interpretative programs

during summer and camping from mid-May to mid-September. Winter offers 13 kilometers of cross-country ski trails.

Founders Museum and Pioneer Village is at Gillespie Road and Highway 61 south of town and has a massive collection of antiques displayed in realistic indoor and outdoor settings, creating an early 1900 Pioneer Village unique to Northwestern Ontario. The village includes a pioneer home, carpenter, cobbler and blacksmith shops, an original one-room schoolhouse, teacherage, church and heritage community hall, along with a replica of a 1908 train station. Visit the general store, village shops and library. Vintage cars and farm equipment are also featured. Well worth a couple of hours.

Paipoonge Museum reflects the pioneer's life of the late 1800s. Homesteading was complete by 1905. A bit out of town. this museum preserves the memory of those who faced the hardships of the frontier. Open 1-5 p.m. early May through August 31, but closed Mondays and holidays. Take Highway 130 west from Highway 61 to the Rosslyn Road corner.

Terry Fox Monument, on a bluff above the highway at the eastern outskirts of Thunder Bay commemorates Terry Fox who lost his leg to cancer. Running on an artificial leg across Canada in 1980 to raise funds for research, his disease recurred and forced him to stop when he reached Thunder Bay. He died less than a year later. His last stretch of highway is now named in his memory: Terry Fox Memorial Highway. Co-located with the Fox Memorial is an outstanding Travel Information Centre. From the Terry Fox Monument, enjoy a wonderful vista of the Sleeping Giant.

Thunder Bay Charity Casino on Cumberland Street provides gaming fun for a variety of good causes. The $30 million, 48,000-square-foot casino was the fourth provincial gaming operation to open, with Sault Ste. Marie being the first. The 13,500-square-foot gaming floor houses 450 slots and 14 table games and offers good dining.

Thunder Bay Community Auditorium, an addition at the Canada Games Complex, is booked nearly every night with

AMETHYST MINES OF ONTARIO

Near Pearl on Trans Canada Highway 11/17 north of Thunder Bay, keep an eye out for signs offering the chance to mine amethyst. It's Ontario's official gemstone, as well as the February birthstone. Ontario's amethyst industry began in the mid-1950s with the discovery of large deposits of the rock near Thunder Bay. The semiprecious gem can be found at the Blue Points Amethyst Mine, Ontario Gem Amethyst Mine, which has a gift shop, and the Panorama Amethyst Mine, the largest amethyst mine on the continent. Watch closely for signage along the road.

cultural events, touring Broadway shows and major performers. The 1,500-seat auditorium hosts numerous international personalities each season. The street in front of the auditorium was renamed to honor Thunder Bay native Paul Shaffer, musical director for the Late Show with David Letterman.

Thunder Bay Symphony Orchestra makes its home in the Community Auditorium and presents a full season of classical and pops concerts.

Magnus Theatre was home to professional community and touring performances on McLaughlin Street for more than 30 years. In 2001, the new "Magnus in the Park" Theatre opened in the Waverley Park area of town. It hosts a variety of locally produced dramatic and comedic performances each season.

Musical and performing arts productions are also offered by schools, colleges and independent arts organizations. Check the Info Centres for current programs.

Marina Park is the embarkation point for two-hour harbor and Kam River tours aboard the weather enclosed motor vessel *Pioneer II*, operated by Stanton Cruise Lines, which also offers some twilight tours and Thursday evening Kam River dinner cruises. An added attraction is a step-off tour on the historic museum tug *James Whalen*.

Three touring routes have been established for travelers trying to navigate Thunder Bay's multi-named streets. They are the Friendship, Memorial and Bayview routes, each offering something of interest to visitors.

Pick up an Architectural Walking Tour Map showing more than two dozen historical buildings at any of the information stops, which also distribute "Hand Made in Thunder Bay" guides to more than 40 arts and crafts studios and galleries in the area.

If you'd prefer a guided tour or plan to arrive with a group, check with Lake Superior Visits, which offers an array of services for visitors in the area, including Great Getaway packages in Winter/Spring and Summer/Fall.

Ghost Walk Thunder Bay offers evening tours of a spookier nature to city sites reputed to be haunted. Fee. There are also other haunted tours. Check with tourism information.

Mount McKay Scenic Overlook on Missions Road offers a 4-kilometer (2.6-mile) hiking trail from the base, with scenic views on the way to a commanding view from the top, which towers 300 meters (984 feet) over both the water body and city of Thunder Bay. An authentic native village was added in 1995. The parkway is operated by Fort William First Nation and a toll is collected.

For golfers, Thunder Bay has 10 courses that include city and privately owned courses from 9 to 18 holes, some a little

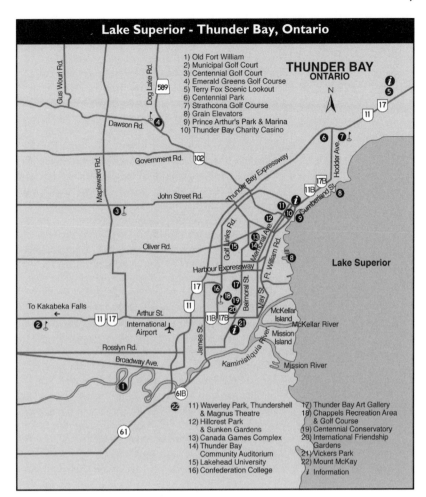

Lake Superior - Thunder Bay, Ontario

THUNDER BAY
ONTARIO

1) Old Fort William
2) Municipal Golf Court
3) Centennial Golf Court
4) Emerald Greens Golf Course
5) Terry Fox Scenic Lookout
6) Centennial Park
7) Strathcona Golf Course
8) Grain Elevators
9) Prince Arthur's Park & Marina
10) Thunder Bay Charity Casino

Lake Superior

To Kakabeka Falls

11) Waverley Park, Thundershell
& Magnus Theatre
12) Hillcrest Park
& Sunken Gardens
13) Canada Games Complex
14) Thunder Bay
Community Auditorium
15) Lakehead University
16) Confederation College

17) Thunder Bay Art Gallery
18) Chappels Recreation Area
& Golf Course
19) Centennial Conservatory
20) International Friendship
Gardens
21) Vickers Park
22) Mount McKay
i Information

more challenging than others. In addition, Eaglequest Golf
Centre provides an indoor, two-tiered 300-foot driving range
and 18-hole miniature golf range for year-round enjoyment.
The 9-hole Bayview and Giant Golf Course is located on
Highway 587, near Pass Lake on the Sibley Peninsula.

Canada Games Complex, built as the site of the 1981
Canada Summer Games, is a multisports facility now serving
as a training facility for world-class athletes. Numerous sports
from swimming to squash are available for public enjoyment,
along with programs for health and wellness, fitness and life-
saving. Fee.

Winter visitors will find plenty of action in the area. On
the nearby Nor'Wester peaks to the west of Thunder Bay,
Loch Lomond offers prime ski slopes and aprés-ski facilities in
winter and is open daily, except closed Tuesdays. Night skiing

is available Thursdays through Saturdays. On the other side of the city, Mount Baldy has the best view of Thunder Bay Harbour and is great for afternoon skiing, or to rent a snowmobile and ride the trails. There are also tubing and horseback riding options. Located off Highway 11/17 some 6 kilometers (4 miles) north on Highway 527. Open Tuesday to Sunday, also Friday and Saturday evenings.

Recreational hiking trails and cross-country skiing are available throughout the region. Kamview is operated by the Thunder Bay Nordic Trails Association. Other challenging ski trails are at Centennial Park, Lappe and the Kakabeka Falls and Sleeping Giant provincial parks cross-country ski areas. Trail guidebooks are available from tourist information centers.

There is a good selection of camping opportunities entering and leaving Thunder Bay. Chippewa Park at the city's south end has been extensively renovated and upgraded under the auspices of Friends of Chippewa Park. With 150 campsites and 18 cabins, as well as a wildlife exhibit of animals in their natural habitats, the park is a favorite for kids. At the eastern end of the city off Highway 11/17, Trowbridge Falls has 145 campsites. Both have tent and trailer sites, electrical hook-ups, laundry facilities, showers, grocery stores and souvenir shops. Just outside of the eastern city, campers will find the Thunder Bay KOA campground on Spruce River Road where Highway 527 intersects 11/17.

In addition to many other area campgrounds, the Thunder Bay International Hostel/Campground (Longhouse Village) offers full facilities and lodging for the visitor. Located 18 kilometers (11 miles) to the east of Thunder Bay off Highway 11/17 at 1594 Lakeshore Drive.

Check out Wild Side Recreations Inc. on Highway 11/17 West, a go-cart facility for drivers of various levels of skill that also offers other activities and a year-round restaurant. Fee.

Nor'West Outdoor Centre is a short jaunt off Highway 61 down Mountain Road. Its 55-acre grounds are available for winter and summer recreation that can be arranged by calling ahead

On Jarvis Bay Road off Highway 61 south of town, Norwest Sled Dog Adventures gives you a chance for a wintertime wilderness trip or up to two-day overnight camping trips into the Ontario back country. There's nothing like it to enjoy the winter. They also offer a unique summer sled dog experience on wilderness trails for families.

Mink Mountain Properties near the international border is a four-season area with hiking and ski trails, biking and winter recreation, access to Lake Superior for water sports, a lodge, dining room and a licensed bar. Turn east toward the lake on Sturgeon Bay Road to Mink Mountain Drive. The view of the islands from the bluff is fantastic.

Notable Museums

There is no admission fee to the Thunder Bay Military Museum, which showcases the heritage of northwestern Ontario. In the Armory on Park Avenue, it is open Monday through Friday and Tuesday evenings.

Thunder Bay Historical Museum houses an extensive collection of artifacts from northwestern Ontario that includes prehistoric Indian, fur trade, mining and shipping relics, with the largest collection of native beadwork in Canada. Open daily from June 15 through Labour Day. In winter, it is open Tuesday through Sunday. On Donald Street East.

Children's Museum for Thunder Bay on Water Street South features hands-on activities and programs for kids throughout the summer.

Northwestern Ontario Sports Hall of Fame and Museum is located on South May Street, with photographs, trophies and some equipment and memorabilia from popular regional sports.

Out of town a bit, Paipoonge Museum reflects the pioneer's life of the late 1800s. Homesteading was complete by 1905. This museum preserves the memory of those who faced the hardships of the frontier. Open 1-5 p.m. early May through August 31, but closed Mondays and holidays. Take Highway 130 off Highway 61 to the Rosslyn Road corner. Fee.

Parks and Public Areas

Thunder Bay offers many wonderful parks, public areas and provincial parklands which preserve incredible landscapes. Many also offer camping and other amenities.

While the Chippewa Park and Wildlife Exhibit has a beach, playground and amusement park, a prime attraction is a 400-meter (1,300-foot) elevated boardwalk overlooking a natural exhibit of timber wolves, bear, deer, foxes and coyotes.

Another spot for an overview of the port of Thunder Bay is from Hillcrest Park, with colorful sunken gardens and a memorial. Head down the hill to see the port up close. At the bottom of the hill, turn south on Water Street then watch on the right for the ore docks, the elevators and Keefer Complex, the multi-million dollar general cargo facility.

Marina Park is at the end of Highway 102, which becomes Red River Road in town. It contains a large full-service marina called Prince Arthur Landing for visiting boaters as well as restaurants and shops at the renovated railway depot and a nearby art gallery. More information on the marinas of Ontario is available from Thunder Bay Tourist Information Centres.

The venerable, refurbished old tugboat *James Whalen* is situated at Kaministiquia River Heritage Park on the Kam. Long a critical part of the icebreaking and salvage operations

of the north shore, the *Whalen* was returned to Lake Superior in 1992 after its last duty on the lower lakes.

Boulevard Lake Park in the city has swimming pools, boating, playgrounds, a beach, tennis courts, picnicking area and lots of room for simply strolling. Boat rentals are available.

At International Friendship Gardens on Victoria Avenue, the city's ethnic diversity is celebrated in flowering plants and monuments. More than a dozen of Thunder Bay's ethnic groups have contributed unique gardens. Going north from Friendship Gardens on Waterloo Street, watch for the signs directing you to the Centennial Conservatory, where you'll Stroll through tasteful landscapes of hundreds of plant species. Open afternoons seven days a week.

Centennial Park and Bushcamp Museum is an 847-acre area on Centennial Park Road, a circa-1910 north woods camp and logging museum, with blacksmith shop, bunkhouse, sauna and cookery. There is a barnyard with farm animals to pet. A narrow-gauge railroad circles the park. The lumber camp is open June through September, although the park is open year-round. Winter sleigh rides and ski trails are available.

Several Lakehead Conservation Areas in the Thunder Bay area offer everything from boating and fishing to hiking by cascading waters. A number access the Lake Superior shoreline. South of town near the international border on Cloud Bay Road off Highway 61 is Little Trout Bay. Silver Harbour is situated on the waters of Thunder Bay 10 minutes east of the city and has a boat launch and picnic area. Within the city, Mission Island Marsh is one of the more popular sites. The area boasts a panoramic view of the Sleeping Giant, Lake Superior and Thunder Bay Harbour, as well as the extensive shoreline marsh that gives the area its name. Trails in Neebing-McIntyre Floodway, The Cascades and Mackenzie Point conservation areas are popular. Wishart Falls' large jackpine boreal forest is about 11 kilometers (7 miles) north of the city and is ideal for skiing in the winter. Hazelwood Lake, about 25 minutes north of the city, is the largest of the conservation areas, providing an excellent opportunity for outdoor family activities A complete map of the conservation areas is available from the Lakehead Region Conservation Authority.

Ontario Parks offers ample opportunity to get close to nature in this area of Lake Superior. Non-residents of Ontario older than 17 must have a Crown Land Camping Permit to stay overnight on Crown land in northern Ontario, available from most Ontario license issuers and Ministry of Natural Resources offices.

At the border and a couple of miles up Highway 593 is Pigeon River Provincial Park, where the focal point is the

Pigeon River and the waterfalls along it with day-use opportunities like hiking and picnicking. Near the Pigeon River Tourist Information Centre take the trail to the Lake Superior shoreline viewing pod or explore the coastal hiking trail to Finger Point Lookout (2.4 kilometers/1.5 miles). These trails and recent improvements to the High Falls Trail are part of the Great Lakes Heritage Coast project, a national undertaking to accent and protect vast areas of habitat of Great Lakes shoreline. The High Falls Trail is accessible from the Information Centre and climbs to a viewpoint above Pigeon Falls. Steep sections have wooden steps. Rated: intermediate.

Other provincial parks in the area are Quetico, La Verendrye, a deep wilderness park for the hardiest of adventurers located inland on the way to Sunset Country, Kakabeka Falls, Sleeping Giant and, at the extreme eastern edge of the Thunder Bay area, Ouimet Canyon provincial parks.

Notable Events

Thunder Bay calls itself the "city of festivals" and hosts major celebrations ranging from the July 1 Canada Day Celebration to events focusing on a wide range of culture and heritage. A sampling follows:

• Fort William Historical Park offers a full summer into fall schedule of annual celebrations, heritage festivals and other significant events commemorating the area's fur trade history.

• Thunder Bay Children's Festival in June brings children from schools in a wide area for a day of fun, learning and adventure.

• Great Rendezvous at Fort William Historical Park in July commemorates the summer gathering of voyageurs, natives and traders at the world's largest fur trade post on the Kam River.

• Canada Day Celebrations are observed in most Canadian cities on July 1, celebrating the founding of the independent nation in 1961.

• Ojibwa Keeshigun at Fort William Historical Park in August celebrates the rich heritage of First Nations people who contributed to the history and heritage of the area.

• Pioneer Days at the Founders Museum south of the city in early September gives participants a feeling for the hardship and deprivation the early area settlers experienced as they moved in, established homes, farms, towns and other improvements.

Where to Shop

For a great variety of Canadian goods, check out Intercity Shopping Centre on Fort William Road, Victoriaville Village Centre on Victoria Avenue, County Fair Plaza on Dawson

DIRECTORY

Tourist Information – Thunder Bay Tourism, 807-625-3960, 800-667-8386; Terry Fox Info Center, 807-983-2041, 800-667-8386; Ontario Tourism, 800-ONTARIO(668-2746)

Where to Stay
Prince Arthur Waterfront Hotel, 807-345-5411, 800-267-2675, 17 N. Cumberland St., offers full service hotel overlooking the waterfront and Marina Park.
Travelodge Hotel Airlane, 807-473-1600, 800-465-5003, 698 Arthur St. and Hwy. 11/17, is convenient for travelers, with all the amenities.
Valhalla Inn, 807-577-1121, 800-964-1121, Arthur Street at Highway 11/17, is big enough for conventions, but offering personal service for travelers.
White Fox Inn, 807-577-3799, 1345 Mountain Rd., is a nine-room bed-and-breakfast inn with fireplace and whirlpool bath units and a gourmet restaurant.

Where to Eat with a Local Flavor
Hoito Restaurant, 807-345-6323, 314 Bay Street, is famous and among the favorites for good Finnish pancakes, hearty meals and language.
Timbers Restaurant, Nordic Dining Room, 807-577-1121, 1 Valhalla Inn Rd. (Valhalla Inn). Two restaurants with scrumptious repasts in pleasant settings.
River Rock Bar and Grill, 807-473-1608, 698 Arthur St. W. (Travelodge Airlane), has fine dining in casual surroundings.
White Fox Inn, 807-577-3799, 1345 Mountain Rd., is a gourmet restaurant at the foot of the mountains.
Armando's Fine Italian Cuisine, 807-344-5833, 28 Cumberland St., has great Italian food, has won the Golden Fork Award several years and also received a Millennium Restaurant of Distinction rating, (Ask Armando to suggest a meal.)

Road, the Arthur Street Marketplace just off Highway 11/17 Expressway and the Grandview Mall off River Street.

Thunder Bay is full of ethnic neighborhoods, especially strong in Finnish and Italian heritage. On East Bay Street, stop by the Finnish Book Store or Fireweed, where author Bill MacDonald of Porphry Press displays his books and works of local artists. Antiquers will want to check out Northern Light Antiques on Cumberland Avenue across from the Prince Arthur Waterfront Hotel. If you're seeking Ontario's official mineral, check the Precious Purple Gemstone amethyst store on East Victoria.

Highway 61 south of town is an area where visitors can discover surprising and interesting stops and shopping possibilities. Thunder Oak Cheese Farm, Ontario's only Gouda cheese producing farm, is located on Paipoonge Concession 6 Road, where Jacob and Margaret Schep make the natural cheese in eight flavors using milk from their own Holstein cows and Dutch family recipes that have won

international awards. Take time to watch the entire cheese-making process in operation and sample selections. The shop is open Monday through Saturday.

A bit farther south of town, Early Snows Bed-and-Breakfast Inn and Pottery offers a nice selection of ceramic goods and other artworks along with a pleasant overnighting possibility. On 3rd Side Road is Camellia's Fine Flowers and Gifts, a quaint shop with quilting and decorating ideas and supplies. In somewhat the same vicinity, Gammondale Farm on McCluskey Drive offers pick-your-own strawberries in season, with great sundaes and other fruity goodies as the reward for your labor. A call ahead on any of their offerings is advised to avoid disappointment. Another nearby farm on Candy Mountain Drive, Belluz Farms-Valley Berry Patch has seasonal crops for the picking and offers kids a half-hour or more of fun finding their way through the cornfield "maze in the maize that's amazing."

Near Kakabeka Falls west on Highway 11/17, Kakabeka Falls Gift and Amethyst Shoppe gives amethyst fanciers the chance to check out "blueberry amethyst" that is mined from a local vein of the deep purple mineral.

Campgrounds

There is a good selection of camping opportunities entering and leaving Thunder Bay. Chippewa Park at the city's south end has been extensively renovated and upgraded under the auspices of Friends of Chippewa Park. With 150 campsites and 18 cabins, as well as a wildlife exhibit of animals in their natural habitats, the park is a favorite for kids. At the eastern end of the city off Highway 11/17, Trowbridge Falls has 145 campsites. Both have tent and trailer sites, electrical hook-ups, laundry facilities, showers, grocery stores and souvenir shops.

West of town at Kakabeka Falls Provincial Park, camping is available from mid-May through mid-September.

Just outside of the eastern city, campers will find the Thunder Bay KOA campground on Spruce River Road where Highway 527 intersects 11/17.

In addition to many other area campgrounds, the Thunder Bay International Hostel/Campground (Longhouse Village) offers full facilities and lodging for the visitor. Located 18 kilometers (11 miles) to the east of Thunder Bay off Highway 11/17 at 1594 Lakeshore Drive.

What's Next

The Circle Tour Route around Lake Superior departs Thunder Bay either south on Highway 61 to the international border or north on Highway 11/17 toward

Sleeping Giant Provincial Park, Silver Islet, Red Rock and Nipigon – depending on your direction of travel. When traveling north of town, keep an eye out for signs directing you to amethyst mines where you can pick your own or purchase Ontario's official gem stone. You'll also want to watch for Pass Lake to enter the road to the Sibley Peninsula, Sleeping Giant and Silver Islet. (See alphabetized listings for Sibley Peninsula and Silver Islet.)

TOFTE, MINNESOTA

Tofte, Minnesota, regional map – page 8.

Population 200-300

Tofte is a small town sitting between Lutsen on the north and Schroeder on the south. Highway 61 bisects the town and gives virtually a complete view of town.

A half-mile southwest of Tofte, Sugar Beach Resort offers individually owned lakeside cabins operated by a homeowners' association. The resort's Valhalla Lighthouse cabin with its 2^1/$_2$-story "lighthouse" tower is surely one of the more unusual rental units on the Lake Superior shore.

The Tofte area has blossomed with visitor comforts. It is home to the highly popular Bluefin Bay on Lake Superior. The old dock for the steamer *America* still stands at Bluefin as testament to the old boat that was once a major cargo and passenger link along the lakeshore.

Although Highway 61 is the only major east/west road through Cook County, much of the north/south traffic moves on four trails: the Sawbill Trail at Tofte, Caribou Trail at Lutsen, Gunflint Trail at Grand Marais and the Arrowhead Trail at the Brule River. These trails are closely connected with the fur trade, logging and mineral exploration. After the Treaty of La Pointe, Wisconsin, was signed in 1855, which released all of northeastern Minnesota from the control of the Ojibway, white settlers moved in and began cutting these trails into the back country.

Today they are the main arteries for vacation travel in the county. These are the roads to the good fishing, the canoe country, vacation resorts and private cabins of those who have found their dreams where the lordly moose roam and loons fill the wilderness nights with their winsome laughter. It has become a popular area for winter enthusiasts who snowmobile, snowshoe and cross-country ski.

What to See and Do

Tofte Town Park with its stone walkways and bridges adds a charming respite to a busy trip.

Fall color arrives along the north shore in two waves, the first peak occurring between mid-September and early October inland from the lake. Drive the trails and back roads

DIRECTORY

Tourist Information – Lutsen-Tofte
Tourism Association Information Center,
218-663-7804, 888-616-6784

Where to Stay
AmericInn Lodge and Suites,
218-663-7899, 800-634-3444, Hwy. 61,
has large rooms and a Lake Superior stone
fireplace.
Bluefin Bay on Lake Superior,
218-663-7296, 800-258-3346, 7192 W.
Hwy. 61, is one of the premiere resort
developments on Lake Superior, with

luxury condos with fireplaces, jacuzzi tubs
and great lake views.
Chateau LeVeaux, 218-663-7223,
800-445-5773, 6626 W. Hwy. 61, offers
condo comfort convenient to all
recreational facilities.

Where to Eat with a Local Flavor
Bluefin Restaurant, 218-663-6200,
7192 W. Hwy. 61, offers north coast
cuisine. Two other restaurants are also
located at the resort.

to see the brilliant reds and oranges. The second season of
color runs right along the shore, following Highway 61. It
usually peaks between the first and third weeks of October.

Sawbill Trail (County Road 2) runs 25 miles (40
kilometers) from Tofte to Sawbill Lake and the Boundary
Waters Canoe Area Wilderness. The highest point directly on
Minnesota's shore, Carlton Peak, now part of the state park
system, towers 927 feet (285 meters) above the lake, a total of
1,529 feet (470 meters) above sea level. Trails wind to the top
for an impressive view of the Sawtooth Mountains and Lake
Superior. In the autumn, the peak offers an outstanding view
of the colorful valley. Access to the trail is from the Sawbill
Trail. Visitors planning to travel inland on Sawbill Trail for a
day or longer visit may want to check Sawtooth Outfitters for
information and canoe, kayak, bike, ski or snowshoe rentals
to expand their pleasure potential. They are also a full-service
sales and service shop for pedalers.

Two other area hiking experiences are Oberg Mountain
(2.25 miles/3 kilometers) and Leveaux (3.4 miles/4.24
kilometers) hiking trails. Both are round trips from the
parking lot 5 miles (8 kilometers) east of Tofte on Forest
Road 336. They offer breathtaking views of Lake Superior
and are especially spectacular during fall color.

Notable Museums

The North Shore Commercial Fishing Museum in Tofte
preserves significant artifacts of fishermen, including an
original fish-cleaning station, fishing skiff and many historic
memorabilia.

What's Next

The Circle Tour continues on Highway 61 either to the northeast to Lutsen and Grand Marais or southwest to Silver Bay, Two Harbors and Duluth.

TOWER-SOUDAN, MINNESOTA

Population: Tower 490, Soudan 200-300

Tower-Soudan, Minnesota, regional map – page 32.

The twin towns of Tower and Soudan on Highway 169 between Ely and Virginia offer some intriguing visits. Tour the Soudan Underground Mine, located in Soudan Underground Mine State Park between the towns. The only underground iron mine in the world open for tours, visitors are guided to a depth of 2,341 feet where the year-round temperature is a constant 50 degrees Fahrenheit. In the nearby Embarrass area, tours of Finnish farms and homesteads explore the importance of this large ethnic group that pioneered settlement here.

Also at Tower-Soudan visit Lake Vermilion, one of the largest lakes in Northeast Minnesota. Visitors may want to reserve a daylong scenic trip on the boat that delivers mail to waterbound residents. Take Highway 77 to find Fortune Bay Resort and Casino on the Bois Forte Ojibway Reservation. The tribe also operates its "Legend House" or *Atisokanigamig* heritage museum and its new championship 18-hole golf course, The Wilderness, that opened in summer 2004 on tribal lands.

DIRECTORY

Tourist Information –
Ely Chamber of Commerce,
218-365-6123, 800-777-7281

TWO HARBORS, MINNESOTA

Population 3,615

Two Harbors, Minnesota, regional map – page 2.

The North Shore Scenic Drive from Duluth meets the Highway 61 expressway at the western outskirt to the city of Two Harbors, whose history as a settlement dates back to 1855. At that time, the area around Agate and Burlington bays (the two harbors) was a well-known Ojibway hunting and fishing ground. Two Harbors owes its growth to the railroad and shipping of iron ore, although it was also a significant logging center.

Highway 61 becomes Seventh Avenue and runs straight through Two Harbors. But it's important to note that the road can be deceptive. Many of the attractions in town like the lighthouse and harbor are in the downtown area, which is closer to the lake. Don't miss the opportunity to follow the directional signs to take you there.

What to See and Do

Two Harbors is fast becoming a destination town with many attractions. You have not seen Two Harbors unless you

head to the downtown and waterfront. Watch for the signs at Seventh Street or Waterfront Drive (Sixth Street) that take you just a few blocks toward the lake side of Highway 61, where viewing areas on the waterfront at Lighthouse Point allow you to watch huge lakers, some as long as 1,000 feet (308 meters), as they load taconite ore.

Paul VanHoven Park includes a gazebo situated on a grassy knoll opposite the historic iron ore docks and within sight of the retired *Edna G.*, the last coal-fed, steam-powered tugboat to operate on the Great Lakes. Retired from service in 1981, the deteriorating *Edna G.* was renovated at Fraser Shipyards in Superior, Wisconsin, to be preserved as a historical interpretative display. Tours of the tug can be arranged at the Depot Museum. This is also the access point to *Grampa Woo* summer boat cruises on Fridays and Saturdays.

Dock #1, once the largest iron ore loading dock in the world, is closest to shore. Two Harbors became the state's first iron ore port in 1884 with the completion of the railway from the town of Tower, located on Minnesota's Vermilion Iron Range. Iron ore is now mined as taconite, a low-grade iron-bearing rock that must first be processed and concentrated before it can be used by the steel mills. Two Harbors is still one of the busiest ore harbors on Lake Superior, visited by the giant ore boats.

The historic R.J. Houle Visitor and Information Center on east Highway 61 was constructed as a ranger fire station and was relocated to Two Harbors in 1977. Another attraction at the site is a hand-hewn totem pole. The sculpture was given to the American people by nationally renowned artist Peter Toth as a tribute to Native Americans.

A 30- to 45-minute walking tour of historic Two Harbors will take you past many of the significant locations in town. Organized by the Historical Society, brochures with the route are available in many places in addition to the depot.

Walkers will also want to check out the Sonju Hiking Trail, a handicapped-accessible trail that follows the lakeshore from the downtown area through Lighthouse Point and takes a beautifully natural route all the way to the Municipal Campground and the 18-hole municipal Lakeview National Golf Course, which offers wonderful lake vistas from its grounds.

Thursday evening concerts in Thomas Owens Park by the Two Harbors City Band are informal affairs, 7:30 p.m., late June through early August. The City Band is the oldest continuous operating volunteer band in the state. In mid-June and mid-December, the summer and winter solstices are celebrated at the lighthouse grounds.

A walk along the east Agate Bay breakwater takes visitors safely out onto the lake about one-quarter mile and provides

Lake Superior - Two Harbors, Minnesota

1) Ore Docks
2) Edna G. Dock
3) 3M/Dwan Museum
4) Depot Historical Museum
5) Two Harbors Lighthouse B&B
6) Breakwall
-) DM&IR Railway
····) Harbor Walking Trail
i Information

TWO HARBORS
MINNESOTA

N

15th St.

4th St.

19

61

11

7th Ave.

7th St.

Waterfront Dr.

Lakeview Dr.

Burlington Bay

61

i

i

1st Ave.

3

4

2

1

Agate Bay

6

5

Lake Superior

an opportunity for stretching the legs or fishing for trout and salmon. Off the west breakwater, accessible only by boat, lie the remains of the *Samuel P. Ely*, a sunken three-masted schooner. The *Ely* went down in 1896 and is one of the oldest recorded shipwrecks on western Lake Superior, as well as a popular dive for scuba enthusiasts.

Lakeview National Golf Course is a par 72 course with 18 holes, 14 of which feature a view of Lake Superior. It has a full pro-shop and lighted cross-country ski trails have been added for winter recreation. It is located across the highway from the Burlington Bay Campground.

East of Two Harbors, Flood Bay is a natural harbor with yet another breathtaking view of the lake. The pebble beach is one of the finest agate beaches on the north shore. It's a great way for kids to let off a little energy. The Minnesota Department of Transportation has provided an excellent wayside area for those who wish to dip their toes in the lake.

Notable Museums

The old Duluth and Iron Range Railroad Depot houses one of the Lake County Historical Society museums. The Depot was extremely active between 1907, when it was built, and the late 1950s. Inside, artifacts, some more than 2,000 years old, are displayed. From the first permanent Minnesota north shore settlement in Beaver Bay, the mining and shipping of ore to the logging era and the recent Veterans Room artifacts, the exhibits help bring local history to life. The museum stresses the three basic industries that "made" Two Harbors: shipping iron ore, logging and fishing.

Of course, one can still catch a ride on the North Shore Scenic Railroad from the Depot. Visitors who arrive in Two Harbors by train will find inexpensive in-town transportation aboard an Arrowhead Transit bus that meets the train. A public transportation service, Arrowhead serves Lake County and Duluth communities with a regular schedule of routes.

On the Depot grounds stands the "Malley," a Mallet-type steam locomotive, one of the most powerful ever built. This forerunner of the diesel hauled iron ore to Two Harbors until 1961. A few feet away is the historic *Three-Spot*. This steam engine arrived in Two Harbors during a storm in 1883 on a scow pulled by a tugboat from Duluth. It was used by the railroad to build the tracks to Tower on the Iron Range and was a workhorse on the logging railroad of the Alger Smith Lumber Company for two decades as the white pine was logged along the north shore.

3M Company had its star-crossed beginnings in 1902 on the northwest corner of Waterfront Drive and Second Avenue in a modest building owned by attorney John Dwan, an original investor in the company. The 3M/Dwan Museum building has been restored to commemorate the company's important place in the history of the north shore. Completely refurbished in preparation for the company's centennial year in 2002, the museum features interactive displays and information on the development and history of the company's many products. The museum is a two minute walk from the Depot and is open daily during the summer, weekends only September to mid-October.

Parks and Public Areas

There is no doubt that Lighthouse Point is the focus of most visitors. Here is ample parking, nice green spaces, benches for sitting to watch ore boats being loaded across Agate Bay and a great boat launch. Here too, Sonju Walking Trail provides a nice shoreline paved pathway.

The Two Harbors Lighthouse, built on Agate Bay in 1892, was acquired by the Lake County Historical Society

Gooseberry Falls State Park

Historically, Gooseberry Falls up the road from Two Harbors, Minnesota, has attracted motorists since early in the 20th century. Efforts were made over a number of years to get a state designation of the scenic area as a park, but it took the 1924 completion of Highway 61 to spur action. Minnesota needed right of way for the road and bridge over the gorge, but also negotiated with the owners to acquire a large part of what became Gooseberry State Park. Constructed during the Great Depression by men in the Civilian Conservation Corp, the granite structures of the park are works of art in themselves. A new visitor center and gift shop is south of the highway near the new bridge, which has a pedestrian walkway for ease of viewing the upstream falls. (See separate Gooseberry Falls State Park listing.)

from the U.S. Coast Guard in 1999 and is now operated as the delightful and popular Lighthouse Bed-and-Breakfast Inn. The nearby Fog Building has been converted into a museum, with a gift shop selling a nice assortment of items. The lighthouse was decommissioned by the Coast Guard in 1969, although it remains a navigational aid to commercial shipping and pleasure boaters. More than 200,000 people a year visit the attractive displays related to commercial shipping and fishing on the Great Lakes. The restored pilothouse from the *Frontenac* iron ore freighter is located on the grounds and other exhibits are nearby. Also nearby, a historic, authentic commercial fishing vessel, the *Crusader*, built locally and christened by Norwegian Crown Prince Olaf, has been refurbished and is on display. Both the lighthouse and depot museums are open daily late April to late October and weekends thereafter.

Along the harbor at Lighthouse Point is a public boat launch with free parking, a convenient telephone booth and an elegant view of the harbor.

Two other parks in town are the Thomas Owens Park with a bandshell in the center in the downtown area and Lakeview Park at the eastern edge, which has a pavilion, washrooms, picnic tables and is traversed at lakeside by the Sonju Trail.

Notable Events
• Summer Solstice at the Lighthouse is celebrated in mid-June.
• Heritage Days features a big parade and other activities in mid-July.

MINNESOTA'S NORTH SHORE TUNNELS

Silver Creek Cliff rises a sheer 300 feet (92 meters) out of Lake Superior's waters. The old highway, built in 1923, used to hug the face of the rock at 125 feet (39 meters) above the waves, providing a breathtaking view of the lake. The privately owned gazebo on the point is often photographed in winter with its intricate icy covering formed by water thrown upward by high, pounding waves just before a freeze.

The Minnesota Department of Transportation opened the tunnel through Silver Creek Cliff in 1994 to improve the safety of the Highway 61 drive. In 2004, work by the Department of Transportation began on a paved bike path, automobile pulloff and viewpoint on the old highway to take in that famous Lake Superior view. A similar tunnel was completed earlier at Lafayette Bluff, a few miles farther on Highway 61.

DIRECTORY

Tourist Information – Two Harbors Area Chamber of Commerce, 218-834-2600, 800-777-7384

Where to Stay
AmericInn Lodge and Suites, 218-834-3000, 800-634-3444, 1088 Hwy. 61, has an indoor pool and enhanced continental breakfast.
Country Inn, 218-834-5557, 877-604-5332, 1204 7th Ave., offers 46 units, indoor pool, sauna and continental breakfast.
Superior Shores Resort and Conference Center, 218-834-5671, 800-242-1988, 1521 Superior Shores Rd. off E. Hwy. 61, offers 144 rooms, suites and lakehomes, pool, Kamloops Restaurant/Lounge and welcomes pets.

Where to Eat with a Local Flavor
Vanilla Bean Bakery and Cafe, 218-834-3714, 812 7th Ave., offers international cuisine, walleye and fresh bakery.
Rustic Inn Cafe and Gifts, 218-834-2488, 2773 Hwy. 61 (east of town), has fresh local fish, prime steaks and great desserts.

Two Harbors Folk Festival in mid-July is three days of music and fun.

• Kayak Festival in early August gives paddlers a full weekend of water-based activities.

• Annual Commemoration of *Edmund Fitzgerald* is held at Split Rock Lighthouse each November 10.

• Winter Solstice at the Two Harbors Lighthouse is celebrated in mid-December.

Where to Shop

In the 700 block along the highway, the Superior Hiking Trail Association gift shop and headquarters are located in the historic Anderson House (See separate listing for Superior Hiking Trail). Also at the corner of the highway and Eighth Street is Sawtooth Mountain Trading Post with many handcrafted gift items. Superior Choice Fish Market in the 600 block has a nice selection of smoked fish, cheeses and curds or prepared takeout.

In the downtown, Wings By the Bay specializes in gift items, souvenirs and a complete selection of quilting supplies, with quilting classes scheduled. In view of the port, the owners, Char and Jerry Wing, generally keep track of the ship traffic due into the docks. Other downtown stops include a jam-packed hardware store, the town's two banks, a cafe and an American Legion club that serves lunches and welcomes the public.

Campgrounds

Adjacent to town, campers can choose from a variety of sites at the municipal Burlington Bay Campground. The

campground is equipped with hookups for motor homes and trailers and affords a beautiful view of the lake and shoreline. It is a perfect location for watching sunrises, sunsets and stars from around the campfire. Burlington Bay is also the site of a Kayak Festival in early August.

What's Next

The Circle tour continues on Highway 61. To the east is Silver Creek Cliff and one of two tunnels carved from lakeside cliffs to realign Highway 61 for safer traffic. See description under the North Shore Tunnels listing. West from Two Harbors lies the Scenic North Shore Drive and Duluth.

Virginia

VIRGINIA, MINNESOTA
Population 9,160

Virginia is a crossroads city where Highway 53 from Duluth meets Highway 169 from Hibbing on the west and Ely to the north.

Virginia, Minnesota, regional map – page 32.

Virginia has long served as a center point of the East Range. Called the Queen City of the Iron Range, it was named after the immense amount of virgin timber that surrounded the city in the late 1800s, but was already firmly established as a mining town by the time lumber barons began harvesting that timber.

What to See and Do
Mineview in the Sky features displays of giant mining equipment and a spectacular viewpoint over the abandoned Rouchleau Mine, and is also an excellent source of area information during the summer.

North of Virginia, the Laurentian Divide cuts across the territory and sends water flowing to three ultimate destinations: Lake Superior, the Mississippi River or northward toward Hudson Bay.

Notable Museums
Heritage Museum gives a nice peek into the city and region's past.

Parks and Public Areas
Olcott Park is always populated by many species of wild birds. The Land of the Loon Ethnic Arts and Crafts Festival is held at Olcott Park in June.

DIRECTORY

Tourist Information – Virginia/ Eveleth, Mountain Iron/Gilbert Chamber of Commerce, 218-741-2717; Iron Trail Convention and Visitors Bureau, 218-749-8161, 800-777-8497

What's Next

Leaving Virginia northward, stay on Highway 169 to visit the town of Ely (see separate listing), perhaps the best known and busiest entry point for the Boundary Waters Canoe Area Wilderness (BWCAW), which *National Geographic* magazine named one of 50 places in the world that everyone should visit in their lifetime. To return to the Circle Tour route on the north shore take Highway 1 out of Ely to Illgen City east of Silver Bay. Sights and points of interest can be found under the Finland, Ely and BWCAW listings.

For an interesting side trip, at the junction of highways 53 and 169 (which continues on to Tower-Soudan, Lake Vermilion and Ely), take Highway 53 north to visit Cook, Orr and Voyageurs National Park on the U.S.-Canadian border to the east of International Falls. Orr is home to the Vince Shute Wildlife Sanctuary, where people can see and learn about black bears in their natural habitat. It is also home to a uniquely styled AmericInn lodging, which features a waterslide in the pool area.

Wakefield - White River

WAKEFIELD, MICHIGAN

Population 2,085

At Wakefield, M-28 meets with U.S. Highway 2 from the lower part of the Upper Peninsula.

Camp inside the city limits at Sunday Lake Campground with modern campgrounds, a boat launch, swimming and day use facilities.

Wakefield Historical Society Museum on Sunday Lake opens mid-June through mid-September, Monday through Saturday afternoons, providing area information for visitors. Wakefield hosts July Fourth festivities, with a nice parade.

Wakefield, Michigan, regional map – page 28.

DIRECTORY

Tourist Information – Wakefield Chamber of Commerce, 800-522-5657; Western U.P. Convention and Visitors Bureau, 906-932-4850, 800-522-5657

WASHBURN, WISCONSIN

Population 2,305

Washburn, found on Highway 13 between Ashland and Bayfield, is a town of lakeside parks, with easy access to fishing, boating, snowmobiling and skiing.

Washburn, Wisconsin, regional map – page 30.

What to See and Do

The town operates Memorial Park and Thompson's West End Park, each with camping, showers, sandy beaches, picnic tables, playgrounds and hook-ups. A boat launch is available at West End Park. Camping is available April 15 to October 15. A walking trail overlooking Chequamegon Bay runs from West End Park to the Washburn Marina, which is a pleasant haven for boaters and other visitors from around the lake. Full service, with diesel and gas, boaters wishing to tie-up a while are advised to call the marina to ensure that space is available. Washburn's heyday saw it shipping enormous amounts of native brownstone from nearby quarries and explosives from a Dupont Corporation plant just outside of town, but the city has since evolved into a center for art.

W X Y Z

BIG TOP CHAUTAUQUA

The cream of Bayfield Peninsula entertainment is found at the Lake Superior Big Top Chautauqua, which offers a summerlong schedule of musical performances ranging from good regional acts to nationally known performers like Willie Nelson, Bela Fleck and the Nitty Gritty Dirt Band. Co-founder Warren Nelson serves as emcee and keeps the shows moving at an pleasing pace. He is also the composer of the special regional house shows that spotlight the history and maritime traditions of the area. To avoid parking problems, Bay Area Regional Transit buses pick up passengers in a number of locations and deliver them to the Big Top, which is located at Mt. Ashwabay Ski Area.

There are two nice parks downtown that invite respite in their green and flowered expanses.

The 80-seat, air conditioned Stage North, offers a variety of live shows and entertainment on a regular basis.

Washburn claims the first "underground" Dairy Queen in the United States. Next to the Dairy Queen is the renowned 80-foot Lombardy poplar, a state champion worthy of a photograph.

Anglers looking for action will want to check with Outdoor Allure Bait, Tackle and Guide Service for charter information.

Mt. Valhalla Recreation Area is located on County Road C, northwest of Washburn and has scenic horseback riding trails, hiking and snowmobile trails and snowshoeing areas.

Eight miles (13 kilometers) toward Bayfield on Wisconsin 13, wax your skis and enjoy 40 miles (65 kilometers) of

groomed cross-country trails at Mount Ashwabay, a ski area
with an acronym name made from the first syllables of
Ashland, Washburn and Bayfield. Turn west on Ski Hill
Road off State Highway 13. Trails vary from old logging
roads to hilly slopes. Mt. Ashwabay has 14 downhill runs for
all skill levels, snowmaking capability, ski rental, instruction,
food and a chalet. Open Wednesday through Saturday for
downhill and daily for cross-country skiing.

Also at Mt. Ashwabay, Lake Superior Big Top
Chautauqua offers unique professional summer entertainment
– culture under canvas. The Big Top features the popular
historical musicals of Bayfield, Washburn and the Chequamegon region and well-known performers under the mirthful
artistry of impresario Warren Nelson. The season runs from
early June through Labor Day. Bay Area Rural Transit buses
provide pickup from various locations in the area.

Self-guided tours of Bayfield State Fish Hatchery are
available year-round on a daily basis. This is one of six northern
Wisconsin hatcheries where visitors are welcome. A variety of
game fish species are reared for release to state waters.

Notable Museums

For a taste of local history and culture, stop at the historic
Washburn Historical Museum and Cultural Center in the old
Washburn Bank Building. It has displays of local historical
families.

Notable Events

• Washburn holds a summer festival each year in late July.
Every five years, a homecoming celebration is held concurrent
with the summer fest.

• In February, the city is site of one end of the Book
Across the Bay 10 kilometer ski and snowshoe race. June sees
the Inland Sea Kayak Symposium in town.

West End Park is the site of the annual Inland Sea Kayak
Symposium, a mid-June event attracting fledgling and
experienced paddlers from throughout the country.

Where to Shop

Visit Bloomquist Gallery on the shore of Lake Superior
about a mile south of Washburn, where the local watercolor
and pastel scenes of noted artist Art Bloomquist are displayed
along with other art by David and Kathi Bloomquist.

In town, stop at Karlyn's Gallery, owned by artist Karlyn
Holman, known for original designs in pottery and
watercolors, as well as art by other area professionals.

Austin Miller Studio & Gallery on the Mt. Ashwabay
road north of Washburn offers works about Lake Superior by

DIRECTORY

Tourist Information – Washburn Area Chamber of Commerce, 715-373-5017, 800-253-4495; Apostle Islands Tourist Information, 715-682-2500, 800-284-9484 ext 9; Bayfield County Tourism, 800-472-6338

Where to Stay
Lodging is limited, but check Redwood Motel & Chalets, 715-373-5512, or Washburn Motel, 715-373-5580, both on West Bayfield St.

Where to Eat with a Local Flavor
Steak Pit, 715-373-5352, 125 Harborview Dr., has tasty steaks and other local favorites.

France Austin Miller, a watercolorist. Her art and limited edition prints are available in many Lake Superior galleries and she also does framing of works at the studio.

Be sure to stop and visit with Richard Avol, owner of Chequamegon Book & Coffee Co., who deals in new and used books and coffee, located across from the Washburn Museum.

What's Next

You'll stay on Highway 13 to depart Washburn. Southward about 11 miles is Ashland. If your route is north toward Bayfield, you'll pass Port Superior Village on Chequamegon Bay as you begin your climb toward Bayfield. This friendly marina provides accommodations and dining at the Portside Restaurant. Next door is Waterford by the Bay, a condo development, and Pikes Bay Marina, bringing the number of slips in these large complexes to more than 400.

Just prior to entering Bayfield, the Wild Rice Restaurant features upscale food and an extensive wine list during the summer months.

WATERSMEET, MICHIGAN

Township Population 1,470

Watersmeet, Michigan, regional map – page 49.

Watersmeet is at the junction of U.S. Highways 2 and 45 in the southwest Upper Peninsula. Near the town are a number of recreation opportunities.

What's Next

The Ottawa National Forest Visitor Center is located in Watersmeet, with full information on the forest's 27 campgrounds, hiking and biking opportunities, canoeing, fishing, hunting or any other recreational activity within this wonderfully scenic area.

Southwest of town, the 19,000-acre Sylvania Wilderness

W X Y Z

Area and Sylvania Recreation Area provide more opportunities for outdoor recreation. The Recreation Area was once the province of the rich and famous, but is now open to the public with a 48-unit campground with showers, beach and picnic areas and boat launches on Clark, Crooked and Long lakes.

Lac Vieux Desert, a large lake south of town, is nestled between Michigan's Ottawa and Wisconsin's Nicolet national forests. This headwaters of the Wisconsin River, home of the world record tiger musky, is great for walleye, muskies, bass, northern pike and panfish. Also in the area is the Cisco Chain of Lakes with 15 lakes interconnected to offer more than 270 miles (360 kilometers) of scenic shoreline and wonderful fishing. Many year-round resorts operate in the area.

Golfers will want to try Gateway Golf Club, a public 9-hole course with lounge and pro shop in the nearby border town of Land O' Lakes, Wisconsin.

West from Watersmeet on U.S. Highway 2, we're entering territory covered under the heading "Big Snow Country." To return to the Lake Superior Circle Tour route, take U.S. 45 north to Michigan Highway 28.

DIRECTORY

Tourist Information – Upper Peninsula Travel and Recreation Association, 906-774-5480; Ottawa National Forest Information, 906-358-4551.

Where to Stay
Lac Vieux Desert Resort & Casino, 906-358-4226, N5384 U.S. 45, offers lodging, a restaurant and gaming action.

WAWA, ONTARIO

Population 3,700

Wawa is located near the northern boundary of Lake Superior Provincial Park on Trans Canada Highway 17 on the eastern shore of Lake Superior. The name is derived from the Ojibway word and imitation of a goose landing on water. Wawa salutes its namesake with an 8.5-meter-high (28-foot), 4,400-pound steel Canada goose statue and log-constructed, red-roofed Wawa Regional Tourist Information Centre at the corner of highways 17 and 101. The big goose commemorates the completion of the final Lake Superior Circle Tour link near this point in 1960.

Travel beyond the "Big Goose" up Highway 101 a couple of kilometers to a downtown fitted with nearly any service needed by travelers. Wawa has shops, restaurants and motels, a hospital, a licensed spirits store, golf course, airport and charter planes.

While in Wawa, pick up a copy of the *Algoma News Review*, one of our favorite hometown papers around Lake Superior. Little in town escapes the eye of owners Bob and Gloria Avis.

Wawa, Ontario, regional map – page 16.

Pukaskwa National & Lake Superior Provincial Parks

Two huge parks lie on the eastern shore of Lake Superior with access near Wawa, Ontario.

To the north is Pukaskwa National Park. It has has limited land access with only one short road, Highway 627, traveling 12 kilometers (7.5 miles) inland to Hattie Cove on the northern end of the park. The remainder is all wilderness, with access only by hiking, canoeing or kayaking rivers or from Lake Superior.

To the south, Lake Superior Provincial Park has more accessible amenities. Here you'll find good campgrounds, beaches, Native American pictographs at Agawa Rock, interesting wildlife and vegetation. A new visitor center at Agawa Bay Campground on the southern end of the park is an awesome stop for families. A visit to Katherine Cove is highly recommended to see the unusual rock formations. Highway 17 penetrates the heart of the entire park. (See separate listings for both parks.)

A few miles from Lake Superior's shoreline, Wawa's economy has relied less on forest products than it has on mining. Gold mining has occurred in the area for more than 100 years and Wawa was the site of the first mining office in Ontario. As the gold rush fizzled, iron ore to stoke the mills at Sault Ste. Marie began to be mined. The Algoma Central Railway was created, and the town of Wawa was born along its line. The discovery of diamonds in the area is the latest buzz on the mineralogical hotline. The information center has a self-guided geology field tour of the area.

The Wawa Airport is a key fly-in entry point to the 12,000 inland wilderness lakes. In addition to outstanding fishing, hunters find an abundance of game in the Canada bush country.

What to See and Do

Mr. Vallee's Park in Wawa was started in 1984 by a local citizen. Here are walkways, a great view of the town and a picnic area on the shore of Anderson Lake. Golfers can try their skills at the Michipicoten Golf Club, near the airport. Wawa Lake has beachfront facilities, including beach houses and playgrounds. Nearby is the Rotary Blasthole Drill, used in the construction of the St. Lawrence Seaway and in local mining operations. It's a part of the Wawa Heritage Walk's pathway along the shoreline of Wawa Lake.

It's worth taking a gander (goose pun intended) at several other sites around Wawa. Young's General Store, about a kilometer from the airport as you enter the city, lives up to its name and seems to make time stand still. Try a pickle straight out of the barrel and sample fresh vegetables right from the crate on the front porch. Be watchful of the many "critters" (bunnies and chipmunks) that scamper among the barrels and boxes. Kids will love the fresh fudge. And bring your camera. Anita Young and her friendly assistants are all local authorities and will be more than happy to assist you with knowledge of the area.

Henrietta, the faithful moose who has stood watch at Young's for years, is back at its post on the front stoop after spending about three years in custody of the Ministry of Natural Resources at a Sault Ste. Marie slammer. Young's has also obtained and repaired the smaller original Wawa goose to its full grandeur and it now stands beside the store on a special perch. There is also a larger-than-life display of the mysterious inuksuk monuments found along the highway. These Inuit "little men" icons guide travelers on their way.

For winter activity, Wawa is the place to visit. A network of groomed snowmobile trails exceeds 560 kilometers (350 miles). With more than adequate snowfall, the season runs from December to April. Snowmobilers visit from throughout the Midwest. Wawa hosts a Lake Trout Ice Fishing Derby each March. The Gold Quest Sled Dog Race is held at the end of February.

The beaches where the Magpie River enters Lake Superior are a sandy delight or, moving a short way south on the Circle Tour Route again, turn west on an unpaved road off Highway 17 about 3 kilometers (2 miles) to see the Magpie Scenic High Falls roar toward Lake Superior. The local Rotary International chapter has improved the site. Prepare to get a little wet from the mist. The road and parking lot accommodate buses. Picnic area and washroom facilities are right at the base of the falls.

Forest Care is the large complex in the vicinity of the turn to the High Falls and is the biggest tree nursery in the province of Ontario. Privately owned, the nursery has innovated methods that ensure greater success in transplanting the 18 million red, white and jack pine, and black and white spruce seedlings it grows each year.

Take the Michipicoten River Village Road 5 kilometers (3 miles) south of Wawa toward Lake Superior to visit the townsite at the mouth of the Michipicoten River. The sign on the highway is hard to spot, so watch carefully for Buck's Marina, a 97-slip full-service marina with showers and lockers at the junction of the Michipicoten and Magpie rivers. Turn left in the townsite for Buck's, which has had an operation on this site for decades. Charter fishing, boat rentals and launch facilities are available. Since Buck's is inland on the river, the marina will guide deeper draft boats if contacted on VHF Channel 68. The channel is dredged to maintain good depth, but Buck's will offer boaters a ferry service if the draft is too shallow. The annual Wawa Salmon Derby, one of the largest on Lake Superior, is held in August. Inquire at Buck's Marina. As a result of the early Jesuit church, the townsite is still called "The Mission."

You'll also want to see Silver Falls, so turn right at the townsite intersection and go to the bridge over the Magpie River. Park just before the bridge to see the falls. The bridge overlooks the confluence of the Magpie and Michipicoten rivers above Buck's Marina.

If you cross the bridge and proceed another kilometer (about a mile) past the hydro dam, you'll find a lookout we discovered that offers a panoramic view of Lake Superior, including the Algoma Marine ore docks to the north and Michipicoten Island on the horizon. This area is unprotected, but there is room to pull the vehicle to the side of the dirt road and there are now signs to mark the way.

DIRECTORY

Tourist Information – Wawa Regional Tourist Information Centre, 705-856-2244, 800-367-9292 ext. 260

Where to Stay
Mystic Isle Motel, 705-856-1737, Hwy. 17 S., has good accommodations overlooking Lake Superior.
Wawa Motor Inn, 705-856-2278,

800-561-2278, 100 Mission Rd., offers a wide choice of lodgings with fireside dining.

Where to Eat with a Local Flavor
Kinniwabi Pines Restaurant, 705-856-7226, Hwy. 17 S., prepares neat cuisine and has patio and deck dining in nice weather.
Cedarhof Restaurant, 705-856-1136, Hwy 17 S., has a hearty Austrian-German menu.

Notable Events
- Wawa hosts a Winter Carnival in February.
- Wawa Ice Fishing Derby is held in late February/early March.
- Canada Day Celebration is held July 1.
- Wawa Salmon Derby is held in late August.

What's Next
Gas up before leaving Wawa, since you're entering a leg of the Circle Tour route with fewer service stations. You'll travel Highway 17 to proceed either north or south on your journey. To the north is White River and Marathon. To the south you'll pass through Lake Superior Provincial Park and several smallish towns on the way to Sault Ste. Marie, some 225 kilometers (140 miles) away.

WHITEFISH POINT, MICHIGAN

Whitefish Point, Michigan, regional map – page 18.

About 15 miles north of Paradise is the Great Lakes Shipwreck Museum at Whitefish Point. This is the only museum dedicated to shipwrecks on the Great Lakes. There are said to be more than 350 known shipwrecks in Lake Superior and probably many more unidentified wrecks. This and Copper Harbor are the sites of the first lighthouses on Lake Superior. It's now automated, but its predecessor began operating in 1849 and was surely a lonely place for its early keepers. The museum has an excellent video presentation on shipwrecks, a gift shop and an exciting beach for agate hunting and swimming. It is known for its material about the famous 1975 *Edmund Fitzgerald* wreck. The bell of the *Fitzgerald* was recovered from the wreck in 1995 and is displayed at the museum in an updated memorial. A good educational stop and well worth the distance to travel.

The restored 1923 Crews Quarters are offered for

overnight stays. Five modern, themed rooms with private baths are available and come with continental breakfast. Reservations are a must.

Next door, the Whitefish Point Bird Observatory documents the distribution and abundance of bird migration and is operated by the Michigan Audubon Society. An exhibit building is located near the Great Lakes Shipwreck Museum, and an elaborate series of wooden walkways through the sand dunes has been constructed to allow the visitor a chance to venture into the sanctuary area and observe wildlife without disturbing dune foliage. Admission is free.

> ### DIRECTORY
>
> **Tourist Information –** Great Lakes Shipwreck Museum, 906-635-1742, 800-635-1742

WHITE LAKE PROVINCIAL PARK, ONTARIO

On the bay of White Lake 72 kilometers (44 miles) east of Marathon on Trans Canada Highway 17, White Lake Provincial Park is an ideal family getaway spot. Inland and sheltered from Lake Superior's sometimes harsh effects, visitors can enjoy camping, hiking, fishing, swimming, boating, interpretative programs and a creative program for the kids. Almost 200 tent and trailer sites are available, but advanced booking is still advisable. The park is the put-in for canoe expeditions paddling down the White River through Pukaskwa National Park to Lake Superior and is open mid-May to late September. Across the lake, the Mobert Indian Reserve (population 232) was the site of an early Hudson's Bay Post.

White Lake Provincial Park, Ontario, regional map – page 14.

WHITE PINE, MICHIGAN

Population 625

South of Silver City on M-64, White Pine was the last copper mining "boom town" in Michigan's fabled Copper Country and existed as a residential site for company employees. Mining of copper ended several years ago with the closing of Copper Range Company facilities, but the town has adjusted, tightened its belt and survives. At the town's shopping area, Konteka Resort and Restaurant offers almost anything a traveler wants, from gifts to lodging, fine dining, a lounge, bowling, snowmobile rental and wildlife viewing from indoor comfort behind large window areas.

White Pine, Michigan, regional map – page 28.

> ### DIRECTORY
>
> **Tourist Information –** Porcupine Mountains Area Chamber of Commerce, 906-885-5399

What's Next

M-64 continues south to a junction with M-28 at Bergland.

WHITE RIVER, ONTARIO

Population 1,000

White River, Ontario, regional map – page 14.

More than 75 kilometers (46 miles) from Lake Superior on the Inland Plateau (the rising topography to the northeast of Lake Superior), White River doesn't receive any climactic benefit from warm lake waters in winter. It gets cold here. In 1935, the mercury is reported to have bottomed out at minus 58 degrees Celsius (minus 72 degrees Fahrenheit). For the record, Environment Canada shows the lowest reading to be minus 51 C (minus 61 F). Some think the thermometer broke that day. Whatever the details, the sign reading "Coldest spot in Canada" still stands unchallenged.

White River is known as the birthplace of Winnie-the-Pooh, A.A. Milne's famous storybook character. Actually, Christopher Robin (Milne's son) really existed, and so did Winnie, a bear cub that traveled to Europe in 1914 with Captain Harry Colbourn, who had bought her in White River. When Milne saw the bear in the London Zoo, where Colbourn left her when he was transferred to duty in France, Milne got the idea for his famous stories.

In White River, a statue of "Winnie the Pooh" reminds visitors of the town's place in history. White River has received a license from the Disney Company to produce exclusive Pooh products, sold locally. Join in the annual Winnie's Hometown Festival the third weekend in August. By the way, Winnie was short for Winnipeg, and yes, "she" was a girl bear.

There are several motels and gift stores in White River. Beyond White River on Highway 17, Obatanga Provincial Park is an area of glacial sand deposits and headwater lakes that feed both the Pukaskwa coastal streams and migrating sandhill cranes. It has camping, canoeing, hiking, bird-watching and a creative playground. The park offers seasonal leasing of campsites. Swimming in Burnfield Lake and fishing in most of the others. Handicapped accessible. Open June to September.

DIRECTORY

Tourist Information – White River Visitor Information Center, 807-822-2794, 888-517-1673 ext. 22

What's Next

If there's a "corner" in this leg of the Circle Route, it occurs at White River. The Lake Superior Circle Tour follows Highway 17 either northwesterly to Marathon or south along the inland boundary of Pukaskwa National Park heading for Wawa. The route to Nipigon is about 272 kilometers (168 miles) and Sault Ste. Marie is a 319-kilometer (197-mile) drive.

INDEX

Notes

Notes

About the Author

HUGH E. BISHOP

Making his home in Two Harbors, Minnesota, and maintaining an interest in almost everything having to do with the North American mid-continent, Hugh Bishop has been poking stories about the Lake Superior region into the back of his mind since 1975. He first encountered the big lake that year as an employee of Erie Mining Company, which had its docks at Taconite Harbor on Minnesota's north shore. Moving to Two Harbors in 1983 gave him much easier access to the stories and the storytellers of the big lake.

Hugh E. Bishop

Bishop is senior writer at Lake Superior Port Cities Inc., publisher of the bi-monthly *Lake Superior Magazine*. After more than a decade of writing for *Lake Superior Magazine* and being closely associated with producing the annual *Lake Superior Travel Guide*, Bishop here presents most of what he has learned and experienced around Lake Superior, making this the most comprehensive guide to the region's sites and scenic beauty.

Also from Lake Superior Port Cities Inc

Haunted Lakes (the original)
by Frederick Stonehouse
Softcover: ISBN 0-942235-30-4

Haunted Lakes II
by Frederick Stonehouse
Softcover: ISBN 0-942235-39-8

Wreck Ashore: United States Life-Saving Service, Legendary Heroes of the Great Lakes
by Frederick Stonehouse
Softcover: ISBN 0-942235-58-4

Shipwreck of the Mesquite
by Frederick Stonehouse
Softcover: ISBN 0-942235-10-X

Julius F. Wolff Jr.'s Lake Superior Shipwrecks
by Julius F. Wolff Jr.
Hardcover: ISBN 0-942235-02-9
Softcover: ISBN 0-942235-01-0

Shipwrecks of Lake Superior, Second Edition
by James R. Marshall
Softcover: ISBN 0-942235-66-5

Lake Superior Journal: Views from the Bridge
by James R. Marshall
Softcover: ISBN 0-942235-40-1

The Night the Fitz *Went Down*
by Hugh E. Bishop
Softcover: ISBN 0-942235-37-1

By Water and Rail: A History of Lake County, Minnesota
by Hugh E. Bishop
Hardcover: ISBN 0-942235-48-7
Softcover: ISBN 0-942235-42-8

Haunted Lake Superior
by Hugh E. Bishop
Softcover: ISBN 0-942235-55-X

Lake Superior, The Ultimate Guide to the Region
by Hugh E. Bishop
Softcover: ISBN 0-942235-67-3

Michigan Gold, Mining in the Upper Peninsula
by Daniel R. Fountain
Softcover: ISBN 0-942235-15-0

Betty's Pies Favorite Recipes
by Betty Lessard
Softcover: ISBN 0-942235-50-9

Shipwrecks of Isle Royale National Park
by Daniel Lenihan
Softcover: ISBN 0-942235-18-5

Schooners, Skiffs & Steamships: Stories along Lake Superior Water Trails
by Howard Sivertson
Hardcover: ISBN 0-942235-51-7

Tales of the Old North Shore
by Howard Sivertson
Hardcover: ISBN 0-942235-29-0

The Illustrated Voyageur
by Howard Sivertson
Hardcover: ISBN 0-942235-43-6

Once Upon an Isle: The Story of Fishing Families on Isle Royale
by Howard Sivertson
Hardcover: ISBN 0-9624369-3-3

Superior Way, Third Edition
by Bonnie Dahl
Softcover: ISBN 0-942235-49-5

Lake Superior Magazine (Bimonthly)

Lake Superior Travel Guide (Annual)

Lake Superior Wall Calendar (Annual)

Lake Superior Mini Wall Calendar (Annual)

Lake Superior Wall Map

Lake Superior Map Placemats

Lake Superior Puzzles

For a catalog of the entire Lake Superior Port Cities collection of books and merchandise, write or call:

Lake Superior Port Cities Inc.
P.O. Box 16417 • Duluth, MN 55816

1-888-BIG LAKE (244-5253)
218-722-5002
FAX 218-722-4096

E-mail: guide@lakesuperior.com
hauntedlakes@lakesuperior.com
www.lakesuperior.com